Pacific Northwest
WEATHER

But My Barometer Says Fair!

A look at those changing and peculiar weather patterns in the Pacific Northwest, large and small

George R. Miller

Pacific Northwest
WEATHER

But My Barometer Says Fair!

*A look at those changing and peculiar weather patterns
in the Pacific Northwest, large and small*

George R. Miller

Frank
Amato
PORTLAND

Dedication

*To my wife Janice who knows far more about
the weather than the average lay person.*

Acknowledgements

Many individuals gave large amounts of their time to make this publication a reality. First of all, I thank my wife Janice for the countless hours she spent in reading and re-reading the manuscript. It was her encouragement that kept me going when I would say, "Ah, this will never go anywhere! Why should I continue?" Her only payment was, now and then, a night out to dinner!

Dr. Daniel Johnson, former Chair, Department of Geography, Portland State University, and himself an author, gave valuable suggestions and corrections as he plowed through the entire manuscript. His only payment was an occasional lunch. Dave Olsen, former Meteorologist in Charge of the Great Falls, Montana, National Weather Service Forecast Office, also a Northwesterner, provided many helpful suggestions. Dr. Larry Hanson, Chair, Science and Math Department, Marylhurst University reviewed the manuscript as did James Little, former Portland television meteorologist, now with the State of Oregon. Both offered valuable comments.

Many others provided helpful suggestions including Peter Christianson, Lewis and Clark College whose comments on the first couple of chapters provided the theme throughout the book. Steve Todd, currently Meteorologist in Charge of the Portland, Oregon Forecast Office, surveyed the chapter on Weather Forecasting. His comments were included. Charles Orwig, former Hydrologist in Charge of the Portland, Oregon River Forecast Center gave valuable assistance for the chapter on Rivers and Flooding. Adair Law, former editor of the Oregon Historical Society Press, suggested the inclusion of a Foreword after looking over the first few chapters. She also provided some clues and routes to follow regarding publishing and encouraged me with the book's title.

I am also indebted to Francine Kirsch, herself an author of several books. Francine recently worked for the Oregon Historical Society where I serve as a volunteer. She helped me write the letters of inquiry and provided expert advice on just what to include. Two individuals at Frank Amato Publications assisted with the book. Jerry Hutchinson did the layout work and Kim Koch provided the editorial expertise.

To all of the above I offer a big Thank You. This book would never have materialized without your gracious help.

Photography and Illustrations: George Miller unless otherwise noted.
Design: Jerry Hutchinson

Softbound ISBN: 1-57188-235-9
Softbound UPC: 0-66066-00489-5

Frank Amato Publications, Inc.
P.O. Box 82112, Portland, Oregon 97282
(503) 653-8108
Printed in Hong Kong
1 3 5 7 9 10 8 6 4 2

Table of Contents

Foreword

It could very well be considered the greatest weather disaster to affect residents of the Pacific Northwest since the arrival of European settlers. Other weather events are mentioned in Native American folklore, but there is no substantiation for these occurrences. Devastating floods, snowstorms, droughts, forest fires and wind storms have also been recorded in meteorological history in this area. Yet, the winter of 1861-1862, by all accounts, should be considered the worst. It is mentioned in diaries, journals, newspapers, and actual accounts of reminiscence. Not just one single event, but a combination of several weather events over a nine-month period brought all the weather elements together to make this period so devastating.

A young country was struggling through a civil war. An even younger state as well as a territory was also divided between Union loyalty and secession beliefs. This topic dominated discussion in the newspapers of the day. Weather was not a daily topic of conversation as it is today. Placid settlers had become accustomed to warm summers, mild winters with an occasional cold spell, and rivers that sometimes ran out of control. Yet, even in the summer of 1861, Mother Nature seemed to be plotting the events of the next nine months.

A fine summer it was; so warm and dry that the projected wheat crop was estimated at only 50 percent of the previous year. *The Oregonian* in its September 12, 1861 issue mentioned, "The weather has been exceedingly warm in this latitude for two or three days past. Large fires are now raging in the woods in back of the city." Light fall rains extinguished the fires and somewhat recharged the dry Pacific Northwest soil. And then came November.

Oregon and Washington settlers in 1861 had no idea of a "jet stream" nor did meteorologists of that time. Yet, this feature silently moved in over the Pacific Northwest bringing with it copious moisture and cold air. Large amounts of snow fell in the mountains of both Washington and Oregon. Heavy mountain snow in November, meteorologists now know, is an ominous sign. The fickle pattern of the jet stream, however, could very well change. And change it did in late November 1861.

The pattern of global winds constantly tries to equalize temperature between cold polar latitudes and warmer equatorial regions. A cold November surrendered to the warm tropical air mass that moved north from lower latitudes during the last few days of the month. The triumph by that warm, moist air, however, turned into a defeat, a devastating defeat, for Pacific Northwest residents, especially those in proximity to rivers.

Today, meteorologists and hydrologists refer to it as a "rain on snow" event. Rain melts snow. A warm subtropical air mass laden with moisture melts it even faster. Throughout Oregon and into southeast Washington, rivers responded quickly to the rapid accumulation of water. No dams were there to control them. Unheeded, they carried the rain and melted snow toward the ocean. With these torrents went houses, barns, bridges, livestock, and probably people. It was a flood of unprecedented nature. Yet, Mother Nature was not through with her fury on the weary settlers. As an army that may venture too far into enemy territory, so it was with the warm, moisture-filled southwest wind. It began to lose the battle as a cold, Arctic air mass steadily moved south into the region around Christmas time 1861. This Arctic air mass would lose a few skirmishes over the next two months, but it would not surrender its hold on the Pacific Northwest until late February 1862. Heavy snowfall was reported throughout the region. Salem newspapers refer to "six weeks of good sledding." Two feet of snow was reported on the ground near Olympia, Washington Territory. Several persons on their way to and from the mines in Idaho perished, some with gold in their pockets, unable to plow through huge snow drifts.

Many of the livestock that survived the floods of late November and early December perished during that cold, snowy winter, especially east of the Cascade Mountains. Upwards of 70 to 80 percent loss was mentioned. Most farmers and ranchers did not have the means, or probably did not think it was necessary, to provide winter feed. After all, a cold period was normally over in a few days, even east of the Cascade Mountains, they thought. That's what had happened in the past. But the winter of 1861-1862 soon made the past forgotten.

Although a slight reprieve was granted in the spring, the mountains that were now covered with additional snow from the cold winter began to lose that snowpack. Rivers rose once again due to melting snow in June. June "snowmelt floods" were recorded at many locations. And then it was over. But for nine months, residents of the Pacific Northwest had endured the worst nature could offer. But was it the worst? For the years past, the author believes it was. For the years to come, maybe not. The Columbus Day storm of 1962 brought death and destruction as did the Christmas floods of 1964. Heavy rain, floods, fire, wind, and drought have historically plagued the region. Yet, several situations combined all the weather elements to make the winter of 1861-1862 the most devastating weather event the Pacific Northwest has ever experienced.

What were the elements? How did they combine? What weather patterns were responsible for these catastrophic events? How did those storms develop? Could it happen again? Read on for some answers.

Introduction

The person's voice on the other end of the line had concern and worry in it. She sounded elderly. I had only begun working for the United States Weather Bureau a few weeks earlier, in January 1960. Thus, I was slightly apprehensive. "But my barometer says fair," she said, "and it is raining outside. Is there something wrong with it? Will I have to return it? I don't want to do that. It was a Christmas gift!" "No," I assured her, "You don't have to take the barometer back. It's set properly. There's nothing wrong with it." "Then why is it raining?" was her reply.

That question was a little harder to answer coming from a meteorologist to someone with limited, if any, knowledge of weather. However, I did my best to explain to her that words on a barometer sometimes are misleading. Generally speaking, high pressure accompanies fair or sunny weather and low pressure is associated with stormy weather. This is not always the case, especially in the Pacific Northwest. "This is one of those times," I explained to her. She seemed a bit more relieved and the conversation ended.

But perhaps that is where it really started. This book is written for that lady and many other lay people like her. It is written for the weather enthusiast and for the person seeking to get a glimpse of how the weather operates. The book contains some historical references to particular weather events in the Pacific Northwest and thereby has some historical value. It is written for anyone whose daily work and play hinges on the weather. You, the reader, are undoubtedly in one or more of those categories.

It begins with a brief overview of the weather elements and how weather operates on a global scale. To understand local effects of the weather, one must understand how it operates from pole to pole. The reader is then guided to weather that is peculiar to the Pacific Northwest, not just the storms, but the hot and cold episodes also.

One chapter touches briefly on a few broad scale topics such as El Niño, global warming, and climate change. However, so much has been written about these topics and so much new material is being discovered, the reader should look elsewhere for more in-depth information. The topic of Pacific Northwest climatology and local effects is incorporated. But here again, not every hill and valley can be explored.

I only hope that you will enjoy reading the material as much as I have enjoyed writing it and developing the figures. Thus, you are left with, "Pacific Northwest Weather: But My Barometer Says Fair!" Enjoy it. I am certain that my elderly caller enjoyed her barometer and found more sunny days than rainy days when it, indeed, said FAIR.

George R. Miller

"Sunshine is delicious,

rain is refreshing,

wind braces up,

snow is exhilarating;

There is no such thing as bad weather,

only different kinds of good weather."

Ruskin

Chapter 1
Weather Elements

Well, it certainly rained a lot yesterday!" "And it is still so cloudy today!" "They say we are going to have some strong winds tomorrow, and then colder temperatures, but the humidity should be lower. It won't seem quite so muggy!" Typical conversations, right? You hear them in line at the supermarket, in the elevator, from a co-worker or the next door neighbor. What those comments are referring to are the elements that make up the weather: Temperature, Relative Humidity, Wind Speed and Direction, Cloudiness, Type and Amount of Precipitation, and Pressure. In this part of Chapter 1 we investigate each of the above weather elements, since we experience most of them every day. We dress for them. We plan our recreational activities around them. They can disrupt our routine so quickly. We want to know what they are going to do. But first, let's look at their effects.

Temperature

Why is it so important? Probably more than any of the other weather elements, temperature affects our daily routine in a myriad of ways, 24 hours each day. I doubt if we would wear a short-sleeved blouse or shorts if the local weather forecaster told us that the temperature was going to

Earthquake Weather

My mother, bless her heart, was a firm believer in the term "earthquake weather." Having moved to the Pacific Northwest from southern California, there could be some basis for her beliefs. Earthquake weather is thought by many to be hot and humid. However, in an article in the Monthly Weather Review, April 1918, a Prof. W.J. Humphreys states that, "the 'earthquake weather' concept is of psychological origin; that the general state of irritation and sensitiveness developed in us during the hot, calm, perhaps sultry weather given this name, inclines us to sharpen observation of earthquake disturbances and accentuates the impression they make on our senses, so that we retain more vivid memories of such quakes while possibly overlooking entirely the occurances on the more soothing days."

Monthly Weather Review, April 1918, with comments by author

be in the 20s. (Although baggy shorts seem to be acceptable attire now, even when the temperature is near or below freezing.) There are thousands of examples of how the temperature affects what we do. What we wear as clothing is certainly temperature-dependent. From an agricultural viewpoint, farmers and fruit growers become concerned if the temperature approaches the freezing point. Many plants are very susceptible to frost damage. On very warm days

with temperatures in the 90s we refrain from strenuous activities in the afternoon.

Temperature can affect how we feel. Have you ever felt irritable when the temperature was too hot? "Oh, I just can't get anything done, it is *so* hot!" Psychologists tell us that our moods can sometimes be weather-dependent. I know people who like it hot and are grumpy when it is cool. And you will find people who like it cool and are miserable if it is hot.

But what about temperature differences? Humans can discern temperature differences to a certain point. No one needs to tell you that if it was 90 degrees Fahrenheit (90°F) yesterday and it is 70°F today, that it is cooler. We can tell. But what if it was 85°F yesterday and 80°F today? Could we notice that difference? Maybe, but we would have a little more difficulty discerning that temperature change. We can distinguish between large temperature differences, like overnight or seasonal, but have difficulty with smaller ones.

We are constantly reminded of the temperature as we go about our daily routines. Time and temperature displays like the one shown in Figure 1.1, give a good approximation of temperatures but sometimes their accuracy is questionable because of exposure and calibration. Radio stations keep us apprised of the temperature several times during the hour.

Figure 1.1 Time and temperature displays give a good approximation of temperatures but often their accuracy is questionable.

Television stations will give the current temperature as well as daily high and low values, not just locally, but nationally and internationally. So temperature is a very important weather element that affects our daily lives in what we wear, eat, the activities we engage in, and where we go. It can combine with other weather elements to produce different effects which are discussed later.

Relative Humidity

"'Tain't the heat, it's the humidity!" My mother always kept telling me that. The problem was, I didn't have the faintest idea what humidity was. Perhaps she didn't either. But those folks from the southern tier of states, the Midwest, and the eastern seaboard of the United States will tell you what humidity is. Basically, it is the amount of moisture in the air relative to the temperature. Hence the term, relative humidity! The amount of moisture (water vapor) the air can "hold" varies directly with the temperature. Warm air can "hold" much more moisture (water vapor) than cold air. As the speed of the molecules increases so does the temperature and the evaporation rate. See Chapter 5. The weather element of relative humidity makes us uncomfortable when it is hot and the air is full of moisture.

Moisture in the air, however, is responsible for many other things that are very important when we talk about the weather. When it condenses, or forms those drops on the inside of your windows, top of your car, or on the roses shown in Figure 1.2, it is releasing heat. The same process occurs when clouds form. Multiply that by several hundred thousand million drops and the result is a considerable amount of heat being released into the atmosphere. Water vapor in the air is in the form of a gas which we cannot see, but it directly affects the earth's energy balance. This water vapor intercepts the longwave radiation emitted by the earth and prevents it from escaping into space much like other gases in the atmosphere.

When we combine the two weather elements of temperature and relative humidity we construct an apparent temperature. The apparent temperature is how you "feel" when you are exposed to a combination of these two weather

HEAT INDEX CHART
Air Temperature (°F)

Relative Humidity (percent)	120	115	110	105	100	95	90	85	80	75	70
15	123	115	108	102	97	91	86	81	76	71	65
20	130	120	112	105	99	93	87	82	77	72	66
25	139	127	117	109	101	94	88	83	77	72	66
30		135	123	113	104	96	90	84	78	73	67
35		143	130	118	107	98	91	85	79	73	67
40			137	123	110	101	93	86	79	74	68
45			143	129	115	104	95	87	80	74	68
50				135	120	107	96	88	81	75	69
55				142	126	110	98	89	81	75	69
60				149	132	114	100	90	82	76	70
65					138	119	102	91	83	76	70
70					144	124	106	93	85	77	70
75						130	109	95	86	77	70
80						136	113	97	86	78	71
85							117	99	87	78	71
90							122	102	88	79	71
95								105	89	79	71

Heat Index values from National Weather Service brochure "Heat Wave"

Table 1.1 The heat index is obtained by combining the temperature and the relative humidity. For example, 90°F and 50% relative humidity gives a heat index or apparent temperature of 96°F.

elements. The result is what is called the heat index and it is displayed in Table 1.1. For example, if the temperature is 90°F and the relative humidity is 60 percent, it would "feel" like it is near 100°F. If we raise the actual temperature to 100°F and keep the same relative humidity of 60 percent, it would "feel" like it was 132°F! Wow! That's hot! We look for relief. How do we get relief?

The body is cooled by the evaporation of moisture off the skin. When the relative humidity is high, the rate of evaporation decreases. That is, fewer water molecules are leaving the surface and we begin to perspire. That's why we fan ourselves when it is hot. We want to push the air loaded with moisture, or saturated, away from our skin and replace it

Figure 1.2 When the temperature is above freezing and the relative humidity is 100 percent, water vapor in the air begins to condense and form dew like that on the two roses below.

Effect of Weather Upon School Department

"It is interesting to note that recent investigations into the effect of weather upon school deportment has shown that conditions of low humidity are accompanied by very many more than the normal number of misdemeanors, while high humidities show corresponding differences. The Oregon school children, experiencing their customary high winter humidities, must be models of deportment as compared with those at Denver and in other cities having low humidities."

USDA, *Climate and Crops: Oregon Section*, July 1900

with air that has less moisture in it so the evaporation process can continue. Thus, the higher the relative humidity and the warmer the temperature, the "hotter" it will feel. It is this condition that can be dangerous. We become susceptible to heat cramps, heat exhaustion, and heatstroke when the temperature and relative humidity are high. Hundreds of people have died when these conditions, called heat waves, persist for several days. The heat wave in the Midwest in July of 1995 was responsible for around 1,000 deaths due to heat-related causes. The Texas and Oklahoma heat wave of July 1998 caused several hundred deaths.

The combination of heat and humidity is seldom a problem in the Pacific Northwest. This part of the country only rarely experiences the conditions found in other sections of the country. Afternoon temperatures that reach into the 80s on a summer day in Seattle or Portland will normally find the relative humidity in the 30 to 40 percent category with even lower values east of the Cascade Mountains. East of the Rocky Mountains, however, the relative humidity is above 50 percent in the summer. When these conditions do occur in the Pacific Northwest, residents feel miserable, unless they have recently moved here from areas east of the Rocky Mountains. We become acclimated to our local conditions or climate. Transport a Pacific Northwesterner into the Midwest in summer, and he or she immediately begins complaining of the humidity. To that local Midwest resident, it would just be another hot, sultry summer day.

Wind Speed & Direction

This weather element is actually a combination of two variables, each important in its own way. First of all, wind is always measured in the direction from which it comes, not in the direction it is going. A south wind means the wind is blowing from the south; an east wind from the east, and so on. Stagnant air conditions due to light winds can cause a build-up of atmospheric pollutants, but brisk winds like those unfurling the flag in Figure 1.3 disperse air particles.

Figure 1.3 Brisk winds, like those unfurling the flag, create ripples that move along the flag. The ripples result from small differences in air pressure on either side of the flag.

Figure 1.4 The Columbia River Gorge is an excellent place for strong winds to occur, creating great windsurfing.

Today, construction of buildings and other structures built in areas prone to high winds must follow strict building codes. For many years this was not the case, but after several destructive windstorms and hurricanes, these codes were introduced to lessen the damage. Windsurfers, like the one shown in Figure 1.4, look for a constant wind speed but are not too concerned with the direction. Strong winds can affect the performance of automobiles and trucks. High-profile vehicles are discouraged from traveling through the Columbia River Gorge during episodes of strong winds. On a lesser note, when I apply a fungicide to my roses, I do it in the early morning or late evening when the winds are light or calm. Landing or taking off in an airplane? Better get the nose of the airplane pointed into the wind for that extra lift. Airport runways are constructed to favor the prevailing winds.

When temperature and wind speed are combined, another apparent temperature is created. It is called the wind chill. The wind chill is usually not taken into account unless the temperature is 40°F or below, but the effects can still be there. On those cold, wet, drizzly, windy days in the Pacific Northwest west of the Cascade Mountains, we actually feel colder than what the temperature is telling us it is. Table 1.2 expresses wind chill as a factor of wind and temperature.

Wind blowing over the skin removes body heat. In calm conditions, a thin layer of air that has been warmed by the body serves to insulate us from colder air. Wind disrupts that layer and the body is then exposed to the colder air. The colder air and the stronger the wind, the greater the effect. People foolish enough to watch a football game when the temperature is near zero and the wind is blowing are

WIND CHILL CHART
Wind Speed (miles per hour)

Air Temperature (°F)	calm	5	10	15	20	25	30	35	40	45	50	55	60
40		36	34	32	30	29	28	28	27	26	26	25	25
35		31	27	25	24	23	22	21	20	19	19	18	17
30		25	21	19	17	16	15	14	13	12	12	11	10
25		19	15	13	11	9	8	7	6	5	4	4	3
20		13	9	6	4	3	1	0	-1	-2	-3	-3	-4
15		7	3	0	-2	-4	-5	-7	-8	-9	-10	-11	-11
10		1	-4	-7	-9	-11	-12	-14	-15	-16	-17	-18	-19
5		-5	-10	-13	-15	-17	-19	-21	-22	-23	-24	-25	-26
0		-11	-16	-19	-22	-24	-26	-27	-29	-30	-31	-32	-33
-5		-16	-22	-26	-29	-31	-33	-34	-36	-37	-38	-39	-40
-10		-22	-28	-32	-35	-37	-39	-41	-43	-44	-45	-46	-48
-15		-28	-35	-39	-42	-44	-46	-48	-50	-51	-52	-54	-55
-20		-34	-41	-45	-48	-51	-53	-55	-57	-58	-60	-61	-62
-25		-40	-47	-51	-55	-58	-60	-62	-64	-65	-67	-68	-69
-30		-46	-53	-58	-61	-64	-67	-69	-71	-72	-74	-75	-76
-35		-52	-59	-64	-68	-71	-73	-76	-78	-79	-81	-82	-84
-40		-57	-66	-71	-74	-78	-80	-82	-84	-86	-88	-89	-91
-45		-63	-72	-77	-81	-84	-87	-89	-91	-93	-95	-97	-98

Wind Chill values from Weatherwise January/February 2002.

Table 1.2 Wind chill values are derived by combining the wind speed and the temperature. For example, a temperature of 20°F and a wind speed of 20 miles per hour gives a wind chill of 4°F.

Figure 1.5 Overcast skies prevent the sun's radiation from reaching the earth and also prevent the earth's radiation from escaping into space.

exposed to dangerous wind-chill conditions. (I was one of those while working in Denver.)

Consider that with a temperature of 25°F and a wind of 10 miles per hour, the temperature your body perceives is 15°F. Increase the wind speed to 20 miles per hour and maintain the same temperature (not uncommon with east winds in the Portland area in winter) and you have an apparent temperature, or wind chill, of 11°F. Brrrrrr!! But if that's cold, pity the friend or relative of yours in the upper Midwest in the winter when a cold norther sets in with a temperature of -10°F and a wind speed of 20 miles per hour. That combination gives a wind chill of -35°F. Now that's cold!

Wind chill is how cold your body "thinks" it is, and it generates heat to compensate for the loss. Air with a low moisture content is a very poor conductor of heat. That's why the advice of many layers of light clothing with a layer of air trapped between each is often better than one thick parka. Wind chill only affects animals. It does not mean that if your car is only protected to zero that it will freeze if the wind chill is -10°F.

Cloudiness

When it is cloudy outside, Figure 1.5, a portion of the sun's radiation (shortwave radiation) is not received at the earth's surface. The clouds reflect it, scatter it, and absorb it so the radiation is prevented from reaching the earth's surface. The result is that cloudy days usually have cooler daytime temperatures than clear days. But cloudiness is an important

weather element in other respects. It, along with the moisture in the air, acts like a free safety on a football team, intercepting those "passes" of longwave radiation emitted by the earth. Not only do clouds intercept them, they send them back to the earth. And with that, you just heard "the rest of the story" as to why it is warmer on a cloudy night than it is on a clear night. Those clouds are directing the radiation that the earth is emitting back to the earth, thus preventing the earth from cooling as much as it would if the sky was clear. Clouds do not have to be very thick to send radiation back to earth. Even very high thin cirrus clouds such as those shown in Figures 1.6a and 1.6b reflect both radiation arriving from the sun and radiation being emitted by the earth.

Clouds prevent us from viewing the sky at night. Sky watchers look for clear nights with no clouds. The amount of cloudiness also affects solar radiation panels and their ability to generate heat or electricity. Cloudiness can also be a factor in a person's attitude, sometimes leading to depression. Studies have shown people's moods can change after prolonged spells of cloudy, gloomy weather,

Figure 1.6a, 1.6b. Even high-elevation cirrus clouds can intercept radiation from the sun and the earth.

Figure 1.7 Snow has excellent insulating qualities that trap the earth's radiation, preventing it from escaping into space.

which often afflict the Pacific Northwest west of the Cascade Mountains in winter. Then with that first sunny day, their spirits are lifted.

Type and Amount of Precipitation

"Rain, rain, go away; come again another day!" I borrow that childhood rhyme every time I hold an outdoor barbeque. Type and amount of precipitation is another weather element, and oh, so very important in a number of ways. Precipitation patterns dictate the different types of climates around the globe and in the United States. Certain plants can only be grown if there is sufficient moisture. The amount of precipitation varies considerably over the earth and even in Oregon and Washington. Precipitation varies from month to month and year to year. Summers in the Pacific Northwest are much drier (well, most of the time) than winters.

If you are a skier, you are not only concerned about the amount of precipitation, you worry about the type. And well you, and all of us, should. It is much easier to drive on wet pavement than snow-covered pavement. Snowpack, as it relates to water supply, is extremely important for irrigation, recreation, fish management, and river transportation. In the Pacific Northwest we are blessed with an abundant snowpack most years. Snow is also a good insulator. The freshly fallen snow in Figure 1.7 provides a protective layer for plants lying below because it inhibits radiation from the earth escaping into space.

But precipitation gets a bit out of control at times, and the amount of precipitation far exceeds what we need. This results in flooding such as in December 1964 and February 1996. At other times there is a deficiency and the result is a drought. The winter of 1976-77 produced very little snowpack in the mountains. Again in the mid 1980s many residents of the Pacific Northwest faced water restrictions during the summer. Just like temperature, the type and amount of precipitation can vary over short distances, and drastically over a few miles.

Pressure

"Oh, darn. My ears just won't pop!" All of us have made that comment while ascending or descending in an airplane or going over a mountain pass in a car. Well, we certainly wouldn't want our ears to literally "pop," but we certainly wish the air pressure outside would equal the pressure inside.

The most precise way to measure the air pressure is through a mercurial barometer, Figure 1.8. Mercury responds quickly to changes in air pressure, and the mercurial barometer can detect minute changes that humans cannot perceive. (Because of the hazards of mercury, however, its use in instruments is declining.) Of all the weather elements, air pressure is the hardest for humans to detect unless, of course, you are traveling over a mountain range, such as the Cascade Mountains or in an airplane that is landing or taking off. In addition to varying with elevation, air pressure also varies during the day, especially in summer, during the week, and during the year.

Let's take a test and see how well you perceive daily pressure changes. The weather guru on television (No matter whether he or she is a real meteorologist) tells you the

Figure 1.8 Mercurial barometers are highly sensitive to changes in air pressure.

barometer reading or the barometric pressure is 30.20 inches. That reading comes from official sources, so it has to be good! You tune in the next day and are sitting on the edge of your chair waiting for today's barometer reading. Here it comes! Wow! 30.10 inches! Now, can you really tell if the pressure was lower or higher than the day before? I don't believe so. Yes, I know the story of Ol' Fido howling in the corner before a big storm and Aunt Martha's rheumatism acting up as the pressure was falling. But maybe Ol' Fido is just hungry and Aunt Martha slept on the wrong side of the bed! It is very difficult for humans to perceive daily changes in air pressure. Yet, small differences in air pressure account for major weather changes.

So, six weather elements combine in various degrees and amounts to make up what we call weather. Some resources refer to a seventh, visibility. But to me, that adds a 4th dimension to what we are talking about. Visibility can be related to human activities. I am going to have enough on my hands to get through the six natural weather elements. Let's not obscure things by adding visibility.

Measuring Weather Elements

In the discussion on weather elements reference was made to their involvement in our daily lives. But how are these weather elements measured? What instruments are used to determine temperature, pressure, wind, and the other weather elements? How does one measure the rain? Books have been written on weather instruments, and my discussion will only "measure" just lightly how the aforementioned weather elements are measured and the instruments used. Some of these instruments are relatively new. Others have been around for about 500 years.

> **Rain**
> *It rained and rained and rained;*
> *The average fall was well maintained,*
> *And when the tracks were simple bogs,*
> *It started raining cats and dogs.*
> *After a drought of half an hour,*
> *We had a most refreshing shower.*
> *And then a most curious thing of all,*
> *A gentle rain began to fall.*
> *Next day but one was fairly dry*
> *Save for one deluge from the sky*
> *Which wetted the party to the skin*
> *And then at last the rain set in.*
>
> Anonymous

Perhaps the first instrument that was used to measure one of the weather elements was a type of hygrometer for measuring the amount of water vapor (moisture) in the air. It was crude and consisted of nothing more than a scales with a few rocks on one side and wool on the other side. As the wool absorbed or lost moisture, the scales would move.

Figure 1.9 A Galileo thermometer. Glass globes containing fluids of different densities react to changes in the density of the fluid in the cylinder.

In 1593, Galileo Galilei invented the first thermometer. It was simply a liquid-in-glass thermometer. However, it used the same principle that thermometers follow today: liquids expand when heated and contract when cooled. Galileo calculated the temperature by the height of the liquid column. Similar instruments are found in speciality stores today, consisting of several glass balls, partially filled with a liquid of slightly different density, that rise and fall within the liquid column depending on the temperature (density) of the fluid in the column. Figure 1.9 is a picture of such a thermometer. (If you are thinking of purchasing one of these instruments, the more glass balls within the column, the greater will be the accuracy of the thermometer.)

The barometer was next. A student of Galileo, Evangelista Torricelli, invented it around 1644. His first experiments used water in a long cylindrical tube with a vacuum at the top. Mercury, however, responds much more readily to changes in barometric pressure, and it was eventually used by Torricelli. The principle has not changed. Mercurial barometers, like the one discussed earlier, are used for precision readings. They are built very similar to Torricelli's, a cistern of mercury below a glass tube with the air at the top removed. Increasing or higher atmospheric pressure pushes the column of mercury up the tube while decreasing or lower atmospheric pressure causes the column of mercury to descend within the tube.

Around 1714, Daniel Fahrenheit developed the Fahrenheit temperature scale (°F) used today. Using a mixture of salt, water, and ice, the lowest point he could bring his solution to was labeled "zero." The second fixed point he used was the body temperature which he set at 96°F. (Fahrenheit could be considered a "cool" guy!) From these two points, he calculated that the freezing point of water would be 32°F and the boiling point, at sea level, would be 212°F.

About 28 years later, Anders Celsius based his temperature scale on the decimal system. He chose 0° as the freezing point of water and 100°, at sea level, as the boiling point of water. For many years this was called the Centigrade scale. By whatever name, it is the temperature scale used throughout the world, except in just a few countries, namely the United States and Great Britain where the Fahrenheit scale is still used. A degree of Celsius (C) is equal to 1.8° Fahrenheit, but to get a Fahrenheit reading from a Celsius (and vice versa) a conversion formula is needed to get the precise temperature. [°F = 9/5°C + 32; °C = 5/9(°F - 32)] Table 1 in Appendices shows both Celsius and Fahrenheit temperatures.

Today's Thermometers

Following Galileo's principle, today's liquid-in-glass thermometers employ either alcohol or, in decreasing use, mercury. Both readily expand when heated and contract when cooled. If the mercury expands and contracts in accordance with the temperature, then there must be a great variance over 24 hours. How are the maximum (highest) and minimum (lowest) values for the day obtained? Would you have to watch it continuously? No. The maximum thermometer has a constriction just above the reservoir of mercury. As the mercury expands it is allowed to move by the constriction. However, when the temperature begins to cool and the mercury contracts, it cannot work its way past the constriction. The maximum reading for that day is recorded. To return the mercury to the reservoir the thermometer is spun several times, using centrifugal force to push the mercury past the constriction into the reservoir.

Minimum thermometers use a slightly different principle. They employ the use of alcohol. Minimum thermometers are mounted horizontally and have a short piece of glass within the tube of alcohol. As the alcohol contracts when the temperature cools, it pulls the small, short piece of glass with it. Then, when the temperature begins to rise, the alcohol expands around the piece of glass. After the minimum reading is noted (or where the piece of glass has finally settled), the thermometer is put in vertical position with the reservoir of alcohol at the top. Gravity pulls the piece of glass down to the current temperature reading, and the thermometer is returned to its horizontal position. The drawing in Figure 1.10 shows an example of maximum and minimum thermometers.

Both the maximum and minimum thermometers are mounted in an instrument shelter. These shelters are box-like with louvers on all four sides. (Figure 1.11) This type of construction allows air to circulate through the shelter. Instrument shelters should be placed free of obstructions and painted white. The door of the shelter will always open toward the north in the Northern Hemisphere and towards the south in the Southern Hemisphere. White objects reflect more of the

Figure 1.11 A standard instrument shelter.

Figure 1.10 Drawing of maximum and minimum thermometers.

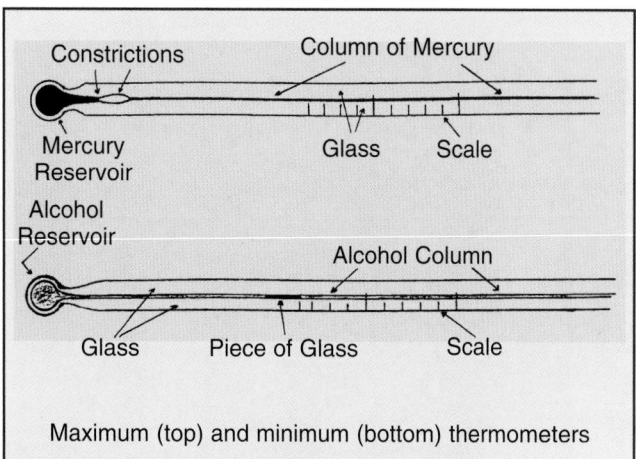

Constrictions   Column of Mercury

Mercury Reservoir   Glass   Scale

Alcohol Reservoir

Alcohol Column

Glass   Piece of Glass   Scale

Maximum (top) and minimum (bottom) thermometers

sun's radiation, but what is the reason for the door to open in different directions in the two hemispheres? A thermometer reacts quickly to sunlight, and any direct radiation allowed inside the shelter could affect the values. Shelters should be placed over natural surfaces, free from irrigation sprinklers and isolated from radiation that may emanate from tall buildings nearby.

The thermometers mounted within the shelter are at a height of around five feet. This height is above the influence that various surfaces may have on the readings, depending on their composition. There can be as much as five to ten degrees difference between a thermometer located at a height of five feet vs. one located at ground level. Daytime high temperature readings at the surface are much higher, and nighttime minimum temperature readings are much lower than temperatures measured at an elevation of five feet. Often around my home on a clear morning in late fall, winter, or early spring, there will be frost on the grass and rocks while the minimum temperature recorded within the shelter is above freezing. Thus, agriculturists are very much concerned about temperatures next to the surface where tender plants are grown.

Temperature can also be measured through the use of a bi-metallic strip. Different metals expand and contract at various rates. If two different strips that react differently are attached and connected through a series of linkages to an arm and a pen, a record of temperature can be traced on a chart. A crescent-shaped cistern filled with a fluid will react similarly to the two metal strips, expanding or contracting with the change in temperature, changing the shape of the cistern, and moving the pen on the chart.

Your author firmly believes in the saying, "All work and no play makes George a dull boy!" He sometimes is gone for a few days visiting relatives, doing research, or relaxing at the beach. My wife is reluctant to take weather readings, except precipitation. Thus, I must find a substitute and that substitute is called a thermograph. A thermograph is used to record temperatures over several days when there is no one to observe the readings each day. A thermograph uses either a bi-metallic strip or a curved cylinder filled with a liquid. A thermograph is shown in Figure 1.12.

Temperature can also be measured electronically through the use of thermisters or thermocouples. A thermister measures the amount of electrical resistance and converts the variance in the readings to temperature. A thermocouple converts thermal energy into electrical energy. Infrared thermometers now measure the amount of radiation an object emits which can be related to temperature. Infrared sensors are used to locate animals and humans where temperatures surrounding the creatures are lower. Remember, your body heat is maintained between 98°F and 99°F. That is warmer than it is on most days outside and certainly at night.

Relative Humidity

Various instruments are used to calculate the amount of water vapor in the air. (We are not talking about rain and

Figure 1.12 A thermograph. Note cistern in lower right of photograph.

clouds, but water vapor as a gas. This invisible gas is present in the atmosphere in various quantities that depend on the temperature of the air.) Improvements to the crude hygrometer mentioned earlier came in the late 1700s. Hair is one element that responds very well to moisture as you have witnessed on those "bad hair days" when moisture has caused hair to become long and scraggly. It is the main element used in many hygrometers today. Hair strands, as they absorb moisture, expand. They are fastened at both ends. Then, through a series of linking mechanisms that are attached to an arm with a pen on the end, a trace is made of the humidity values on a chart which is attached to a drum, driven by a spring-wound clock. A combination of the thermograph and hygrometer is called a hygrothermograph and one is shown in Figure 1.13.

The amount of moisture in the air can also be measured through the use of two thermometers. The device is called a sling psychrometer. Two thermometers are placed side by side.

Figure 1.13 A hygrothermograph. The cistern measures the temperature and the hair element measures relative humidity.

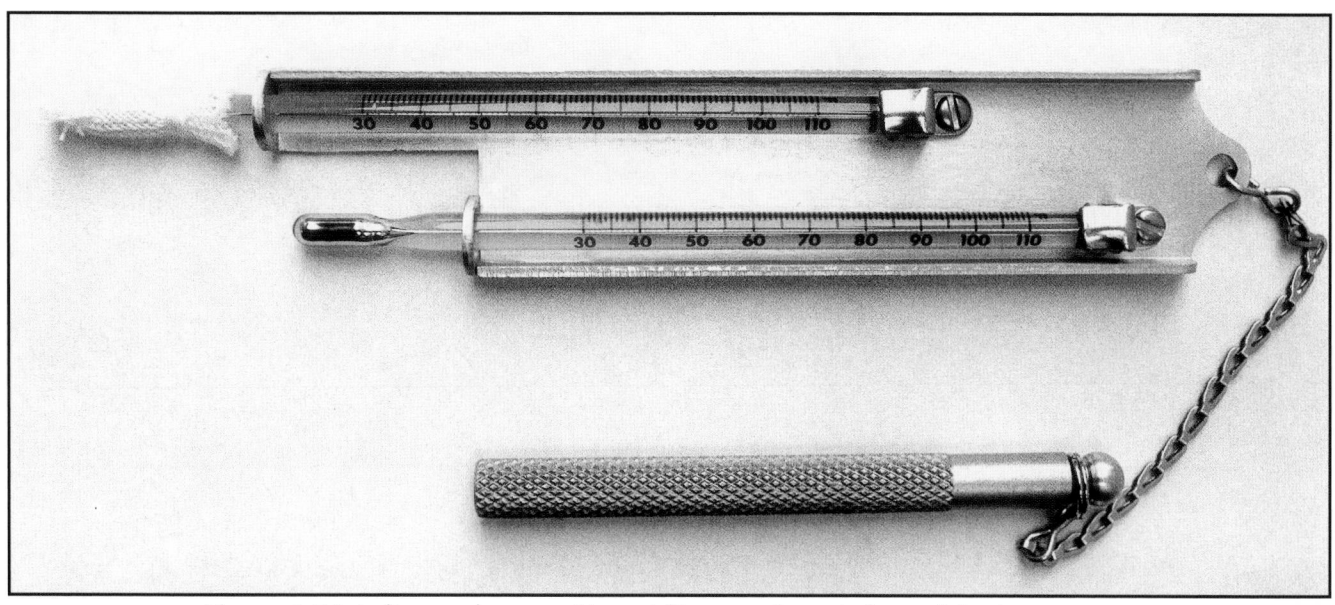

Figure 1.14 A sling psychrometer. Note wicking over the end of one of the thermometers.

A piece of cloth is tied around the reservoir of mercury or alcohol on one of the thermometers. The end of that thermometer is then placed in a small container of water to saturate the piece of cloth. Both thermometers are then twirled around and around. Water evaporating off the piece of cloth will cool that thermometer, lowering its temperature. After ten to twenty seconds, the temperature of both thermometers is noted. The one with the piece of cloth around it will have a lower temperature, called the wet-bulb temperature. A sling psychrometer is shown in Figure 1.14. One can readily see that the drier the air, the lower will be the wet-bulb temperature as more moisture from the cloth is evaporated which results in more cooling.

Relative humidity can also be measured electronically through a hygrister. Electrical resistance varies as the humidity varies, so by measuring this change in resistance, the humidity can be calculated. There are far more sophisticated methods of measuring the amount of water vapor in the air, but all employ the same principle that when moisture evaporates, it cools the surface from which it was attached.

Measuring the Wind

Wind is measured using an anemometer. The anemometer was developed in the 1800s. Before that adjectives such as moderate, gale, light were used. The Beaufort Wind Scale was developed in the early 1800s by Admiral Beaufort of the British Navy. It was based on the amount of wind that affected the canvas sails used on a frigate. It has since been modified to include waves at sea and flags, tree limbs, trees, etc., on land. Wind is expressed in miles per hour (mph), nautical miles per hour (knots), or in meters per second. Table 2 in Appendices converts these values. (The term "knot" was used by early mariners long before other methods were used to indicate the speed of vessels. A rope with knots in it would

be thrown overboard and the number of knots that passed were then counted.)

Most anemometers employ the use of cups that rotate at different rates depending on the speed of the wind. Others use a propellor-type system. A wind vane indicates the direction. Both types of anemometers are shown in Figure 1.15 as they appear on the Morrison Bridge crossing the Willamette River in Portland, Oregon. Lately acoustical anemometers have been developed that very accurately measure wind velocity.

Sky Cover or Cloudiness

The amount of cloudiness was measured mostly with the human eye until a few years ago. Estimation of the amount

Figure 1.15 Two types of anemometers: propellor-type and wind vane with cups.

Figure 1.16 An Automated Surface Observing System (ASOS).

of sky cover and height of the clouds was recorded. Now, automatic instruments such as the Automated Surface Observing System (ASOS) shown in Figure 1.16 at Astoria, Oregon, can detect the amount of cloudiness over one location up to elevations of around 12,000 feet. For aviation purposes, visual observations of the amount and type of cloudiness are still preferred over automatic weather stations that only record the amount of cloudiness over one point. Satellites, using both visual and infrared observations, map cloudiness over the entire globe, but it is a view from space rather than from the earth, and subsequently all the cloud layers may not be detected.

Measuring Precipitation

The most common method of measuring precipitation is done manually using a rain gauge. The standard rain gauge used by the National Weather Service has an 8-inch opening which is funneled down to a 2 1/2-inch tube. Figure 1.17 is a picture of this rain gauge with the funnel and tube removed. A rain gauge stick is inserted in the opening and the total amount of precipitation that has fallen is indicated in hundredths of an inch. There are other precipitation gauges similar to this that are constructed to measure rainfall in tenths of an inch. Other gauges used to measure precipitation include a storage gauge, a tipping bucket gauge, and a recording weighing gauge. Storage gauges were used extensively in remote locations up until several years ago, but their use is diminishing as they are replaced by automatic weather stations. Storage gauges are filled with an antifreeze solution so that snow falling into them melts. The antifreeze solution also inhibits evaporation. A technician visits the site once a year and the total amount of precipitation that fell since the last visit is weighed and the gauge emptied.

A tipping bucket gauge, Figure 1.18, is constructed so that as precipitation from a funnel falls into one side of a small open bucket it fills the bucket with 0.01 inch of precipitation. As side BDC fills up, it tips down allowing side

Figure 1.17 A standard 8-inch rain gauge with tube, funnel and measuring stick.

CDA to tip up and fill. This causes the mechanism to tip and empty its contents, allowing the other side to then fill with another 0.01 of an inch, tip, and so on. The number of "tips" corresponds to the amount of precipitation, measured in

Figure 1.18 A schematic showing a tipping bucket rain gauge. As side BDC fills up, it tips down allowing side CDA to tip up and fill.

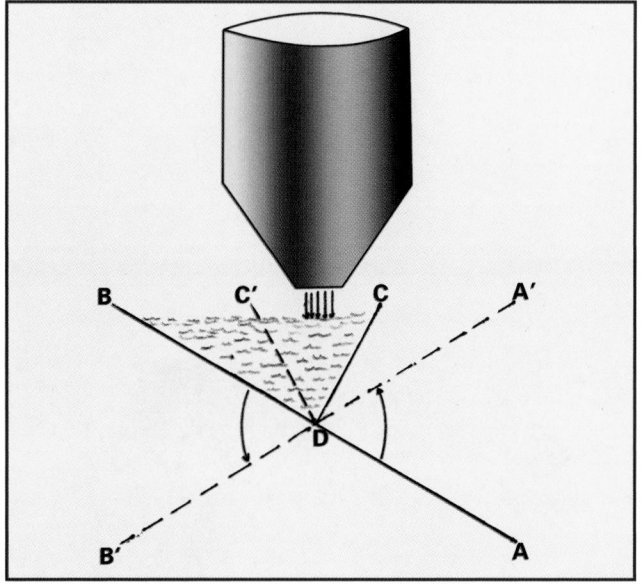

hundredths of an inch. This type of gauge is used in many small weather stations.

A recording weighing gauge also uses an antifreeze solution similar to the storage gauge. Precipitation falling into the opening accumulates and the amount pushes down on a scales. The total weight of the precipitation and the antifreeze is recorded on a chart. Recording weighing gauges need to be attended to more often than the storage gauges since the containers are much smaller.

In most cases snow is simply measured with a normal ruler. The ruler is inserted in the snow and the amount recorded in inches & fractions. If it is snowing at the time of observation, a clear board, called a snowboard, is placed on the snow so the new amount that falls can be recorded at the next observation or when it quits snowing. In remote areas some government agencies actually measure the weight or density of the snow along what are known as "snow courses" through mountainous terrain. This requires individuals to trek through these mountains stopping at various sites to measure the weight of the snow. The weight of the snow on an undisturbed remote small area can also be measured automatically. The value is transmitted, usually via satellite, to a ground receiving station. This instrument is not measuring the depth of the snow, only the water content of the snow. Such a station is located below Timberline Lodge on Mt. Hood in Oregon near the 5,000-foot elevation and is shown in Figure 1.19 in the foreground. The long cylinder in the back, left, is a storage gauge.

Measuring Pressure

Air pressure is measured by a barometer and is usually expressed in inches of mercury or millibars. Table 3 in Appendices converts these values. Evangelista Torricelli inserted a hollow tube of glass with the air removed into a dish of mercury. It is the same principle used in mercurial barometers today. The height of a column of mercury in a glass tube with a vacuum at the top reacts to changes in pressure on a reservoir full of mercury. As air pressure increases and pushes down on the mercury in the reservoir, the column of mercury rises

within the tube. If the atmospheric pressure decreases the column of mercury will retreat into the reservoir leaving a greater gap at the top, or lower pressure. A diagram of a mercurial barometer is shown in Figure 1.20.

Another kind of barometer, like the one many people have in their homes, is called an aneroid barometer. The term aneroid means without liquid. This barometer works on the principle of a cylinder or diaphragm that also contains a vacuum. The cylinder is connected through a series of linkages to a pen that indicates the pressure. As the pressure increases or causes the cylinder to constrict, the needle indicates a higher pressure. As the pressure decreases, the cylinder expands and the needle points to a lower pressure. An aneroid barometer is shown in Figure 1.21. These barometers usually have words included on them such as "stormy," "changing," "fair," and "hot." However, this often does not reflect the true state of the weather outside as was explained to the caller many years ago. A barometer need not be hung outside since air pressure inside the home very quickly assumes outside values. (I can still remember how excited I was when my sister gave me a barometer for Christmas many, many years ago. That same barometer still hangs in our home today.)

Figure 1.20 The principle of a mercurial barometer. As air pressure increases and pushes down on the reservoir of mercury, the mercury column rises in the tube. As pressure lowers the column retreats.

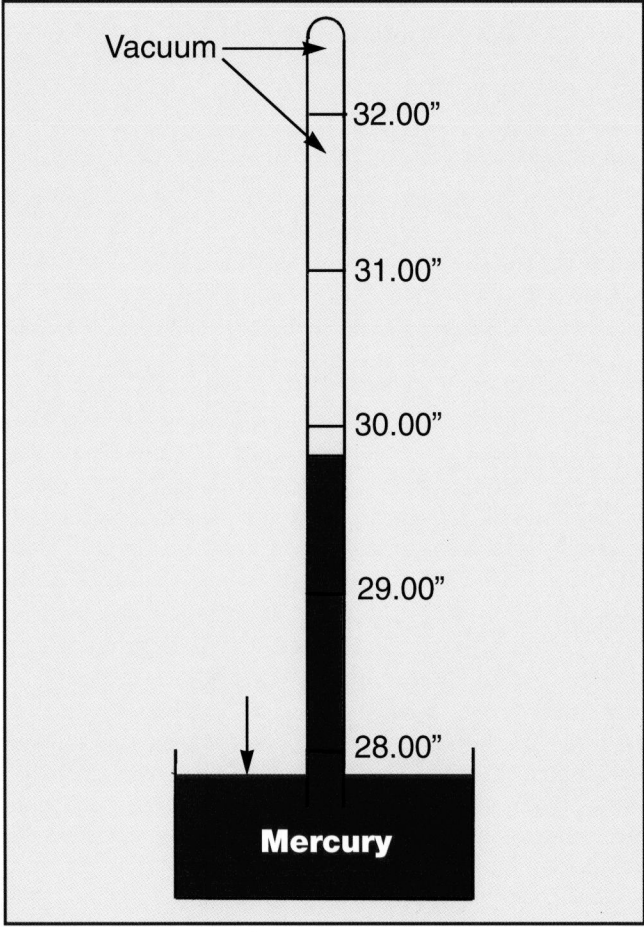

Figure 1.19 A "snotel" site below Mt. Hood, Oregon, maintained by the Natural Resources Conservation Service.

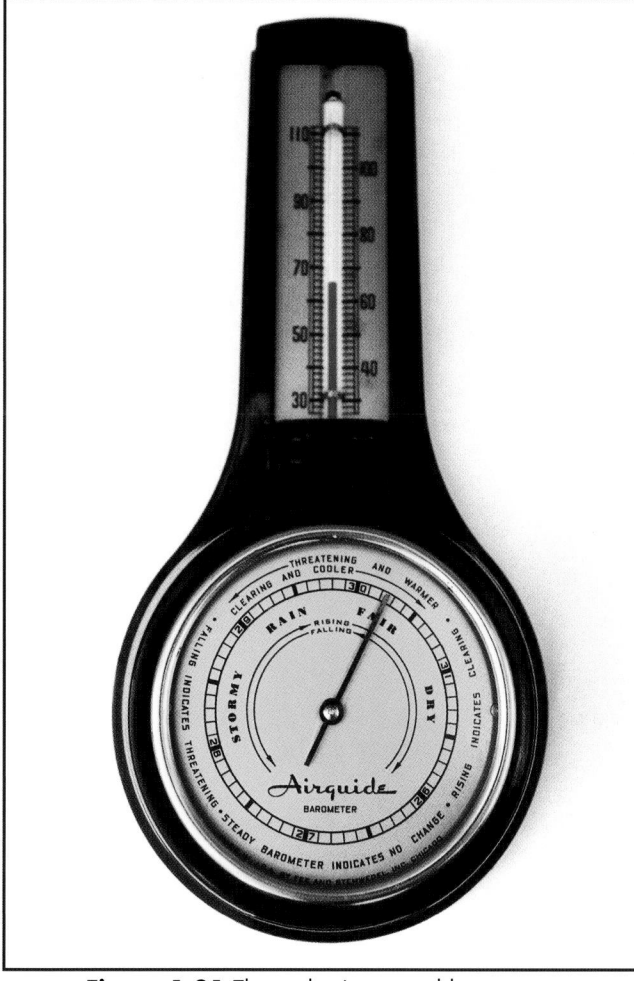

Figure 1.21 The author's aneroid barometer.

Other Measurements

Early meteorologists knew that the atmosphere extended well above the surface of the earth. Thus they soon began looking for methods to obtain information from these heights. Kites were used extensively in the late 1800s and

Figure 1.22 The shape of today's kites is far different from kites used by meteorologists in the late 1800s and early 1900s.

early 1900s to obtain measurements above the surface of the earth. They were generally of a box-like construction, often quite large, and far different from the kites shown in Figure 1.22. Recording instruments were attached to the kite or at various levels on the wire. When the kite was retrieved, the information from the recording instruments could then be viewed and analyzed. With the development of aircraft, meteorologists were able to receive the same information from the air overhead by installing instruments on the aircraft.

In the late 1930s a very effective instrument was developed to obtain temperature, moisture, pressure, wind speed and direction from altitudes above the surface of the earth. The instrument is called the radiosonde, and it is still used extensively today around the world to obtain weather data above the earth's surface. It consists of a large balloon filled with hydrogen or helium gas. An instrument package is attached to the balloon by a long piece of string. Inside the package is a small barometer, a thermistor and a hygrister. The package contains dry cell batteries and a miniature transmitter.

As the balloon ascends into the atmosphere it transmits temperature and relative humidity signals back to the receiving station that sent it aloft. The balloon is filled with a measured amount of gas that causes it to rise at a predetermined rate. The barometer inside the package has a pen that is attached to a bar. This bar contains very small reference points that correspond to the pressure. A pen moves slowly across the bar as the instrument gains altitude moving into lower pressure. Since the instrument package was calibrated at the factory which made it, its height can be determined from the reference points on the bar. Figure 1.23 shows a radiosonde being prepared and then launched from Salem, Oregon.

"Radiosonde" an Officially-Adopted Weather Bureau Term.
In 1938, the Weather Bureau officially adopted the use of the term radiosonde as an instrument that was carried aloft by a balloon and transmitted the information back to the receiving station. The term was also used in French and German literature.

Monthly Weather Review October 1938

The instrument package attached to the balloon is tracked by a detector which takes azimuth and elevation readings every minute. Thus, the balloon's position can be determined and from that data, the wind speed and direction above the surface of the earth can be calculated. The balloon keeps rising until it bursts somewhere around 20 miles high or 100,000 feet. Once that happens, a parachute opens and the instrument package drifts back to earth. Many are retrieved, and they can be refurbished and sent aloft again. Stations that send these instruments aloft in the Pacific Northwest include Quillayute and Spokane, Washington; Boise, Idaho; Salem and Medford, Oregon.

Since it was developed around 1940, radar has been used extensively to detect areas of precipitation. A basic radar, Figure 1.24, sends out a pulse of energy at a certain frequency. A portion of this energy is reflected off precipitation or any particles of sufficient size in the atmosphere and returns to the detector portion of the antenna. Radar signals, or radar beams as they are called, are sometimes affected by atmospheric conditions that result in erroneous returns called anomalous propagation.

Lately the development and deployment of a type of radar known as the Doppler radar has given meteorologists a much clearer picture of what is happening within clouds. Doppler radars work on the same principle as other radars; that is, transmitting a signal and detecting a return signal. Doppler radars, however, detect a change in frequency of the return signal depending on whether the particle is moving away from or toward the radar. The signal detected by particles moving away from the radar returns at a slightly lower frequency (longer wavelength). Those particles that the wind is transporting toward the radar reflect the signal back to the radar at a slightly higher frequency (shorter wavelength). This is similar to the change in the tone of a train whistle as the train approaches and then moves away. The ability of a computer to analyze this return signal has helped meteorologists to detect heavy areas of precipitation, hail, wind shear, and even the formative stage of a tornado.

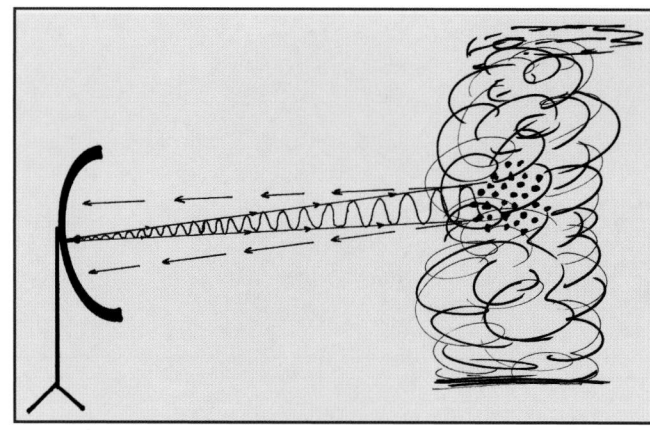

Figure 1.24 A radar sends out a pulse of energy, a small portion of which reflects off precipitation, and travels back to the radar.

Several instruments used to measure the weather elements have been briefly discussed. These are by no means all the instruments that are used today. Several have become quite sophisticated and are used in weather stations located in remote areas. Many inexpensive weather stations are available for use as home weather stations. It suffices to say that weather must be measured in its initial state before any type of weather forecast can be made. Even before the above instruments were developed, early observers used their visual observations of clouds, wind, and how they felt to determine the weather's initial state.

Figure 1.23 A radiosonde being checked before launch, filling the balloon with helium, and ascending into the atmosphere transmitting back data.

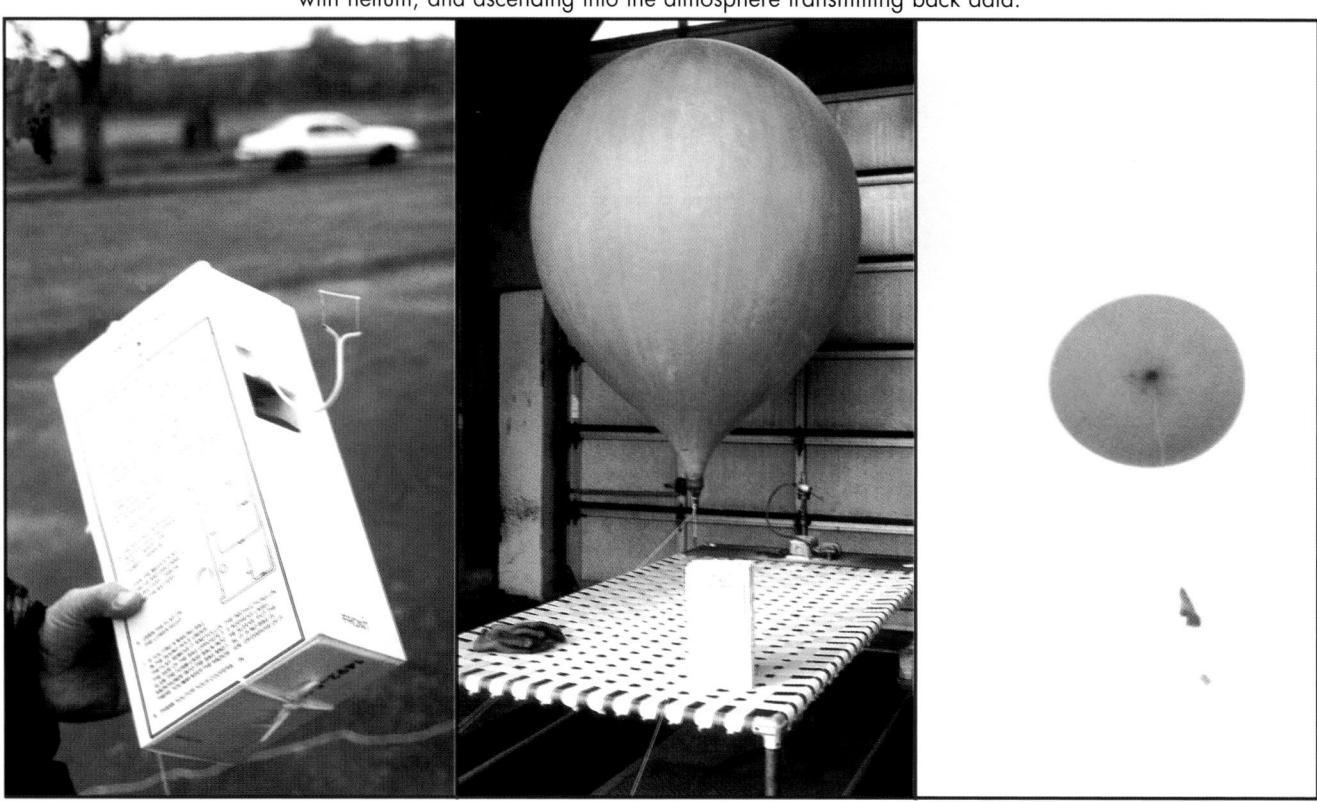

Chapter 2
Earth-Sun Relationship, Energy Balance, Atmosphere Composition

One small star, one small planet. Compared to other stars, the sun is relatively small. Compared to other planets in the solar system, earth is also relatively small. It seems to be the right combination. Perhaps there are other combinations. But for life on earth – the sun is it! It is our source of energy.

The sun is a vast nuclear reaction that emits energy in all directions. The earth intercepts only a very small portion of that energy as it revolves around the sun. However, that small portion is enough. If the earth were closer to the sun, it would be too hot, like Venus, the second planet from the sun. If it were farther away, like Mars, the earth would be too cold. So, the earth and the sun have a longstanding relationship that accounts for the right energy balance and the variance in weather from summer to winter.

Electromagnetic Spectrum

But what kind of energy? The sun emits energy in the form of radiation. This radiation covers the range of the electromagnetic spectrum, Figure 2.1, from very short wavelengths (gamma rays) to extremely long wavelengths (radio waves.) Radiation from the sun travels through space at the speed of light, 186,000 miles per second or nearly 300,000 kilometers per second. You can think of this radiation that has traveled through a vacuum to get here as little packets, pulses, or waves of energy. This is not a true analogy, but good enough. A depiction of wavelength is shown in Figure 2.2.

Fortunately for life on earth, the sun's temperature is around 6,000°C or 10,000°F. Why are we fortunate? At this temperature a large portion of the sun's radiation (around 44 percent) is emitted in wavelengths from 0.4 micrometers to 0.7 micrometers or the visible portion of the electromagnetic spectrum and not in the other wavelengths that may be damaging. But just how long is a micrometer? Take one of the hairs from your head. (I have to be careful, because age has taken too many of mine!) Now, if you can, divide it, not in segments, but dissect it down the middle from one end to the other (we're "splitting hairs," now) about one hundred times! You get the picture that the wavelength of visible light is very short. Another 48 percent that also is in the good range is emitted in the infrared portion. Ultraviolet is around 7 percent (the damaging rays) which leaves only 1 percent to the other wavelengths. Hotter stars emit most of their energy in the shorter wavelengths of the electromagnetic spectrum and cooler stars in the longer wavelengths with still enough visible light so we can see them.

The sun, however, is not the only object that emits radiation. The earth and everything on it emit radiation. That includes you and me and all our shrubs, trees, cats, dogs, etc. But the earth is much cooler than the sun so the radiation it emits is mostly in the infrared band with wavelengths of 5 to 20 micrometers. Energy that is in the wavelength from infrared to the long radio waves is often referred to as longwave radiation, and that of shorter wavelength as shortwave

Figure 2.1 The electromagnetic spectrum.

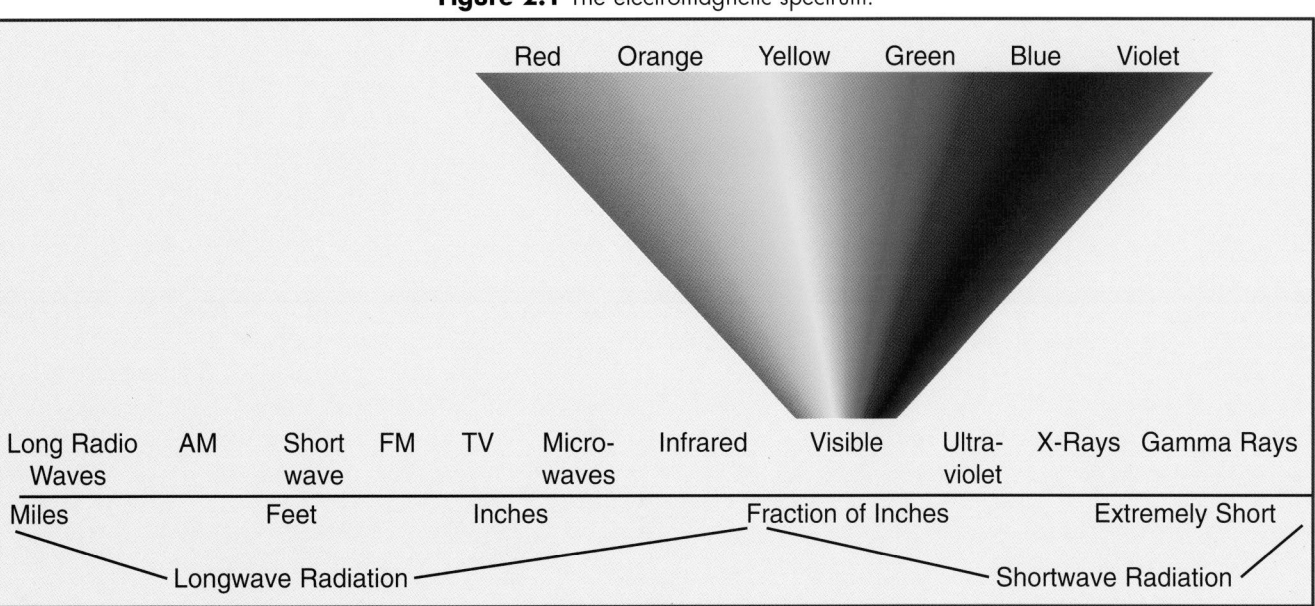

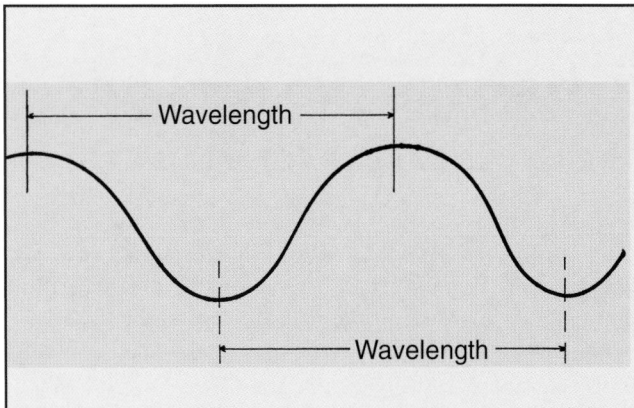

Figure 2.2 Wavelength, be it electromagnetic waves or ocean waves, is measured from ridge crest to ridge crest, or from trough to trough.

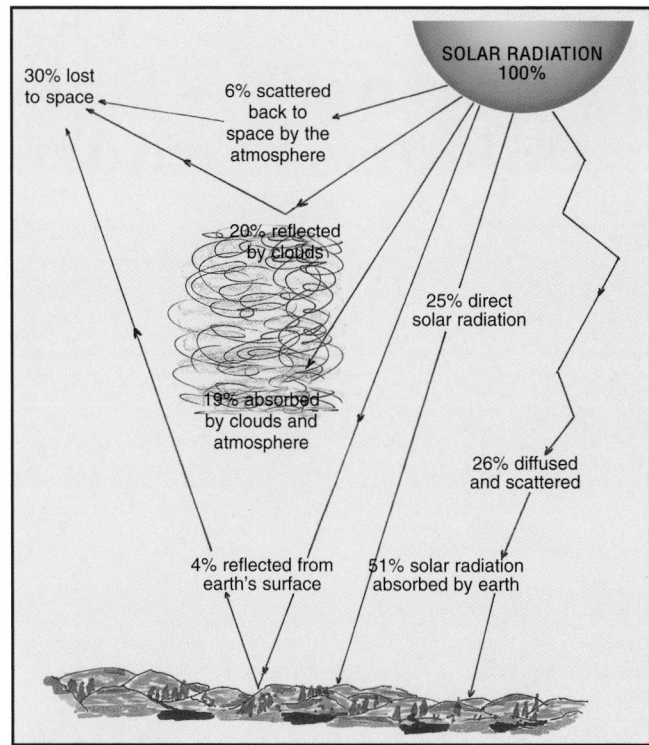

Figure 2.3 Only 25% of the sun's radiation reaching the earth strikes it directly. An additional 26% reaches it after being scattered through the atmosphere. A total of 19% is absorbed by the clouds and the atmosphere itself.

radiation. Thus, the reference is frequently made to the sun's radiation as shortwave radiation and to the earth's as long-wave radiation. Through the use of satellites, scientists are now able to measure very accurately the amount of infrared radiation the earth emits and also the exact amount of radiation received from the sun. These values are very important when we consider the earth's energy balance.

If you are wondering about the other wavelengths, your favorite radio station in the AM band is emitting radiation that is miles from one wave crest to the next. Shortwave and FM radio, including television, transmit signals that are measured in feet and inches from one wave crest to the next. At the other end of the spectrum, the dangerous gamma rays are very, very short.

Earth's Energy Balance

Throughout the years the sun and the earth have maintained an "energy balance" that is favorable for life on earth. That is, the radiation that has reached the earth from the sun has been balanced by what leaves. Otherwise, our earth would warm or cool (if no other factors are involved) depending on whether there is a surplus or a deficiency. It is this disruption of the energy balance (more entering or more leaving) that may be the cause of global warming or cooling.

If we take the radiation from the sun that reaches our planet and its atmosphere and attach a figure of 100 percent to it, then, like pieces of a pie, we can begin dividing up what happens to it when it reaches the earth. This is diagramed in Figure 2.3. First, 6 percent is immediately scattered back to space by particles in the atmosphere. Then, an average of 20 percent is reflected by the clouds back to space. My goodness, we are already behind by 26 percent! Another 4 percent finds its way directly to the earth, but "hates it" and immediately leaves by the closest exit (reflected) back out to space. The result is that 30 percent of the radiation from the sun never gets a chance to heat the earth. It is reflected back to space by atmospheric particles, clouds, and the earth's surface.

But not all of the solar radiation that hits the clouds is reflected. Some, approximately 19 percent, is absorbed. Another 26 percent of the radiation reaching the earth and atmosphere is probably as confused as I have been driving in San Francisco or Los Angeles, and it is scattered and diffused (bounced around) until it finds the earth's surface. The final 25 percent, after leaving the sun, knows exactly where it is going and ends up at the earth's surface, willing to stay, after a journey of around 93,000,000 miles.

The result is that slightly more than one-half the solar radiation received from the sun (51 percent) is finally absorbed by the earth at its surface. The rest is (1) scattered back to space or into the atmosphere, (2) absorbed by the clouds and other particles in the atmosphere, and (3) reflected off clouds and other particles to end up who knows where. But, when we add in that 19 percent absorbed by the clouds in the atmosphere we have a 70/30 ratio. Not too bad! We gain 70 and lose 30. Oh, if our stock market ventures only went so well!

The above figures are averages (except for the 100 percent) as you may well have guessed. On clear days, more radiation from the sun arrives at the surface. On cloudy days, there is less. Also, depending on where you are, the amount of radiation that is reflected varies. Some surfaces absorb more radiation than other surfaces and, conversely, some reflect most of the radiation they receive. That brings us to albedo.

Figure 2.4 Sand along the Pacific Ocean in Washington and Oregon contains magnetite which reduces its reflectivity.

Albedo

Albedo is the amount of energy reflected by a surface compared to the amount that it receives. Surfaces like fresh snow and white clothing have a "high" albedo. Freshly fallen snow reflects up to 90 percent of the radiation it receives and thick clouds around 75 percent. Sand, especially the white sands like those in New Mexico and on tropical golf courses, can reflect nearly 50 percent of the radiation they receive. The darker sands, however, like those along the Pacific Coast of Washington and Oregon, shown in Figure 2.4, which contain magnetite, have a much lower albedo.

What surfaces then, would have a "low" albedo? Why certainly, they would be freshly plowed ground and dark clothing. A grassy field has an albedo of around 20 percent. The albedo of water varies greatly due to its turbidity and the angle at which the sun's rays strike it. Forests, such as those shown in an early photograph of Mt. St. Helens in Washington State in Figure 2.5, have low albedos.

Figure 2.5 Heavily forested areas have low albedo as the sun's radiation is dispersed among the leaves and needles. Snow has a high albedo. (Photo taken by author many years before Mt. St. Helens erupted on May 18, 1980.)

Overall, the earth's average albedo is around 30 percent due to its many different surfaces and, as mentioned earlier, the earth's atmosphere is part of this entire picture. That figure, 30 percent, has already been introduced when we discussed incoming radiation from the sun. Remember, 30 percent was immediately lost to space.

Asphalt is certainly a good absorber of the sun's radiation. It can get very hot during the day and, when walking across it after dark, you can feel the infrared radiation emitted from it. So it absorbs the sun's radiation during the day, then retransmits it very well at night. I remember driving the lonely roads of Nevada at dusk when the surrounding desert was cooling. Coming to the top of one hill I was greeted by several cows that had settled down in the middle of the asphalt road where it was still warm. The screech of tires on blacktop warmed the surface further, and the cows drifted to the side of the road. In my rearview mirror I could see them beginning to mingle once again in the center of the road to catch more of that longwave radiation being emitted by the earth.

In the above case, the albedo of the asphalt was low as it converted most of the sun's visible light into heat and very little was reflected back to space. But it was also a very good emitter of infrared radiation at night. Such surfaces are referred to as "blackbodies." A blackbody does not necessarily have to be black. It must absorb all the radiation it receives and then retransmit. In doing so, it maintains a constant temperature over a 24-hour period. The earth, because it is not warming up or cooling down, is very much like a black body. Remember, it is not just the earth we are speaking about, but the earth and its atmosphere. Many scientists now maintain that the earth's surface and the atmosphere are not transmitting as much radiation as they receive and are warming slightly.

What about plastic? What kind of an albedo does it have? I have tried putting a layer of black plastic on the ground to warm my soil in the spring. It does get warm underneath the plastic as incoming radiation from the sun is absorbed. But it is serving another purpose; it is also preventing the earth's radiation from being emitted back into space.

Over the course of one earth day or 24 hours, the earth receives energy from the sun, converts it to heat, and then transmits it to space. In the early morning hours, the sun begins to heat the earth. By noon, the sun is at the zenith and incoming radiation reaches a maximum. After that, it begins decreasing, eventually reaching zero as the sun sets. The earth, however, is constantly radiating heat. The progression of the sun's incoming radiation versus the earth's outgoing radiation for a station in middle latitude near the vernal equinox or the autumnal equinox is plotted in Figure 2.6 for a day. Note that the two curves cross around mid to late afternoon, which is usually when the daily maximum temperature occurs. Up until that time the earth is storing more heat that it is transmitting. As solar radiation continues to decrease after this time, the earth's

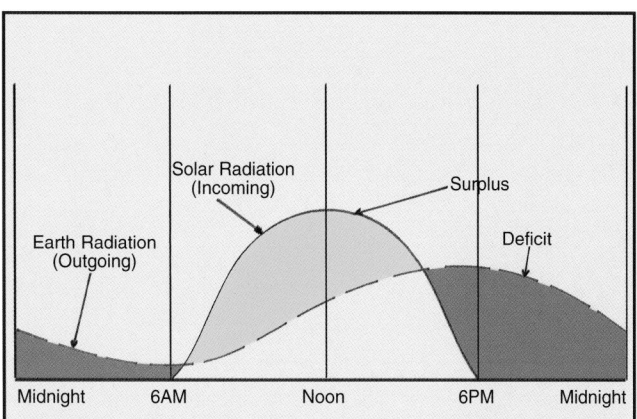

Figure 2.6 Incoming (solar) radiation is plotted against the outgoing (earth's) radiation for a day for a station located at middle latitude and near the vernal or autumnal equinox.

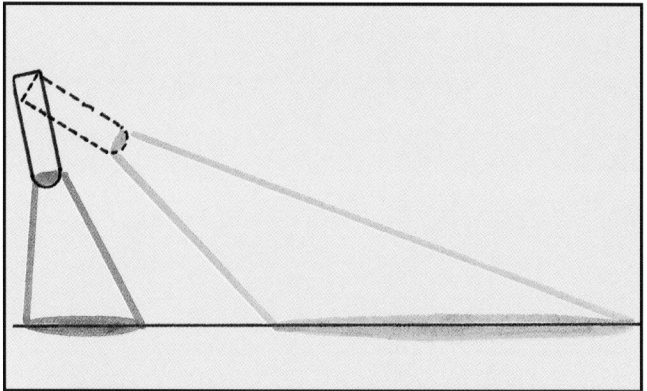

Figure 2.7 A flashlight shining nearly straight down will illuminate objects more clearly than if pointed in a more horizontal position. The intensity of the sun's radiation acts similarly as it strikes the earth's surface.

radiation also begins to decrease. In the morning, the two curves intersect shortly after sunrise, or the usual time of minimum temperature. The intersection of the two curves will move slightly with the seasons. Less solar radiation in winter would result in the curves intersecting earlier in the afternoon (maximum) and later in the morning (minimum). With more solar radiation in the summer the intersections of the curves would shift in the opposite directions. This, of course, assumes clear skies and no change of air mass.

The earth, then, receives radiation from the sun that warms its surface. However, this warming is not the same throughout the year. In summer, the northern hemisphere is warmer than it is in winter. We call this variance seasonal change.

Reasons For The Seasons

Several years ago, so I am told, a survey was taken of some college graduates. A startling percentage of them could not explain why the earth has seasons. The reasons for the seasons are very simple. Imagine you are walking along a dark street at midnight. There is no moon. No streetlights. You do have a flashlight, thank goodness! You shine the light straight down so as not to step on something and trip. The light is bright and you can see objects directly below and in a short distance in front of you very clearly. You cannot see what lies farther down the street, however. To do that you shine the light out ahead of you. But now the light becomes diffused and scattered. You can't see small objects as well, but you can see more area, but not as clearly as when the light was shining straight down. The same effect occurs when you switch your headlights to the "high-beam" position. You can see farther, but not as well directly in front of the headlights than when they are "low-beam." The flashlight experiment is depicted in Figure 2.7, variations of which appear in practically every meteorological text.

Light from the sun as it strikes the earth is similar to light from that flashlight. Since the earth is round (well, nearly so) more direct light reaches the equatorial areas than the polar regions because of the angle at which radiation from the sun strikes the surface. It is mostly perpendicular at the equator

and at a very low angle at the poles. When the sun's rays shine directly on an object or location, more energy is received there than if the sun's light strikes it at an angle. This difference in the angle that the sun's rays strike the surface of the earth leads us to the reasons for the seasons.

The earth and the sun form an imaginary plane that intersects both the earth and the sun. You can think of this plane as your living room floor. It is flat. The walls around the living room are constructed perpendicular or at an angle of 90 degrees to the floor. Off in the corner is that lamp with a shade that you just never seem to be able to get "straight" or parallel to the walls and perpendicular to the floor. It looks always to be slightly tilted. If the lamp shade is sitting on the floor you can imagine it to be the earth. The earth in its journey around the sun on this imaginary plane is also tilted from a line that is perpendicular to the plane. The tilt of the earth's axis (an imaginary line that runs through the center of the earth and exits at each pole) is 23.5 degrees.

The earth, in addition to having its axis tilted 23.5 degrees from the perpendicular, is also revolving around the sun. It is not at the same place in space today as it was yesterday. It has moved! And it moves in an elliptical orbit around the sun on this imaginary plane, with the distance varying from 91,400,000 miles in early January to 94,500,000 miles in July. (Yes, that's right! The earth is closer to the sun in the Northern Hemisphere winter than it is in the Northern Hemisphere summer.) Figure 2.8 is an illustration of the earth's motion around the sun with a slight variation in distance from summer to winter.

You can take Figure 2.8 for granted, or you can do your own experiment. With the house empty (you do not want other family members seeing you do this crazy experiment) place a lamp on the living room coffee table. (Not that crooked lamp we used earlier, however, or you might get confused.) The new lamp becomes the sun. Now take a broom handle and tilt it 23.5 degrees away from the walls and the lamp and walk around the coffee table, being careful not to knock over any other lamps or pictures off the wall. (The author assumes no liability for this experiment!)

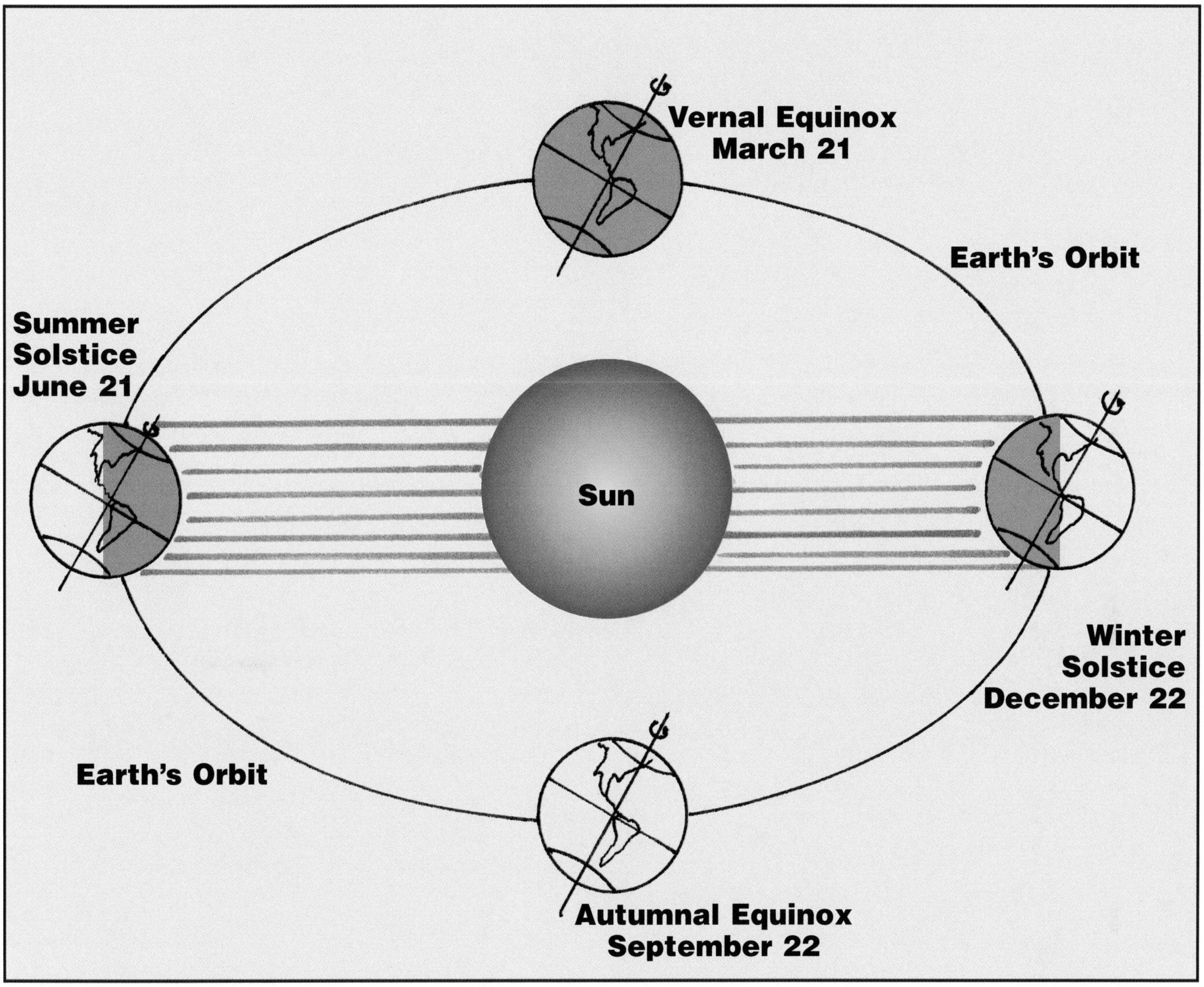

Figure 2.8 Reasons for the seasons: The earth is tilted 23.5 degrees on its axis and revolves around the sun.

If you looked closely, you noticed that on one side of the coffee table the top half of the broom handle was tilted away from the lamp, while at the opposite side of the coffee table, it was tilted toward the lamp on the coffee table. The bottom half of the broom handle reacted just the opposite. This experiment clearly explains why it is summer in the Northern Hemisphere (winter in the Southern Hemisphere) in July and winter in the Northern Hemisphere (summer in the Southern Hemisphere) in January.

Now, back to this business of radiation, absorption, and reflection. If the north end of the earth's axis is tilted toward the sun, that hemisphere will receive more solar radiation than the other hemisphere which is pointed away from the sun. Remember, the more direct the sun's rays are as they strike the earth, the greater will be their impact. Areas near the north pole and south pole actually are not receiving any radiation when the axis is tilted away from the sun in January (north pole) and July (south pole.)

In between those two times when the earth's axis is tilted toward and away from the sun, it passes through two other phases—the spring equinox, around March 21 or 22, and the fall equinox around September 21 or 22. Both hemispheres at these two points in the earth's journey around the sun receive the same amount of light. If you were at the north or south pole, you would see half a sun, but not for long. Depending on whether it was spring or fall, the sun would either rise in the sky (spring) or settle out of sight below the horizon (fall).

Portland, Oregon, for instance, is located near latitude 45 degrees north (actually 45°30"N.) What would be the sun angles above the horizon for late June and late December? Figure 2.9 will help with this answer We know the earth is tilted at 23.5 degrees. Around June 21 the sun has reached its greatest journey north. (This is really not a true statement, since the sun does not "come north," but we refer to it as such, since it is near this date that the axis of the earth is pointed toward the sun in the Northern Hemisphere.) The sun is at the zenith or directly overhead at noon at 23.5 degrees north latitude or the Tropic of Cancer. If we add 23.5 to 45 we get 68.5, or rounded up to 69 degrees for the sun in

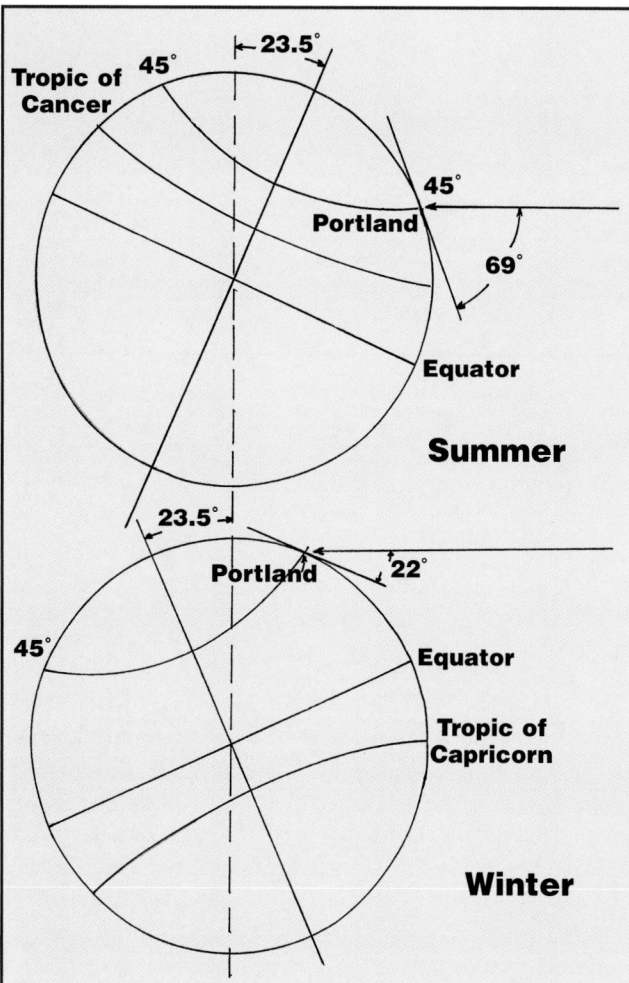

Figure 2.9 The angle of the sun's rays reaching the earth varies as the earth revolves around the sun. At Portland, Oregon, the angle reaches around 69° in late June but decreases to near 22° in late December.

Portland at noon on June 21. Conversely, around December 21, just before Christmas, the Northern Hemisphere is tilted away from the sun. The Southern Hemisphere is tilted toward the sun which is directly overhead at noon at the Tropic of Capricorn or 23.5 south latitude. We can subtract that 23.5 degrees from 45 degrees and get 22.5 or rounded down to around 22 degrees at Portland in late December, and this, remember, is noon. Well, no wonder it is warmer in June than December—we get more direct sunlight.

In the Northern Hemisphere we refer to June 21 (or 22, depending on the year) as the "longest day" of the year and December 21 (or 22, depending on the year) as the "shortest day" of the year. These are not true statements since a day is regarded as 24-hours long. Our reference is, of course, to the hours of daylight, of which there are more in June than December. Sunrise and sunset tables confirm this reduction in daylight hours. However, close examination of these tables reveals that the sun continues to set earlier in the day in the northern hemisphere until around December 5 and then begins to set a little later.

(Our time here is measured in seconds.) In the morning, however, the sun continues to rise later in the morning until around January 5, when it then begins to rise earlier. The gain in the evening is offset by the loss in the morning from early December to early January. It is not until after January 5 that we can truly say, "The days are getting longer," when actually we just mean there is more daylight. In the northern hemisphere summer the opposite occurs. The sun begins rising a little later each day

after about June 13 but continues to set a little later each day until nearly July 1. After that date, the days begin getting "shorter" or less sunlight.

This variation is caused by the earth's journey around the sun. When the earth is at its closest point to the sun (perihelion) on January 5, it is traveling slightly faster through space than when it is at its farthest point (aphelion) around July 5. Thus from around December 21 to

January 5, its orbital speed is accelerating slightly. Conversely, from around June 21 to July 5, its orbital speed is slowing down. These minor variations in speed, the relative position of the earth to the sun, the rotation of the earth, and tilt of the axis all combine to produce this discrepancy in sunrise and sunset times.

In summary, our earth is tilted on its axis and revolves around the sun once every 365 1/4 days. Energy is received from the sun in the form of electromagnetic radiation mostly in the visible and infrared portion of the electromagnetic spectrum. The earth and everything on it emit radiation, but mostly in the infrared region of that same spectrum. Radiation from the sun is reflected, scattered, and absorbed as it enters the earth's atmosphere.

Differential Heating

The surface of the earth receives different amounts of radiation depending on where you are on the surface. Radiation from the sun is converted to heat as it strikes the earth's surface. Areas near the equator receive more radiation than areas near the poles because the sun's rays are more perpendicular to the surface at the equator. Thus, these areas become hotter. Basically, this is referred to as "differential heating." It is differential heating on a global scale. It is the basic cause of weather across the planet. Differential heating is also manifest on much smaller scales such as on a regional scale down to what might be happening in your own back yard, from cement to a grassy lawn.

But what exactly is heat? Heat is a form of energy. If we could look very closely at the air around us and even ourselves, our clothes, the computer on which we are working, we would see a composition of billions and billions of tiny atoms and molecules scurrying around in all directions, much like my hive of bees does when I take away some of their honey. But, unlike my bees that don't collide with one another, the atoms and molecules are continually bouncing off other atoms and molecules. The energy associated with this movement of the atoms and molecules is called kinetic energy. Heat, then, is the total kinetic energy of all the atoms and molecules that compose a substance, or the amount of heat absorbed by a substance.

Temperature is different from heat. When we speak of temperature, we are talking about the average kinetic energy of the motion of the atoms and molecules. Those atoms and molecules are not all moving at the same speed.

Heat vs. Temperature
Heat: *The amount of energy absorbed by a substance.*
Temperature: *A measure of the motion of the molecules of the substance.*

Temperature refers more to intensity. The atoms and molecules that are moving very fast will have an average speed that is higher than those that are moving at a slower speed. When substances cool, the speed of the atoms and molecules that comprise the substance is reduced. Slower speeds mean a slower average speed, and thus less kinetic energy or a lower temperature. Let's see if a simple comparison clears this matter up.

It has been a tough day at the office. Stress, deadlines, and uncooperative coworkers make you want to take a hot bath and have a hot cup of tea before bedtime. You run the bathtub full of hot water and put a tea kettle on the stove and bring it to a boil. Now, which container, the tub or the tea kettle, has the hottest temperature? Why, the tea kettle, of course. You could not get into a tub full of boiling water and you would not want a cup of lukewarm tea. However, which container has the most heat? You got it! The tub does. Although the water in the tea kettle is hotter (its atoms and molecules are moving faster) than the water in the bath tub, there is more heat in the tub. Ahhhh! That makes you feel good. So, heat is total, temperature is average.

Heat Transfer

In our discussion so far we have learned that the areas near the equator receive more radiation from the sun than the polar regions because of the angle of the sun's radiation as it strikes the earth. Heating is more intense in the equatorial regions. There is a surplus of heat in this area and a deficiency at the poles. Figure 2.10 shows this difference. More heat is lost at the poles through radiation than is gained and more heat is gained at the equator from radiation than is lost. But the tropics do not keep getting hotter and the polar regions do not keep getting colder. It is at a latitude of about 37 degrees, north and south, that the amount of incoming heat equals the amount lost to space over a year's time. Heat, then, must be transferred from one area to another so that regions from 37 degrees north of the equator to regions 37 degrees south of the equator do not keep getting hotter and regions above and below that (depending on the hemisphere) toward the poles, do not keep getting colder. And how is this transfer of heat accomplished? It is done by conduction, advection or convection, and radiation.

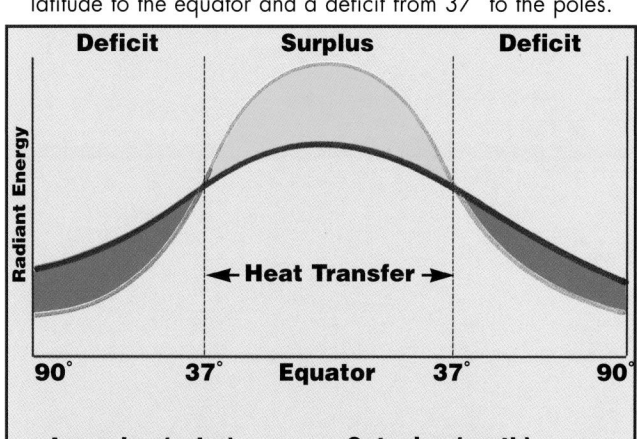

Figure 2.10 There is a surplus of heat energy from 37° latitude to the equator and a deficit from 37° to the poles.

I enjoy a hot cup of coffee in the morning, but if I let it sit and forget about it, it gets cold. Here is an excellent example of how heat is transferred, using the above three methods. Conduction takes heat from the coffee into the bottom of the cup and then onto the coffee table. Heat also is conducted to the sides of the cup and then radiated from around the side of the cup. Heat is also lost to convection at the surface of the coffee. If you hold your hand around the hot cup of coffee, you feel the heat that is being conducted to your hand. Hold your hand an inch or so away from the cup and you feel heat that is being radiated. Place your hand over the top of the cup and you feel heat that is being transferred by advection, or in this case convection. (Advection refers to the horizontal movement and convection to vertical movement of atoms and molecules.) Figure 2.11 illustrates this through convection A, radiation B, and conduction C.

Another example is my fireplace. I like to build hot fires that heat up the bricks, or heat transfer by conduction. When I stand in front of my fireplace, I feel the heat that is being radiated from the fire. If I were to climb up on my roof and stand by the chimney, I would feel heat that is being convected up the chimney. Or, more simply and safer, some fireplaces or wood stoves have fans in them that blow (advect) the heat into the room. A furnace blows (advects) heat out through the heat ducts.

The earth and the atmosphere above it are constantly exchanging heat via these three methods with other areas. It is this exchange of heat, or heat transfer, that keeps the tropics from getting hotter and the polar regions from getting colder. Wind and ocean currents transfer large amounts of heat from the tropics to more northern and southern latitudes. Water,

however, is a poor conductor of heat and heats up much more slowly than land. Radiant energy penetrates farther into water than, for example, a granite surface. Thus, the energy is distributed, or dispersed, through a volume of water. The radiant energy that strikes the granite surface immediately heats the surface. Heat must be transferred to deeper layers through conduction. The air above the surface is warmed through radiation and conduction as this heat is being transferred by air molecules colliding with other molecules.

Water in rivers, lakes, and oceans is generally mixing, and the heat is thus being transferred by convection and advection. An additional factor is that more evaporation is occurring over water than over land. Evaporation is a cooling process. Figure 2.12 depicts the concept of differential heating on a smaller scale than the global scale discussed earlier. Water, although it heats up much more slowly than land surfaces, also retains its heat longer. Oceans are often referred to as giant "heat sinks" where tremendous amounts of heat are stored.

Heat that is transferred by radiation does so at the speed of those electromagnetic waves. On that first warm spring day, you stand and face the sun and feel its warmth. The rays from the sun are heating your face, not the air. The air still has the chill of winter in it. Then as you go inside your face transmits that energy through infrared radiation. It feels warm.

To summarize, different areas on the earth receive different amounts of heat. Heat is a form of energy and temperature is a measure of that heat. Heat is transferred by various methods such as conduction, convection (advection), and radiation. It is this heat transfer, or exchange, that is responsible for our weather.

Atmosphere Composition and Atmosphere Zones

The earth and the area surrounding it have been divided into four spheres: lithosphere, hydrosphere, atmosphere,

Figure 2.11 A hot cup of coffee or tea is losing heat via convection at the surface, A. by conduction into the side of the cup and table, C. and radiation out the side, B.

Figure 2.12 Differential Heating. Ground surfaces heat up much more quickly than water surfaces. Radiant energy penetrates farther into the water, mixing occurs, and more evaporation of water molecules cools the surface.

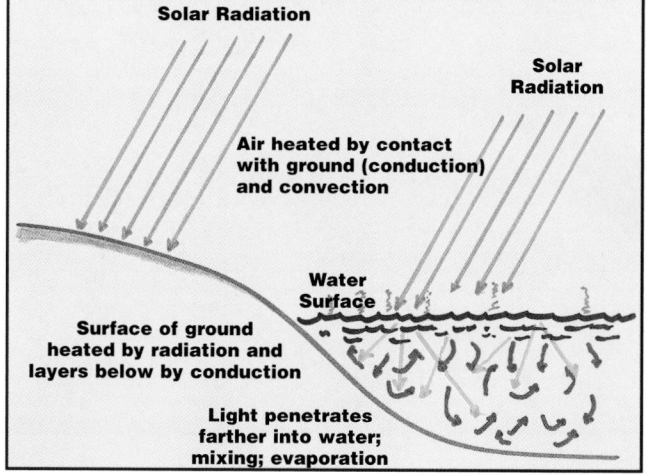

and the biosphere. The lithosphere is the solid, or rock, portion of the earth. The ground we stand on is part of the lithosphere. The hydrosphere is the water, or liquid portion. All the rivers, lakes, and oceans make up the hydrosphere. The oceans cover roughly 70 percent of the earth's surface, leaving 30 percent to the lithosphere. The atmosphere, or the air we breathe, is the gaseous portion. Containing a variety of gases in various quantities, it is, for the most part, invisible. The biosphere constitutes the animal and plant life on our planet.

Weather occurs in the atmosphere portion but is greatly affected by the lithosphere and the hydrosphere. The lithosphere takes on many forms, and classification of them is left to the geologists. But since land heats up faster than water, the lithosphere has a profound effect on circulation patterns. The lithosphere also extends many thousands of feet above the mean level of the oceans which disrupts movement of air in the atmosphere. Those two items, where and how high, are the two items of main concern when we factor the lithosphere into weather. The hydrosphere supplies the atmosphere with moisture through evaporation from the surface of rivers, lakes, and mainly the ocean, Figure 2.13. The biosphere, or you and I and all the animal and plant life forms that live here, does not have an effect on the weather although man's role in the scheme of things, many think, is becoming more influential. But weather certainly has an effect on all life forms.

Atmosphere Composition

The atmosphere, as we mentioned, is a gas. But what kind of a gas? Early in the earth's development it was probably mostly hydrogen and helium and quite warm. Scientists speculate that most of it escaped into space.

Meanwhile, volcanic eruptions began adding water vapor and carbon dioxide and some nitrogen, much as they do today. Most of the carbon dioxide became locked up in the rocks. The sun's action on water vapor began increasing the oxygen content. A large portion of the water vapor condensed out to form the hydrosphere. What was left was mostly nitrogen. And that gas accounts for a large portion of our atmosphere today.

Roughly 78 percent of our atmosphere today is nitrogen. Oxygen takes up another 21 percent. The last 1 percent is comprised of a host of other gases such as argon,

> **Atmosphere Composition**
> Nitrogen 78%
> Oxygen slightly less than 21%
> Argon, Neon, Helium, Krypton, Xenon 0.9%
> Variable gasses:
> Water Vapor varies from near zero
> at poles to 4% near equator.
> Carbon Dioxide 0.03%

neon, helium, hydrogen, and xenon in relative decreasing quantities. These gases are called permanent gases.

There are other variable gases, a few of which become very important to meteorology and climatology. The first is water vapor. You may not have thought of water as a gas, but it is. It is of extreme importance to our topic of weather. It varies in composition from near zero in polar and desert regions to around 4 percent by volume in the tropical regions. Without water vapor in our atmosphere, life on earth would be pretty tough, to put it mildly. Regarding meteorology, water vapor is the most important gas in our

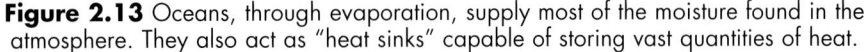

Figure 2.13 Oceans, through evaporation, supply most of the moisture found in the atmosphere. They also act as "heat sinks" capable of storing vast quantities of heat.

atmosphere. It condenses to form clouds and precipitation. It intercepts longwave radiation from the earth. The total amount of water vapor in the atmosphere is pretty much fixed. There is, however, some speculation about this amount. Water molecules constantly escape our earth and head into space. Volcanoes add water molecules from deep within the earth to the atmosphere when they erupt, and there is some evidence that meteors and debris from dead comets are also adding to the supply.

Carbon dioxide is another very important gas in our atmosphere. However, it is present in even smaller quantities than water vapor and is measured in parts per million (PPM). Methane, in even smaller quantities, and carbon dioxide are extremely important to a liveable planet since they trap the earth's longwave radiation and prevent it from escaping into space. Ozone, occurring high in the stratosphere, intercepts the ultraviolet radiation from the sun that can be harmful to life on earth. At high altitudes its effect is beneficial, but the ozone created by human activities near the surface of the earth can be harmful.

Atmosphere Zones

The atmosphere of the earth is divided into layers. The lower layer is called the troposphere. The troposphere is where most of the weather on earth occurs. An average figure for the depth of the troposphere is around 11 kilometers or 35,000 feet. But that figure varies daily, seasonally and latitudinally. On the average, temperature normally decreases at about 3.6°F for every 1,000 feet in elevation as one goes higher in the troposphere. The temperature decrease is a result of the expansion of the air due to less pressure and because the air is farther (higher) from its major heat source or the earth's surface.

The layer directly above the troposphere is called the stratosphere. In the stratosphere, temperature stops decreasing with elevation and either remains constant (isothermal), or even increases with elevation, a phenomenon that is called an inversion. Most of this increase of temperature (or the fact that the temperature does not continue to decrease with elevation) is thought to be caused by the presence of the gas ozone. Ozone intercepts the ultraviolet radiation from the sun and thus serves to warm this layer of the atmosphere.

The top of the stratosphere is around 30 miles (50 kilometers) above the earth's surface. The pressure here is quite low, on the order of one millibar, or one-thousandth of what it is at the earth's surface. Air particles that reach into the stratosphere often remain there for many years since effective mixing between the stratosphere and troposphere is inhibited because of the presence of an inversion.

There are other layers above the stratosphere such as the mesosphere and thermosphere. These layers contribute very little to the weather we observe on the earth, although scientists have observed lightning strokes from the top of very large thunderstorms into these higher layers of the atmosphere above the stratosphere.

Figure 2.14, although not to scale, shows a cross-section of the earth's atmosphere and those various layers. This figure also shows the temperature distribution with elevation. The boundary between the troposphere and the stratosphere is called the tropopause. The height of the tropopause is quite variable in both time and space. It varies latitudinally, being higher at the equator than it is at the poles. This, of course, is due to the greater amount of solar radiation received at lower latitudes, resulting in much warmer temperatures there. The tropopause varies with the season, being higher over the Northern Hemisphere during the summer than during the Northern Hemisphere winter. The tropopause also can vary on a daily basis, sometimes quite rapidly, as weather fronts and low pressure areas move through a location.

Winds that normally show an increase in speed with elevation in the troposphere often reach their maximum at or just below the tropopause. This is the location of the jet stream. Winds generally decrease in speed with elevation in the stratosphere, and often reverse direction from prevailing winds in the troposphere.

In summary, the air we breathe is comprised mostly of nitrogen. There are scant amounts of water vapor present in the air compared to oxygen and nitrogen, but it is this small amount of water vapor that causes weather and is so important in the field of meteorology. We also know that most of the earth's weather occurs in the troposphere and that the upper boundary of the troposphere is called the tropopause. Above the tropopause is the stratosphere, an area where cloudiness is almost absent and that is penetrated only by the tops of very large thunderstorms.

Figure 2.14 Most of the earth's weather occurs in the troposphere. Directly above that layer is the stratosphere. The tropopause separates the troposphere from the stratosphere.

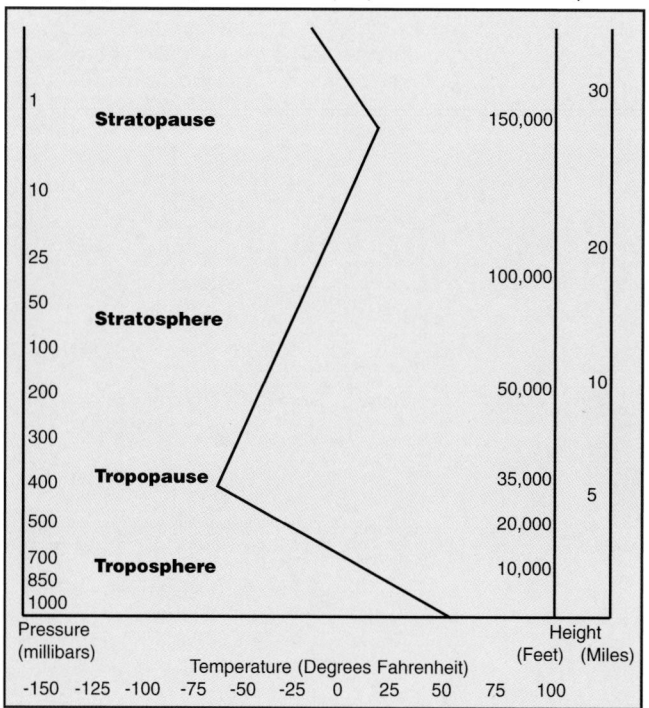

Chapter 3
The Earth's Major Wind Belts

Wwith nothing to do on a lazy, warm summer day you may have watched an eagle or hawk or some large bird just floating around and around, only moving their wings infrequently. "How does that bird stay aloft?" you may have asked. Well, our bird is pretty smart. It knows where the thermals are located in the atmosphere, much like the bird in Figure 3.1. It knows where there are rising columns of warm air to keep it aloft. It also knows where there are descending areas of cool air, and it stays away from those.

Warm air, since it is lighter than cold air, rises. Cold air, which is heavier and more dense, sinks. You've experienced that. The upstairs of a home is always warmer than the basement. Those ceiling fans are placed there to divert the warm air down toward the floor. You are instructed to lie on the floor if there is smoke in the room because the smoke, being warm, will most likely rise to the ceiling, leaving the air next to the floor somewhat cooler and breathable. But here our lesson on what to do if you find yourself in a smoke-filled room ends, and our lesson on the earth's major wind belts begins.

The Hadley Cell

We have learned that the earth receives more solar radiation near the equator than at higher latitudes so the air in those areas near the equator is warmer. That air, because it is warm, rises. It rises to great heights. Once it gets to the height of the tropopause it begins to spread out toward the north pole and south pole. At the poles, the air has cooled enough in its high altitude journey north and south so that it begins to sink and flow back toward the equator. This basic circulation is referred to

as the Hadley cell, named after George Hadley, an English meteorologist. It is depicted in Figure 3.2, showing warm air rising near the equator and descending in the polar regions.

Hadley, as early as 1735, speculated that air was rising at the equator and sinking at some latitude to account for the trade winds. This would be one large convective circulation, with the heated air at the equator rising, flowing northward, cooling, sinking, and then returning to the equator. Hadley speculated that the air was sinking around 30 degrees north and south latitude. He was right. Thus, the simple one-cell circulation has been expanded north and south to include the poles, but it follows Hadley's basic circulation theory. In reality, however, it is not that simple. I suspect Hadley thought so also. There are complications. Our earth is rotating on its axis about once every 24 hours. This complicates the simple Hadley cell or one-cell type of circulation and breaks it up into what are called the earth's major wind belts.

The Earth's Major Wind Belts

Around 1835 a French scientist, Gustave-Gaspard Coriolis, theorized (and then expressed mathematically) that because of the earth's rotation, particles in motion, if projected towards a certain spot, would end up to the right of that spot in the Northern Hemisphere. (Some have said that he was an officer in the war with England and his cannon balls kept ending up to the right of their target. Oh, well!) The result is that a force was named after Coriolis, and it is called the Coriolis force, or, since it is not a true force, the Coriolis effect. It causes particles that are in motion on a

Figure 3.1 Large birds know where to find thermals or rising columns of warm air.

Figure 3.2 A basic Hadley cell for the earth. Air rises at the equator, flows toward the poles, sinks, and flows back to the equator.

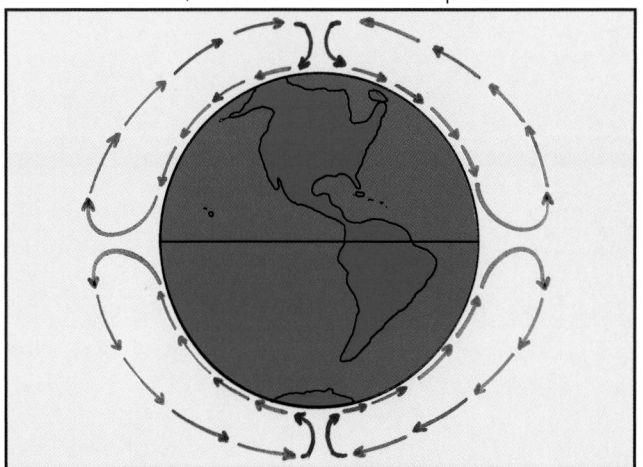

rotating earth to curve to the right in the Northern Hemisphere and to the left in the Southern Hemisphere.

Any particle (in our case, since we are talking meteorology, we will say a parcel of air) that is set in motion in the Northern Hemisphere will begin curving to the right. (Now I did not say that was the reason for your slice or hook off the golf tee! Consult your golf pro for that solution.) The magnitude of the Coriolis effect is a function of latitude and the speed of the parcel. The faster a parcel is moving, the greater the Coriolis effect acting on it. Additionally, since we indicated that it was a function of latitude, the magnitude varies from zero at the equator to a maximum at the north pole and the south pole. Mathematically, it is expressed as: **2w(sinlat)v**, where "w" is the angular speed of the earth's rotation, multiplied by the sine of the latitude, (sinlat) multiplied by the speed of the parcel, "v." Since the Coriolis effect is a function of the latitude, the effect is zero at the equator because the sine of 0° is zero, and the sine of 90° is 1.

If you could get far enough "above" the north pole and look down, you would see the earth rotating in a counter-clockwise direction. Conversely, if you could get far enough "below" the south pole and look up, you would see the earth rotating in a clockwise direction. This motion is what causes particles in the Northern Hemisphere to be deflected to the right and in the Southern Hemisphere to the left.

To illustrate this, take a piece of paper, cut it into a circle. Place it on the table in front of you. Put a mark in the center (the north pole) and rotate the paper in a counter-clockwise direction around the center, all the while pulling a marker or pencil directly toward you. You appear to be drawing a straight line, but when you look at the paper it is a curved line, or should be. From the line's starting point in the center, it will show a curve to the right.

Now, start at the outside of the circular piece of paper and draw the line away from you towards the center of the paper, still rotating it in a counter-clockwise direction around a point. This indicates you are starting from the equator. The curve should be very small or gentle to start with and get sharper as you draw the line "north" or towards the center of the paper. The lines you draw on the piece of paper should look similar to those in Figure 3.3. You can get even braver and rotate the paper in a clockwise direction and draw the line, pretending you are in the Southern Hemisphere.

Thus, if a parcel of air leaving the north pole curves toward the right, it might begin as a north wind, but soon turn into a northeast wind. The simple one-cell circulation has just taken its first "hit." The air that descended at the north pole and started moving south began curving to the right, and air that descended at southern latitudes near the south pole began moving north and curving toward the left. Those winds become the polar easterlies or polar northeasterlies in the Northern Hemisphere and polar southeasterlies in the Southern Hemisphere.

There are two other parts to the earth's major wind belts. If we take a look at a map of the world, we will notice

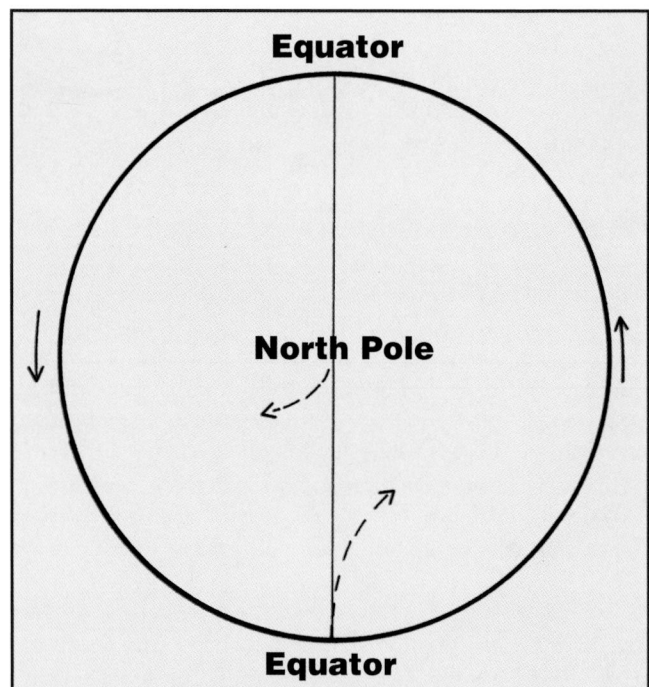

Figure 3.3 Objects in motion in the Northern Hemisphere will show a curvature to the right due to the Coriolis effect, with the greatest curvature at the pole and zero at the equator.

that around latitudes 20 to 30 degrees north and south we find mostly deserts. Northern Africa, in the northern hemisphere, and Australia, in the southern hemisphere, are good examples of this. At this latitude, the simple one-cell circulation suffers its second "hit." Some of the air that started north and south after rising near the equator begins descending at these latitudes, precisely what Mr. Hadley thought. This descending air has a tendency to "pile up" much like when you spill a box of sugar on the counter. There is more in the center of the spill than at the edges. Air will "pile up" the same way, creating areas of high pressure at the surface around the globe at these latitudes. Meteorologists and climatologists refer to these areas as the subtropical high-pressure areas and they are present in both hemispheres.

If you keep pouring more sugar on top of the pile, you will notice that it does not stay on top, but spreads down the sides. (You do not have to literally go through this experiment.) That is also what happens to our area of high pressure. It begins to spread out—some to the east, some to the west, some to the north, and some to the south. But wait a minute, didn't we say that parcels of air that are in motion turn to the right in the Northern Hemisphere? We certainly did. Thus air that flows out from the pile-up does so in a clockwise manner. Thus, you can see that air has a tendency to flow clockwise around an area of high pressure in the Northern Hemisphere and counter-clockwise around an area of high pressure in the Southern Hemisphere. Figure 3.4 shows a two-dimensional sketch of a high-pressure circulation.

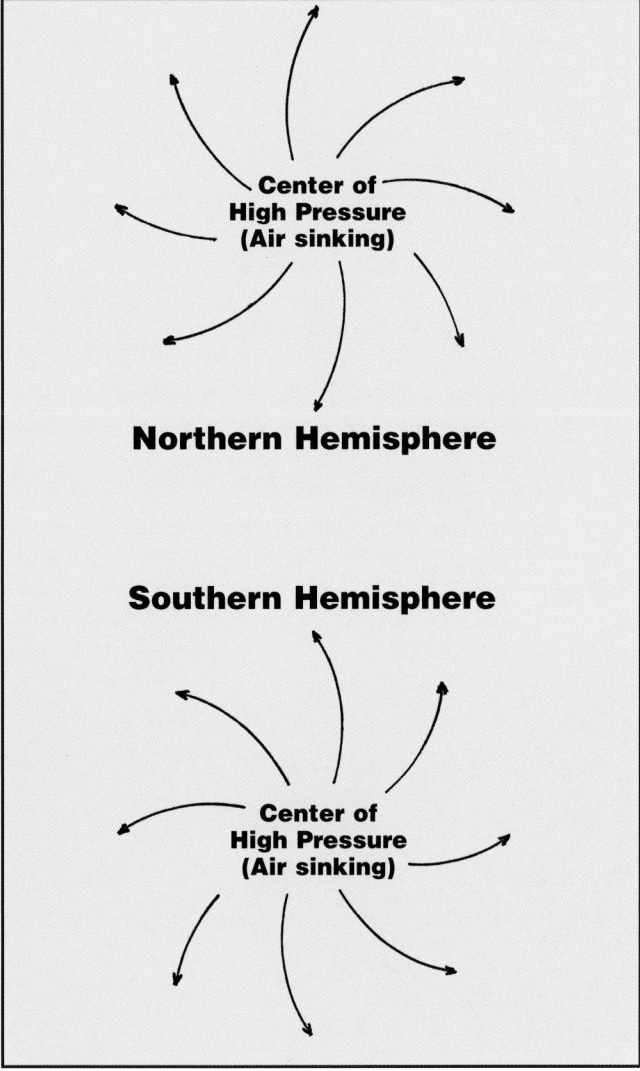

Figure 3.4 Within areas of high pressure, the air is sinking and flowing outward, clockwise in the Northern Hemisphere; counter-clockwise in the Southern Hemisphere.

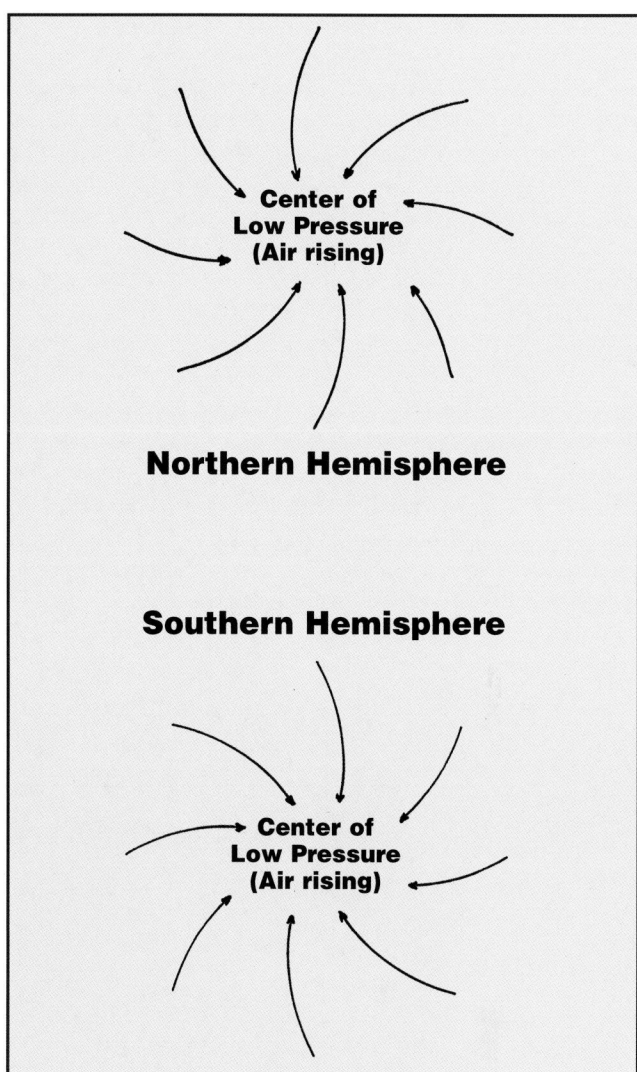

Figure 3.5 Within areas of low pressure, the air is rising and flowing inward, counter-clockwise in the Northern Hemisphere; clockwise in the Southern Hemisphere.

Well, we just "messed-up" the one-cell circulation some more. Now let's look at the air that begins to flow north in the Northern Hemisphere (south in the Southern Hemisphere) from this subtropical high-pressure area. It is forced to curve to the right in the Northern Hemisphere (left in the Southern Hemisphere) and becomes the westerlies, or as referred to by some, the prevailing westerlies or southwesterlies. We now have that second major wind belt that surrounds the globe, and it is present in both the Southern and Northern Hemispheres.

Back now to our polar easterlies or northeasterlies in the Northern Hemisphere. As these cool or cold winds begin moving south, they encounter the southwesterlies that are warm and flowing north. These two wind belts do not like each other, and they have been battling for thousands of years along an imaginary line called the polar front. First the polar winds are victorious, then the westerlies score a win. Portland, Seattle, and thousands of other cities and towns in the area from roughly 35 degrees north and south to around 60 degrees north and south get caught in the middle. The result is that air is being forced aloft near this polar front because, as we already know, the colder air sinks and warmer air rises up over it. These colliding air masses generate areas of low pressure where the air is rising. Figure 3.5 is a two-dimensional illustration of areas of low pressure in the Northern and Southern Hemispheres. Note that the curvature is opposite due to the lower pressure in the center which overcomes the Coriolis effect.

But what about the air that started south from the subtropical high-pressure area in the Northern Hemisphere? It started curving to the right because of the Coriolis effect and now has become the northeast trade winds. In the Southern Hemisphere, air that started moving north, out of the subtropical area of high pressure began turning to the left, and now becomes the southeast trade winds. The trade winds constitute our third major wind belt.

However, with northeast trade winds blowing on one side of the equator and southeast trade winds blowing on the other side, we again have two wind belts coming together. But these two wind belts have similar properties (warm and moist) so they do not go into battle. What happens, then? When two air streams come together, they cannot go down into the earth. They are forced to rise. Now isn't that a coincidence? From the very start we said that air was rising near the equator from the heating at the surface. Now we have discovered another reason why it is rising. That reason is the converging of two different air streams.

The area where these northeast and southeast trade winds meet is called the Intertropical Convergence Zone or the ITCZ. It is a very important feature regarding weather in and near the tropics since its position varies with the seasons. The ITCZ is farther north in July than it is in January. This zone migrates north and south in response to the earth's movement around the sun and the change in the area receiving the most heat. Because of the converging air masses near the ITCZ and the rising air, this area is known for its light winds.

The area is frequently called the doldrums. For most of the time weather is pretty much the same here. Some call it dull and monotonous; hence the term, "Down in the Doldrums."

Additionally, the area between 20 degrees and 30 degrees north and 20 degrees and 30 degrees south, where the air is descending, is also known for its light winds. When early maritime explorers sailed into these areas they would encounter very light or calm winds for several days but certainly not enough to fill their sails. It is reported that the horses they had on board would either have to be killed for food or thrown overboard because there was nothing to feed them. Hence, this area is referred to as the "horse latitudes." It is also the area where most of the earth's deserts are found. Figure 3.6 shows the earth's major wind belts including the ITCZ and Polar Front.

When the air pressure around the surface of the earth is examined, we realize that the continents, ocean currents, mountains, and ice fields all contribute to form major areas of low and high pressure. These are semi-permanent, meaning that for the most part, they are located in the same

Figure 3.6 The earth's major wind belts showing the polar front, the Intertropical Convergence Zone and areas where air is rising or sinking.

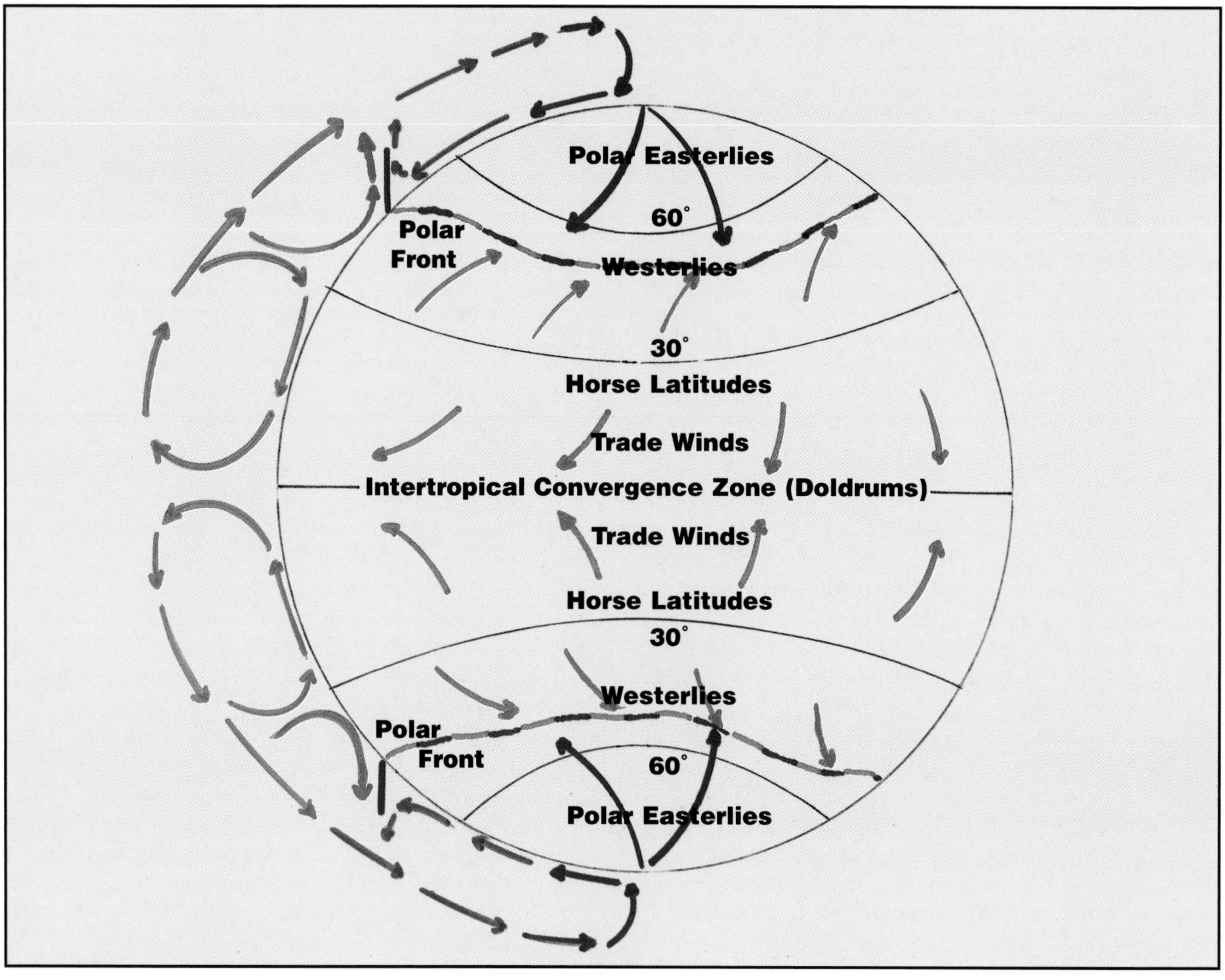

region year after year. Figure 3.7 shows the average wind flow and locations of major pressure centers and ITCZ for January in the Pacific Ocean and adjacent land masses. Note in particular the location of the Pacific high-pressure area. It is relatively small and located between southern

California and Hawaii. The Aleutian Low is quite prevalent and covers most of the Gulf of Alaska and the Bering Sea. There is a large area of high pressure over the Asian continent where the air is cold and dense. This area, although not shown, extends westward to eastern Europe. Note also that a weak area of high pressure exists over the western portion

of the United States. This is also due to cooler, more dense air over this area in the winter months. With air flowing out of an area of high pressure into an area of low pressure, the flow along the coasts of Washington and Oregon becomes prevailing southerly in the winter months. In the Portland area and at the mouth of the Columbia River the prevailing flow is mostly southeasterly in the winter months. This is due to the influence of the Columbia River Gorge, a gap in the Cascade Mountains, and the gap in the Coast Range Mountains at the mouth of the Columbia River. A similar effect in prevailing winds is noted through the Strait of Juan de Fuca separating Washington from Vancouver Island in British Columbia. Terrain features can cause many other local variations in the wind flow.

The average wind flow and locations of major pressure centers and the ITCZ for July are shown in Figure 3.8. Major changes have occurred. In the Northern Hemisphere the large area of low pressure centered around the Aleutian Chain and in the Gulf of Alaska has retreated northward into the Bering Sea and weakened. The Pacific

Figure 3.7 Average wind flow and the location of pressure centers and the Intertropical Convergence Zone for January over the Pacific Ocean.

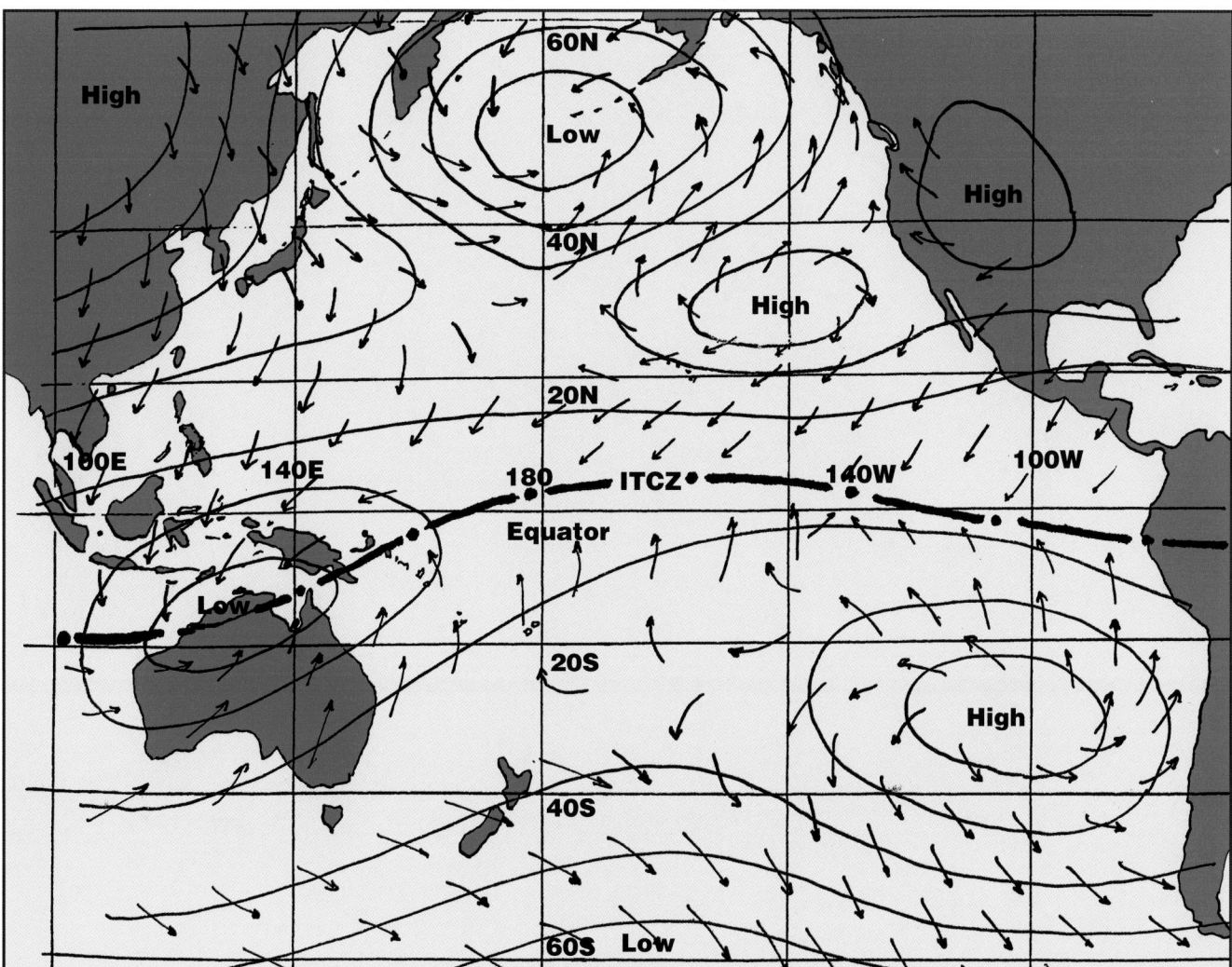

high-pressure area between Hawaii and continental United States has expanded northward and intensified. The cold high pressure over Asia has been replaced by an area of low pressure. Thus, the wind flow in this area off the Asian coast has completely reversed from northerly in January to southerly in July. The weak high-pressure center over the western United States has dissipated. An area of low pressure has developed over the southwestern portion of the United States due to the intense surface heating in this area and the air subsequently rising. Thus, there is a difference in air pressure between the subtropical high pressure off the coast of the Pacific Northwest and the surface low over the desert Southwest. Air flows from high pressure to low pressure, and this produces the prevailing north to northwesterly winds along the coasts of California, Oregon, and Washington in the summer months.

In the Southern Hemisphere, the low over Australia has been replaced by an area of high pressure. Off South America, the location of the center of the surface high-pressure area changes very little, but the high-pressure area has increased slightly in intensity resulting in a stronger southerly flow off the coasts of Ecuador and Peru. The ITCZ also changes from July to January, locating itself farther north in the Northern Hemisphere summer and retreating south in the Northern Hemisphere winter, especially in proximity to large land masses.

As depicted in Figures 3.7 and 3.8 that show the major pressure centers over the Pacific Ocean and surrounding land masses, air flows outward from areas of high pressure into areas of low pressure at the surface. In actuality, these areas of high pressure and areas of low pressure are three-dimensional. They extend upward into the atmosphere. If we looked at the North Pacific area of high pressure in three-dimension we would see air on the eastern edge of this large mound (near the North American continent) that is not only flowing outward but is also sinking.

On the western edge of this same feature (near the Asian continent), the air is flowing out from the high-pressure center but it is also rising. After having traveled many miles through the sub-tropical regions the air has increased

Figure 3.8 Average wind flow and location of pressure centers and the Intertropical Convergence Zone for July over the Pacific Ocean.

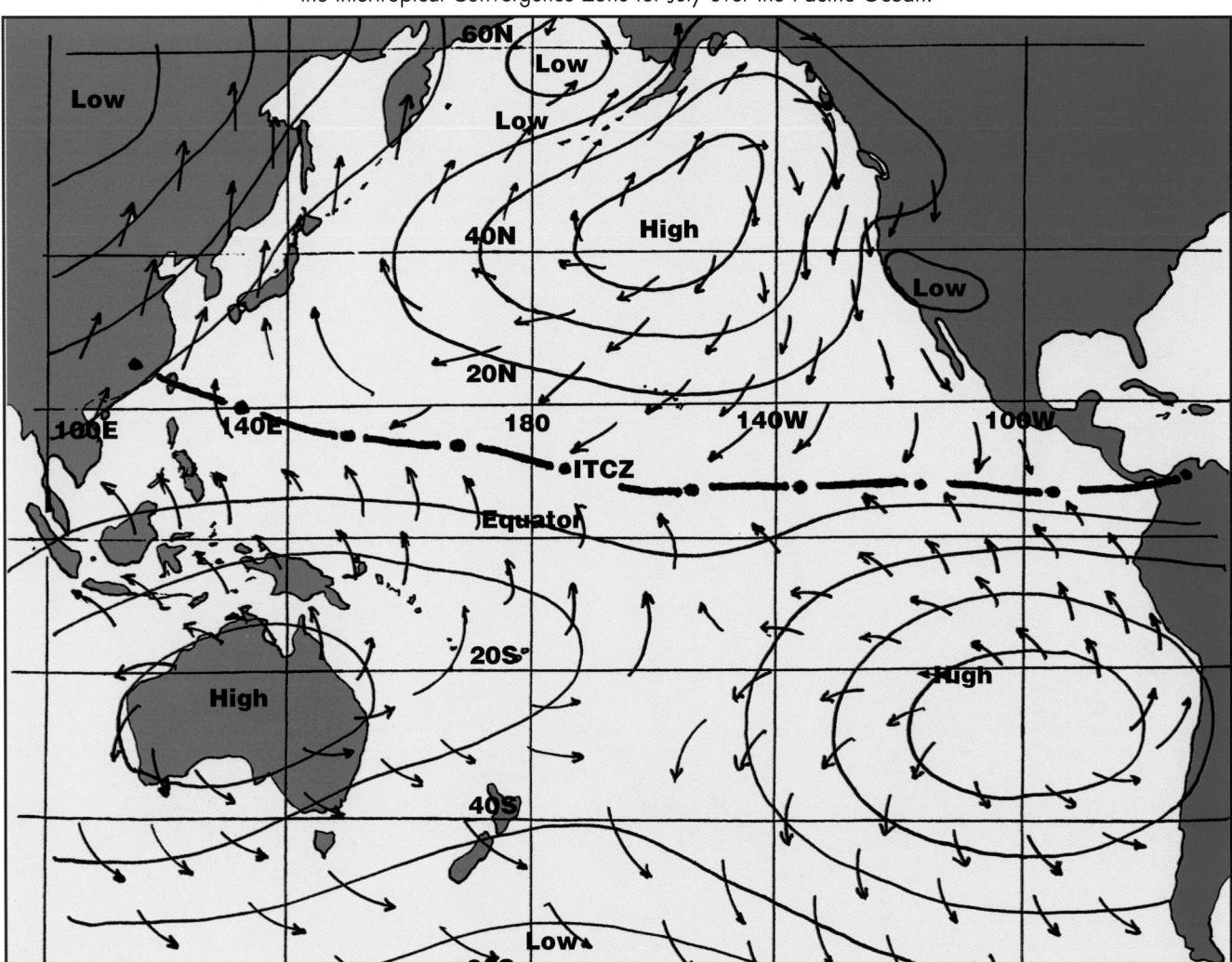

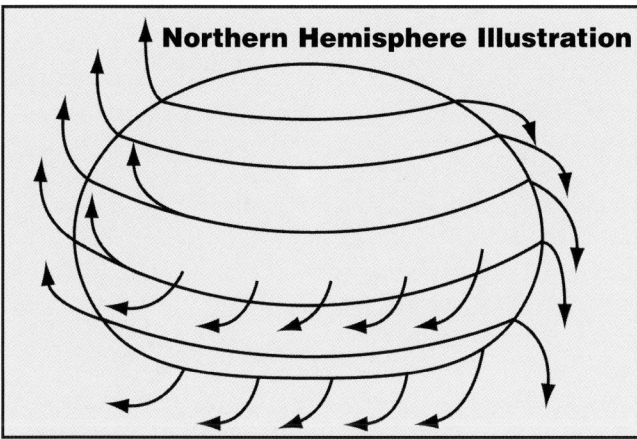

Figure 3.9 In large areas of high pressure, air is flowing outward. The air is also sinking on the eastern edge of the high-pressure area but rising on the western edge.

its moisture content. As it arrives on the western edge of the large Pacific high, it begins to rise. Thus, we can readily see that air on the eastern side of these large areas of high pressure is sinking and flowing outward, while on the western side the air is flowing outward but also rising, as depicted in Figure 3.9. This accounts for entirely different summer weather at the same latitude depending on which side of the high-pressure area one is located. The large area of high pressure that is called the Bermuda High in the North Atlantic is an identical feature, bringing subsiding air to the coasts of Portugal and Spain and rising, moist air to southeast United States.

In summary, heated air rises and air that is cooler sinks. Air flows from areas of high pressure into areas of low pressure. As it does, this air is subject to the Coriolis effect, which deflects it to the right in the Northern Hemisphere and to the left in the Southern Hemisphere. In meteorology when we speak of any semi-permanent area or any of the three major wind belts, we must remember that these are average conditions. Differences, sometimes major, change conditions from the average.

Jet Streams

Perhaps one of the most talked about aspects of weather is the jet stream. For the most part, we blame it for all the cold rainy weekends that weather forecasters promise us. "Well," they will say, "the jet stream is plunging south and pushing those storm fronts toward us. Looks like another lousy weekend ahead!" True, but only partially so. Middle latitude storms do, indeed, follow the jet stream. It is a steering mechanism. It is that westerly current of air, the westerlies, we talked about earlier. But jet streams are not omnipotent or omnipresent. They are important, but sometimes their importance is exaggerated.

As early as the 1890s, the Weather Bureau (now the National Weather Service) was experimenting with kites to explore the air at levels above the surface. Balloons had shown that the air "up there" was moving faster than at the surface. The Weather Bureau hoped to achieve an altitude of one mile and hopefully to 10,000 feet or nearly two miles using kites with instruments attached to them. These were box kites similar to the kite shown in Figure 3.10. On September 19, 1897, a kite reached a height of 9,885 feet above sea level at the Blue Hill Observatory in Massachusetts. Approximately three miles of wire were used to attain this altitude.

So, meteorologists were already looking up to determine what effect winds aloft had on the weather. Although the existence of prevailing westerly winds around the globe was accepted in the late 1930s and early 1940s, it was not confirmed until World War II. Pilots flying at altitudes approaching 20,000 feet westward toward Japan would frequently have to turn back after encountering extreme head winds. Then, on their return, they landed earlier than expected. What they had encountered was a portion of the jet stream. The Japanese had also discovered this current of air. They launched balloons with explosives attached to them anticipating that the strong westerly current of air would carry them to the Pacific Northwest where they would start forest fires. The westerly flow, however, is far more complicated than what was speculated in the *Monthly Weather Review* in 1898 on page 38.

The jet stream is normally depicted as a continuous ribbon of air that circles the globe from west to east. Part of the time this is true. But like the major pressure centers, the jet stream is not static. It moves, on a daily basis and on a seasonal basis. In the topsy-turvy world of our atmosphere, it can even blow from northeast to southwest or from southeast to northwest. It can be very strong for several days or weeks, and then almost disappear. The jet stream can split into two, sometimes three, or even four branches. In the Northern Hemisphere the jet stream is weaker in summer than it is in winter. That is, the wind speeds on average are less. But what is the overall cause of the jet stream?

Figure 3.10 Around 1900, kites were used extensively to obtain meteorological readings above the surface. They were mostly box-like structures similar to the kite shown below. Often several kites were used in tandem, attached with piano wire to a ground site.

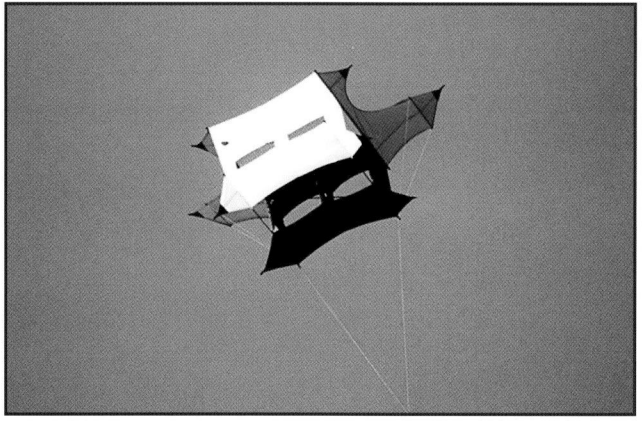

We have already talked about differences in temperature or differential heating. It is this difference in temperature across a region (usually colder to the north and warmer to the south) that produces differences in pressure in the middle

and upper levels of the atmosphere. A difference in pressure causes the wind to blow. Without getting too involved with mathematics, it suffices to say that when you change the temperature of a volume of air, you also change its pressure, and when you change the density, you also change the pressure and temperature. Once the air starts flowing from high pressure to low pressure, the Coriolis effect causes it to turn to the right in the Northern Hemisphere.

Very simplistically, the cause of the jet stream is shown in Figure 3.11. Here we have two columns of air, one cold and the other warm, with the same number of molecules. (In this case it is 20, although a column of air in the real world contains billions of molecules.) The pressure at the surface will be the same, since pressure is defined as the weight of a column of air above a point. (Pressure gets "released" in the next chapter.) If you were located at the 500 millibar level, however, or around 18,000 feet, the pressure in Column A is less than in Column B since above 500 millibars there are only 5 molecules in Column A and 10 in Column B. Air, then, will begin flowing from Column B,

Figure 3.11 A difference in temperature causes the jet streams. At 500 millibars, for instance, air molecules flow from the warm column of air (the equator) toward the cold column (polar areas). Once in motion, the Coriolis effect occurs.

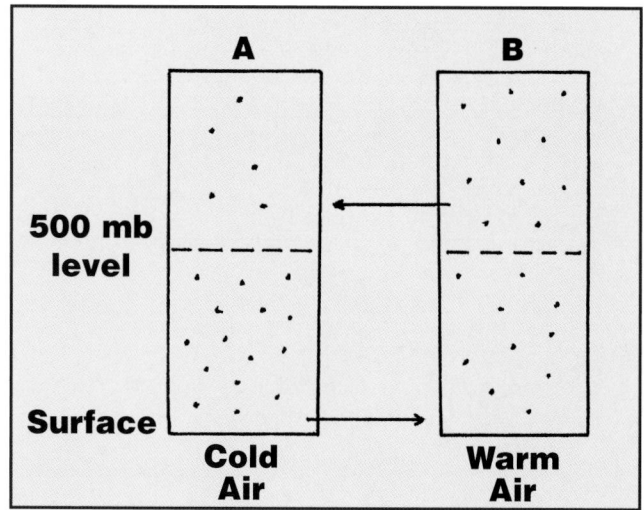

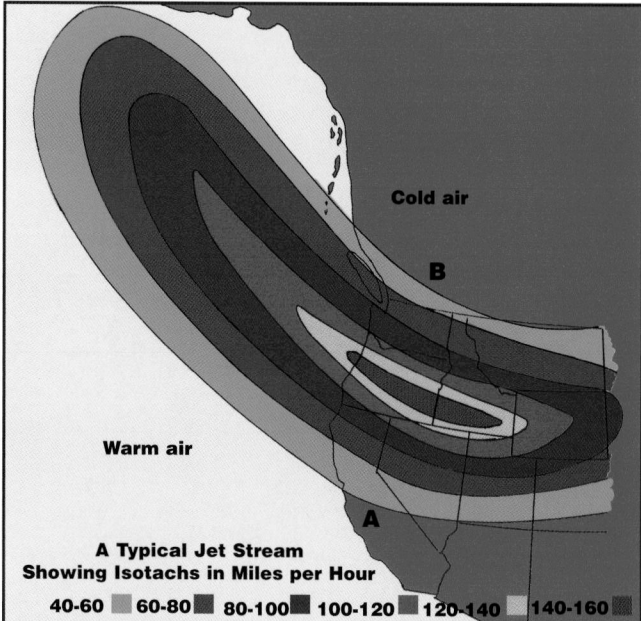

Figure 3.12 The jet stream on weather maps is usually depicted as a two-dimensional figure with the strongest winds located in the center.

the warm column, to Column A, the cold column, at 500 millibars. But if two of the molecules leave Column B, what happens to the air pressure at the surface? Aha! You're right! It lowers. So then at the bottom of the columns (the surface), air begins flowing from the cold column toward the warm column. This is precisely what happens in the atmosphere and why great temperature differences cause great pressure differences which causes the jet stream.

Now let's turn our attention to the westerlies we discussed earlier. In the Northern Hemisphere, air that flows north from equatorial regions toward the north pole is pulled to the right because of the Coriolis effect. This is true at all levels of the atmosphere. However, at higher elevations above the friction level (around 5,000 feet) the winds frequently reach a point where they are blowing parallel to lines of equal temperature (isotherms) separating cold air to the north and warm air to the south. In this case the Coriolis effect equals the force that is caused by a difference in pressure (temperature). When that temperature contrast is large, so is the difference in pressure. The result is a stronger jet stream. This is certainly true in the fall, winter, and spring seasons in the Northern Hemisphere. During these months large temperature differences exist on a latitudinal basis separating cold air near the north pole from warmer air in the tropical regions.

The jet stream is mostly portrayed as a two-dimensional feature. Television meteorologists will show you its location on their weather maps, and pictures in books give the same image. The jet stream depicted in Figure 3.12 traveling from the Gulf of Alaska across Oregon into Wyoming is one of those two dimensional pictures. Meteorologists draw lines of equal wind speed called isotachs to determine the location of a jet stream or the strongest winds.

But a jet stream is three-dimensional. If we take a cross-section of the jet stream in Figure 3.11, we would see that it looks much like an onion when we cut it in half. The layers of the onion would compare to the isotachs, getting stronger towards the center. (No, I am not saying the center of the onion is stronger than the outside!) But the jet stream winds are strongest in the center as shown in Figure 3.13. Note also in this figure that the isotachs are more closely spaced near the top of the jet or higher in elevation. This is often the case since jet streams, or the strongest winds, are frequently found just below the tropopause. For airplanes flying in this location, it can be very turbulent if wind speeds decrease rapidly with elevation. Pilots flying jet aircraft try to avoid these areas since it is frequently where clear air turbulence is found.

Although the jet stream may have wind speeds of near 200 miles per hour, the jet stream itself, that ribbon of air, is moving much more slowly. In Figure 3.14 a parcel of air labeled "P" enters the jet stream over the Pacific. At this time, the core of the jet stream, or center of strongest winds, is slightly offshore. By the second day this parcel of air has accelerated to a point over Oregon, and the core of the jet stream has moved slowly from its location slightly offshore to a position over Oregon and Idaho. On the third day, the parcel of air has completed its journey through the jet stream and is found somewhere over the Great Lakes, but the core of the jet stream has only moved to near the Wyoming-Montana border. Thus, air parcels travel through the jet stream, while the entire jet stream itself is not moving nearly as rapidly as speeds within it.

If you have ever dropped a small piece of wood or a leaf into a stream and watched as it moved downstream, you observed it accelerating when it enters a faster flow, but slows down when the stream broadens. The stream itself has not moved, only the water flowing through it. The jet stream is therefore much like a river where the strongest flows are in the center and weaker flows along the shoreline or near the bottom. In fact, the analogy has been used to depict the jet stream as, "that river of air above us."

So far, our discussion of jet streams has been about the polar jet stream. This phenomenon is generally located above the polar front, where the northeasterly polar winds at the surface are doing battle with the warmer southwesterly winds also at the surface. There is a secondary jet stream that is located generally on the equator-side above the subtropical high-pressure areas and higher in the atmosphere than the polar jet stream. Meteorologists refer to it as the subtropical jet. Combinations can occur and jet stream configuration can often be complicated. Figure 3.15 is a reproduction of a jet stream pattern that occurred several years ago during winter. One branch migrated north into the interior of Alaska, then began curving south and then southwest, where it exited the North American continent at the tip of southeast Alaska. Another branch of the jet stream is shown heading east-northeastward into Washington from the central Pacific Ocean. Still another jet stream, probably the subtropical jet stream, is shown entering Southern

Figure 3.14 Jet streams change or move their locations and orientations slowly. It is the parcels of air within the jet stream that are moving rapidly.

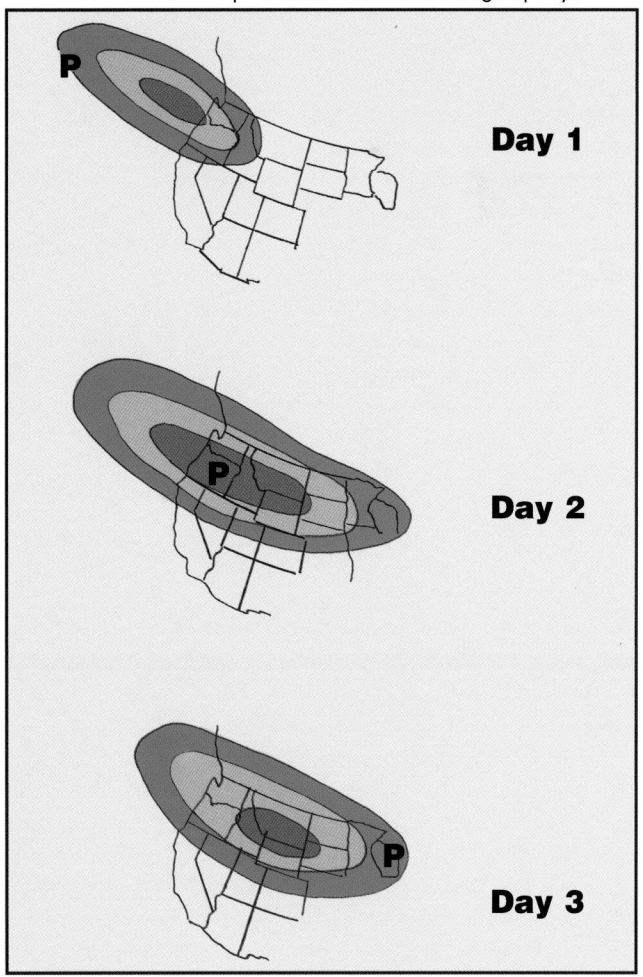

Figure 3.13 A cross-section through a jet stream will show an isotach pattern with strongest winds usually located directly below the tropopause with the tightest gradient in this area.

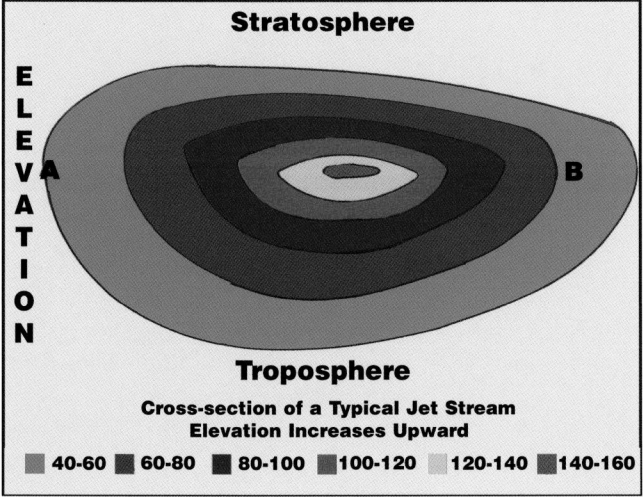

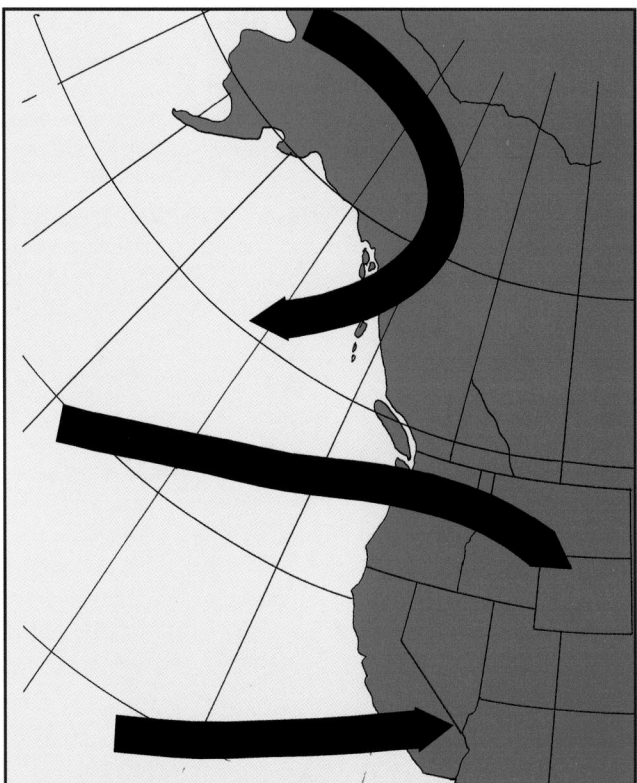

Figure 3.15 A complicated jet stream pattern as it appeared over western North America and the eastern Pacific Ocean several years ago.

California from the west-southwest. Thus, jet streams can take on many forms.

In summary, there are some points we want to remember about jet streams:

1. They are in most cases not continuous around the entire globe, but broken up into segments.

2. They normally blow from west to east due to temperature differences across them and the Coriolis effect, but often blow from different directions.

3. Although wind speeds may be very high (strong) within a jet stream, the jet stream itself is moving much more slowly.

4. Jet streams are generally at a lower altitude during the colder months of the year and at a higher altitude during the warmer months of the year.

5. Jet streams are generally at a higher latitude during the warmer months of the year and at a lower latitude during the colder months of the year.

6. Jet streams can "split" into two different segments, one veering to the left, and one to the right.

7. Often there can be more than one jet stream, sometimes two polar jet streams, or a polar jet stream and a subtropical jet stream.

We know that weather fluctuates on a daily, weekly, and monthly basis. Generally speaking, in this discussion we are talking about the middle latitudes and, to some extent, the polar latitudes. (Variances in tropical weather

are often more subtle or related to tropical disturbances or movement north and south of the ITCZ.) But what is responsible for those few days or even weeks of sunny, warm weather or cold, stormy weather at middle latitudes? These changes are related to the jet stream, but it is the troughs and ridges moving along this jet stream that are responsible.

Troughs and Ridges

If you have ever taken a topographical map that shows elevation lines and gone hiking in the mountains, you experienced ridges and valleys. Looking at a weather map reveals a similar situation, only on weather maps they are referred to as troughs and ridges. Troughs and ridges account for most of the periods of stormy weather and fair weather we experience.

In the Northern Hemisphere where the jet stream curves south or migrates into lower latitudes, it usually brings with it cold air at the middle and upper levels of the troposphere. When the jet stream bulges north, warm air accompanies it at these same levels. Figure 3.16 shows a ridge over the western portion of the United States, a trough approaching the coast, and a ridge extending along 155W north into Alaska.

But how are troughs and ridges determined? Contour lines, such as those shown in Figure 3.16, are similar to the lines on that topographical map. They show the height above mean sea level of a constant pressure surface. In Figure 3.16 the 500 millibar surface has arbitrarily been chosen as our constant pressure surface, since it is a level used frequently by meteorologists in analyzing weather charts. The values shown are the heights in meters. They are

Figure 3.16 A ridge of high pressure over the western United States, a trough of low pressure approaching the coast and a ridge near 155W.

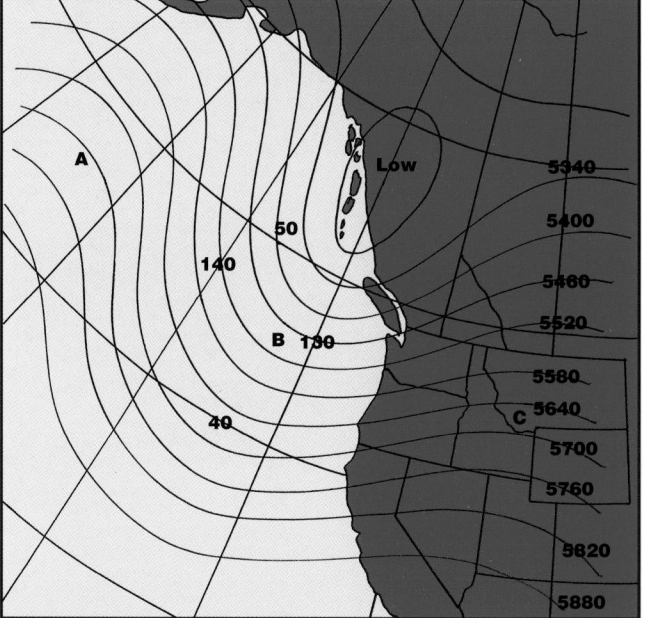

the elevations to which one would have to rise in the atmosphere above mean sea level to arrive at a pressure of 500 millibars since pressure decreases with altitude. The 5760 line passes through Northern California into the extreme northwest tip of Nevada. Everywhere along this line one would have to ascend to a height of 5,760 meters, or around 18,900 feet, to reach a pressure of 500 millibars. The 5580 line passes through northwest Oregon and into northern Idaho. At all points along this line one would have to ascend to only 5,580 meters (18,300 feet) to reach a level of 500 millibars. This is referred to as a lower height. Same pressure, but reached at a lower height in the atmosphere.

In middle latitudes, a trough (or an area of lower height values) is usually associated with an area of lower pressure (stormy weather) at the surface and colder air aloft. A ridge is usually associated with an area of higher pressure (fair weather) at the surface and warmer air aloft. Hence we have the terms, "trough of low pressure aloft" or "ridge of high pressure aloft." If we start upward in an area of low pressure at the surface, we start out with a lower value to begin with, so we do not need to go as high to reach this level or pressure of 500 millibars. (We assume here that the rate of decrease with elevation is the same at all points.) Conversely, if we start out in an area of high pressure at the surface and go upward, we would have to go to a higher elevation before reaching a value of 500 millibars, assuming again that the decrease in pressure with elevation is the same everywhere.

Note in Figure 3.16 that the values continue to lower as we move to a higher latitude or toward the polar regions and toward the center of low pressure, in this case somewhere over the Queen Charlotte Islands along the coast of British Columbia. This is indicative of the fact that colder air normally lies in the Polar regions and warmer air in the more tropical regions.

Troughs and ridges move along through the jet stream, sometimes rapidly, sometimes slowly. They are often referred to as short wave troughs and short wave ridges. These short waves, however, have nothing in common with the electromagnetic spectrum discussed earlier. Meteorologists do track them since they are responsible for the day-to-day changes in the weather that we experience. A two-dimensional cross-section of the ridge-trough-ridge that was shown in Figure 3.16 is shown in Figure 3.17. The letters A, B, and C correspond to the same locations as shown in Figure 3.16 and the heights of the 500 mb surface are shown in meters.

Meteorologists will often draw ridge lines and trough lines on a weather map. A ridge line shows the maximum curvature of the contour line. On either side of a ridge line, the height that one has to ascend to get to a constant pressure surface decreases. A trough line also indicates maximum curvature of the contour lines. Higher values are found on either side of a trough line. Trough and ridge lines do not have to be oriented strictly north to south. They can be northeast to southwest, southeast to northwest, or even

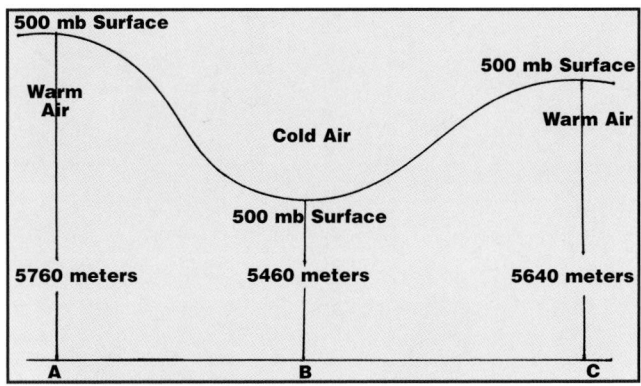

Figure 3.17 A cross-section of the letters shown in Figure 3.16 with cold air located in a trough and warm air in a ridge. Height of the 500 millibar surface is in meters above mean sea level.

oriented east-west. Additionally, these trough and ridge lines do not have to be straight lines, but can show curvature. The passage of a trough line over a weather reporting station is very often accompanied by showery, stormy weather.

You will hear meteorologists refer to short wave troughs and ridges by a plethora of names such as "wiggles," "systems," "disturbances," "dips," "minor upper air troughs (ridges)" etc. Whatever the name, they bring the day-to-day variations in our weather. There could be a long period of warm, dry weather that is broken up by a day or two of rain and then some more warm, dry weather. The day or two of rain was caused by a short wave trough. Figure 3.18 is a hypothetical 500 millibar map showing numerous troughs and ridges. How many can you locate?

Ridges and troughs can be small features that cover only one or two hundred miles, or they can be larger and cover several thousand miles. In the latter they are referred to as long wave ridges and long wave troughs. Again, there is no relation to the electromagnetic spectrum. Short wave troughs and ridges meander through long wave troughs and ridges. In cases such as these, the movement of the jet stream is slow, although the jet stream itself may have very strong winds blowing through it. These long wave features are also called Rossby waves, by the meteorologist C. G. Rossby, who devoted much study to understanding them and developed equations regarding their movement. In Figure 3.18, a long wave trough is located along the west coast of the United States. One short wave trough extends southwest from the low center near the mouth of the

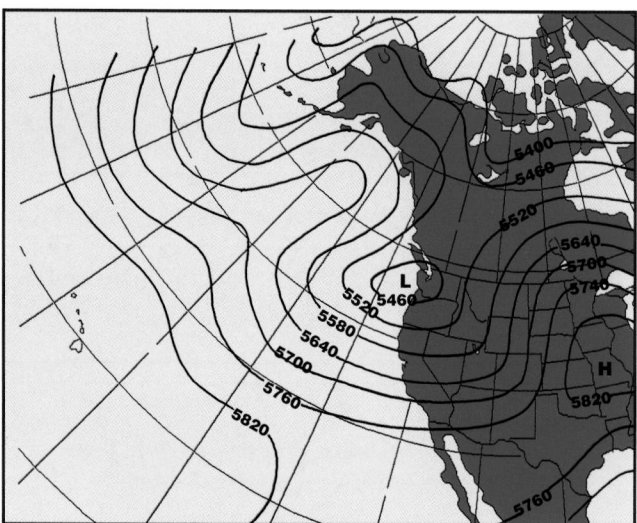

Figure 3.18 A 500 millibar chart showing many troughs and ridges.

Columbia River and another southeastward from northeast Oregon across southern Idaho, into northern Utah and southeastward across Colorado.

Long wave ridges that pass over an area account for extended periods of fair, cloud-free, warm, rainless weather. Whereas if a long wave trough is moving slowly over an area, cold, stormy, unsettled, showery, rainy weather is usually the rule. These long waves generally move slowly in an easterly direction. At times they remain stationary and they can even retrogress, or move in a westerly direction. They may be present for weeks, then over a few days dissipate, only to reappear in a different location.

Cut-off Lows and Cut-off Highs

Occasionally cold air that advances too far south or warm air that advances too far north will get "cut off" from the main jet stream. These situations are like an army that advances far ahead of its reinforcements and gets surrounded by the enemy. What happens? Unless reinforcements are sent in, the army may wander around for several days, finally weakening and then taken captive. So it is with the pockets of warm air and cold air that get cut off. Meteorologists refer to them as "cut-off lows" or "cut-off highs." Closed lows (cut-off lows) often bring cold air to lower latitudes and closed highs (cut-off highs), warm air to much higher latitudes.

An example of the formation of a cut-off low is shown in Figure 3.19. Day 1 shows a trough of low pressure approaching the West Coast with its pool of cold air identified in blue. The solid black lines are constant height lines or contour lines, and the solid red lines are isotherms. Notice in Day 2 how the trough has become elongated. The cold air in the trough is pushing farther south. By Day 3 it has plunged too far south and become cut off over northeastern Arizona and northwestern New Mexico. The cold air is now completely surrounded. The northern portion of the trough continues to move on east across the northern

tier of states and southern Canada in the jet stream. This cut-off low may wander aimlessly around for a few days until its supply of cold air is completely modified by air around it.

In some cases, "reinforcements" do arrive in the form of another short wave trough that will "pick up" the wandering cut-off low, and carry it safely "home" to the jet stream. You might think this is a fitting and nice end to the story. For meteorologists and weather forecasters, it is not! Cut-off lows and cut-off highs often have a mind of their own and meander aimlessly before they weaken or are "rescued," which makes forecasting the weather associated with these phenomena somewhat difficult to say the least.

"But My Barometer Says Fair"

The caller was absolutely correct. It was raining outside and her barometer did say "FAIR." Oh, if only weather and weather forecasting were as simple as the words on a barometer! But they definitely are not. Although areas of high pressure at the surface (ridge of high pressure aloft) are generally associated with warm, sunny, dry weather, that is not always the case as we see from this example shown in Figure 3.20. A warm ridge of high pressure has

Figure 3.19 The formation of a cut-off low.

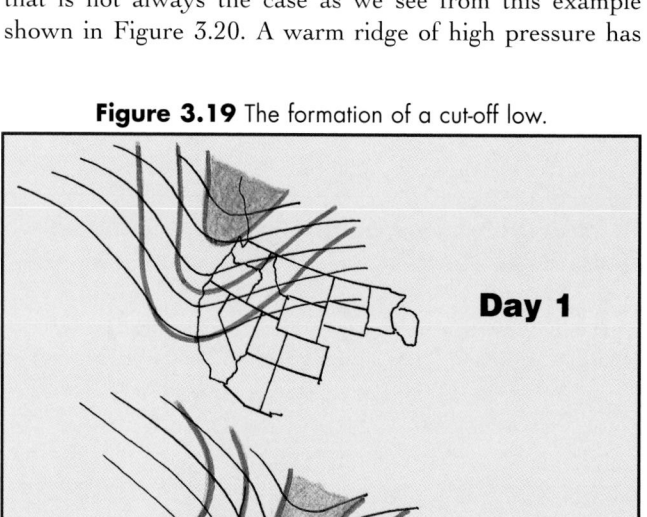

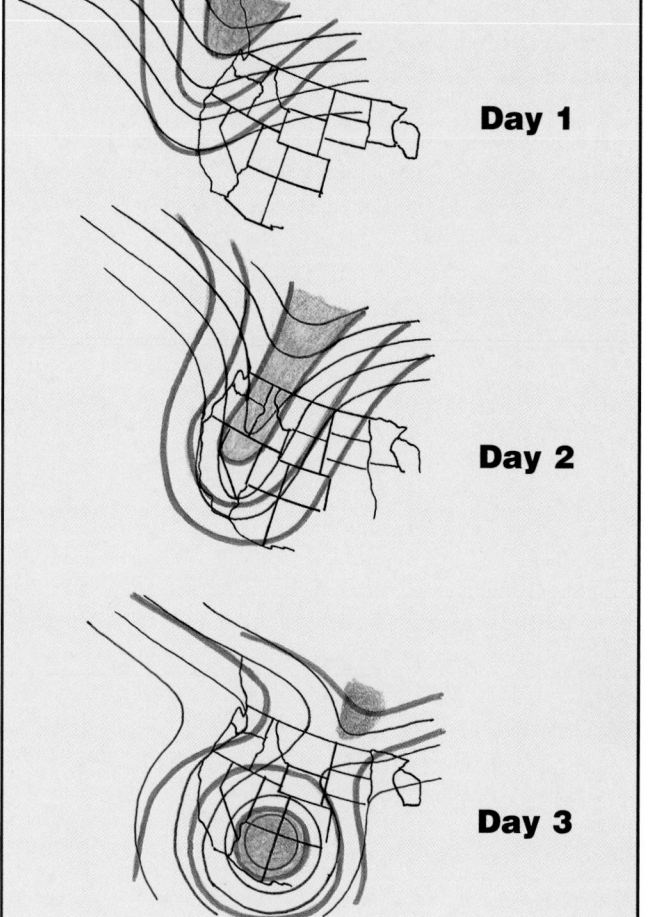

Day 1

Day 2

Day 3

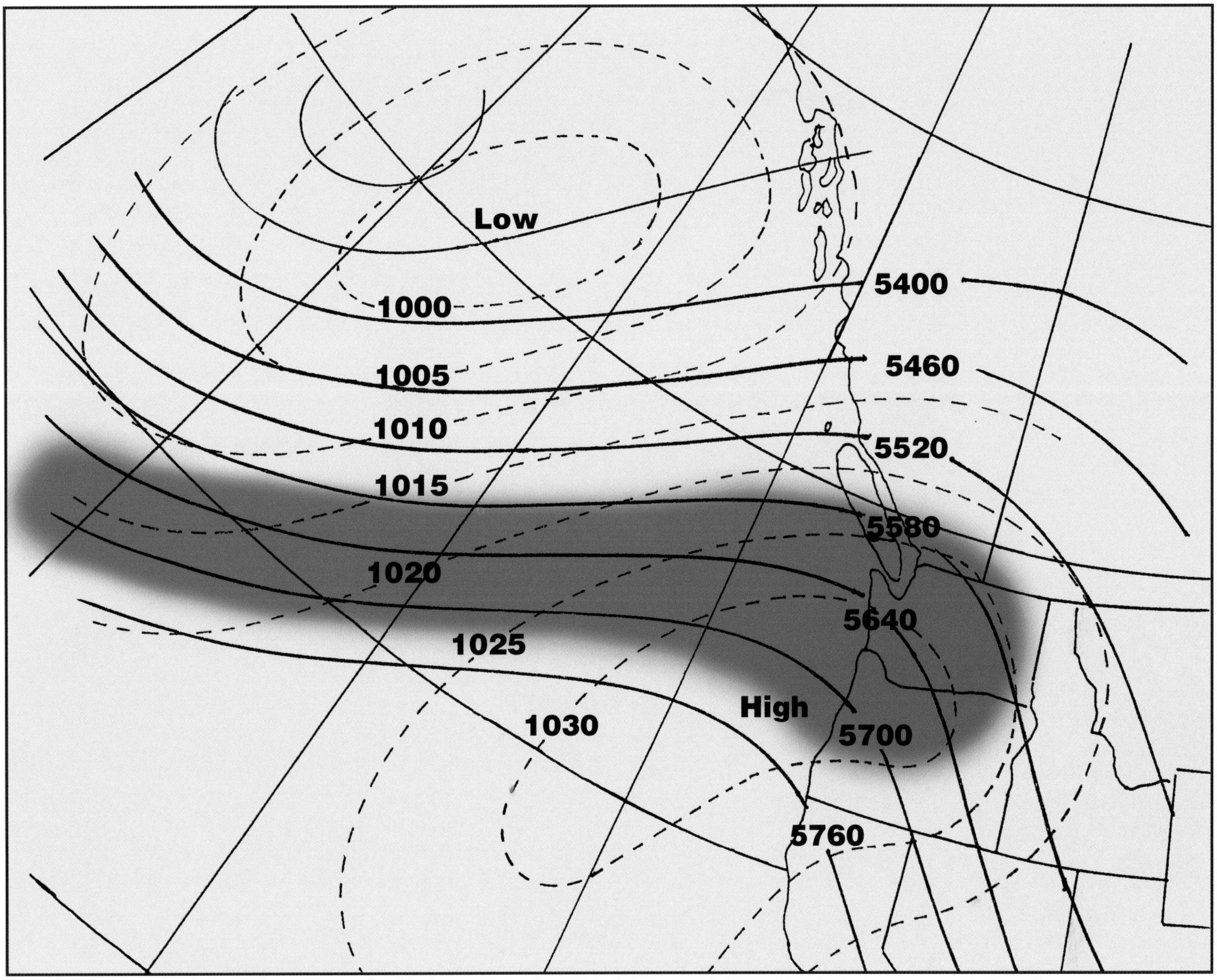

Figure 3.20 An example of what meteorologists refer to as a "dirty ridge." High pressure, both surface and aloft, has built into the Pacific Northwest, yet the flow aloft contains sufficient moisture (green) to produce clouds and rain. (Dashed lines are surface isobars; solid lines 500-mb contour heights.)

pushed into the Pacific Northwest. High pressure has preceded it at the surface with a value of 1030 millibars or 30.40 inches of mercury, well into the "FAIR" category on home barometers. Yet, sufficient moisture is flowing through the ridge of high pressure, often from lower latitudes, to continue the cloudy, rainy weather. The pattern often confuses meteorologists who see the approaching surface high and warm ridge and immediately forecast clear, sunny weather that turns out to be gray, cloudy, cool and rainy. The situation is not unusual, especially in the Pacific Northwest, where warm moist air aloft will override cold dense air with high pressure at the surface. The pattern often occurs with a northwesterly flow aloft after the passage of a short wave trough. Meteorologists have given it the term "dirty ridge!"

Now, you might ask, if there is such a term as "dirty ridge," can we then have a "clean trough?" The answer is, "Yes, we can." In this case, there is insufficient moisture to cause clouds and rain even though the barometer needle is pointing to stormy and a short wave trough may be passing through the area. I guess we are right back to that old cliche: "Don't believe everything you see!"

In this chapter we have looked at the major weather features around the earth and have seen how they are formed. We have talked about troughs and ridges as being the producers of weather. We have identified ridge lines and trough lines as areas of maximum curvature in contour lines. The latter term, we found out, represents an elevation to which one must rise to reach a certain designated pressure. We are aware that troughs and ridges move along through the jet stream as short wave features on our weather map. We discussed the importance of long wave features that give us persistent fair or stormy weather, and then we were "cut off" from the main westerly flow and briefly examined those pesky lows and highs that leave the jet stream to wander off by themselves, which I am sure you are ready to do after all the ups and downs in this chapter.

Chapter 4
Atmospheric Pressure

I have not tried the device described in the text box. It would be nice if weather and weather forecasting were that simple. But, alas, they are not. Pressure, however, is a very simple concept as the article shows. In fact, the mercurial barometer shown in Figure 1.20 uses precisely the same

> ### The Farmer's Barometer
> *Take a common glass pickle bottle, wide mouthed; fill it within three inches of top with water; then take a common Florence oil flask, removing the straw covering, and cleansing the flask thoroughly; plunge the neck of the flask as far as it will go, and the barometer is complete. In fine weather the water will rise into the neck of the flask even higher than the mouth of the pickle bottle, and in wet and windy weather it will fall to within an inch of the mouth of the flask. Before a heavy gale of wind, the water has been seen to leave the flask altogether at least eight hours before the gale came to its height. The invention was made by a German and communicated to a London Journal.*
>
> *Oregon Statesman,* December 11, 1865

principle: Air pushing down on a cistern of mercury pushes the mercury column up the tube. Conversely, lower pressure allows the mercury column to descend down the tube. We know from the discussion on weather elements that pressure varies, and sometimes we can correlate that variance with what the weather is actually doing. But low atmospheric pressure does not always mean rain, and high atmospheric pressure does not always mean fair weather as I tried to explain to the elderly caller on the other end of the telephone.

Pressure Defined
Our atmosphere is held to the earth by gravity, the same force that keeps you from floating off into space. When you step on the scales (No, you do not have to!) you are generating a force downward. Our atmosphere also has weight and exerts a force downward and, actually, in all directions. This force is called pressure. Simply put, air pressure is the weight of the column of air above a certain point. It is related to the number of molecules in that column. The more molecules there are and the denser they are packed, the greater the weight.

Pressure is expressed in a variety of ways. The scale most commonly used is "inches of mercury." That's the value that is displayed on weather programs and given over the radio. It merely reflects the height of the mercury column within the tube that is labeled on the outside in inches.

Meteorologists, however, convert the inches of mercury to millibars as a way to express pressure. A conversion is found in Table 3 in Appendices.

Of all the weather elements discussed in Chapter 1, pressure is the only one that consistently decreases with elevation. There are no exceptions. But the rate of decrease can vary. There are horizontal differences in air pressure and these produce wind. These differences are sometimes hard to detect. If the pressure at Portland was 10 millibars higher than it was in Seattle, you would not detect that change driving from one location to the other. Vertically, however, the pressure change is more dramatic. Driving up into the mountains this change is very discernable. If you take an elevator to the top of a building 500 feet high, the pressure will have decreased about 0.5 inch. Over the short time the elevator took to get to the top floor, you may have noticed the change in air pressure. Pressure decreases rapidly with elevation at first, roughly 0.01 inch for every 10 feet on the average and then more slowly, finally dribbling off even more slowly the farther you get from the earth, or in the upper regions of our atmosphere, hundreds of miles above the earth. If you have climbed to the top of Mt. Hood (roughly two miles high) you probably found a pressure of around 700 millibars. You would have climbed through roughly one-third of the atmosphere. Two-thirds of it was still above you. If you are really into this mountain climbing and reached the top of Mt. Rainier just under three miles high, the pressure you experienced there was

Figure 4.1 Pressure in the atmosphere decreases rapidly with elevation at first and then more slowly the higher in elevation or farther from the earth.

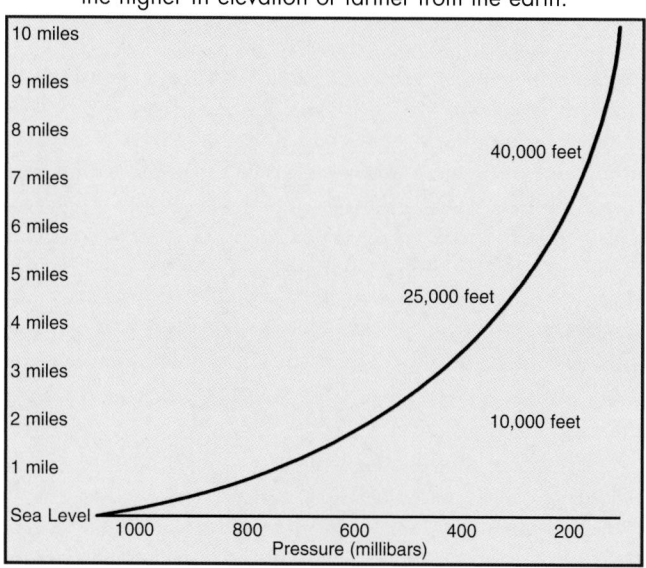

near 600 millibars. Flying in a jet plane at 35,000 feet, roughly 80 percent of the earth's atmosphere (that is, 80 percent of all the air molecules) is below you, and the pressure outside the plane is about 200 millibars. Figure 4.1 depicts the average decrease in pressure with elevation.

What are some relative values of pressure at the earth's surface? The highest pressure ever recorded was 1084 millibars or 32.01 inches of mercury in Siberia. A "strong" high pressure center, where air is sinking and piling up, has a pressure of around 1030 to 1040 millibars, 30.42 to 30.71 inches of mercury. The average pressure on the surface of the earth is around 1013 millibars or 29.92 inches of mercury. A strong low-pressure area would be in the neighborhood of 990 millibars to 980 millibars, or 29.24 to 28.94 inches of mercury. The lowest pressure ever recorded in Oregon occurred on January 9, 1880, at Astoria. It was 963 millibars or 28.45 inches of mercury. The lowest atmospheric pressure ever recorded at the surface of the earth was in the center of Typhoon Tip in October 1979. That value was 870 millibars or 25.70 inches of mercury. I suspect that pressure would make your ears pop, along with numerous other things!

But what happens to air pressure when the air is heated or cooled? Since our atmosphere is a gas, it follows certain "rules" or "laws" that gases follow where temperature, pressure, and density (mass per unit volume) are related. The pressure of a gas (P) is equal to the density (p) multiplied by the temperature (T) multiplied by a constant (K) or, P=pTK. Ugh! Sounds complicated, and to a certain degree, it is, so let's try to simplify it. If we increase the temperature of a gas and maintain the same pressure, we must lower the density (fewer molecules). Subsequently, if we increase the density (more molecules), we must decrease the temperature to maintain the same pressure. If we increase the pressure, we must either increase the density or the temperature, or both. If we decrease the density and decrease the temperature, the pressure must also decrease. This is what happens in a trough of low pressure aloft with its associated cold air.

If two quart jars could be filled with the same number of molecules, one with cold molecules and the other with warm molecules, the pressure at the bottom of each jar would be the same. However, most of the cold molecules in the one jar would be concentrated near the bottom of the jar, while the warm molecules would show a greater distribution throughout the jar. This is simply shown in Figure 4.2. This depiction is basically what happens in the atmosphere. In arctic air masses that are comprised of very cold, dense air, the pressure is higher at the surface and normally decreases quite rapidly with elevation, since most of the molecules are near the surface. In this same air mass, they thin out quickly with elevation much like those cold molecules in the one quart jar. In those large subtropical areas of high pressure, there is a very deep column of warm air molecules. This, together with the fact that this air is sinking and pushing downward, explains why these areas have higher pressure than surrounding areas.

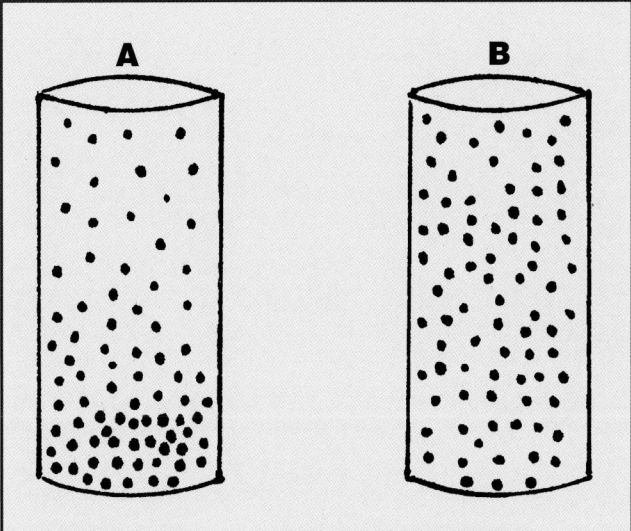

Figure 4.2 Given the same number of molecules, the pressure at the bottom of both jars is equal but the molecules decrease rapidly with elevation in jar A.

Pressure Gradients

As we have noted, the pressure at the surface of the earth is not the same everywhere. There are permanent areas of high pressure and permanent areas of low pressure. Air flows from high pressure to low pressure. The statement is analogous to taking a ball to the top of a hill and letting it roll down like the two stick figures have done in Figure 4.3. Released at the same time, the ball on the steeper hill has already gone farther than the ball on the more gentle slope. As a skier, I know that if I tackle a steep slope, I will go faster and probably get out of control. That's why I relax and enjoy a more gentle slope where I can go slower. So it is with the wind. The greater the "pile-up" of air (higher

Figure 4.3 A pressure gradient is analogous to the steepness of a slope. The ball released by the stick figure on the steep slope will roll faster than the one released by the figure on the gentle slope.

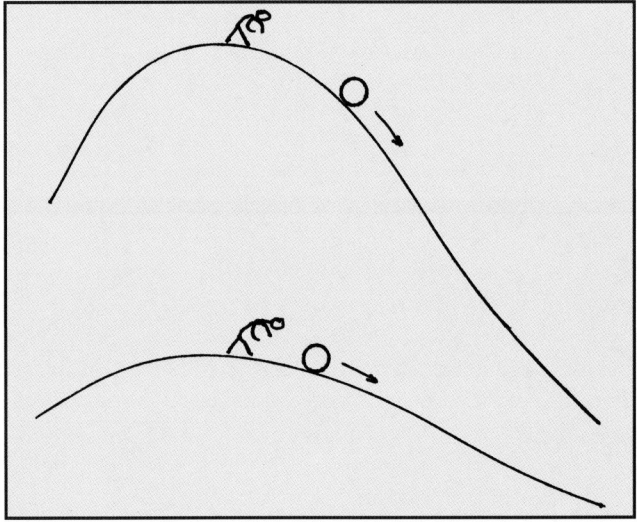

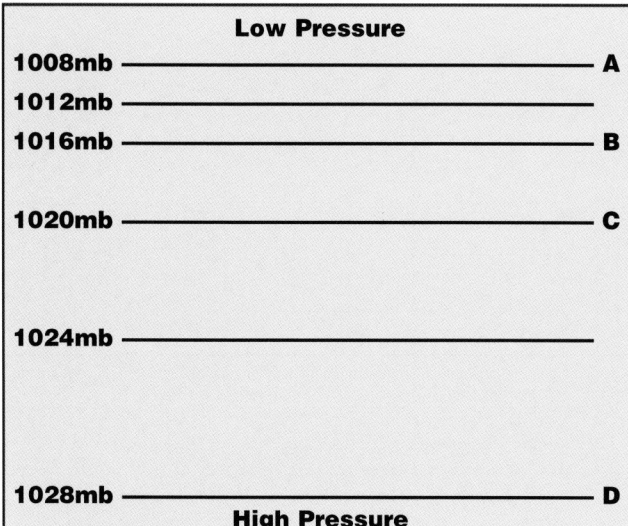

Figure 4.4 Pressure gradient depends on the distance between isobars or lines of constant pressure. The pressure gradient is the same from points A to B and from C to D but the distance between isobars is much greater from C to D.

pressure) the greater is the tendency for the atmosphere to want to equalize the pressure, causing it to flow from the higher pressure to the lower pressure.

This steepness of the slope can be thought of as the pressure gradient. It is the pressure gradient, or the difference in pressure between two locations, that sets the air in motion. The steeper the slope, the faster the ball will roll and the faster the skier will travel. The greater the pressure gradient, the faster the wind will blow. On your contour chart, remember, when the hill you are climbing is steep, the lines of equal elevation will be closely spaced. Slip and you might tumble down the hill. So it is with isobars or lines of constant pressure. The closer they are spaced, the greater the pressure gradient, and the faster the wind is blowing.

In Figure 4.4 the pressure gradient is the same (8 millibars) between A and B and from C to D. However, the distance between the two points is much greater from C to D. Thus, the wind will be blowing much stronger from B to A than from D to C. Meteorologists use pressure gradients to estimate just how fast the wind will blow. A certain difference in pressure between two locations will produce a wind speed of a certain value. Pressure gradients are normally thought of as positive values. Let's say the pressure at Portland is 1016 millibars and the pressure at Seattle is 1008 millibars. The pressure gradient would be 8 millibars or 1016 minus 1008. If the pressure at Seattle was 1016 millibars and at Portland 1008 millibars, the pressure gradient would still be 8 millibars, but meteorologists might refer to it as a "negative" gradient. The absolute value is still the same, 8 millibars. The addition of a plus or minus would simply make reference to the direction from which the wind is blowing. In the latter case the wind would be blowing from Seattle to Portland.

Reducing Pressure To Sea Level

You may have already wondered that since pressure decreases with elevation, would it always be lower in the mountains, and what effect would that have on a weather map? (Well, maybe you haven't, but we are going to discuss this, anyway!) Would there always be a low-pressure area over mountains? If meteorologists analyzed their weather maps with the actual measured pressure, the answer would be yes. But the real answer is "NO" because meteorologists adjust that value. Pressure must be relative to mean sea level. Weather observations taken at Denver (5,280 feet), or Salt Lake City (4,500 feet), or any other station above mean sea level must be "reduced to sea level." Actually the term "reduced to sea level" is somewhat of a misnomer since the value is actually increased rather than decreased, or reduced. What happens is the estimated decrease because of the elevation (approximately one inch of mercury for each 1,000 feet) must be added to those station pressures taken at Denver, Salt Lake City, and other stations above mean sea level to make their readings compatible with stations at sea level. A better term is "corrected to mean sea level." So, the readings of pressure that are taken at elevations above mean sea level have added to them that decrease in pressure with elevation mentioned earlier, taking into account the temperature at the location and a few other minor variables. This is shown in Figure 4.5. Station A at sea level needs no correction, but stations B, C, and D need corrections added to the station pressure they record, thus correcting the value to what might be recorded if the stations were at sea level, B', C', and D'.

Sometimes for meteorologists it is not so much the actual air pressure that is important, but whether the pressure is rising or falling. A barograph keeps a record of the pressure for a week or more. It consists of a cylinder or can with a chart on it that is driven by a clock. A pen, connected through various linkages to a drum with the air removed (vacuum), makes a mark of the air pressure on the chart as it turns. Some barographs are called micro-barographs and those need to have a new chart installed every day. They are used to record very small changes in air pressure. A barograph is shown in Figure 4.6.

Figure 4.5 Stations above mean sea level that take barometric pressure readings need to have their measurements increased by applying a pressure and temperature correction that converts the reading to mean sea level.

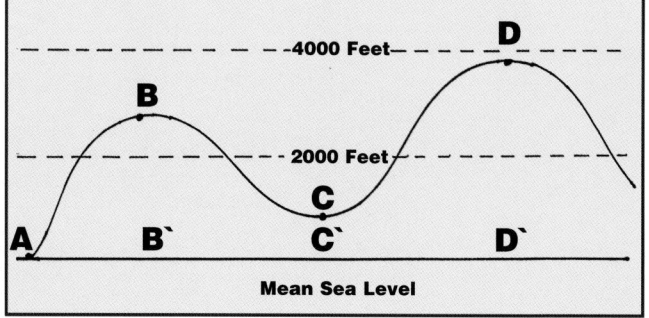

Figure 4.6 A barograph records the barometric pressure.

Surface pressure, in addition to varying greatly on a daily or weekly basis as low- and high-pressure areas move through a location, also varies over a 24-hour period, especially in middle latitudes. At night when the air is normally cooler and the air is more dense, the pressure will be higher than it will be in the middle of the afternoon when surface heating is at·a maximum. The afternoon air is lighter and rises. This variance in pressure over a 24-hour period is greatest in summer with warm days and cool nights. A graph of the 24-hour pressure change at a middle latitude station assuming no change in air mass is shown in Figure 4.7.

Other Forces Acting on the Wind

So far, we have talked about two forces that act on the wind, namely the Coriolis effect and the pressure gradient force. At the surface of the earth there is another force which acts to reduce the wind speed. That force is friction. Friction acts to pull the air back. Friction is a force your tires must overcome when you move away from a stop sign. It is readily apparent that friction will be greater if the surface is uneven. Also, the effect of friction decreases the higher one goes in the atmosphere. Meteorologists often refer to the boundary layer as the layer above which very little friction occurs. It has been given

an arbitrary depth of 50 millibars above the surface. However, we cannot go to a certain height above the ground and state, "Friction has no effect above this height." Its effect, however, is greatly diminished the higher one goes in the atmosphere, but the effect is still there. Mountains and mountain ranges that rise to great heights have a profound effect on the wind flow.

Once air is set in motion by a difference in pressure, the Coriolis effect begins acting on it by pulling it towards the right in the Northern Hemisphere and towards the left in the Southern Hemisphere. Air, then, does not normally flow directly from high pressure to low pressure or perpendicular to the isobars but at an angle across the isobars. The result of these three forces is shown in Figure 4.8. Note the pressure gradient force pulling the wind across the isobars, the Coriolis effect pulling it to the right (Northern Hemisphere) and friction pulling the air back. Flow across isobars is also depicted in Figures 3.7 and 3.8 which showed the major pressure centers over the Pacific Ocean. Because of all this we have air that is spiraling out from areas of high pressure and air that is spiraling in towards areas of low pressure at the surface and flowing across the isobars at about a 30-degree angle in middle latitudes.

But what happens above the boundary layer where friction is much less or even absent? The pressure gradient force first pulls the wind toward lower pressure. The Coriolis effect then tries to pull it away. The result is that in regions above the boundary layer, the pressure gradient force is balanced out by the Coriolis effect. The "tug-of-war" reaches a stalemate. This causes the wind to flow parallel to the contour lines and not directly from high to low pressure. If the flow is in a straight line, we call this wind the geostrophic wind. This wind is illustrated in Figure 4.9. If the flow is curved, such as around a ridge of high pressure aloft or around a trough of low pressure aloft, another force acts on the parcel and that is the centrifugal force, which is pushing (or pulling) the parcel outward. (That's the same force that keeps the water in the bucket as you swing it over your head if you are fast!) We call the curved wind that flows parallel to the contour lines the gradient wind. An example of a gradient wind is illustrated in Figure 4.10.

Figure 4.7 The pressure at a middle latitude location varies over a 24-hour period, assuming no change in air mass, reaching a high value near 7 a.m. and a low value near 4 p.m.

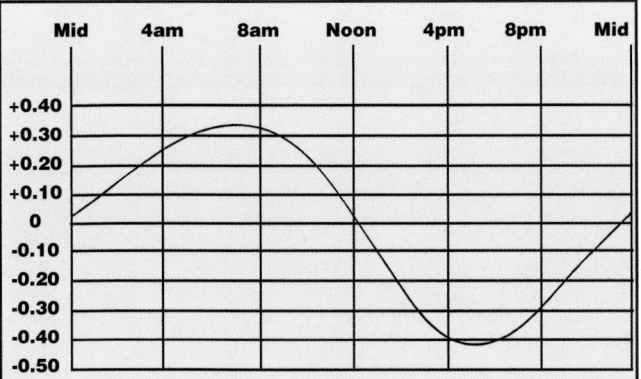

Figure 4.8 Forces acting on parcel of air at the earth's surface in the Northern Hemisphere. PGF is the pressure gradient force; CF is the Coriolis effect, and F is friction.

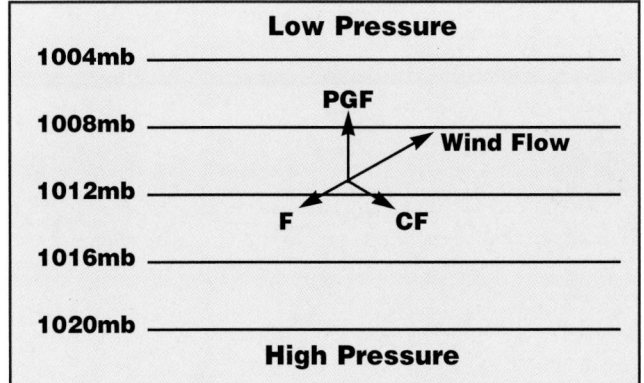

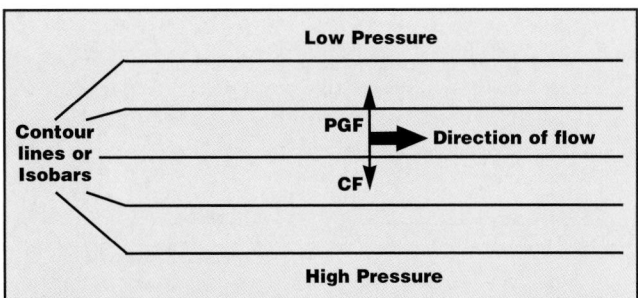

Figure 4.9 The geostrophic wind occurs in a straight line flow when the Coriolis effect (CF) is balanced out by the pressure gradient force (PGF) and friction is absent.

Feeling winded?! You don't have to be too confused by all of this. Remember that wind flow is normally not directly from high pressure to low pressure but is slightly across the isobars at the surface. The angle that the wind crosses the isobars is least near the poles and greatest near the equator. Near the equator, the Coriolis effect is of a smaller magnitude, and all that is acting to slow the wind down is friction. Thus winds near the equator often blow almost directly across isobars.

With an increase in elevation, the wind begins to blow more parallel to the contour lines since the higher we go, the less effect friction has on the air parcel. In Figure 3.16 the wind would be flowing along the lines of constant height. Hence, jet streams do not blow directly into low-pressure areas but between areas of strong temperature differences. Remember that pressure is a function of temperature. The greater the temperature difference between two locations, the greater the pressure difference will be. Thus, a strong jet stream will have large temperature differences across it, which is what causes it to blow.

The gradient wind can have an effect on the surface wind when strong winds aloft get transported to the surface through instability or mixing in the atmosphere. Also, when pressure gradients are very strong, as they can be in very strong low-pressure areas or very strong high-pressure areas, the pressure gradient force can become the dominant force, overpowering friction and the Coriolis effect. Winds in this case can blow directly across the isobars at the surface. Terrain features can also enhance the wind flow.

Dust fall at Portland, Oregon
On the morning of January 17, 1930 there was observed in Portland a very unusual deposit of dust. It covered the snow which lay on the ground at that time, giving it a reddish brown color. It lay on the pavements in such quantities that persons coming into the office from the street left tracks on the office floor at every step. The dust was so fine as to enter around closed windows. Investigation showed that all of Oregon was covered by snow at the time, for the deposit occured during the memorable cold period; therefore investigation was carried into Washington, and it was learned that severe dust storms occurred in several counties of eastern Washington on the 16th.

It will be noted that the dust was not carried to a sufficiently high level to take it over the Cascade Mountains but that enough came through the Columbia Gorge, carried by a strong east wind, to reach Portland and as far as Forest Grove, about 30 miles west of Portland." At this station the wind was mostly from the east on the dates mentioned, the average velocity for the two days being 16.3 miles per hour. Through the Columbia Gorge the velocity was undoubtedly much greater than this.

Edward L. Wells
Monthly Weather Review, February 1930

Venturi Effect

One other item needs to be mentioned before we reach the "horse latitudes" of this section on pressure and wind. As air, or any fluid, moves through a constriction, it speeds up. It is referred to as the Venturi effect and is depicted in Figure 4.11. Contours, or lines of equal height on a weather map, that are closely spaced indicate a stronger wind flow than where the contours are widely spaced. The Columbia River Gorge between the east and west sides of the Cascade Mountains is an excellent example of the Venturi effect at the surface. Winds accelerate as they blow through this gap in the Cascade Mountains. The Venturi effect is also very manifest as wind blows through and around buildings in a downtown location.

Figure 4.10 An example of gradient wind where the Coriolis effect (CF) and the centrifugal force (Cfg) are balanced out by the pressure gradient force (PGF).

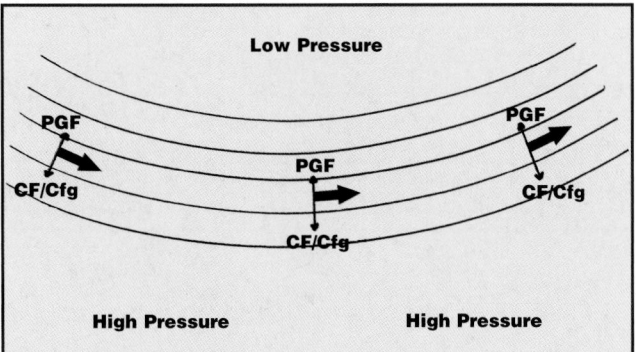

Figure 4.11 Air that passes through a constriction will accelerate, then decrease and fan out once it passes through the constriction. The Columbia River Gorge is an excellent example of this.

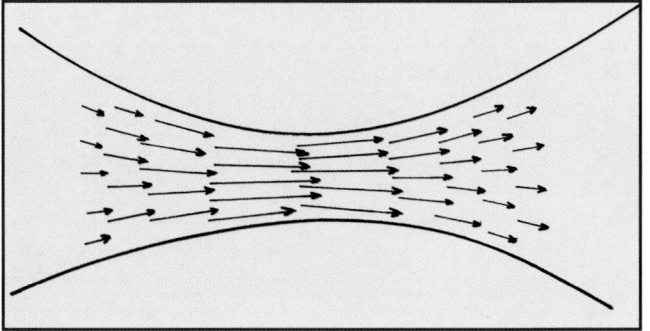

Chapter 5
Moisture, Relative Humidity, Change of State

In the section on Weather Elements it was mentioned that as far as meteorology was concerned, moisture (water vapor) was the most important gas in the atmosphere. Now we will see why. We will learn how the amount of moisture in the air varies, and how temperature affects that amount of moisture. Also, as water changes from ice to water to water vapor and back again, very important processes are occurring. This chapter investigates those processes.

Moisture

Water is unique among the substances on earth. It can exist in three different phases side by side. We know it in the solid form as ice, in the liquid form as water, and in the gaseous stage as water vapor. As a solid, the molecules are linked together in a uniform manner much like a troop of soldiers. Spacing is uniform among the soldiers (molecules) and they are linked together perhaps with one arm on the shoulder of the person on one side and one arm stretched ahead to the soldier in front. The application of heat weakens the bond holding the molecules together in the solid state, and it changes. In the liquid state, the molecules are free to move at random but are still somewhat confined. We can think of this as the same

group of soldiers not at attention or marching together, but perhaps free to move about the parade ground on their own. Additional heat frees the water molecules even more and they become less concentrated. They are moving around at random—invisible—much like the soldiers might do if they are told they have a free weekend. They scatter! This is the gas phase. The three phases are depicted in Figure 5.1.

The last phase, the gas phase, is often overlooked. We do not think about water occurring as an invisible gas, water vapor. When I was young, I always wanted it to snow in the winter. (That is not the case now, except up in the mountains!) My mother would tell me, when it was very cold outside, and I was looking for it to snow, "George, it is too cold to snow." What she was telling me, although she probably did not know it, was that she thought there was not enough moisture in the air to make snow flakes. She was wrong, bless her heart. It is never too cold to snow. The air always contains some moisture. There are always some water vapor molecules present, but the ability of the air to "hold" or "contain" moisture varies with the temperature, because of the speed of the molecules.

When we talk about the ability of the air to hold or contain moisture, we are talking about the number of water vapor molecules the air can contain, or simply stated, saturation. (Remember, air cannot hold moisture like a pan holds water.) However, if we place a pan of water on the counter, eventually all the water in the pan will be gone. It will have evaporated. (You cannot use this, however, as an excuse for refusing to dry the dishes!) All the water molecules in the pan will have escaped into the air right above the pan. This air above the pan, although it may contain more water molecules than the air around it, is not saturated because it is continually mixing with the air in the room. It can take in more of those refugee water molecules.

If we put a lid over the pan, Figure 5.2, to prevent any foreign air from getting into our experiment, the water molecules will still escape into the air between the surface and the lid above them. There are a few water molecules that may escape into this air, find it not to their liking, and go back to the water. But for the most part, more water molecules will leave the pan than return. This exchange is always taking place between the water and the air above it. If the air is not saturated above the water, more water molecules will escape from the surface than will return from the air to the water. The lid on the pan prevents the air within the pan from mixing with the other air in the room. Eventually, as enough water molecules escape, the air above the water in the covered pan becomes saturated. For each molecule escaping from the water into the air, another one is leaving the air and

Figure 5.1 Water exists in three different phases. As ice, the molecules are bonded together; as water they are confined but not so bonded; as water vapor, they are free to move about at random.

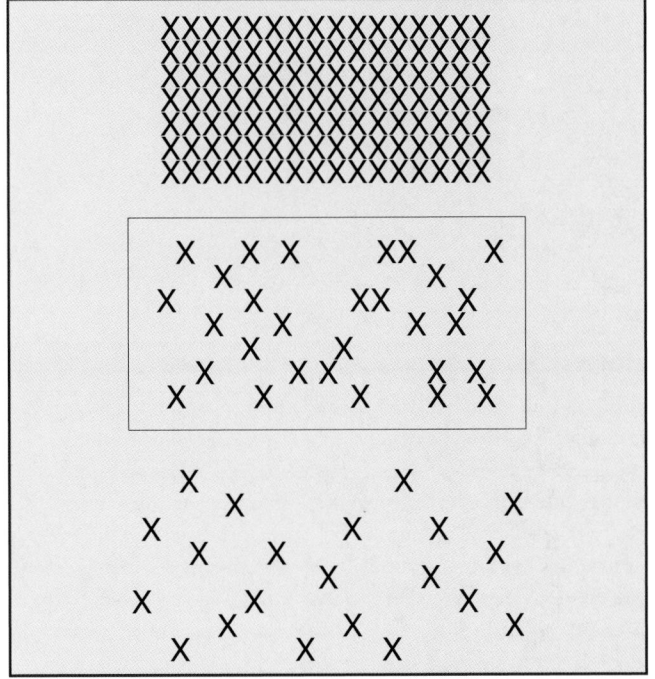

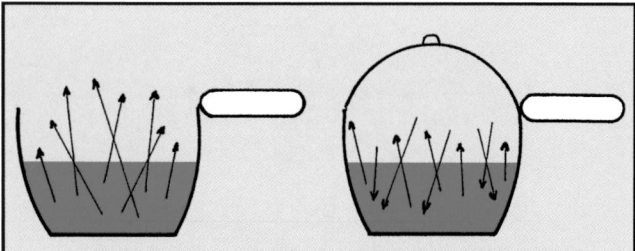

Figure 5.2 If an uncovered pan of water is left open, all the water molecules will eventually escape into the air above. Placing a lid over the pan prevents the air inside from mixing with air outside. The air underneath the lid will soon become saturated.

Temperature		Grams of water per kilogram of dry air
Celsius	Fahrenheit	
-40	-40	0.1
-30	-22	0.3
-20	-4	0.75
-10	14	2
0	32	4
5	41	6
10	50	8
15	59	11
20	68	15
25	77	20
30	86	28
35	95	37
40	104	47

Figure 5.3 The air's ability to hold moisture varies with the temperature.

returning to the water. It is in a state of equilibrium. The air has reached saturation.

If we raise the temperature of the air above the pan, (that is, increase the speed of the molecules) its ability to hold or contain moisture increases. We express this ability to have moisture (water vapor molecules) as grams of water per kilogram of dry air. At 50°F the air can hold about twice as much moisture (twice as many water vapor molecules) as it can at 32°F, or a value of 4 grams versus 8 grams. At 95°F it can hold nearly 10 times as much moisture or water vapor molecules than it could hold at 32°F. Note the values in Figure 5.3 that show the approximate amount of moisture the air can hold at various temperatures, assuming the same air pressure.

Saturated air is air that contains all the moisture it can hold at that temperature. Air that is not saturated can still hold additional moisture, and it is referred to as dry air, or unsaturated air. These two definitions regarding saturated and unsaturated air need to be kept in mind as we move through the other topics in this chapter. Dry air does not mean that there are no water vapor molecules present. It simply means that the air is capable of having more water vapor molecules added to it. Remember, it is never too cold to snow!

Relative Humidity

Simply stated, relative humidity is the amount of moisture in the air compared to the amount it could hold at that temperature. Those last three words are very important. It means that humidity is directly related to temperature. As was stated in Chapter 1, Weather Elements, the term is "relative" humidity.

Refer again to Figure 5.3. Note that at 59°F the air can hold a quantity of about 11 grams per kilogram. If that amount of moisture is present, the air is saturated and the relative humidity is 100 percent. Let's see what happens, however, if we raise the temperature to 86°F but do not change the moisture content. At 86°F the air can hold around 28 grams per kilogram. That is quite a bit more. But we did not increase the available moisture, only the air's ability to hold moisture by increasing its temperature. The air still contains only about 11 grams of moisture. It is not

saturated. It is referred to as dry air. We arrive at a relative humidity of around 39 percent simply by dividing 28 into 11. That is one way of computing relative humidity.

Gigantic Snowflakes

About 4:30 pm on January 10, 1915, Berlin (Germany) experienced a brief fall of snow during which snowflakes of very considerable dimensions occured simultaneously with those of more usual size. On this occasion a large number of snowflakes had diameters of 8 to 10 centimeters (3 to 4 inches), and these giant flakes fell with both a greater speed and more definite paths than did the smaller flakes. They did not have the complicated fluttering flight of the latter. In form the great flakes resembled a round or oval dish with its edges bent upward. During flight they rocked to this side or that, but none were observed to turn quite over so that the concave side became directed downward. The temperature was but little above freezing.

Monthly Weather Review, February 1915

We can measure, or compute, the relative humidity by other methods. Pressure, remember, is the force exerted by the air molecules. Since water vapor is a gas, its molecules are also exerting pressure. The pressure the water vapor molecules are exerting on your skin and everything around you is called the vapor pressure. The more water vapor molecules in the air, the higher the vapor pressure. Saturated air contains a certain amount of water vapor molecules, and the pressure exerted by these water molecules is called the saturation vapor pressure. If we compare the vapor pressure to the saturation vapor pressure, we can compute the relative

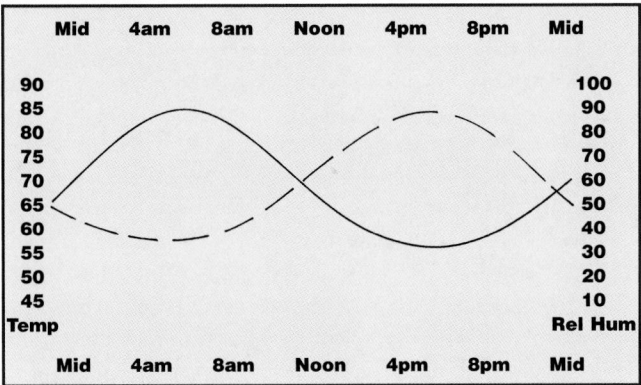

Figure 5.4 Temperature varies inversely with relative humidity over a 24-hour period with no air mass change. Solid line is relative humidity; dashed line is temperature.

humidity. Since it is no simple task to measure the vapor pressure, there has to be an easier way to compute the relative humidity, and there is. It is called the dewpoint. That topic is examined later. Right now, let's hope you are not "saturated!"

The above example of taking air at 59°F and raising its temperature to 86°F is precisely what happens over the course of an average summer day in many western valleys of the Pacific Northwest. In the early morning hours around sunrise, 59°F is a normal summer temperature. It is not unusual for the temperature to climb to 86°F by mid to late afternoon. From this, it is very easy to see why the relative humidity is higher in the hours around dawn, when the temperature is at its lowest value. Furthermore, it is easy to see that the relative humidity decreases to its lowest value during the late afternoon, when the temperature is at its highest. Figure 5.4 shows the daily distribution of temperature and relative humidity. Note that the temperature and relative humidity are inversely related. That is, when one goes up, the other goes down, assuming no addition or subtraction of moisture.

Change of State

Up to now, we have concerned ourselves with molecules escaping from the water's surface into the air and back to the water. Several significant processes occur during these transitions. As we mentioned, water has the ability to exist in three different forms—ice, water, and water vapor. Each time that it goes from one form to another, heat is either "taken in" or "released." But exactly what do we mean by the terms "taken in" and "released?"

Let's start with evaporation. When I moved from Utah back to Oregon, I had a change of state. But the "change of state" we are going to be talking about is totally different. Those water molecules that were escaping from the pan into the air above the pan were evaporating. Scientists refer to this as a "change of state." The molecules went from a liquid state to a gaseous state, or from a semi-organized arrangement to a random arrangement. But just as we often need a cup of coffee or a glass of juice to get us moving in the morning, something is needed to get the molecules moving, or

moving faster. Something is needed to loosen the bond between them. That something is heat. It took heat to get those molecules moving fast enough to escape. That heat came from the water.

A good example of evaporation and loss of heat is when you step out of the shower or the bathtub in the morning, or out of a swimming pool on a hot summer afternoon. You immediately feel cool and you look for a towel to dry off and throw over your shoulders. But why do you feel cool? Those molecules in the liquid state are evaporating off your skin into the air and becoming water vapor molecules. Like a thief in the night, they take something with them. They take your body heat, and that is why you feel cool. Why those little rascals!

This process is called evaporational cooling and it is depicted in Figure 5.5. Evaporation is a cooling process that adds heat to the atmosphere. Wait a minute! A "cooling process" that "adds" heat to the atmosphere? Did you miss something? No, you did not. It takes heat to complete this evaporation process. In fact, it takes 585 calories of heat per gram of water to get all those molecules moving fast enough to escape at a temperature of 68°F. (A calorie is the amount of heat needed to raise the temperature of one gram of water one degree Celsius.) The figure may not sound like much, but multiply it by several thousand or millions or trillions, and you get a tremendous amount of heat. Water that evaporates from the surface of the ocean or a lake is adding large quantities of heat to our atmosphere. Your body, as the water molecules escape into the air, is adding heat to the atmosphere.

But what happens to this heat? The atmosphere has the capability of storing it as latent heat. The term "latent" means hidden. Well, the atmosphere does not literally store it behind the mountains or under the prairies or in back of the clouds, but I assure you, it is out there waiting for a rainy day. (No pun intended.) The heat stored is in the energy of the molecules.

There are other ways that the atmosphere stores heat other than through evaporation. You may have watched a new fall of snow disappear even though the temperature

Figure 5.5 Water molecules that leave a surface, such as your skin, need a certain amount of heat to get them moving. That heat is supplied by your body. As they leave, the molecules take the heat with them.

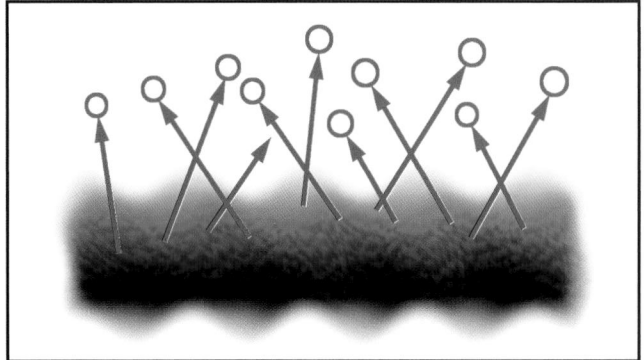

Figure 5.6 The build-up of rime on this tree is a good example of deposition as tiny water droplets change directly to ice. (Photo courtesy Jack Bird, Medford, OR.)

is a good example of deposition. Water vapor molecules are going directly from the gaseous state to the solid state to coat the windows of your car with frost. Rime as it appears on the tree in Figure 5.6 is often a combination of tiny supercooled (existing as a liquid below freezing) water droplets and water vapor molecules turning to a solid as they strike the tree.

Water vapor molecules that go from the gaseous state to the solid state release this stored heat back into the atmosphere. You may have heard the phrase, "It is warming up and starting to snow." Some of the warming may be coming from the formation of snowflakes. Those molecules that went from the solid state to the gaseous state and used heat now release the heat into the atmosphere. We call this heat "sensible" heat, or "useable" heat that the atmosphere is now able to use. Look at it this way. You have a certificate of deposit (CD) worth $2,000, but you go out and buy one of those fancy big-screen televisions and borrow on that $2,000 to pay for it. The $2,000 is still there, but you can't use it. It is latent. Pay off that loan and it becomes useable.

When water molecules go from the liquid to the solid, or freeze, they also release the same amount of heat (80 calories per gram) it took to get them from the solid phase to the liquid phase. Orchardists use this method to prevent the delicate fruit or blossoms from being destroyed by below freezing temperatures. They sprinkle the entire orchard with water. As the water freezes near the blossom, enough latent heat is released as sensible heat to maintain a temperature very close to freezing, but above the critical point for the fruit. An orchardist, however, must continue to spray to continue the freezing process and continue the release of heat. If the orchardist stopped sprinkling, the temperature would rapidly cool to the outside air temperature since no heat is being added to the environment around the fruit blossoms. The field in Figure 5.7 near Prineville, Oregon, that is being irrigated shows water that has frozen to plants. The temperature near the ground was slightly below freezing in the early morning hours.

Figure 5.7 As water goes from liquid state to a solid state, enough heat is released to keep tender plants and blossoms just above the freezing mark, thus preventing damage.

was well below the freezing point. The molecules went from a solid state in the snow directly to a gaseous state, or water vapor. They skipped the liquid state. It is like those s oldiers at attention, arms locked together, on the parade ground. They scattered in all directions on Friday afternoon when they heard, "Disssssmissed!" The process is called sublimation. This also used up some heat to the tune of about 665 calories per gram. Heat is also needed to melt the ice in that cool glass of ice tea. This melting process, as water molecules go from a highly organized arrangement (ice) to that semi-organized arrangement (water), uses up 80 calories per gram that the atmosphere also stores. Wow, you must be saying! What a glutton, this atmosphere! What does it do with all that stored heat? Eventually, it gives it all back. Doesn't keep a penny, or in this case, a calorie. It is very generous, but that generosity can be disastrous as we will soon find out.

But how does it give it back? It does it through the reverse processes. Snow is not frozen water droplets, but simply stated, is frozen water vapor. That is perhaps not the most accurate statement, but it tells us that those molecules of water vapor are capable of skipping the liquid phase and returning directly to the solid phase or state. The process here is called deposition (sublimation in some texts). Frost

Figure 5.8 depicts what happens when the various changes take place. Perhaps the greatest amount of heat that becomes available is through the process of condensation. When water vapor molecules change from the gaseous state to the liquid state, that same amount of energy it took to get them in that state is released. The release of latent heat by condensation is the primary source of available energy that contributes to the strength of hurricanes, thunderstorms, and middle latitude storms. This heat that is released back into the atmosphere as sensible heat warms the atmosphere.

All of the above processes (evaporation, condensation, sublimation, deposition, freezing and melting) are going on continuously. Water in large quantities evaporates from the oceans of the world into the atmosphere. The oceans lose this heat but the atmosphere stores it. The water vapor is then transported thousands of miles by global winds only to condense (releasing the heat) and fall as precipitation that eventually finds its way back to the ocean or into the soil. The process is called the hydrologic cycle. It's that old saying: "All rivers run to the sea, but the sea does not fill up." (Well, *most* rivers run to the sea, anyway.)

In this part of Chapter 5 we have looked at moisture in three different forms: solid, liquid and gas. We have seen that warm air is capable of holding much more moisture than cold air because of the speed of the molecules. As the three different phases constantly rearrange themselves in the atmosphere, they use and release heat. Water vapor molecules exert a pressure and that pressure, or the amount of water vapor molecules present, is a measure of the relative humidity, which itself is dependent on the temperature.

Wet-bulb, Dry-bulb, and Dewpoint Temperatures

Manually, the amount of water vapor there is in the air at a given temperature is measured through the use of a sling psychrometer. The use of a sling psychrometer was discussed in Chapter 1 under Measuring Weather Elements. It suffices to say that the movement of air over the moistened cloth causes evaporation which lowers the temperature of that thermometer.

The temperature of the thermometer with the piece of cloth around it, after we have twirled the thermometers, is called the wet-bulb temperature. The wet-bulb temperature is the temperature that air assumes by the evaporation of water into it. That is exactly what we did when we twirled that thermometer around and around. The water molecules in the cloth evaporated into the atmosphere, taking heat from the thermometer with them. Thus, the air close to the thermometer cooled and became saturated. It could not "hold" any more moisture. When it could not hold any more moisture, water stopped evaporating off the piece of wet cloth and the wet-bulb temperature was reached. After computing the wet-bulb temperature, a whole host of possibilities is open to us in finding just how much moisture there is in the air around us, but only at that temperature.

With the wet-bulb temperature and the dry-bulb temperature (that was the thermometer without the piece of cloth and sometimes referred to as the ambient air temperature) we can compute the dewpoint temperature. The dewpoint temperature is different from the wet-bulb temperature. It is the temperature to which air must be cooled in

order for the air to become saturated or for condensation to begin at that pressure and temperature. The dewpoint temperature is a good indication of the overnight low or minimum temperature, providing there are no changes to the air mass at that location. Once the ambient or free air temperature reaches the dewpoint temperature, the overall temperature cools much more slowly. When the air temperature reaches the dewpoint temperature, dew, fog and clouds are likely to form, which begins releasing heat back into the atmosphere, accounting for the reduced rate of cooling.

The dewpoint temperature is a much better indicator of how much moisture is in the air than the term relative humidity. Picture a snow scene like that in Figure 5.9 with the temperature 30°F, dewpoint temperature 27°F, and relative humidity 88 percent. Now shift your vision to a scene in the desert of eastern Oregon, where the temperature is 80°F, the dewpoint temperature is 30°F, and the relative humidity about 16 percent, Figure 5.10. Which air mass has the most moisture in it? If you answered "the desert," you are well on your way to understanding this section. Even though the

Figure 5.8 In all actions from left to right, heat is lost by the environment; in all actions right to left heat is gained by the environment.

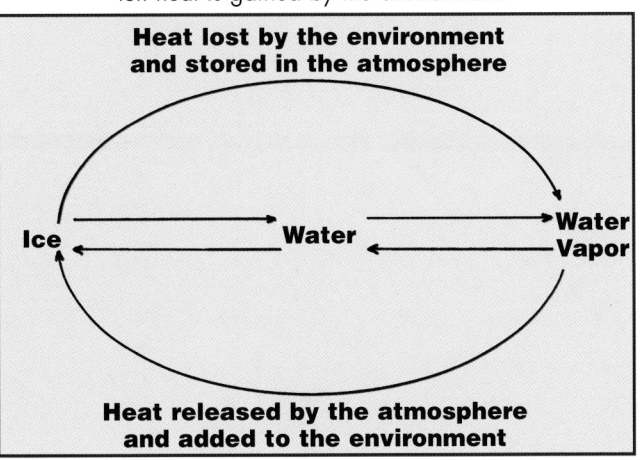

Figure 5.9 Temperature 30°F, dewpoint temperature 27°F, relative humidity 88%.

relative humidity is higher in the snow scene than it is in the desert picture; even though the cold air was almost saturated, the desert air holds more moisture, because the dewpoint temperature is higher. The dewpoint temperature is a true measure of how much moisture there is in the air. For all practical purposes, it can never be higher than the temperature. The two can read the same, but for simplicity, and this book, the dewpoint temperature can never be higher than the temperature.

Adiabatic Lapse Rates

For the most part, air is constantly in motion. It is either being transported horizontally (advection) or going up and down (convection). But remember what happens to the pressure as we go higher. It decreases. We also know that if we warm a parcel of air next to the surface, it wants to rise, since warm air is lighter than cold air. Okay, let's do just that, but first let's construct what we call an environmental sounding.

Meteorologists can measure the actual distribution of temperature and moisture above the ground. One way of doing this is with an instrument called the radiosonde discussed in Chapter 1, Weather Elements. Once we know the actual distribution of temperature and moisture with elevation (we call it the environmental sounding or the

Figure 5.10 Temperature 80°F, dewpoint temperature 30°F, relative humidity 16%.

environmental lapse rate), we can determine the stability of the air. (A lapse rate is the rate at which temperature decreases, or increases, with elevation.) The environmental lapse rate is the actual distribution of temperature and moisture with elevation. One is shown in Figure 5.11 as the solid dark line. (Blue horizontal lines are pressure elevations and the diagonally red lines are isotherms in degrees Celsius.) Environmental soundings vary from place to place and from day to day, and parcels of air respond differently to different environmental lapse rates.

Balloonists heat the air inside their balloon to make it rise. We do not have a balloon, so let's take some unsaturated air (dry air, remember) and enclose it in a large cellophane bag. This will be our parcel of air. Now, let's move this air up and down through the atmosphere, or through our environmental sounding. In Figure 5.12 the values on the left at the various elevations correspond to the temperatures and pressures of our environmental sounding. This represents the actual distribution of temperature with elevation to 2,000 feet as measured. If we give our cellophane bag of air a push upward, it will cool at a rate of 5.4°F for every 1,000 feet it ascends. This rate of cooling is the dry-adiabatic lapse rate and the cooling is due to expansion of the air. As the cellophane bag full of air rises in the atmosphere, the pressure outside decreases and the air inside the bag pushes out and the bag expands. The air molecules within the bag are spread over a larger area, and the temperature within the bag lowers. It still has the same amount of heat that it had at the surface, however. The heat is simply spread throughout a larger volume. We have just sent our cellophane bag through an adiabatic process. The term adiabatic means no gain or loss

Figure 5.11 An environmental sounding in black. Horizontal blue lines are height in millibars and red lines running diagonally are isotherms in degrees Celsius.

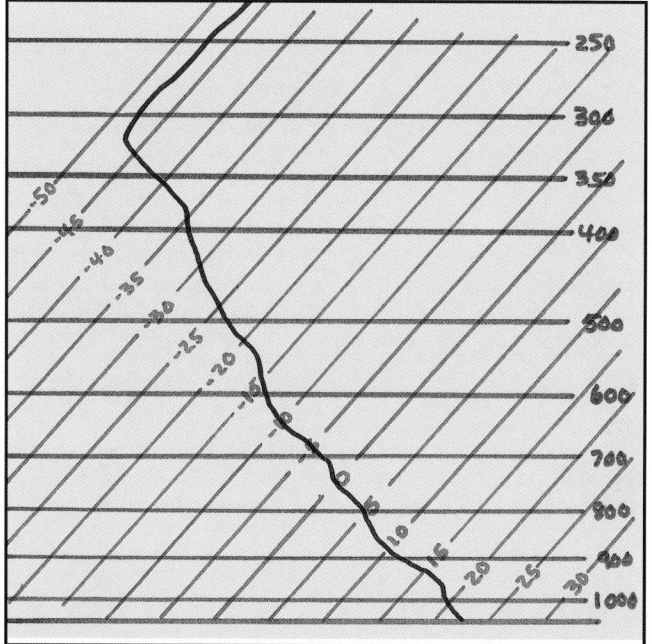

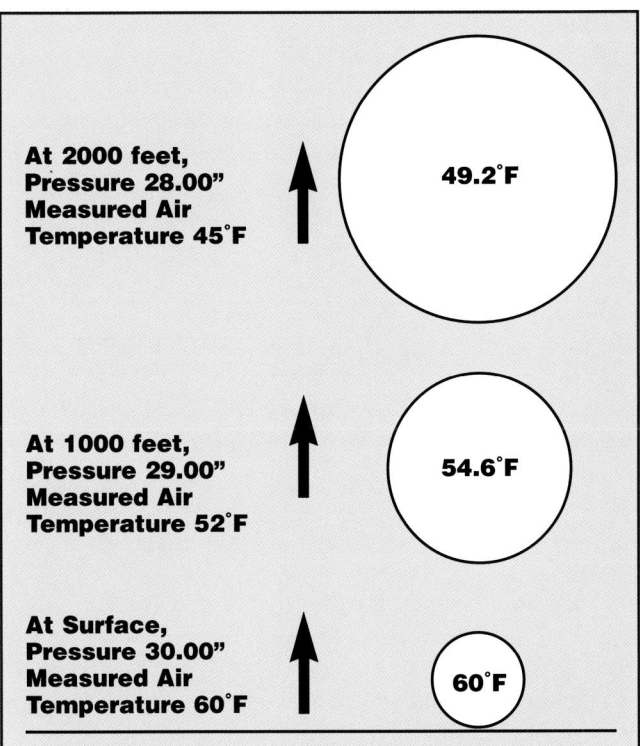

Figure 5.12 A parcel of dry air, if forced to rise, will cool at a rate of 5.4°F/1000 feet. It expands due to less air pressure, but still has the same amount of heat. If warmer than the air around it, it will continue to rise.

At 2000 feet, Pressure 28.00" Measured Air Temperature 45°F — 49.2°F

At 1000 feet, Pressure 29.00" Measured Air Temperature 52°F — 54.6°F

At Surface, Pressure 30.00" Measured Air Temperature 60°F — 60°F

of heat. Remember, we did not say temperature, we said heat or heat energy.

Our environmental sounding in Figure 5.12 measured the temperature at 1,000 feet as 52°F. The temperature of the air inside our cellophane bag, however, only cooled to 54.6°F. Thus, it is warmer than the air outside. Yes, it is only 2.6°F warmer, but that is plenty. Air that is warmer than the air around it will continue to rise. At an elevation of 2,000 feet, the outside air temperature (our environmental sounding) is 45°F, but the temperature of the air within the bag has cooled to 49.2°F, more than 4°F warmer than the outside air. This is known as an unstable condition or an unstable atmosphere. The cellophane bag full of air will continue to rise, expand and cool until the temperature outside of it equals the temperature inside the bag. The reverse process happens if we pull our cellophane bag back down to the surface. As it descends, the pressure outside increases, the volume of the bag decreases, and the temperature of the air inside the bag increases at 5.4°F for every 1,000 feet we pull it down, but we have not lost or gained one calorie of heat.

Let's begin the process again using the same environmental sounding, only this time we will assume that the air within the cellophane bag is saturated. The temperature and the dewpoint temperature are the same. If we force the bag of air aloft it will also expand and cool, but it will do so at a different rate. That rate is 3.3°F for every 1,000 feet it rises. This rate varies with elevation, but the average is 3.3

degrees over the lower portion of the atmosphere. It is called the moist-adiabatic lapse rate. We can follow these changes in Figure 5.13. At 1,000 feet the temperature within the bag would have lowered to 56.7°F, or 4.7°F warmer than the air outside the bag whose temperature is 52°F. That is substantial, and the air will continue to rise requiring no help from us. At 2,000 feet, its temperature would have decreased to only 53.4°F or almost 8°F warmer than the outside air that was measured at 45°F. This is also known as an unstable condition, or an unstable atmosphere. It manifests itself in the large billowing clouds that reach high into the atmosphere and result in showers and thundershowers.

But wait a minute! If the air was saturated when we started out, it had to have had a dewpoint temperature the same as the actual temperature of 60°F. Yes, it had. Now, didn't we just say that the dewpoint temperature could not be higher than the actual temperature? That's right, we did, so the dewpoint temperature also decreased to 56.7°F at 1,000 feet. At 56.7°F the air cannot hold as much moisture as it could at 60°F, since the air's ability to hold moisture decreases as the temperature decreases. What happened to the moisture? Have we lost it? Well, in a way we have "lost" it, or certainly the atmosphere lost it.

If you guessed or figured out that it condensed into raindrops and fell to the earth (or the bottom of the cellophane bag) you were absolutely correct. If we continue to cool

Figure 5.13 A parcel of moist air (saturated), if forced to rise, will cool at a rate of 3.3°F/1000 feet. It expands due to less air pressure, but still has the same amount of heat. If warmer than the air around it, it will continue to rise.

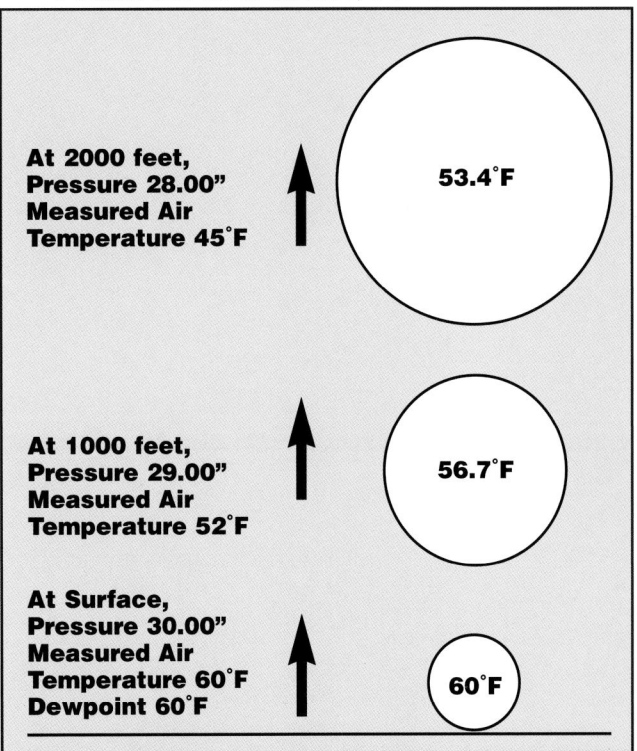

At 2000 feet, Pressure 28.00" Measured Air Temperature 45°F — 53.4°F

At 1000 feet, Pressure 29.00" Measured Air Temperature 52°F — 56.7°F

At Surface, Pressure 30.00" Measured Air Temperature 60°F Dewpoint 60°F — 60°F

air that is saturated, the moisture condenses out as dew, clouds, fog, or precipitation. Now, remember what happens when those water vapor molecules go from the gaseous stage to the liquid stage. The latent heat that the atmosphere had stored for a "rainy day" became sensible heat as it was released into the environment. This release of heat is precisely why the moist-adiabatic lapse rate is less than the dry-adiabatic lapse rate. The released heat warms the air within the parcel.

Now, since the prevailing wind flow at middle latitudes is from the west, air is generally forced up and over the Cascade Mountains in Washington and Oregon or the Sierra Nevada Mountains in California. It may start out as unsaturated air, but quickly reaches the saturation point as it is forced aloft. Once saturated, it cools at a slower rate, but as it cools, some of its moisture content is deposited on the west side of the mountains as rain and snow. And now you have "the rest of the story," or a good idea why it is normally drier with more sunshine east of the Cascade Mountains than it is on the west side. Once air begins descending, the atmospheric pressure increases and the air is warmed by compression. If no moisture is added (remember, we lost some on those drizzly west slopes), it will warm at the dry-adiabatic lapse rate almost immediately as it descends on the leeward side of the mountains.

Suppose the environmental sounding changes, as we know environmental soundings do, and assumes the values on the left side of Figure 5.14. This environmental sounding is warmer than the previous one and has a smaller decrease

Figure 5.14 A parcel of dry air, if forced to rise, will cool at a rate of 5.4°F/1000 feet. It expands due to less air pressure, but still has the same amount of heat. If cooler than the air around it, it will descend.

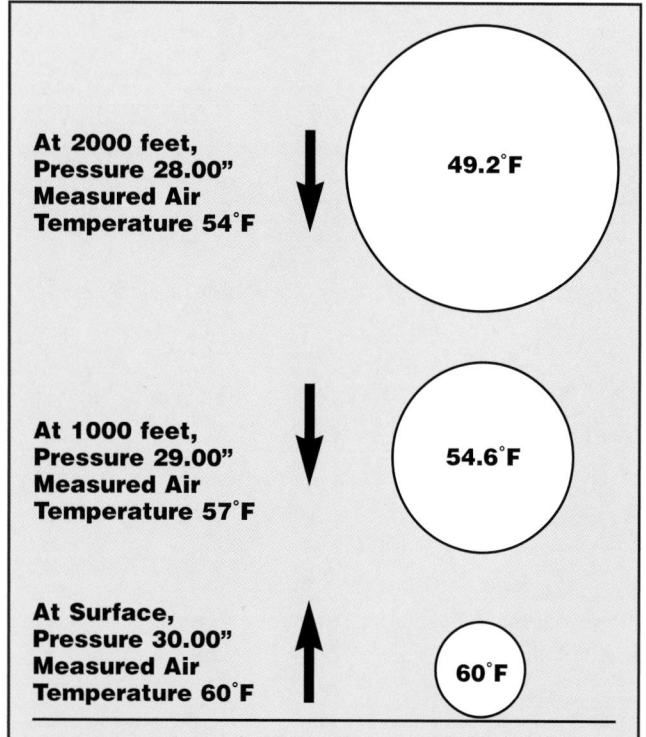

At 2000 feet,
Pressure 28.00"
Measured Air
Temperature 54°F

49.2°F

At 1000 feet,
Pressure 29.00"
Measured Air
Temperature 57°F

54.6°F

At Surface,
Pressure 30.00"
Measured Air
Temperature 60°F

60°F

in temperature with elevation. That is, the temperatures at 1,000 feet and 2,000 feet are warmer than the previous environmental soundings. If the air is unsaturated and we give it a push upward, it will expand and cool to a temperature of 54.6°F at 1,000 feet. This temperature is cooler than the outside air which was measured at 57°F. It is cooler by 2.4°F. We could keep pushing or forcing our bag of air up to 2,000 feet, cooling it to 49.2°F where the outside air was 54°F. However, once we stopped applying that force, what do you suppose our cellophane bag of air would do? Right! It will want to sink back down. A parcel of air that is cooler than the air surrounding it will sink. We could use this same experiment with air that is saturated. If pushed aloft through our environmental sounding, the moist (or saturated air) would cool at a rate of 3.3°F for every 1,000 feet it rises. At 1,000 feet, its temperature would be 56.7°F, or only 0.3°F cooler than the outside air, but this is enough. If we kept pushing it upward to 2,000 feet, its temperature would be 53.4°F, or 0.6°F cooler than the environmental air. Once we stop applying a force to keep it aloft, it will also want to return to its original position. This is known as an absolutely stable atmosphere. It is very common in the early morning hours.

Most of the processes that take place in our atmosphere are adiabatic processes. Well, truthfully, they are "pseudo" adiabatic processes. By pseudo we mean that we cannot wrap cellophane around our parcel of air. It is free to mix with the air around it, and it does precisely that. We know that precipitation falling through a parcel of air can also warm or cool the air and that melting and evaporation also have some effect. But the approximation is still very close. Also, air parcels do not necessarily assume the shape of circles.

Air can be stable or unstable at a given temperature depending on the moisture content. We call this air conditionally unstable. For air to be conditionally unstable, the environmental sounding (the actual distribution of temperature with elevation as measured) must decrease between 5.4°F per 1,000 feet and 3.3°F per 1,000 feet.

Figure 5.15 is an example of air that is conditionally unstable. The environmental sounding or actual distribution of temperature with elevation is again shown on the left. Dry (unsaturated) air that rises will cool at 5.4°F per 1,000 feet reaching a temperature of 54.6°F at 1,000 feet and to 49.2°F if we keep pushing it up to 2,000 feet. This air is cooler than the surrounding air, and it will want to sink back down as the arrows to the left of the bag show. The figures in parentheses, however, are if the air started out moist or saturated at the surface with both a temperature and dewpoint temperature of 60°F. Again, if forced to rise, notice that at 1,000 feet it reached a temperature of 56.7°F, or more than 1°F warmer than the outside air, while at 2,000 feet it only cooled to 53.4°F, yet was more than 2°F warmer than the surrounding environmental air. This saturated air will continue to rise, unlike the dry or unsaturated air that wanted to sink. We say that this air is

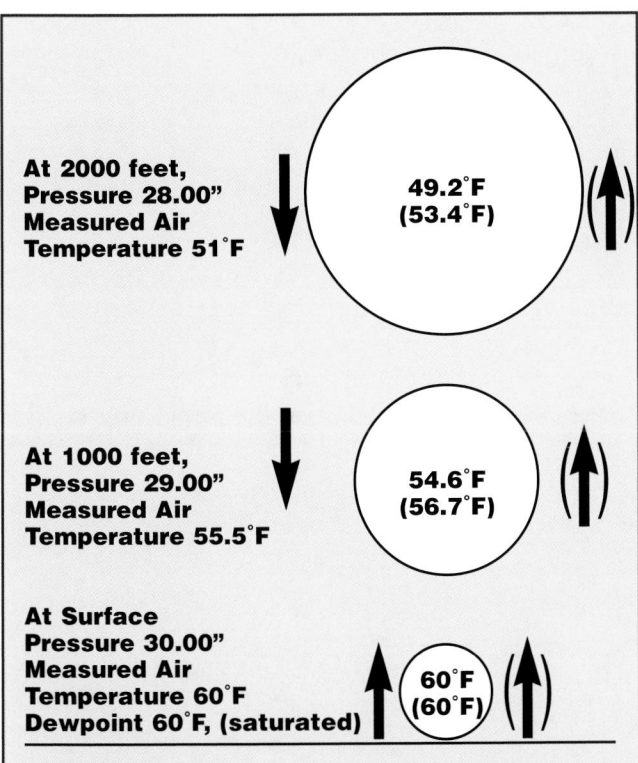

At 2000 feet,
Pressure 28.00"
Measured Air
Temperature 51°F

49.2°F
(53.4°F)

At 1000 feet,
Pressure 29.00"
Measured Air
Temperature 55.5°F

54.6°F
(56.7°F)

At Surface
Pressure 30.00"
Measured Air
Temperature 60°F
Dewpoint 60°F, (saturated)

60°F
(60°F)

Figure 5.15 Conditionally unstable air is air that is stable if it is dry (unsaturated) and forced to rise, but unstable if it is saturated and forced to rise. The saturated air is warmer than the air around it, but the unsaturated air is cooler. (Temperatures and arrows in parentheses indicate saturated air.)

conditionally unstable, meaning that if it was dry (unsaturated), it would be stable, but if it was moist (saturated) it would be unstable. Conditionally unstable air occurs frequently in actual atmospheric conditions.

From the above exercises, it is clear that there are several things that can occur to change the stability of the atmosphere and they are occurring all the time, sometimes together, sometimes on their own. First, we can make the air more unstable by bringing in cooler air aloft and thus changing the environmental sounding. In this case the temperature would show a larger decrease with elevation. We can also make the air more unstable by bringing in warmer air at or near the surface, or simply by heating the air near the surface on a hot summer day. This also results in a larger decrease in temperature with elevation. The latter is the process that occurs in the tropics when showers most often occur in the mid afternoon. In this case, the environmental sounding has not changed, except immediately near the surface where the sun's radiant energy has warmed the surface which has warmed the air near the surface, making the air unstable.

To make the air more stable, we do just the opposite. Spring and summer showers usually dissipate after dark. That is because the air near the surface has cooled, making the air more stable. If warmer air is brought in aloft, that reduces the decrease in temperature with elevation, which

reduces the instability of the air or increases the stability of the air.

There are two other ways we can change the stability of the air that relate directly back to the term conditionally unstable. Those two ways are by adding moisture to the air mass or taking moisture away. We can make the air more unstable by bringing in air that has a higher moisture content or simply more water vapor molecules, thus bringing our air to a state of saturation. Or, we can make air that is moist more stable by bringing in air that has less moisture. Fluffy cumulus clouds might start out strong in the morning hours, but dissipate upon reaching very dry air aloft. This is precisely what is happening to the cloud in Figure 5.16. Notice that the base of this cloud is dark and intact. Sufficient moisture is present at lower levels to cause the cloud to build. However, notice that at the middle and top of the picture the cloud is being reduced to fragments, indicating that it has reached a layer of drier air and the moisture supply has been reduced or cut off entirely. Conversely, if some moisture is added to clouds they will increase or grow and showers and thundershowers will be the result.

Air that is forced aloft by mountains or some other process may start out cooling at the dry-adiabatic lapse rate if it is unsaturated. As it rises, it cools and soon reaches the

Figure 5.16 A towering cumulus cloud as a result of unstable moist air in the low levels, but the infusion of drier air at middle levels has greatly reduced the instability, causing the cloud to dissipate.

Figure 5.17 The flat base to a cumulus cloud is called the lifting condensation level (LCL), where the temperature and the dewpoint temperature are the same.

dewpoint temperature. Clouds begin to form. This level is called the lifting condensation level (LCL) or the level at which condensation begins. The flat bases to the cloud in Figure 5.16 and to the clouds over the city of Portland in Figure 5.17 clearly show this level. The height of these clouds can be quite accurately determined if the surface dewpoint and air temperature are known. Once air becomes saturated, however, it will continue cooling as it is forced aloft over the mountains, but now at the moist-adiabatic lapse rate. This is a very common occurrence as air off the Pacific Ocean, which may have a temperature and dewpoint temperature of only a few degrees difference, ascends the Coast Range Mountains and the Cascade Mountains.

So far in our discussion we have talked about three lapse rates: The environmental lapse rate, dry-adiabatic lapse rate, and the moist-adiabatic lapse rate. There are two others. One is called the standard lapse rate, or sometimes called normal lapse rate. It is an idealized, or computed average, vertical distribution of temperature with elevation. It is the lapse rate depicted in Figure 2.14. The second is the super adiabatic lapse rate, or simply stated as just a super lapse rate. This is a lapse rate that is greater than the dry-adiabatic lapse rate of 5.4° for every 1000 feet. Because of intense heating near the earth's surface the air immediately next to the surface becomes much hotter than the air above it. You will find super lapse rates over hot asphalt surfaces,

deserts, and even in valleys west of the Cascade Mountains on hot summer afternoons.

Warm air is lighter than cold air. But what about warm, moist air? Is it lighter or heavier than warm, dry air? To answer this question, we need to think of the moisture as water vapor, not water. We think of water as being heavy, and it is. But water vapor is lighter than some other gases. We can see this by comparing molecular weights of the various gases. Nitrogen, remember, comprises most of the volume of the air we breathe. It has a molecular weight of 28. Oxygen is the other main gas and its molecular weight is 32. Water vapor has a molecular weight of only 18. If we take away 15 molecules of nitrogen, we have lost a molecular weight equivalent to 420. If we take away another 5 molecules of oxygen, we have lost an additional molecular weight of 160 for a total loss of 580. Now, if we replace those 20 molecules of nitrogen and oxygen with 20 molecules of water vapor, we only replace it with a molecular weight of 360. The total change has been a loss of molecular weight equivalent to 580 minus 360 or 220 total. Thus warm, moist air is lighter than warm, dry air and you should move quicker and faster on those hot, humid days. And all along you thought it was the moisture in the air that made you move slowly, feel drowsy, and want to take a nap, which I am sure you feel like doing now, after this lengthy chapter.

Chapter 6
Air Masses, Fronts and Middle-Latitude Storms

Differential heating of the earth causes daily and seasonal weather changes. Cold air is always trying to work its way south from the North Pole and north from the South Pole. Warm tropical air is trying to move in the opposite directions. It would be correct to say that these two air masses do not like one another since each is trying to push the other out of the way and they collide.

The Pacific Northwest Indian legend of the warm Chinook Wind caused by the Chinook brothers and the cold east wind caused by the Walla Walla brothers is pretty much as things are today in the Pacific Northwest. Cold, arctic air will invade the area only to be replaced by warm southwesterly winds.

These two different brothers (air masses, if you will) collide where the polar easterlies (northeasterlies) and the westerlies (southwesterlies) come together. The area is called the polar front. It is not a continuous zone, just as in a war between two countries there is not a continuous battlefield. It is, however, a battleground in the Northern Hemisphere between warm air wanting to move north and cold air looking for a warmer climate. Warm air masses vs. cold air masses. But what exactly is an air mass?

Air Masses

An air mass is a large body (mass) of air with essentially the same characteristics or properties of moisture and temperature. That does not mean that the temperature and dewpoint temperature are the same throughout the air mass. Local conditions, such as elevation or even a small water source, will cause minor variations. Properties will also be different around the periphery of the air mass.

Air masses form mostly over regions where the air can become stagnant, or remain in the same location, for several days. That is why the tropics, the polar regions, and the horse latitudes are favorable locations. In these areas there generally is little air movement or semi-stagnant conditions. In the belt of westerlies where Oregon and Washington are located, the weather is too variable and air masses do not readily form in the middle latitudes. There are exceptions to this such as over the ocean. In long transit over an ocean, an air mass assumes the characteristics of that ocean.

Basically, there are four major types of air masses: Polar or Arctic (Northern Hemisphere), Tropical, Maritime, and Continental. These types refer to Polar as cold; Tropical as warm; Maritime as moist; and Continental as dry. Oh, if only the atmosphere would think along lines that simple. But alas, it does not. Those four types combine to form others. When maritime air combines or mixes with polar air, we call it maritime polar, or an "mP" air mass. When maritime air combines or associates with tropical air we call it a maritime tropical (mT) air mass. (Guess which air mass caused all those flooding problems in the Pacific Northwest in November 1965 and February 1996!)

> ### The Chinook Wind
>
> *Long, long ago, the warm west wind was caused by five Chinook brothers. They lived far down the Columbia River, near the Pacific Ocean. The cold east wind was caused by the five Walla Walla brothers. They lived east of the mountains, near the meeting of the waters...*
>
> *All these wind brothers blew very hard over the country. Sometimes the warm Chinook wind would dash over the camps, blow down trees, tear up the earth, and fill the air with dust. Then the cold Walla Walla wind would come along and freeze everything with its icy breath. So the people led a miserable life.*
>
> *One day, the five Walla Walla brothers sent a message to the five Chinook brothers. 'We challenge you to a wrestling match,' they said.*
>
> *The Chinook brothers accepted and Coyote was chosen as judge and would cut off the head of the losers. One by one the brothers fought. Each time the Chinook brother was defeated and soon all five were dead. The cold Walla Walla winds must have blown relentlessly for a period until the son of one of the five Chinook brothers slain became old enough and strong enough to challenge the five Walla Walla brothers. This he did, and one by one he defeated the Walla Walla brothers until only one was left. 'One of us must remain alive,' the last Walla Walla brother explained.*
>
> *Coyote said, 'I will let you live. But I make a law that hereafter you shall blow only lightly. You can never again blow so hard and so cold. No longer will you freeze people to death everytime you breathe on them.'*
>
> *Then Coyote turned to the young Chinook. 'I make a law that you shall blow hard only at night. You shall blow first on the mountain ridges to warn the people that you are coming. Then you shall come down to the valleys and take off the snow quickly.'*
>
> *Ever since then, the cold wind has blown lightly in the winter, and the warm Chinook wind has blown early in the spring. Then it carries off the snow in a rush.*
>
> *Indian Legends of the Pacific Northwest,*
> Ella E. Clark

Continental air has a low moisture content. That makes sense, since it forms in an area removed from the oceans. A continental polar (cP) air mass causes those chilling Columbia Gorge winds out of the east and the equally as cold northeast winds out of the Fraser River Valley into northern Washington during the winter. Those winds cause very cold temperatures in valleys west of the Cascades, into northern California, and to the coastal strip of Washington and Oregon. In summer, the desiccating dry, hot east winds are of continental tropical (cT) air mass origin. This is also the air mass that brings the 90-, and 100-degree heat to the valleys west of the Cascade Mountains and even to the coastal areas. However, the majority of air masses affecting the Pacific Northwest are maritime polar (mP). This area is not visited by many of the other air masses. We have to wait for the "specials!" But it is the specials that give us the extreme heat and extreme cold and the very heavy rains. Figure 6.1 shows the source regions of air masses that affect the Pacific Northwest.

An air mass can remain over its initial location for several days and even weeks. A continental polar air mass that forms over the interior of Alaska or the Northwest Territories of Canada in winter is continuously losing heat via radiation to space, allowing the air to become very cold. At lower latitudes stagnant conditions will lead to air masses that are warm and loaded with moisture if they are over water, and hot and dry if they are over land.

Once an air mass begins moving out of its "home" or initial location, it is modified in the layers next to the earth's surface and, of course, around its periphery. A very cold air mass moving south out of Canada will gradually warm as it passes over land that is warmer. Thus, the conditions (temperature and moisture content) along the leading edge of the air mass will be different from the conditions elsewhere within the air mass. A cold, polar (arctic) air mass that is relatively dry in the lower layers will gradually warm and increase its moisture content as it travels out over the Gulf of Alaska on its way to the Pacific Northwest as shown in Figure 6.2. This needs to be kept in mind when Pacific Northwest snowstorms are discussed.

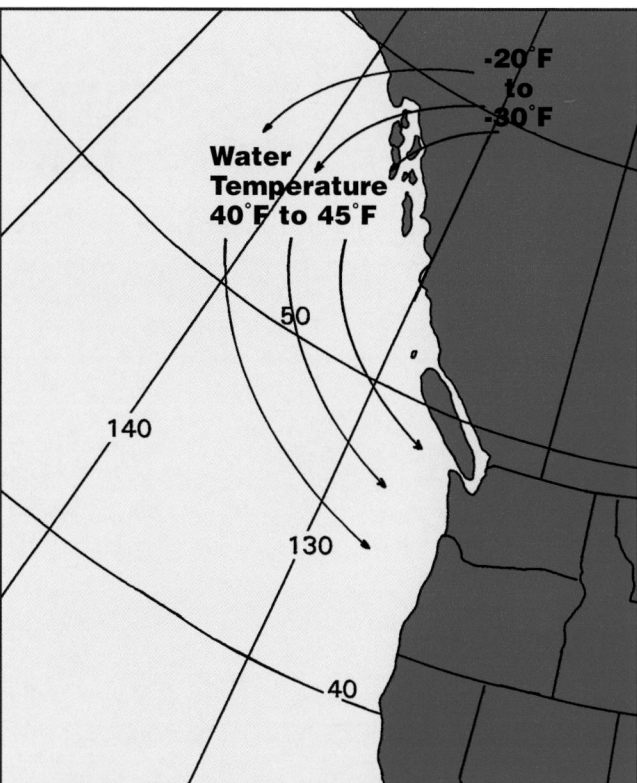

Figure 6.2 In winter, very cold air from the interior of Alaska and Canada is modified considerably in the lower layers as it moves out over the warmer Gulf of Alaska.

One more designation is made to differences between air masses and this is a "k" or a "w" to the original designation. For instance, if the air mass is designated "mPk" it means that it is a maritime polar air mass that is colder (k) than the surface over which it is moving. Most of the air masses that arrive in the Pacific Northwest from off the ocean in summer are mPk air masses. In summer, the land is warmer than the ocean offshore, thus cooler air is advancing over warmer land. In the winter the antithesis is often the case. The temperature of the land is normally colder than the temperature of the ocean during the colder months of the year. Thus, most air masses that arrive in the Pacific Northwest in winter from the west have the designation "mPw," indicating that in the lower layers they are warmer (w) than the surface over which they are moving.

Fronts

The dividing line between two air masses with different characteristics is called a front. A polar front is the boundary where warm air moving north from southern latitudes (Northern Hemisphere) meets cold air moving down from the north. Figure 6.3 is an example of a middle-latitude area of low pressure encircled by isobars with a cold front and warm front emanating from the center. An arrow indicates the direction of storm movement.

If the cold air is "winning" or advancing or displacing the warm air, the front is called a cold front. Conversely, if the warm air is advancing and displacing the cold air, the

Figure 6.1 Air masses that affect the Pacific Northwest.

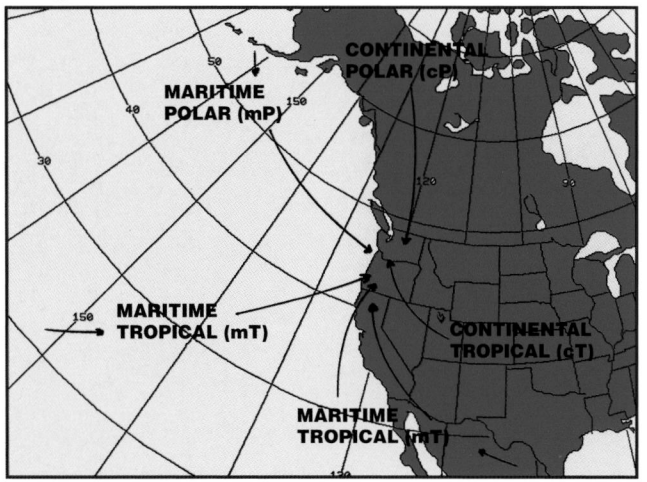

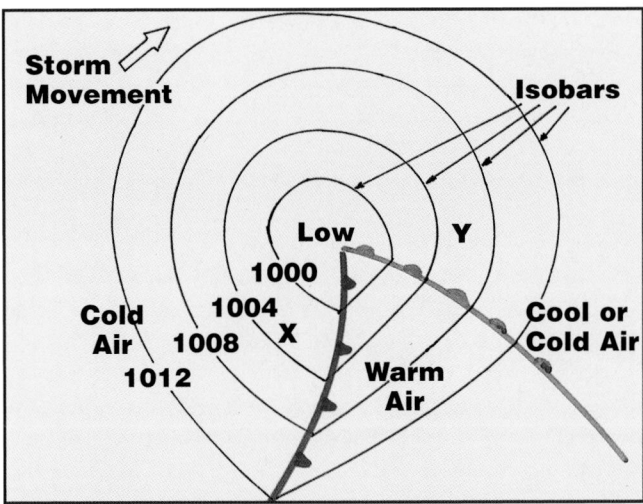

Figure 6.3 An idealized middle latitude low pressure area showing cold front (blue), warm front (red) and isobars.

front is called a warm front. If neither is gaining ground, or they are oscillating back and forth, then the front is called a stationary front. A blue line, with small barbs, indicates a cold front on weather maps, and a red line, with small mounds, is the correct symbol for a warm front. The side on which barbs or mounds appear is the direction the fronts are moving. A stationary front has alternating red and blue colors, barbs, and mounds. This is an idealized picture, and often Mother Nature has not read the text or looked at the pictures. Thus, not all storms and storm fronts look exactly like this. But let's try to keep things simple.

If we take a cross-section of this storm from point X to point Y across both the cold front and warm front, we have what is shown in Figure 6.4. Cold air is heavier, or denser, than warm air. Thus, as a cold front advances, the cold air hugs the surface, and the warmer air is forced aloft. This forced ascent causes the air to cool. The temperature of the air soon reaches condensation, clouds form and precipitation begins. Basically the same thing occurs when the warm air is advancing and displacing the cold air, but the slope of the frontal surface is different. Since the warm air is lighter,

it is pushed aloft over the cold air that is still hugging the surface. The result is a long, sloping surface. This factor makes warm fronts much harder to locate than cold fronts on weather maps. A station located on a mountain top might show the invading warm air long before valley stations feel its effect. This effect can be observed in areas of Washington and Oregon where there are mountains.

With this in mind, what precisely are the characteristics of cold fronts and warm fronts? There are several clues that identify when one or the other passes a location. Let's look at the cold front first. If colder air is more dense, the pressure of the cold air is greater than the pressure of the warm air. Our first clue, then, regarding the passage of a cold front would be a rise in the air pressure, as the cold air begins to replace the warm air. After the passage of a cold front, the air is usually sinking. This normally results in a decrease in cloudiness, which is another indicator of a cold front passage. Also, since the air is sinking and "piling up" on the surface, this contributes to an increase in pressure.

With cold air replacing the warmer air after the passage of a cold front, there would be a decrease in temperature. So, a drop in temperature is another clue that a cold front may have passed your location, especially if the temperature is dropping during the day when it is supposed to be rising. The decrease in cloudiness mentioned previously is normally associated with a decrease in the amount of moisture, and the fact that the air is subsiding, or sinking. Since the dewpoint is a measure of the amount of moisture in the air, a decrease in moisture content is associated with a decrease in the dewpoint temperature.

In Chapter 3, troughs or regions of lower pressure in the upper atmosphere were introduced. These same features (troughs) appear on surface weather maps. A trough as it passes over a location moving west to east or from the left side of your paper to the right side, will have southerly winds ahead of it and northwesterly winds behind it, provided the trough itself is oriented north-south or nearly north-south.

The isobars that define where a trough on the surface weather map exists will appear much like the letter "V" with

Figure 6.4 A cross-section from Point X to Point Y in Figure 6.3. The boundary between two air masses is where warm air is being forced aloft over cold air.

the apex pointing away from the center of lower pressure towards higher pressure. Cold fronts are normally found in this apex. Thus, another characteristic of a cold front is a shift of the wind in a clockwise rotation in the Northern Hemisphere or, for example, from a southerly to southwesterly to westerly to northwesterly direction. Remember, wind is measured in the direction from which it is coming. Figure 6.5 should help with these characteristics as it graphically and in tabular form shows what happens when a well-defined cold front passes a location.

In summary, the passage of a cold front in the Northern Hemisphere can be detected in several ways: (1) Rise in air pressure, (2) Decrease in cloudiness, (3) Decrease in temperature, (4) Decrease in the dewpoint temperature, (5) Shift of the wind in a clockwise direction, usually from a southerly component to a northwesterly component. Sometimes, the exact passage of the cold front is associated with the most intense shower activity, and perhaps a brief thunderstorm.

As mentioned, warm fronts are much harder to detect on weather maps than cold fronts. That is especially so in the Pacific Northwest where the terrain is interrupted by mountains. In the area from the Rocky Mountains east, warm fronts are much easier to locate and somewhat well defined. Pressure ahead of a warm front is usually falling, due mainly to the advection of warmer, lighter air into the area. The pressure is also falling ahead of a warm front because this area is in the path of the advancing low pressure center that is bringing lower pressure with it. The warmer, lighter air is forced aloft over the cold air. The pressure will likely fall as the warm front advances toward the station, then remain steady, or fall slightly after it passes, but begin to fall more rapidly again as the cold front approaches. Pressure changes are not the best way to locate warm fronts.

Cloudiness is also not a good indicator, since overcast clouds will likely occur before and continue after a warm front passes a location. Precipitation, however, will often be heavy before the passage of a warm front, then decrease after the passage, but quite often still continue. On rare occasions in the Pacific Northwest, a warm front may be preceded by precipitation, and after its passage the skies will become clear to partly cloudy with some sunshine. This is only temporary, since cloudiness will begin increasing as the cold front advances, but it can account for missed temperature forecasts. The decrease in cloudiness and increased solar radiation will allow the temperature to rise above what may be expected with a dense cloud cover.

By far the best indicator of a warm front passing by a location is an increase in temperature. Remember, the warm air is displacing the cold air, but since the warm air is lighter, it will be forced aloft over the cold air. Accompanying the increase in temperature there will often be an increase in the dewpoint temperature. The warmer air is capable of containing much more moisture. In the Northern Hemisphere, because warm air is advancing from the south, there will be a wind shift in a clockwise direction from easterly or northeasterly to southerly or southwesterly. This is another characteristic of a warm frontal passage. Figure 6.6 depicts the characteristics of a warm front.

In summary, warm fronts are usually preceded by falling pressure as the warmer, lighter air is forced aloft over a location. Then, after the passage of the warm front the pressure will fall more slowly or show little change until the cold front gets closer to the station. Meteorologists call this area the "warm sector." A rise in temperature and often a rise in dewpoint temperature will accompany a warm front. The wind will shift in a clockwise direction from easterly to southerly. Steady, sometimes heavy precipitation will decrease to light, intermittent precipitation or, as mentioned, quit entirely and the sky will clear or become partly cloudy.

Stationary fronts are precisely that, fronts that show very little movement. In some meteorological terms they are referred to as "quasi-stationary" fronts, but the connotation is the same. There may be minor movement back and forth, like armies on the battlefield, with first one advancing a little, then falling back as the other advances a little. For the most part, stationary fronts remain over an area for several hours, and in some extreme cases days, accounting for very heavy rainfall.

Figure 6.5 The characteristics of a cold front. Weather parameters at A will be replaced by those at B as the front passes over that location.

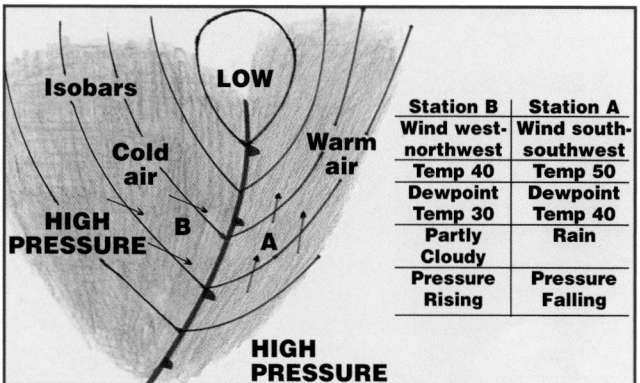

Figure 6.6 The characteristics of a warm front. Weather parameters at A will be replaced by those at B as the front passes over that location.

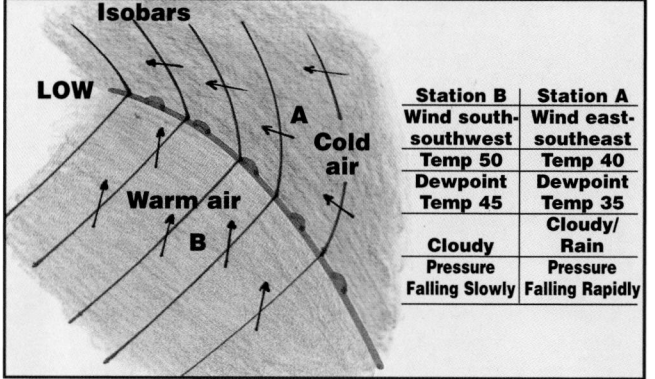

Stationary fronts are generally oriented parallel to the wind flow at higher elevations, such as 500 millibars. Mountain barriers can also cause fronts to become stationary, or at least to slow down. To get moving, stationary fronts need a shove, like many of us. An approaching shortwave trough or another area of low pressure often provides that shove.

Remember, Figures 6.3 through 6.6 are "textbook" illustrations of how the ideal cold front and the ideal warm front should look. Unfortunately, this is not the case every time. As mentioned, Mother Nature has not always read the textbook, and the actual positions of the fronts on weather maps and the weather associated with them show variations from these illustrations.

Occluded Fronts

Cold fronts usually advance faster than warm fronts. (Don't you have more energy on cold, crisp days than on hot, muggy days? Yes, yes, I know that according to molecular weight of air, you should move faster on the hot, humid days because the air is lighter, but generally we do not!) Since cold fronts are usually moving faster than warm fronts they will "catch up" with the slower moving warm fronts. The result is what is called an occluded front or an occlusion. In this case, the warm air gets pinched or pushed aloft leaving the two cold or cool air masses to battle it out. There are two types of occlusions: warm occlusions and cold occlusions. In the case of the cold occlusion, colder air is displacing air that is not quite as cold or just cooler at the surface. A warm occlusion would have cool air replacing cold air at the surface.

Weather associated with occlusions is similar to the weather that accompanies cold fronts and warm fronts. Characteristics of an occlusion passing a location are similar to those of a cold front if it is a cold occlusion. The pressure at a location will fall as an occlusion approaches and will rise after the occlusion has passed. The difference in pressure is mainly due to the location of the isobars as they move over a station and the rising air on one side and sinking air on the other side. Following a warm occlusion, the surface temperature will show a slight increase. Figure 6.7 depicts the ideal "textbook" structure of cold and warm occlusions. Sometimes the atmosphere can take things into its own hands and create what are called by meteorologists "instant occlusions." These are usually formed as a trough of low pressure approaches a low pressure center with its associated cold and warm fronts.

Most of the fronts that move off the Pacific Ocean into the Pacific Northwest are of the occlusion variety. In winter the land is generally colder than the Pacific Ocean. An air mass approaching the Pacific Northwest attains the same temperature as the ocean in its lower layers. The result is that most of the occlusions that affect the Pacific Northwest in the winter are warm occlusions. (On weather maps, however, they are often drawn as cold fronts, not because the surface temperatures lowers, but due to colder air following aloft in the upper trough.) The opposite occurs in the summer. The land is warmer than the ocean. As an air mass travels across the ocean and approaches the

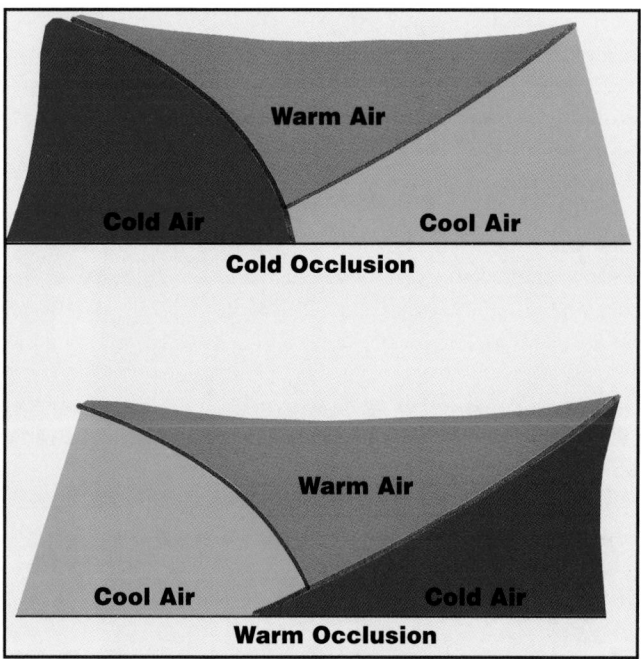

Figure 6.7 Examples of a cold occlusion (top) and warm occlusion (bottom).

Pacific Northwest, the air in contact with the ocean attains that temperature. A cold occlusion is usually the result.

Meteorologists and weather people are a colorful bunch which is why cold fronts are drawn in blue and warm fronts in red on weather maps. Occlusions are drawn in purple and areas of precipitation shaded in green. Although the same color is shown throughout the different air masses, it must be remembered that temperature normally decreases with elevation, except along frontal boundaries where a temperature inversion may exist. Horizontal properties may be the same, but vertical properties can, and do, change.

> **January 31, 1806 camped at Fort Clatsop**
> *"The Winds from the Land brings us cold and clear weather while those obliquely along either coast or off the Oceans bring us warm damp cloudy and rainy weather. the hardest winds are always from the S.W."*
> The Journals of the Lewis & Clark Expedition
> Volume 6, Gary E. Moulton, Editor.

Middle-Latitude Storms

Cold fronts, warm fronts and occluded fronts are all parts of what are called storms that move along the polar front, usually at latitudes between 35 degrees and 65 degrees in both hemispheres. These are the storms that you read about in the newspaper or see pictures of on television of heavy rain, snow and wind. These same storms sometimes spawn tornadoes, but that is another topic. Middle-latitude storms show an entirely different structure than hurricanes and typhoons. There is virtually no temperature difference horizontally through hurricanes and typhoons, except perhaps a warm core in the center. Middle-latitude storms thrive and grow (intensify) on temperature differences horizontally across the storm. In fact, the stronger the temperature difference, usually the stronger the storm and the stronger the jet stream.

But before we get too deeply into this section, we should define what exactly we mean by a "storm." To some people, the term storm refers only to one small portion of a large area of low pressure. A middle-latitude storm can cover thousands of square miles and cause widespread damage all along the west coast from California to Washington and east to Idaho. People in Eugene, Oregon for instance, who had trees blown down in their yards and who lost some shingles might say, "That sure was a strong storm that went through here last night!" On the coast at Long Beach, Washington, where major damage might have occurred, headlines may read, "Storm Disrupts Traffic; Destroys Several Buildings." That might seem like there were two separate storms, but to the meteorologist it was a strong storm that occurred over several thousand square miles. So who's right? We are going to look at the structure of these storms, where they come from, and how they get started.

In the Pacific Northwest, and probably elsewhere in the country or world, you may hear the statement, "Oh, the storms we have here come from that direction." I have heard that remark many times from coastal residents, fishermen, and even from persons who live east of the Cascade Mountains. What they are referring to, or what they really mean, is the wind that precedes a storm or area of low pressure. The storm centers usually do not come from that direction, only the winds. A vivid example of this is the area around Long Beach, Washington, Figure 6.8. Here, surface wind flow associated with the low-pressure area is strongly affected by winds flowing out of the Columbia River ahead of Pacific storms. The result is a strong southeasterly wind in this area that is blowing into the center of the advancing low-pressure area that still may be hundreds of miles off shore to the west-northwest, moving towards the coast. Examples of this type of wind flow can be found in numerous areas along the coasts of Washington and Oregon where there is a gap in the Coast Range Mountains to the east.

So, our reference to the term storm in this discussion will be to the entire area of low pressure. Of course it would be folly to draw a line somewhere distant from the center of lowest pressure and say, "This is where the storm ends." We cannot do that. When we talk about the center of the storm, however, we can be definitive. The center of the storm is the point of lowest pressure at the surface. When reference is made to a storm's direction of movement (For example, "This type of storm moves in from the west") reference will be to direction of movement of the center of lowest pressure.

But what causes storms to form in the first place? Why do they form in one location and not in another? As two air masses come together, most often along the polar front, the warm air will try to push north and the cold air will try to

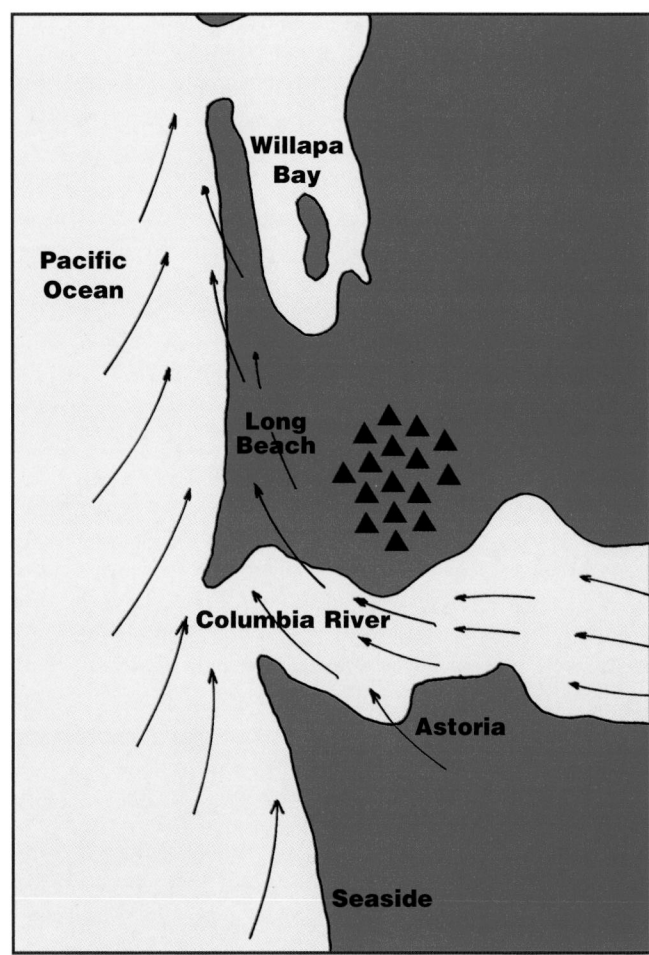

Figure 6.8 An example of strongest winds from a southeasterly direction ahead of a Pacific storm that is approaching from the west. The topography at the mouth of the Columbia River greatly affects the flow.

move south in the Northern Hemisphere. This usually sets up a circulation around a point, or the center of the developing storm. Meteorologists refer to it as a "wave."

As the pressure around a wave decreases, meteorologists analyzing weather maps can draw concentric circles (or near-

Benjamin Franklin Recognizes Storm Movement
1743. In September Benjamin Franklin, then Postmaster General, from the reports of numerous postmasters and from the fact that at Philadelphia, Pa., a storm prevented observations of an eclipse of the moon, while at Boston, Mass., the eclipse was over an hour before the storm began, deduced the progressive movement of a hurricane storm moving up from the West Indies. This is the first recorded instance in which the progressive movement of our storms as a whole was recognized.
Monthly Weather Review March 1909

ly concentric circles) or isobars (lines of constant pressure) around the point with the lowest pressure. The three stages usually referred to in storm development are depicted in

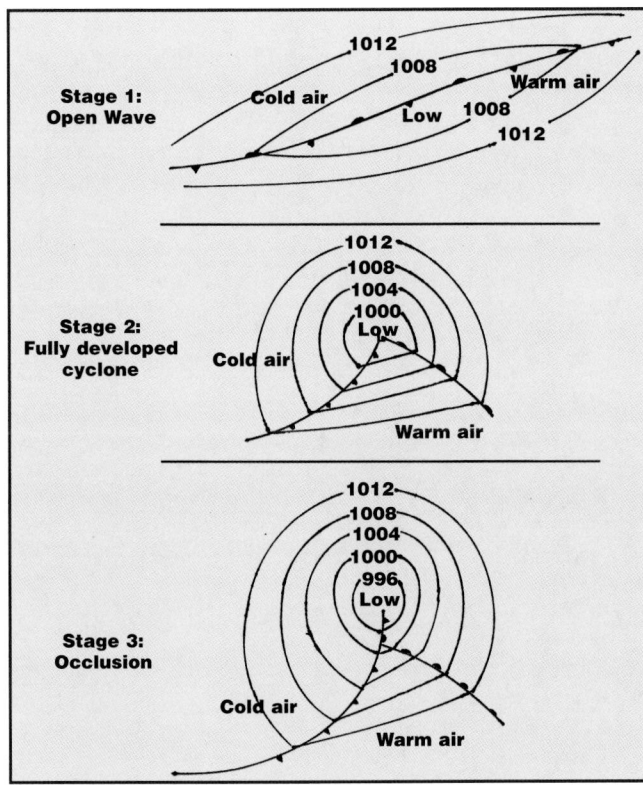

Figure 6.9 The three stages of cyclone development.

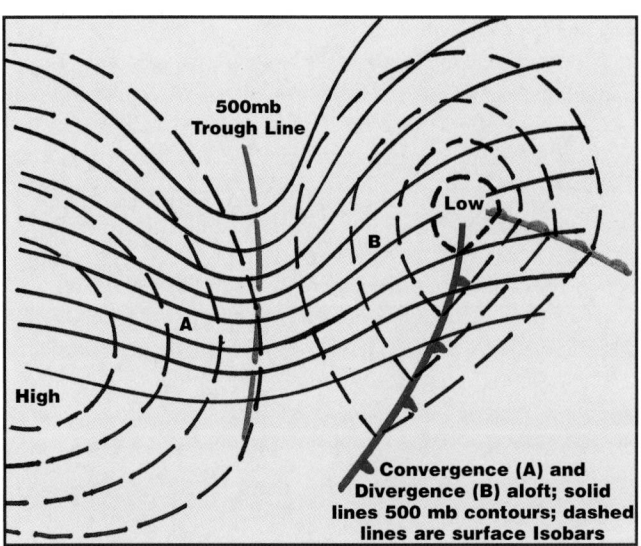

Figure 6.10 Surface storm formation is located below areas where air streams or contour lines are diverging, at middle and high levels of the atmosphere such as at B in the above diagram.

Figure 6.9. The first constitutes a wave along a stationary front, or a front that has stalled and shows little movement. In the second phase, warm air has begun to progress north and cold air is beginning to advance south in the Northern Hemisphere. This stage is a fully developed low-pressure area, or storm. The third stage is the occlusion stage. This is the most intense stage of a middle-latitude storm. Once this stage has been reached, storms begin to weaken. Often the next wave will develop along the trailing edge of the cold front.

But it is not at the surface of the earth that all this action is taking place as depicted in Figure 6.9. The formation of a storm is manifest through several layers of the atmosphere. In fact, strong storms are found where there is also a very strong jet stream simply because of the strong temperature contrast. There are other processes occurring that contribute to storm development and those are convergence and divergence.

The regions of high pressure at the surface of the earth are where the air has piled up. Much of this air has come from higher levels in the atmosphere where the wind flow or streamlines are converging. If you have ever been on a freeway traveling along at 65 mph and come to a place where six lanes funnel down to four, you have been involved with convergence and had to slow down. You had no place to go.

The same thing happens in the atmosphere, but the results are entirely different since air can keep moving. Note the location of the letter A in Figure 6.10. This figure shows a trough of low pressure at 500 millibars (solid lines) with the trough line illustrated as a series of dashes (purple) and

an area of surface low pressure (dashed lines) with its attendant warm and cold front. Remember, the locations of the cold and warm fronts show the leading edge of those air masses at the surface. The contour lines, representing the wind flow at 500 millibars in Figure 6.10, are converging, or coming closer together at A while at B they are diverging or spreading apart. Air particles converging at A have two options. (You had only one, slow down and wait! But that is not one of our air molecule's options.) One option those air molecules have is to accelerate through the trough. Another option is to look for somewhere else to go when the "crowd gets too thick." We do this, also. "Too many people! Let's get out of here!" Many of the air molecules at this elevation, when they are converging, take the exit that is marked "down." In other words, they descend. Air that is descending is stable and tends to "pile up" at the surface creating higher pressure, which can be seen at the surface below this area of convergence at 500 millibars.

We know that air is circulating in a counter-clockwise rotation toward the center of a surface low-pressure area in the Northern Hemisphere. The molecules are coming together. They look for someplace to go and take the elevator marked "up." When stuck in a traffic jam, we wish that our car would sprout wings and go up like James Bond could do in his movies. That is precisely what is happening around the point marked B in Figure 6.10, again in the vicinity of the jet stream. The streamlines at 500 millibars at this point are diverging or spreading apart. Other air molecules rush up from below to take the place of those that "went their separate ways" in the diverging air streams. Air that is rising, we now know, is cooling. When it reaches the dewpoint temperature, condensation begins to occur, releasing heat, and usually creating a more unstable atmosphere. Precipitation is the result. As the air molecules rush up they, in turn, leave somewhat of a void at the surface. Air molecules near the surface rush in to fill this void. A favorable location for a storm to develop, then, would be where there are diverging air streams aloft and converging air streams at the surface. Meteorologists look for areas where this is occurring as a clue to storm development.

With storms that are developing, forming, or intensifying, there is much more air rushing up immediately ahead of the storm than there is air filling in at the surface. Again, fewer molecules mean that the pressure is lower. When the fall of pressure reaches a certain value (that is, much more air ascending than is being brought in) a term called "meteorological bombs" is introduced. These are storms that are intensifying, "deepening" in meteorological language, at a very rapid rate, or greater than one millibar decrease in their central pressure each hour for 24 hours. The Pacific Northwest has its meteorological bombs which we will discuss later.

There are many locations on the surface of the earth that are reporting the pressure of the air. If those stations are in the mountains, or above mean sea level, we know their readings must be converted to a reading that is relevant to sea level. Over the oceans there are pressure readings taken also. Those vessels that are hauling goods and materials back and forth between Asia and the Pacific Northwest take weather reports. In fact, there are thousands of merchant ships that are part of a weather collection program including the Coast Guard, Navy and others that observe the weather. There are also a number of buoys that are both anchored to the ocean floor and others that are drifting with the ocean currents. All send pressure readings,

along with reports of other weather elements and ocean conditions, to satellites that are passing overhead that retransmit the data to a receiving station on land.

From these data, meteorologists draw weather maps. If it is a surface pressure analysis, they draw a line connecting all those stations that have the same pressure. That line is

> ### Corps of Discovery on the North Side of the Columbia River
> *"November 22, 1805 a moderate rain all the last night with wind, a little before Day light the wind which was from the SS.E. blew with Such violence that we were almost overwhelmned with water blown from the river, this Storm did not Sease at day but blew with nearly equal violence throughout the whole day accompanied with rain. O! how horrible is the day waves brakeing with great violence against the Shore throwing the Water into our Camp &c. all wet and Confined to our shelters."*
> The Journals of the Lewis & Clark Expedition, *Volume 6*, Gary E. Moulton, Editor

called an isobar. Isobars connect points of equal pressure. They are usually labeled in millibars, such as 996, 1000, 1004, 1008, including higher and lower values. That is the standard separation, but isobars can be drawn every millibar to get a more accurate or precise picture of the pressure field. If we draw a 1008 millibar isobar around a low pressure center, it will take on the shape of a circle. (Well, almost a circle. Mother Nature doesn't make it that easy and the circles generally become distorted.) Inside that isobar labeled 1008 millibars there might be one with a value 1004, another with a value of 1000, and so on until we get to the center of the storm. So, storms with many isobars around them will be large and intense. The isobars will be packed closely together (a stronger pressure gradient) and the wind will be stronger.

Isobars are drawn on a weather map to show the areas of high and low pressure as they would appear if the earth were totally flat with no mountains. When we leave mean sea level and go to higher elevations in the atmosphere, meteorologists also draw maps that look similar but that are slightly different. These maps are drawn at a constant pressure value or a constant pressure surface. That simply means that everywhere on the map the pressure is the same. The lines meteorologists draw are not isobars, but are called contour lines. These maps are similar to the topographical maps that show elevations, because contour lines also show elevations which indicate the height of a constant pressure surface above mean sea level.

Refer again to Figure 6.10. Troughs, or short waves, in the upper atmosphere lag behind areas of low pressure on the surface weather map at mean sea level. The higher one goes in the atmosphere, the greater the lag. It will not be as much at 700 millibars as it is at 500 millibars. It will lag even more at 300 millibars than at 500 millibars. Thus, you can see that storms have a slope to them. The trough in the upper atmosphere that is associated with the low pressure at the surface will not be directly over that area of low pressure. Remember that the leading edge of the cold air advancing behind the cold front at the surface was not vertical, but sloped up to the left of the picture. Thus, the cold air aloft is associated with the trough of low pressure aloft. Storms that do not show a vertical sloping structure to them (that is with the upper low or trough directly over the surface low or trough) are usually weak to begin with, or in the weakening process.

In this section we have talked about middle-latitude storm development. The more intense the storm, the more isobars there are packed closely together surrounding it. Middle-latitude storm development depends on where the areas of convergence at the surface and divergence aloft are located. A storm at the surface of the earth is associated with a trough of low pressure aloft and may cover thousands of square miles. The center of the storm, however, is definitive and is the area of lowest pressure.

Pacific Northwest Windstorms

It was late February in the year 1543. Bartolome Ferrelo, sailing under the flag of Spain, was struggling to move north very close to what is now the California/Oregon border. His

> **Bartolome Ferrelo near the California-Oregon border 1543**
>
> On 28 February, the storm increased in intensity, with huge waves breaking over the ships, so that the two ships without sterncastles were nearly swamped. In these straits, the sailors made new vows to the Virgin—this time to Our Lady of Guadalupe—promising another pilgrimage if they were saved from the storm.
>
> As though in answer to their prayers, the wind shifted to the north, and the ships were able to begin running back toward their island haven. The seas remained high, and the waves broke over the bows with crashing blows, 'and passed over them as though over a rock.'
>
> *Juan Rodriguez Cabrillo* by Harry Kelsey

vessel was being battered by strong south-southwesterly winds that were pushing it closer and closer to the rocks along the shoreline. Heavy rain was lashing the vessel. The crew members were praying, believing they would soon die. Suddenly, the wind shifted to northwesterly and the rain and wind lessened. Disaster was averted and the vessel and crew were saved. They retreated southward.

Ferrelo and his crew were probably the first Europeans to witness the passage of a strong Pacific cold front or perhaps an occluded front. Its associated low-pressure center was located somewhere north of their position. Since that time, thousands of storms and storm fronts have struck the Oregon, Washington and California coasts. Many of them have caused devastation

and death. Were they different from other storms elsewhere in the world? Was the storm Ferrelo experienced out of the ordinary? Probably not as far as Pacific Northwest windstorms are concerned.

The Pacific Northwest and Northern California are located in the belt of westerlies. Most storms travel in this band of strong winds that we call the jet stream. We know also that this band is not stagnant, but shifts north and south and gets large humps and dips (troughs and ridges) in it. The Pacific Ocean is a source of moisture, one ingredient necessary for a "good" storm. A good storm, you say? Let's talk like a meteorologist for a few minutes.

A good storm is one that has a very low central pressure. It has strong winds associated with it. It "kicks up" big waves over the ocean. But not all storms are good storms. Each is different. The direction from which they strike the Pacific Northwest and their intensity all vary. There is no difference, however, in how Pacific Northwest storms are formed than with any other storm in other parts of the world at middle latitudes. The conditions that cause "our" storms to form exist in other parts of the country. What enters into the picture is the geography of the Pacific Northwest and the direction from which the storms approach this part of the continent.

Your author has divided Pacific Northwest storms into two categories. Those two categories are "Columbus Day-type" storms, and for the lack of anything imaginative, "normal" storms. "What's the difference?" and moreover, "What's a Columbus Day-type storm?" Aren't all storms the same? In structure you are basically correct. Columbus Day-type storms and normal storms develop in much the same way. There is divergence aloft and convergence at the surface. There is the presence of a jet stream. There is a strong temperature contrast. There is the low-pressure center at the surface followed by a trough of low-pressure aloft containing colder air. It is the direction from which the storm approaches the Pacific Northwest that distinguishes one type from the other, and what happens before and after the storm.

First, we will discuss those normal storms, that is, your "everyday, run-of-the-mill" Pacific Northwest windstorm. With these kinds of storms the clouds increase, thicken and lower; the wind increases, shifts direction from southerly to westerly, and then decreases; the pressure drops and then rises as the storm front passes; the rain comes down, heavy for a brief period of time, then lessens or quits; and it is all over. This type of storm can occur any month of the year, but is more prevalent during the fall, winter and spring seasons. This was probably the type of storm Ferrelo and his crew experienced. Yet, this type of storm can cause destruction, devastation, and even death during any month of the year.

Normal Pacific Northwest storms approach our coast from a southwesterly, westerly or northwesterly direction or even a northerly direction, Figure 6.11. (Remember, we are talking about the center of lowest pressure.) Oh, I suppose

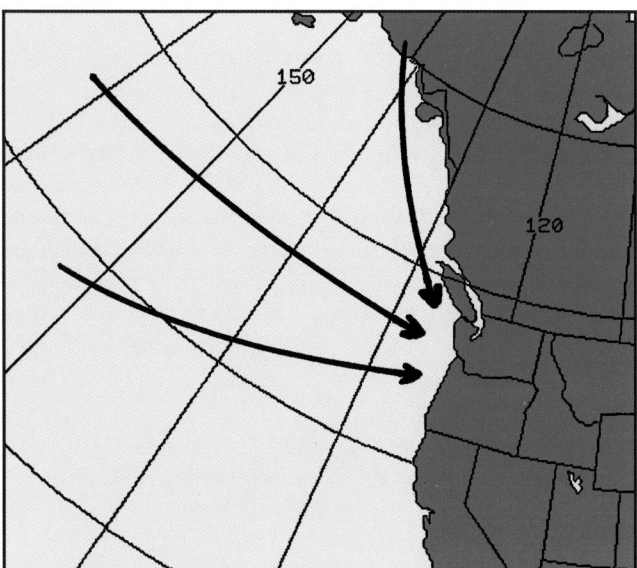

Figure 6.11 Normal Pacific Northwest windstorms arrive from the southwest, west or northwest.

we could get a maverick that slips in from the east, but very rarely. Let's focus our attention on those that approach our area from the Pacific Ocean. As these storms approach the coast, the pressure gradient or difference in pressure from south to north increases, meaning that the surface pressure falls much faster around Vancouver Island or along the coast of Washington than it does along the coasts of Oregon or northern California. The following is an example.

Tatoosh Island is on the northwest tip of the Olympic Peninsula. For starters, let's give it a pressure of 1010 millibars. At Newport on the Oregon coast, the pressure is 1020 millibars, resulting in a pressure gradient of 10 millibars between the two locations. Six hours later, the pressure at Tatoosh Island may have fallen to 1006 millibars as the storm approaches, but at Newport it may have fallen to only 1018 millibars. Now what's our pressure gradient? Of course, 12 millibars. When the pressure gradient between two locations increases, the wind will increase. All of this is happening as the pressure over the entire area is falling, but at different rates at different locations depending on which way the center of the low pressure is headed and where that area of divergence aloft is located.

If we draw isobars around the center of low pressure that is approaching Vancouver Island or northwest Washington, we would see that their orientation is north-northeast to south-southwest, or south-southwest to north-northeast, however you want to look at it in the area ahead of the storm. In other words, the isobars will intersect the coastline at about a 30 degree angle. Remember that the area of lowest pressure (the storm's center) is still to the west of the coastline over the open ocean (Figure 6.12) and moving in an easterly direction as depicted by the arrow. Surface winds, because of friction, are blowing across the isobars at roughly a 30-degree angle, or in this case nearly parallel to the coastline, into the center of low pressure.

If the pressure continues to fall at the same rate at Tatoosh Island (4 millibars in six hours) and at the same rate at Newport (2 millibars every six hours) you can see that the pressure gradient will continue to increase and so will the southerly winds. That is one of the characteristics of normal Pacific Northwest wind storms—falling pressure accompanied by increasing southerly wind.

As the storm center approaches Vancouver Island or northwest Washington, the cold front or occlusion we talked about earlier will move onshore. Recall that one of the characteristics of cold fronts or occlusions is a shift in the wind followed by a rising pressure. Now, with the pressure rising at Tatoosh Island, what happens to the pressure gradient between that location and Newport? Why sure, it decreases, or weakens, or becomes less. This is an oversimplified situation as the cold front or occlusion may still be approaching Astoria, Oregon. The pressure at that location may still be falling. Thus, the winds may still be increasing on the Oregon coast, but are now decreasing on the Washington coast as rising pressure to the north lessens the pressure gradient.

There is one other factor that causes the winds to be stronger along the coast prior to the passage of normal Pacific Northwest windstorms. If there is a southwesterly component to the wind as it approaches the coastal terrain, the air will be deflected to the north. There is some convergence to the air streams here that causes a slight acceleration to the wind. This effect has been related to me by several fishermen who fish areas off the coast. They indicate that they will frequently encounter stronger winds than reported by land observation stations out to about five miles from shore. This is especially so near headlands such as Cape Blanco on the southern Oregon Coast, Heceta Head

Figure 6.12 With normal Pacific Northwest windstorms, the strongest winds are ahead of the occlusion or cold front from a southerly direction and then shift to a westerly direction and weaken as the front passes on east.

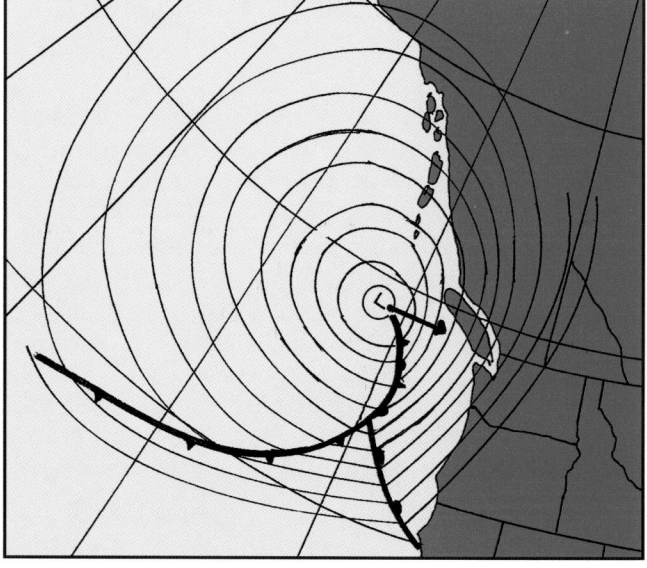

on the central Oregon coast, and near Destruction Island off the Washington coast. This converging of the streamlines occurs prior to the passage of the frontal system and may well account for some of the extreme wind speeds that are reported with normal Pacific Northwest windstorms. It is illustrated in Figure 6.13.

Figure 6.13 Coastal terrain causes air streams to converge near the coast which results in a slight increase in the wind speeds in this area ahead of normal Pacific Northwest windstorms.

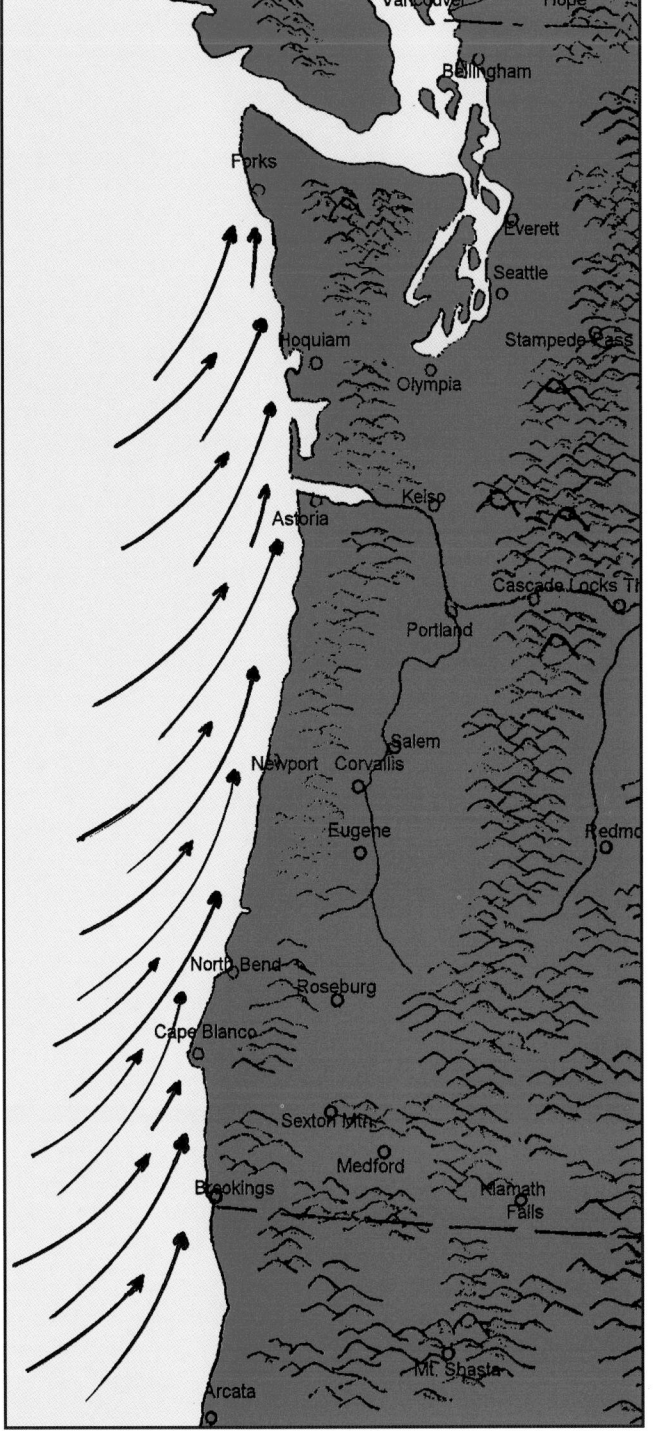

To summarize, the strongest winds associated with normal Pacific Northwest storms normally occur as the storm is approaching the coast and the pressure is falling. They occur in advance of the cold front or occlusion. After the storm center and storm front move inland, the pressure gradient relaxes, or decreases, and the winds shift clockwise from southerly to southwesterly, westerly, or even northwesterly direction and decrease. There can be a slight fall of temperature at the surface, but Pacific Northwest storms are not known for large temperature variations across them at the surface. Usually, what they

> **The Afternoon and Evening of October 12, 1962**
> *We both noticed the brick building we were in shaking or vibrating slightly in the wind. Power was gone, and we later ventured outside to the instrument shelter to take our hourly readings. We could hear objects striking the building next to us and see others flying by.*
> Author's personal account of the Columbus Day Storm while on duty with the U.S. Weather Bureau

are noted for is the much cooler air aloft associated with the upper air trough of low pressure. The cooler, or colder, air aloft lowers the snow level in the mountains. This is, of course, the textbook case. Again, Mother Nature sometimes is lax about doing her reading! But the above conditions occur most of the time with most Pacific Northwest windstorms. Now, what about that other classification? Those Columbus Day-type storms?

If you were living in the Pacific Northwest on October 12, 1962 (Columbus Day), you know about the Columbus Day storm. Even if you moved to the area later, or were born after that date, you probably have heard someone mention the infamous Columbus Day storm. It is one of those natural events that is fixed in the minds of local residents in the Pacific Northwest. As my dad may have said had he been here, "It was a dandy!" In meteorological terms, it was a meteorological bomb. It was a very intense storm and probably the strongest storm to affect the Pacific Northwest in recent history.

Total damage in 1962 dollars was over 200 million. Twenty-four people lost their lives. It affected the area from Northern California to British Columbia. Wind gusts in the Portland, Oregon area and other locations in the Willamette Valley were measured at over 100 miles per hour. Along the coast, they were measured at 130 miles per hour with estimates as high as 170 miles per hour. Millions of trees were blown down in the forests. Power and telephone service was interrupted for many days. At the time I was a young, upstart meteorologist at the Portland Weather Bureau Office who thought he "knew everything there was to know" about the weather. I was wrong!

So, what made this storm so strong? Simply stated, it was the intensity of the storm, the direction from which the center of the storm approached the Pacific Northwest, and its proximity to the coastline. The track of the storm, or the center of lowest pressure, approached Oregon and Washington from the south-southwest. It moved north just off the coast. Figure 6.14 shows the track or path of Columbus Day-type storms. This is different from the normal storms we have just talked about that approach from the southwest, west or northwest.

The Columbus Day storm started out like any other storm. It went through the three stages of storm development discussed earlier. There was plenty of warm, moist air left over from a dissipating Pacific typhoon (Freda). Cold air was lurking in the Gulf of Alaska. The two came together over the central Pacific Ocean, underneath a strong westerly jet stream. The storm reached its maximum intensity just off the coast. Its formation and movement across the Pacific Ocean was rapid, approaching 50 miles per hour, and intensifying at a rate exceeding one millibar per hour. It was a meteorological bomb. On the morning of October 12, the center of low pressure was located just off the California/Oregon border.

If we place a surface low-pressure center just off the California/Oregon border, the isobars circling around that center will have an orientation from south or southeast to north or northwest through much of Washington and Oregon. The low-pressure area will also be elongated toward the north. The isobars will be more closely packed around the southern quadrant of the storm. A typical Columbus Day-type storm will look similar to the one depicted in Figure 6.15. This type of orientation favors an easterly wind over much of the area. But the Coast Range and the Cascade Mountains disrupt this easterly flow at the surface. It generally is weak, except in those areas where there is a gap in the mountains such as at Astoria, at the

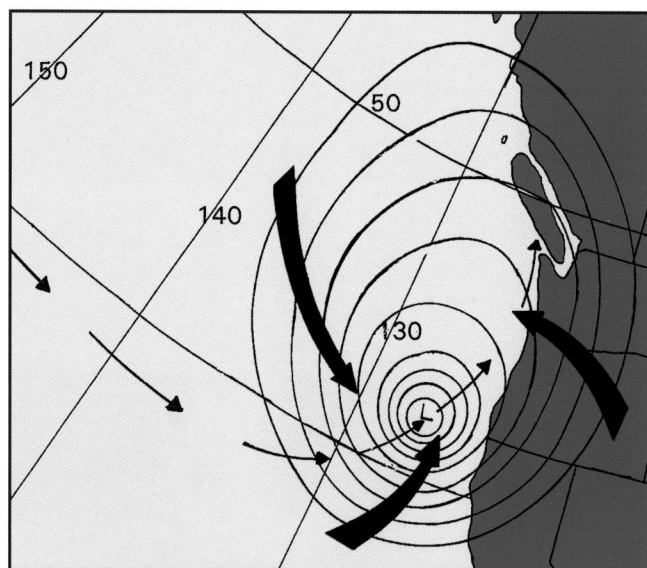

Figure 6.15 Movement of storm center approaching the coast and the surface wind flow associated with Columbus Day-type storms.

mouth of the Columbia River for the Coast Range Mountains, and Portland, at the opening of the Columbia River Gorge, for the Cascade Mountains. Here, the easterly winds can be quite strong ahead of this type of storm.

As the center of low pressure moves north along the coast, the surface pressure ahead of it will fall rapidly. This takes us back to those areas of convergence at the surface and divergence aloft. That characteristic is no different with normal wind storms than it is with Columbus Day-type wind storms. That coupling is still needed for storm development or intensification. The wind flow aloft is diverging, creating massive upward motion of the air over a large area.

Once the center of lowest pressure off the coast moves north, the isobars change their orientation to a more southwest-northeast orientation, and in extreme cases even to a west-east orientation. Now, as the low center moves north, the pressure is rising rapidly behind it, but still falling rapidly ahead of it. This fall of pressure to the north and rise of pressure to the south creates a very strong pressure gradient from south to north. Figure 6.16 shows how the orientation might look for a storm center just off the northwest tip of Washington, 12 to 18 hours after its position off the California/Oregon border.

Mountain ranges do not become a hindrance now, but an enhancement to the wind as the Venturi effect funnels the wind between north-south oriented mountain barriers. The Willamette Valley, oriented north-south, is one location where geographical features act to increase the wind speed. In this case, the pressure gradient force becomes so strong that the Coriolis effect is minimal, and the winds blow almost directly across the isobars from higher pressure in the south toward much lower pressure in the north. It is in this area of the storm, the south quadrant, that the strongest winds associated with Columbus Day-type storms occur.

Figure 6.14 The path or track of Columbus Day-type storms that affect the Pacific Northwest.

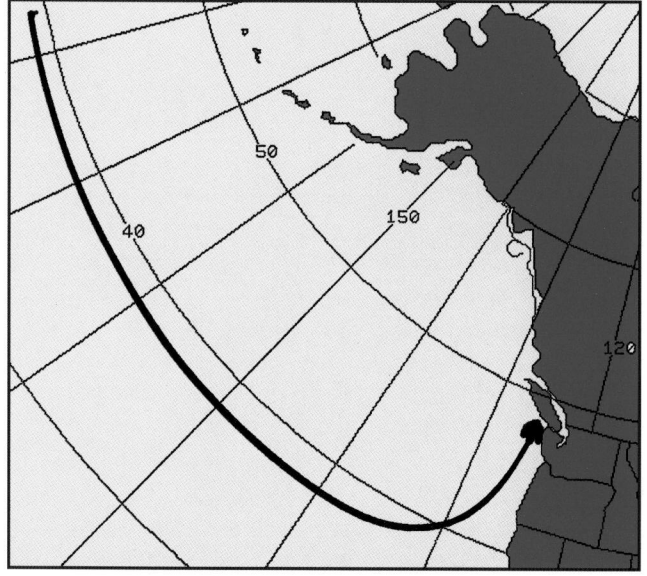

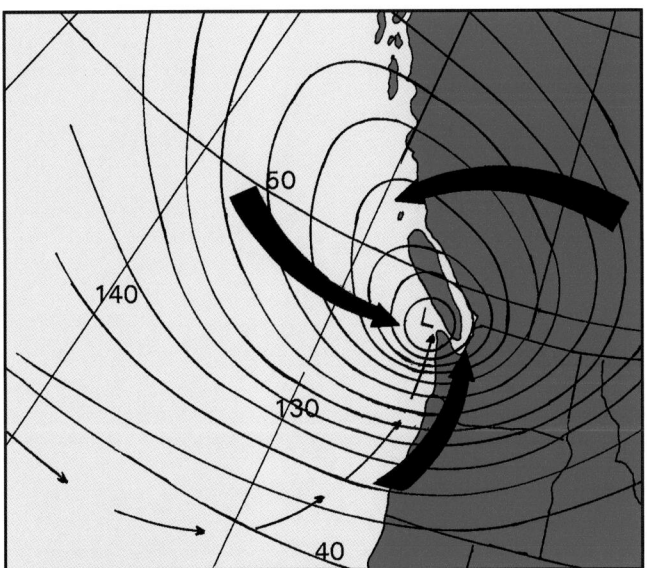

Figure 6.16 Location of storm center and wind flow associated with Columbus Day-type storms about 12 hours after position off California/Oregon border.

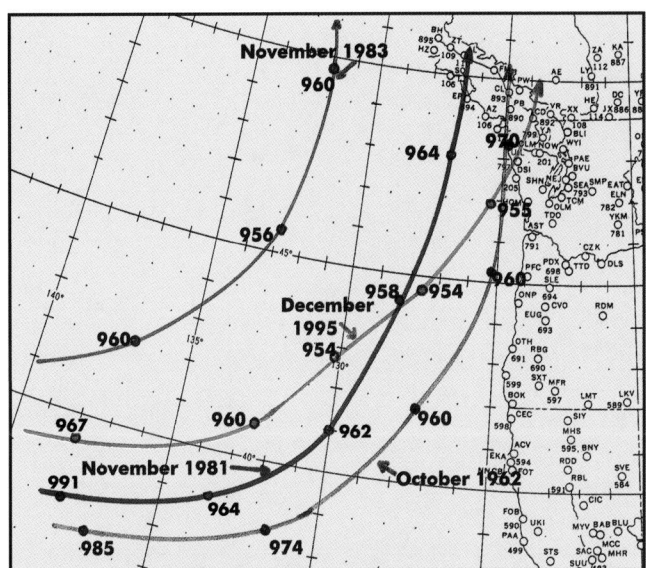

Figure 6.17 Tracks of some recent storms of the Columbus Day-type. (Pressure values are every 6 hours and do not reflect lowest values.)

Surface winds associated with normal Pacific Northwest storms will increase with a falling barometer, and then decrease as the pressure rises, shifting from a southerly direction to a more westerly direction. In contrast, winds associated with Columbus Day-type storms will shift from an easterly or southeasterly direction to a more southerly or southwesterly direction. They will increase markedly from that direction as the pressure rises rapidly.

Storms that belong to the Columbus Day variety favor the fall season; that is, from the end of September to the early part of December. It is during this time of year that we often find the greatest contrasts in air masses. The polar regions are cooling and the sub-tropics are still warm. Columbus Day-variety wind storms will form under a strong westerly jet stream of around 150-200 miles per hour across the Pacific Ocean near latitude 40°N. This jet stream usually takes a turn to the north near the coast during this season of the year. Thus, these storms move rapidly toward the coast and then curve north. Their northward deflection is partly due to the presence of a lingering warm summer ridge of high pressure over the western portion of the United States and rapidly intensifying storms often show a curvature to the left.

Another factor in the destructive power of these types of storms is the proximity of the center of low pressure to the coast. The Columbus Day storm of 1962 moved north between 130°W and the coastline and had a central pressure that reached 956 millibars. A similar storm on November 13, 1981 had a central pressure that was slightly lower at 954 millibars. However, its northward track was slightly farther off the coast, just east of (inside) 130°W. Had it been closer to the coast, destruction would likely have been greater than for the Columbus Day storm. Figure 6.17 shows the tracks of four recent storms of the Columbus Day variety with central pressures at six-hour

intervals noted in millibars. The mid-December storm of 1995 that was superbly forecast by Pacific Northwest meteorologists, began curving northward farther offshore and had more of a southwesterly trajectory as it approached the coastline. The November 1983 storm had a very low central pressure but its track was much farther offshore and the effect on the Pacific Northwest not as great.

Another characteristic of Columbus Day storms is that they often travel in "pairs." When referring to the term pairs it does not mean that two of them are occurring at the same time, or that "they do not want to venture out alone." It means that one intense storm may be followed by a more intense storm 24 to 36 hours later. The first storm could fall into the category of a normal storm and the second into the category of the Columbus Day-type storm. Figure 6.18 is a trace of barometric pressure for the Portland Weather Service (Weather Bureau in 1962)

Figure 6.18 Trace of barometric pressure at Portland, Oregon for October 10-13, 1962. (Courtesy National Weather Service, Portland.)

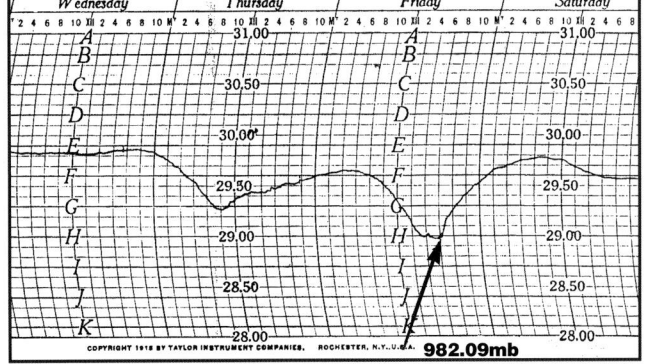

Air Masses, Fronts and Middle-Latitude Storms | 71

Office. There is a fall of pressure with the first storm as it approached the coast on Thursday and then a more rapid fall with the Columbus Day storm on Friday. Strong southerly winds at Portland began with the rapid rise in pressure between 5:30 and 6:00 PM with the Columbus Day storm. Normal storms can also display this characteristic of occurring in pairs, and sometimes as many as three or four, one right after the other.

There is one other difference in the two types of storms, and that is the temperature after the low center has moved north-northeast along the coast. Both storms develop over the Pacific Ocean because of contrasting air masses. However, after the passage of the occlusion or cold front associated with normal wind storms, there will usually be a drop in the freezing level and rise in surface air pressure due to the advection of colder air aloft into the Pacific Northwest. The abrupt pressure rise associated with Columbus Day storms is not directly related to the advection of colder air, but due to the movement of the low-pressure area north. Often, with Columbus Day variety storms, there will be a rise in temperature at the surface associated with the strong southerly winds and rising air pressure, indicative of a warm occlusion. This warming will only be temporary, however, as cooler air from the associated trough of low pressure aloft moves onshore and the freezing level lowers.

On a personal note, I was working at the Weather Bureau Office on N.E. Marine Drive the night of the Columbus Day storm. At this particular location, very strong east winds preceded the storm, blowing out of the Columbia River Gorge. As the center of the intense low moved north just off the coast, the winds shifted quickly to the south, increased in velocity, and the pressure started to rise. With the power gone and only flashlights to guide us, my observing partner and I stumbled out to the instrument shelter to check the readings. It felt warm. What our instruments showed us was far and above what we had expected. The temperature had shown a marked increase.

Note again the differences in the two storms. With normal Pacific Northwest storms, the strongest winds occur out ahead of the storm with falling barometric pressure. With Columbus Day-type storms, the strongest winds occur behind the storm in an area of rising pressure. Normal wind storms are usually associated with a colder air mass immediately following the front. With Columbus Day variety storms the surface temperature will often rise with the passage of a warm occlusion only to fall later as cooler air aloft is advected onshore with the upper level trough of low pressure.

Of supreme importance to the occurrence of strong winds in the Pacific Northwest is where the center of low pressure crosses the coastline and where the low pressure reaches its maximum intensity. A storm center can move onshore near the mouth of the Columbia River, passing west to east, bringing strong winds to Oregon, but only

light winds to Washington. Such was the case on January 9, 1880. This storm produced the lowest pressure reading ever recorded at Portland, 28.556 inches of mercury or 967.2 millibars. Also, the lowest pressure reading ever recorded in Oregon occurred with this storm at Astoria. Here, the mercury lowered to 963 millibars or 28.45 inches of mercury. Strong, damaging winds were reported throughout Oregon but mostly light winds over much of Washington, and heavy snows in the Evergreen State. The track of the storm, or perhaps two storms that merged (Figure 6.19), brought it onshore in proximity to Astoria and then east just north of the Columbia River into southeast Washington where northeast winds shifted abruptly to southerly and then shifted back to northeast. Snow even preceded the storm at Astoria.

Columbus Day-type storms, although favoring the fall months, are certainly not confined to that season of the year. Several destructive storms have developed in a trough of low pressure aloft off the coast and moved rapidly north-northeast. A recent example is the January 16, 2000 storm. Other destructive storms have occurred, even in the summer. One such storm, which killed several fishermen, occurred off the Northern California and Southern Oregon coast in August 1972. This storm developed in a long wave trough just off the coast and intensified as it moved rapidly north. Wind gusts of over 75 miles per hour were recorded, which are very strong for the Pacific Northwest in August.

Most Pacific Northwest wind storms fall into one of the two above categories. There are some, however, that may

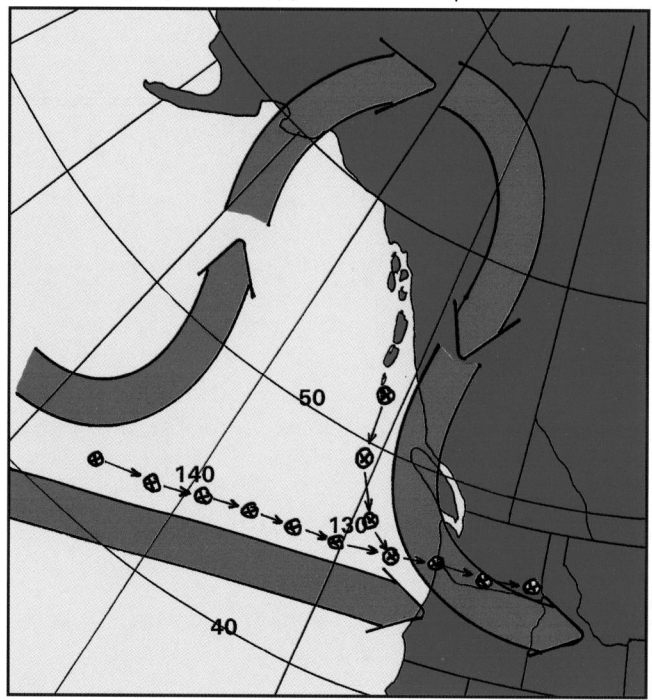

Figure 6.19 The author's suggested weather pattern for the period around January 9, 1880 showing location of jet stream (red) and track(s) of surface low-pressure areas.

approach from a more southwesterly direction and possess characteristics of both. These storms often have strong southeasterly winds ahead of them at a coastal location where the barometer is falling. As the storm center moves northeast and inland into western Washington, the strong southeasterly winds can shift to strong southerly or southwesterly with a rising barometer. This type of storm lies in that gray zone between the normal storms and the Columbus Day-type storms. They are more prevalent in late winter and early spring. Figure 6.20 is an example of such a storm. This type of storm, if entering western Washington and moving northeast, will sometimes show intensification in the Puget Sound area to the lee of the Olympic Mountains. This intensification has resulted in very strong, damaging winds in the Puget Sound area. If the low center moves onshore along the Oregon Coast and thence northeastward into eastern Washington, only light winds will occur in western Washington, but strong southerly winds in Oregon. Two examples are the March 27, 1963 storm and more recently the February 7, 2002 storm.

It is not unusual to find Pacific storms with a central pressure equal to the Columbus Day-type across the Pacific and Atlantic oceans at various times during the colder months of the year. These storms, however, are far removed from land. Thus, it is not entirely the strength of the storm but its proximity to a location, and in the case of the Pacific Northwest, the coastline. Even the normal storms can attain intensities and associated wind speeds that are near the Columbus Day-type storms. Usually, the closer one is to the center of the storm, the greater the wind speed. Other factors such as the Venturi effect can contribute to strong winds as well as instability in the atmosphere that transports strong winds aloft down to the surface. This is often the case east of the Cascade Mountains, especially in the higher desert country of eastern Oregon.

In summary, wind storms that affect the Pacific Northwest for the most part can be categorized into two types: those that approach from a westerly direction, and those that approach from a more southerly direction. Structure-wise they look the same, with divergence aloft and convergence at the surface ahead of the storm, and convergence aloft and divergence near the surface behind the storms. Strongest winds associated with these storms occur at different times with the passage of each. Strong wind storms can occur any month of the year, but favor those seasons of the year when temperature contrasts are the greatest. For Columbus Day-type storms this is predominately the fall and early winter season.

The discussion so far has focused on wind. Pacific Northwest storms, like storms everywhere, bring a combination of wind and rain. If the freezing level is low enough, the precipitation will fall as snow in the Cascade Mountains and higher elevations of the Coast Range Mountains. Most of the frontal characteristics mentioned earlier are displayed with the passage of each storm. However, these frontal passages are not all of the "textbook" variety. Yet their persistent occurrence is the main reason that the Pacific Northwest will struggle through extended periods of stormy weather with little, if any, sun to brighten those winter days with minimum daylight.

Often, a long-wave trough will position itself off or along the Pacific Northwest coast. The jet stream will assume an orientation like that shown in Figure 6.21. It is depicted as brown in this figure. In this case, a series of storms with their associated occlusions will travel through the long-wave trough and pass over the Pacific Northwest. The temperature contrast at the surface between these storms is minimal, since the trajectory over

Figure 6.21 A weather pattern showing a persistent long wave trough along or just off the West Coast.

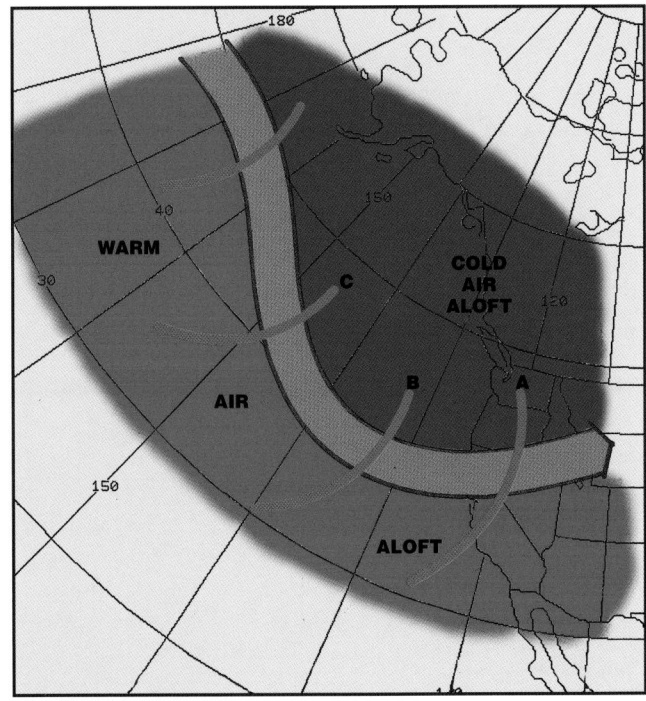

Figure 6.20 Some Pacific Northwest windstorms fall into a "gray" zone between normal and Columbus Day-type storms. In such a case, equally as strong winds can occur ahead of the storm as occur after the center passes.

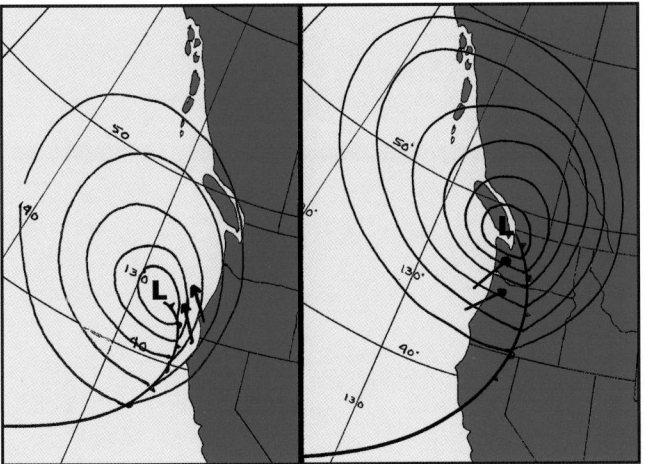

water has greatly modified the air in the lower layers making it almost homogeneous.

In Figure 6.21, Storm A is traveling through the Pacific Northwest. Storm B has reached the "bottom" of the long wave trough and will follow Storm A. Storm C is probably intensifying slightly as it approaches the bottom of the long wave trough and will follow a path similar to Storms A and B and could very well be followed by yet another storm that is moving over the "top" of the long wave ridge. While these storms are moving rapidly through the long wave trough, that feature (the long wave trough) is very likely moving slowly eastward. Such a pattern may account for an extended period of cloudy, stormy weather filled with episodes of precipitation and separated by only short clearing periods. The frequency of these storms can be every 18 to 24 hours, and they are usually drawn as occluded fronts. Additionally, there will be very little fluctuation of the freezing level between each storm. Because the temperature contrast between these storms is slight, they will generally not be intense. This weather pattern could persist for several days.

There is yet another weather pattern that favors continued storminess along the west coast of the United States. Referred to by meteorologists as a "high index" pattern, there is very little amplitude, if any at all, to the long wave features. The jet stream in this case is very strong, on the order of 150 to 200 miles an hour from a westerly direction. Storms that develop under such a jet stream move rapidly eastward toward the coast, often at speeds of 50 miles an hour. There is a marked temperature contrast north to south at both the surface and higher elevations with this pattern. East and west, however, across these storms the temperature contrast is not as great. The storms are generally moving so fast there is little time for the warm air to be advected north and the cold air to be advected south.

Figure 6.22 depicts this type of weather pattern and shows the jet stream in brown and surface isobars in thin black lines, and surface frontal systems in their appropriate colors. Note that Storm A has moved onshore and is followed closely by Storm B, which is followed by Storm C and so on. This pattern will often be around for several days and even weeks and is another cause for the miserable, cloudy, dreary, damp weather the Pacific Northwest is famous for in the winter. There is very little sunshine associated with such a weather pattern. Some breaks in the low and middle cloudiness will occur after the passage of each storm, but high-elevation cloudiness will already be increasing ahead of the next storm. Freezing levels may show slightly more fluctuation with this pattern than the earlier long wave trough, but only on the order of one or two thousand feet. The area of low pressure is elongated in the Gulf of Alaska, while the surface high pressure is flattened out to the south underneath the warm air aloft.

In both the above cases, due to the relatively long trajectory over water, the air mass next to the surface has a temperature that closely resembles the ocean temperature, or around 45-50°F in winter. The air mass is usually near saturation. Thus, a good estimate of the freezing level can be made by using an adiabatic lapse rate between the moist and the dry rates mentioned earlier, or a rate of around 3.5°F decrease per 1,000 feet. The snow level, or level at which snowflakes turn to raindrops, is usually 1,000 to 1,500 feet below the freezing level. This level varies especially if colder air at the surface from east of the Cascade Mountains is being advected through mountain passes. In both the above two cases a person can usually escape the damp, dreary weather west of the Cascade Mountains by traveling to places east of those mountains where less precipitation and more sunshine are found. But even in a strong, moist, westerly flow, some cloudiness and precipitation will persist east of the Cascade Mountains, especially on the west-facing slopes of mountain ranges in eastern Washington and eastern Oregon.

We know that the above weather patterns can persist for long periods of time, but what finally causes them to dissipate or change? If the long wave trough is migratory, it could continue its slow movement eastward into the middle of the country taking its cold, cloudy, stormy weather with it and leaving a long wave ridge in its place. Very often the change is the result of changes in the weather pattern occurring half-way around the globe that are responsible for changes locally. Weather is very seldom normal, but fluctuates between wet and dry, cold and warm. Perhaps, also, Mother Nature just gets tired of all the moaning, groaning, and complaining we do and decides it's time for a change! And I suspect this is a good time for a change, or at least a break in this long wave regime!

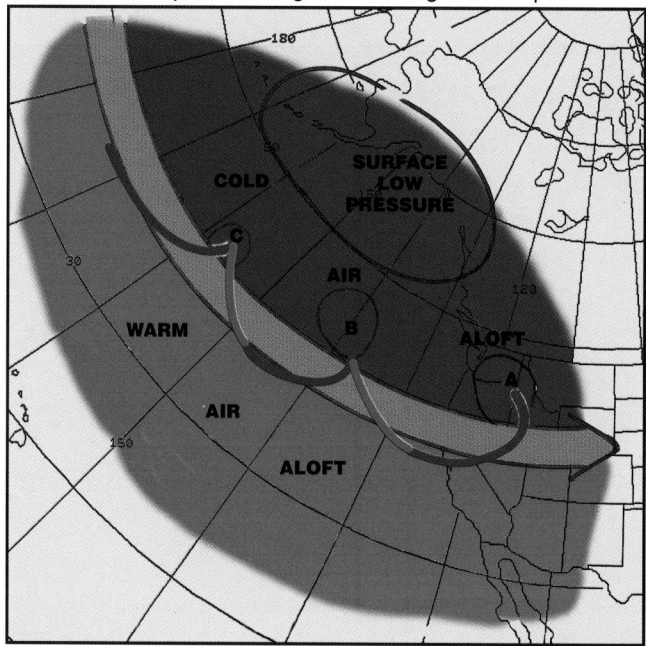

Figure 6.22 A persistent weather regime with a strong west-to-east jet stream across the Pacific Ocean. It is referred to by meteorologists as a "high index" pattern.

Chapter 7
Pacific Northwest Snowstorms and Hot Spells

The two quotations refer to an invasion of cold arctic air into the Pacific Northwest. Generally these invasions only last for a few days, west of the Cascade Mountains, as the prevailing westerly flow from the Pacific Ocean returns. East of the Cascade Mountains their presence is more frequent and often lasts longer. But there have been episodes when the arctic air has persisted over most of the Pacific Northwest for weeks

Heavy Snow in Western Oregon
The past week closed with one foot of snow generally on the level country and from one and one-half to two feet, on the higher grounds, with an 'upward tendency.'
     Statesman, Salem, Oregon, February 27, 1862

Corps of Discovery, Fort Clatsop, January 1806
Jan. 25. It is now perceptibly colder than it has been this winter. Jan 26. The snow this evening is 4 1/2 inches deep; the icicles continue suspended from the eaves of the houses during the day; it now appears something like winter, for the first time this season. Jan. 27. The sun shown more brightly this morning than it has done since our arrival at this place; The snow since 4 p.m yesterday has increased to the depth of 6 inches, and this morning is perceptibly colder than we have had. I suspect the mercury would stand at 20° above zero; the breath is perceptible in our room by the fire..
    The History of the Lewis & Clark Expedition, Volume III
                edited by Elliot Coues

and even months. Such was the case with the two observations, when Salem residents remarked of "six weeks of good sledding" in January and February 1862, and the Corps of Discovery experienced a full two weeks of cold weather at their camp near present-day Astoria, Oregon.

However, snowstorms are not your normal, everyday occurrence west of the Cascade Mountains in Washington and Oregon during the winter. East of the Cascade Mountains, snow occurs more frequently. Many winters, have passed, however, without any snow on the west side of these mountains in Oregon and Washington at low elevations. Why is this so? Washington and Oregon are located at the same latitude as the Dakotas and Minnesota. Yet snowfall and cold temperatures occur with regularity in those areas of the country. Also, those areas get far colder temperatures in winter as cold arctic air roars down from northern latitudes.

Three geographical features prevent lowlands in western Oregon and western Washington from frequent heavy snows and invasions of cold arctic (polar) air. Those three features are the Rocky Mountains, the Cascade Mountains, and the Pacific Ocean. Take those away and Oregon and

Washington would experience much colder temperatures. But before we get too deeply into this snowdrift, we should define what we mean by a snowstorm or what is a significant or substantial fall of snow.

This can vary. A snowfall of one or two inches at rush hour can disrupt traffic considerably in the Portland, Seattle, or even the Spokane or Eugene metropolitan areas, and snow advisories are issued. At night or in the middle of the day, in rural areas, or certainly in areas east of the Cascade Mountains, the problem of snowfall is not as great as it is in the city. A substantial fall of snow that warrants a winter storm warning is four inches or more for low elevations west of the Cascade Mountains in 12 hours and six

Friday, January 13, 1950 "Blizzard" in Southwest Washington
It was January 13, 1950. I was in the 7th grade at Kelso Junior High School in Kelso, Washington. We had been dismissed early because of the snow and the buses came to pick us up. We lived five miles out of town and the bus had some difficulty getting to where we lived. Actually, it did not get that far since a moderate hill which the bus could not navigate separated the bus from our home about one-quarter mile distant. The driver let us off and cautioned us to be careful.
There was a younger girl who lived close by and she, too, left the bus. I remember the two of us trekking through snow that was at least knee deep and often up to our waists on that short journey home with the snow still swirling around us. The girl found her way home and I proceeded to my home, to my mother who was anxiously waiting. That evening I remember the wind had ceased and the snowflakes were softly falling as we sawed wood to add to the warm fire. The snow was piled to two feet.
                    The Author

inches in 24 hours. These are National Weather Service criteria and the criteria may vary in each area. There have been times, however, when four to six inches have been greatly exceeded.

On January 13, 1950, substantial snow fell in northwest Oregon and southwest Washington. In many locations the snow accumulation was 10 to 20 inches in 24 hours. Strong northeasterly winds pushed the snow into deep drifts and halted traffic on most major highways from northern Oregon through western Washington into the Puget Sound area. But how did the Pacific Northwest get into this situation? What arrangement of the surface isobars and the upper wind flow came together to produce a foot of snow in the above areas?

Snowfall West of the Cascade Mountains

For snow to occur in the valleys west of the Cascade Mountains, the air must be cold enough. That is, it must be near or below the freezing point. But where does this cold air come from? It should be of continental origin, from northern latitudes; the same place from which those areas east of the Rocky Mountains receive their cold air. More specifically, it is a continental polar air mass. That is, it comes from the interior of Alaska and/or the Northwest Territories of Canada. It may sit there in the far north for a number of days before it starts to move. Then, for that air to get into the Pacific Northwest, the flow of air aloft (the jet stream) must be out of the north, or north-northwest.

A typical weather pattern for cold arctic air to invade the Pacific Northwest is a ridge of high pressure at middle and high levels of the atmosphere (10,000 to 30,000 feet) in the Gulf of Alaska. (Figure 7.1) Here the warm air associated with the ridge pushes north, creating a north-north-westerly flow of air aloft from out of the interior of Alaska down along the British Columbia coast into Washington and Oregon. If there is a cold air mass lurking over Alaska or the Northwest Territories, it will move south assisted by the northerly flow of air aloft. The orientation of this flow aloft is critical. If the ridge axis is near the coast, cold air will plunge south into the United States east of the Rocky Mountains. If this axis is farther west the trajectory of the air is over too much ocean. If the trajectory is more north-westerly, Montana, the Dakotas, and Wyoming will get the brunt of the cold air and the Pacific Northwest will be spared since most of the cold air in this case would flow south, east of the Rocky Mountains. Figure 7.2 shows an arctic high-pressure area poised to move south into the Pacific Northwest. If Figure 7.1 (the upper wind flow) is

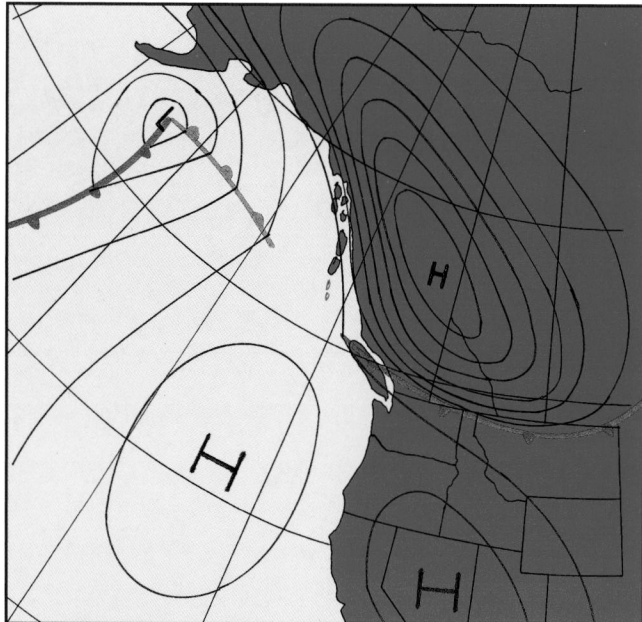

Figure 7.2 An arctic air mass poised to move south into the Pacific Northwest.

superimposed on Figure 7.2 (the surface isobar pattern), the stage is set for cold arctic air to plunge south into western Washington and Oregon.

Since this air is of continental origin, its moisture content is low and it is very cold (dense) so it hugs the surface. The Rocky Mountains and the Cascade Mountains act as barriers. The cold air looks for the easiest route. That route is south through the Fraser River Valley and other valleys in British Columbia and finally, the Columbia River Gorge to western Oregon and southwest Washington. If this cold air mass is deep enough, and the flow aloft has a northerly or northeasterly component, it will cross over mountain ridges. Also, since the ridge aloft with its warmer air is far to the west, cold air aloft will usually accompany the surge of cold air at the surface. Double trouble!

The leading edge of this continental polar air mass is called the arctic front. Sometimes this front is well defined with all the characteristics associated with cold frontal passages. There will be a shift of the wind to a northerly direction, a drop in the temperature, and rapidly rising barometric pressure. The wind shift, however, can sometimes occur in a counter-clockwise direction. That is, it could shift from a southerly direction to an easterly, northeasterly, or northerly direction, especially at locations east of the Cascade Mountains, contrary to the normal Pacific cold frontal characteristics stated earlier regarding a shift in the wind. There might be a few snow flurries associated with the passage, but the air quickly clears after the front has passed as the dewpoint temperature drops rapidly, indicating much less moisture content to the air.

At other times the arctic front is very hard to locate on the weather map. The winds do shift, but gradually. The temperature drop is more subtle and the barometric pressure

Figure 7.1 An upper air pattern favorable for arctic air to invade the Pacific Northwest.

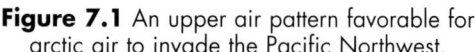
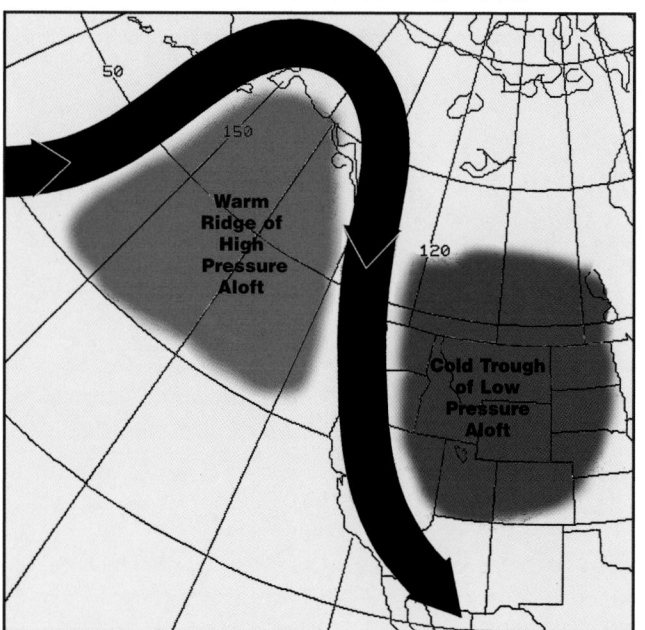

takes a slower rise, indicating that more mixing has taken place with other air along the leading edge of the air mass. In this case, one could say that the arctic air sort of seeps into the Pacific Northwest through gaps in the mountains. The strength of the arctic front is directly related to the strength of the cold air mass that is following. The colder the air mass, the more dramatic will be the change. Snowfall accumulations associated with the passage of the arctic front through Washington and Oregon are generally light. The temperature and dewpoint temperature are low. Thus, there is not much moisture available to cause snow to form. But this can change quickly.

If the front meets some resistance in displacing the warmer air and slows down, the fall of snow can be more substantial. Such was the case in Eugene, Oregon in February 1969 when up to two feet of snow fell with the passage of an arctic front. By slowing down, more warm air with a higher moisture content is allowed to rise up over the cold air.

Origin of the Word "Blizzard"

According to an article in the Weekly Record, *published at Sturgis, South Dakota, January 6, 1899, the word "blizzard" was in use at least as early as 1867. In that year the* Hutchinson County Herald *gives an account of the blizzard that suddenly approached the town of Vermillion, calling it by that name as one in common use when applied to a sudden change from warm and balmy weather to a blinding snow with cold northwest winds.*

The old settlers of South Dakota take exception to the statement that the word 'blizzard' originated with a Chicago newspaper, The Advance, *on the 8th of January 1880. Previously, however, in the fifties and sixties, a Dakota blizzard was called "pouderie" among French settlers, meaning powder mill—the force of which will be appreciated by anyone who has had a blizzard burst upon them.*

Monthly Weather Review, December 1898 and August 1930

Usually, however, the arctic front keeps moving south due to the northerly flow of air aloft. Most of the high pressure settles in east of the Cascade Mountains and that is when the east wind (Coho Wind) out of the Columbia River Gorge begins to "chill Portlanders to the bone." Or, if you are located near the border of Washington and Canada where the Fraser River flows into the upper Puget Sound area, such as Bellingham, Washington, you will feel the effects of this arctic air.

Once the area is covered with cold arctic air, almost anything can happen. The average time a continental polar air mass remains over the Pacific Northwest is around 4 to 6 days. Sometimes its stay here is less, and sometimes it is more. Lewis and Clark recorded in their journals a cold period, (meteorologists today call them "arctic outbreaks") that started around January 25, 1806 and continued into the first week of February 1806 while the Corps of Discovery was camped at the mouth of the Columbia River near Astoria, Oregon. Other

historical references during the brutal winter of 1861-62 indicated the arctic outbreak began around Christmas in 1861 and lasted through February 1862 west of the Cascade Mountains. More recently, during the winter of 1949-50 it arrived around mid December 1949. Except for a few cases when it warmed up slightly, it remained until early February 1950.

Since a heavy snowfall west of the Cascade Mountains with the passage of an arctic front is uncommon, there must be other conditions or weather patterns for heavy snow to occur. Basically, the weather map shown in Figure 7.3 is the final product. But what sequence of events leads up to conditions like those shown in Figure 7.3?

There are two distinct weather patterns and several combinations of both that can bring snow to valleys west of the Cascade Mountains. Perhaps the one most looked for by meteorologists in the Pacific Northwest is that pattern referred to in Figure 7.1. Air flow aloft into the Pacific Northwest is out of the north-northwest as a long-wave ridge of high pressure is positioned throughout the Gulf of Alaska. A weak short wave trough of low pressure aloft moves over the "top" of this long wave ridge, or through Alaska, and begins heading south-southeastward toward Washington and Oregon. At the surface, a weak low-pressure area begins forming in the northeastern Gulf of Alaska, slightly ahead of the trough aloft. The tandem of convergence at the surface and divergence aloft draws the low south-southeastward, all the while intensifying it. Figure 7.4 is a schematic of conditions at the surface and aloft midway through the process. These surface low-pressure areas now are afforded numerous options, and forecasters sometimes pull out their hair wondering which option or path the low will take.

Figure 7.3 Position of low-pressure center at surface and location of arctic air for potential heavy snow in northwest Oregon, western Washington and east of the Cascade Mountains.

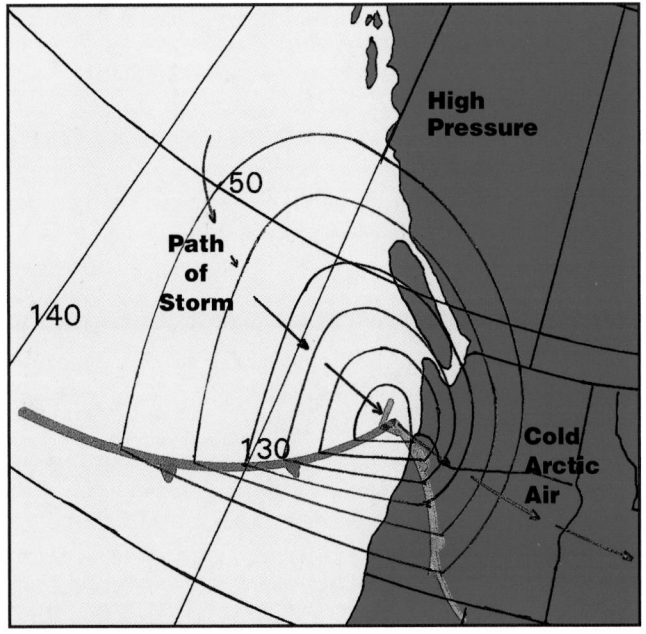

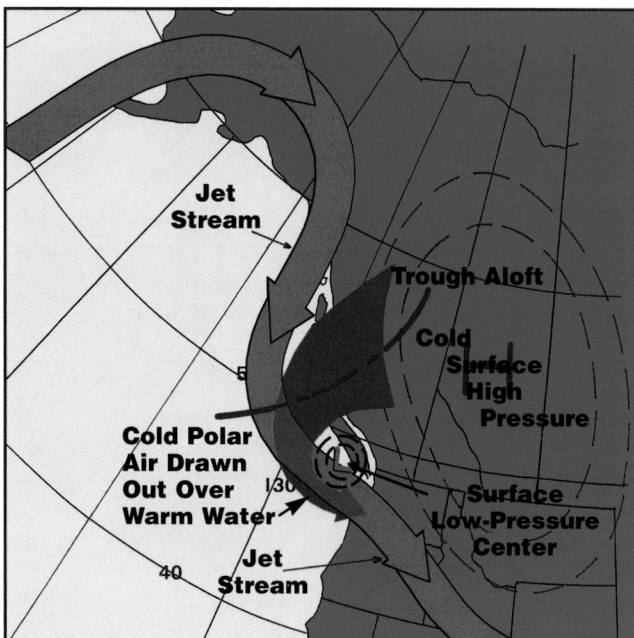

Figure 7.4 Location of upper short wave trough and surface low-pressure center and high-pressure center favorable for heavy snow at low elevations west of the Cascade Mountains.

If the low center slows down and intensifies, cold arctic air is drawn out of the interior of British Columbia around the low. In doing so, it comes in contact with the warmer Pacific Ocean. This modifies the cold arctic air by causing an increase in its temperature. Warmer air has a greater ability to contain moisture. Thus, the arctic air circulating out of British Columbia around the center of the low pressure area in the vicinity of Vancouver Island arrives at the coasts of Washington and Oregon warmer, but with more moisture. It is called a modified continental polar air mass, the modifications coming from increasing its temperature and adding moisture.

The track of the center of low pressure is now very critical. If it moves southeast across Washington, the air does not have an opportunity to pass over much water. Thus, its moisture content does not increase by very much. If it continues moving south along the coast, the fall of snow will be along the coast with only scant amounts inland. If it moves more south-southeasterly across Oregon, most of the snow will fall over the interior of western Oregon and Washington. If the center of low pressure is too far offshore, the trajectory around the storm will allow the air to increase its temperature to above the freezing point or around 40°F, since its stay over water is longer. In this case the result is usually a substantial fall of snow above about 1000 feet and a very cold rain at lower elevations in the valleys west of the Cascade Mountains.

This type of weather pattern probably results in more forecasts of snow that do not materialize, or that occur in areas other than where it was forecast, than any other type of pattern. There have been times when several inches of snow were forecast for the interior of western Oregon and did not occur. But as the low moved south along the coast,

Tillamook, Newport, and other coastal locations in Oregon were shoveling three to six inches of "rain, occasionally mixed with snow." Depending on the track of the surface low-pressure area, scant amounts can fall in the Portland area while Salem and Eugene farther south receive from three to six inches. The Seattle area has its own particular problem due to its proximity to Puget Sound and wind flow that often converges around terrain features in the area. Thus, snowfall amounts can vary considerably in western Washington as well as western Oregon.

Snow does not always arrive, however, from a low-pressure area and a high-pressure area that are moving down from northern latitudes. There is another weather pattern that brings snow to the areas west of the Cascade Mountains. In this case, cold arctic air is well entrenched over the Pacific Northwest. Radiosonde observations reveal that the entire atmosphere from the surface upward is below freezing over a large portion of the Pacific Northwest except, perhaps, the southwest corner of Oregon near the coast. East winds are blowing out of the Columbia River Gorge and the Fraser River. Mittens, wool scarfs, Long Johns, and winter boots have been removed from the depths of the closet. The furnace just does not want to keep the house warm. The temperature outside is 25 to 30 degrees but it "feels like" it is zero because of the wind chill. This time, however, instead of arriving from the north, the low center arrives from the west.

Occasionally, the advance of warm air north into the Gulf of Alaska that forms the long-wave ridge of high pressure aloft is so strong and so far north that the southern portion of it weakens and allows the westerlies, or jet stream, to penetrate "underneath" the ridge of high pressure. A split in the jet stream occurs somewhere over the central Pacific Ocean. This is not unlike that army whose forces advanced too far into enemy territory and then found itself cut off from its supplies. The ridge becomes cut off from its supply of warm air or the antithesis of the cut-off low mentioned earlier.

As the westerlies (jet stream) advance toward the coast, they bring with them an area of low pressure at the surface (Figure 7.5). Where this storm moves inland is again very critical regarding the location of the heaviest fall of snow. If the low center crosses the coastline near the California-Oregon border and advances east, there will be a substantial snowfall in areas both west and east of the Cascade Mountains, decreasing the farther north a location is from the track or path of the low-pressure center. If the movement of the low is eastward through northern California, then southern Oregon will receive the precipitation and the northern portion of western Oregon will only receive high and middle cloudiness and very little precipitation.

Should the low-pressure center move inland farther north, the zone of heavy precipitation will also shift north. When the track of the low-pressure center on January 13, 1950 is examined, it follows more closely this weather pattern as well as the January 9, 1880 storm. In central and southern portions of western Oregon these storms produced

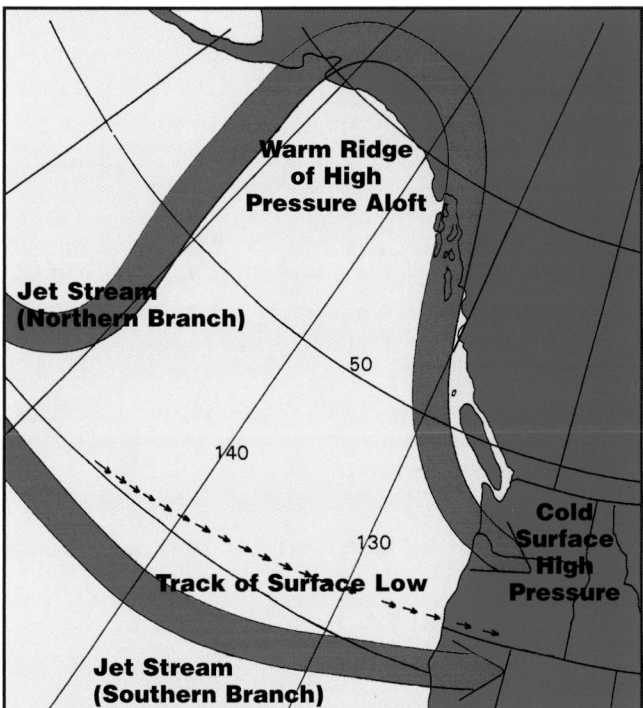

Figure 7.5 Location of surface and upper air features associated with heavy snow when arctic air is over the Pacific Northwest and storm arrives from the west.

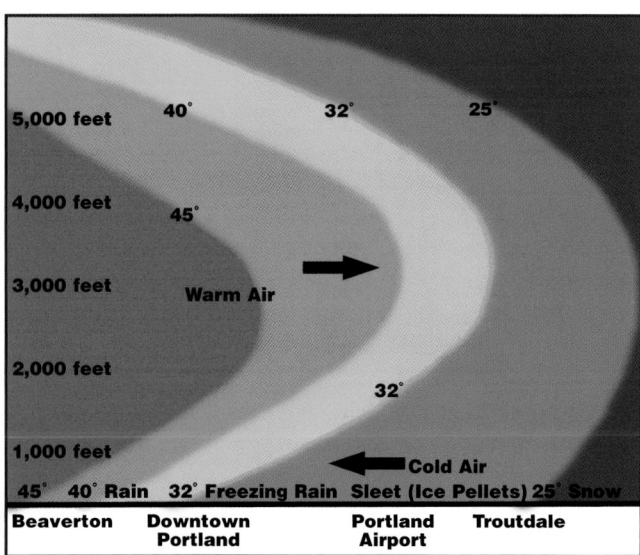

Figure 7.6 A typical cross-section through the Portland, Oregon metropolitan area during the "breaking up" of a cold spell.

rain while areas farther north in the northern portions of western Washington received only light amounts of snow. A warm front separated rain at Eugene, Oregon from heavy snow in Portland on January 13, 1950. Heavy snow also fell north into the Seattle, Washington area. The track of this low-pressure center would eventually take it east-southeastward across Oregon while the January 9, 1880 storm moved east along the Washington-Oregon border.

The "breaking up" of a cold spell can often bring a substantial snowfall to western valleys. Keep in mind that warm air rises and cold air sinks. Over a period of time, the flow of air aloft over the Pacific Northwest shifts from a northerly to a northwesterly to a westerly to a southwesterly direction as the ridge of high pressure aloft, 700 millibars or higher, moves over and then east of the area. This southwesterly flow of air is warm and it begins to ride up over the dome of cold air that has hung around and plagued the region for several days. Often as this sequence of events is progressing the low pressure center may never move inland but stall along the coast of Washington and Oregon or move very slowly north along the coast and end up in the vicinity of Vancouver Island. It is this type of movement of the low-pressure center that results in severe ice storms in the valleys west of the Cascade Mountains, especially the Portland metropolitan area. Here the freezing rain can last for more than 24 hours as cold air filters out of the Columbia River Gorge from east of the Cascade Mountains.

What happens when air is forced aloft? It cools, reaches the dewpoint (condenses), and clouds and precipitation form. The precipitation usually begins as snow since the depth of cold air is several thousand feet. Figure 7.6 shows a cross-sec-

tion of the Portland area during the "break-up" of a cold spell. Troutdale at the mouth of the Columbia River Gorge is receiving snow. The entire air mass above this city is below freezing. The precipitation starts out as snow high above the city. The Portland Airport, with a temperature below freezing, is receiving sleet or ice pellets. High above the airport, the precipitation is likely starting out as snow and melting as it falls down through a layer of air above freezing, but then freezing as it falls through the layer of air next to the surface that is below freezing. In portions of downtown Portland the layer of below freezing temperatures is very shallow and of insufficient depth for the raindrops to freeze before they strike the surface. Thus, when these raindrops strike a cold surface that is below freezing (highways, cars, trees, streets, etc.), they freeze. Hence the term freezing rain. Beaverton, away from the influence of the cold air flowing out of the Columbia River Gorge, is having plain old warm rain.

This cross-section is not unique to the Portland area. It can be shifted north or south with different towns, usually in a north-south line, rather than an east-west line as Figure 7.6 shows. The figure can even be moved to areas east of the Cascade Mountains using towns in the Columbia Basin as examples. The figure also depicts the transition as a sharp line. In reality, that is not the case at and above the surface. Rain and snow falling through the air, mixing and turbulence all stir up the atmosphere making the transition diffuse. It is not uncommon for freezing rain, ice pellets and snow to be occurring at the same time at one location.

This transition during the breaking up of a cold spell can last for a few hours, sometimes half a day, sometimes longer than 24 hours. Since the southwesterly flow of air aloft is usually bringing in an area of low pressure at the surface from the Pacific Ocean, the pressure gradient of high pressure east of the Cascade Mountains to a low-pressure area off the coast is maintained. This continues to supply cold air from east of the mountains. Only when the pressure east of the Cascade Mountains lowers does the cross-section above dissipate. This type of weather pattern generates the forecast in the Portland area of: "Rain at times today, except freezing rain near the mouth of the Columbia River Gorge." It sometimes takes days to "scour out" all the cold air east of the Cascade Mountains. Figure 7.7 shows the destruction caused by an ice storm in Portland, Oregon.

At locations farther south of Portland in the Willamette Valley, and to the north of Portland into Puget Sound, and along the coasts of Washington and Oregon, the transition is usually quicker. But even in these areas, severe ice storms (Silver Thaws) have occurred. In these areas since the supply of cold air is not replenished by cold air flowing out of the Columbia River Gorge, warming is generally quicker. Some of the warmer air aloft will be pulled down to the surface by the rain that is falling. Turbulence in the atmosphere also results in mixing. An additional supply of heat is added as water vapor sublimes to form snowflakes.

Snowfall East of the Cascade Mountains

East of the Cascade Mountains, conditions are different from on the west side, and snow occurs regularly during the winter months, November through March, and often at times into April. Here, the area is not influenced as much as western Oregon and Washington by storms moving in off the Pacific Ocean. The Cascade Mountains act as a barrier. East of these mountains the terrain is generally higher and there is less cloudiness and less moisture. Because of this, there is more longwave radiation escaping from the earth allowing the air to become cooler than the air west of the Cascade Mountains during those colder winter months. The temperature is normally below the freezing point throughout most of the atmosphere from the surface to higher elevations.

Much of the precipitation east of the Cascade Mountains from November through March falls as snow.

There are times, however, when warm southerly winds bring air with temperatures in the 40s and even low 50s. In these cases, the precipitation falls as rain rather than snow. Normally, there will not be as much precipitation compared to stations west of the Cascade Mountains. That is because, for the most part, the air is generally colder and its ability to hold moisture is reduced. Yet, snow is not unusual at places such as Bend, Burns, Lakeview or Pendleton in Oregon and Yakima, Spokane, or Wenatchee in Washington, when a storm system moves through the area. There are times when heavy snowstorms do occur east of the Cascade Mountains, and these generally occur in the fall and spring, when the air temperature is only slightly below freezing. Such a snowstorm is shown in Figure 7.8 which occurred in Lakeview, Oregon, many years ago.

East of the Cascade Mountains, because of the variance in terrain, a snowfall of three to four inches, or more, can occur in relatively small areas and often where the low level winds are favorable for upslope conditions. Thus, a low-pressure area moving east along the border between California and Oregon would be in a favorable location to cause substantial snowfall in the area around Klamath Falls, Oregon, and locations to the north. Because Lakeview, Oregon is located just to the west of the Warner Mountains, downslope winds may decrease the amount of snow that falls in this area as the low-pressure center moves east, south of the area.

Similar occurrences happen just east of the Cascade Mountains in Washington with a low-pressure center that may move east across central Oregon or along the border between Oregon and Washington. In this case, low-level winds would be easterly. On January 13, 1950, Yakima and Kennewick, Washington received five to seven inches of snow while Wenatchee, farther north, received less than an inch. Often, locations east of the Cascade Mountains in Washington will get a substantial fall of snow due to cold air already over the area and southwesterly winds aloft bringing in warmer,

Figure 7.7 The ice storm or freezing rain on February 2, 1916 in Portland, Oregon broke power lines and tree limbs. Oregon Historical Society neg., #cn0325 8 010

Figure 7.8 Heavy snow can fall east of the Cascade Mountains as is shown in this attempt to shovel out a snowbound train near Lakeview, Oregon. Oregon Historical Society neg., #cn022030

more moist air. Yakima, Wenatchee, and the Tri-Cities areas are prime locations for this occurrence.

There are many possibilities for a substantial snow event at low elevations in the Pacific Northwest. These events are highly dependent on the track of the low-pressure center involved, the moisture content of the air, the exact location, and the extent of the cold air. At any location or valley where cold air is trapped near the surface and is of sufficient depth, precipitation that begins to fall usually falls as snow. Often, the Columbia River Gorge receives very heavy snow because of cold air that is "trapped" or present in the Gorge that is overrun by a warmer southwesterly flow of air filled with moisture. The cold air in the Columbia River Gorge is continually replenished at lower elevations by the colder air located east of the Cascade Mountains while warmer air is moving in aloft. Bonneville Dam holds the single day total of snowfall for Oregon with 39 inches recorded on January 9, 1980.

Even in metropolitan areas, the amount of snow that falls is highly variable. The West Hills of Portland, located at elevations of around 1000 feet, can receive much more snow than the core area of the city, which is only slightly above sea level. The Seattle area also has its elevation changes that result in more snow at one location than other locations close by. Here, the Puget Sound Convergence Zone is a definite factor in where and how much snow will fall. Snow is therefore a function of elevation, temperature, and moisture content. Those elements can vary considerably over a short distance.

Heavy Snowfall in the Mountains

In the mountains, forecasting snow is a lot easier. Weather patterns that are favorable for a heavy (greater than six inches in twelve hours) fall of snow in the Cascade Mountains are similar to snow events in lowland areas. This type of pattern has a ridge of high pressure in the Gulf of Alaska, but the wind flow can assume a slightly longer trajectory over water before entering the Pacific Northwest. (Figure 7.9)

There are subtle differences to this pattern as opposed to the pattern favorable for heavy snow at low elevations west of the Cascade Mountains. The ridge of high pressure does not extend as far north into Alaska. The trough of low pressure in the upper atmosphere (often a long wave trough) is just off or along the coast and moving east very slowly. There is a surface high-pressure area underneath the upper ridge aloft in the Gulf of Alaska and an area of surface low pressure over southwest British Columbia. Thus, the wind flow throughout most of the atmosphere into the Pacific Northwest is perpendicular to the north-south mountain range, and copious amounts of precipitation are deposited as snow at elevations above 2,000 feet and often down to 500 to 1,000 feet if the air is cold enough. One to two feet of snow in 24 hours can occur in the Cascade Mountains if the trough of low pressure remains stationary and the trajectory over water is of sufficient duration to saturate the lower layers. This is the type of weather pattern

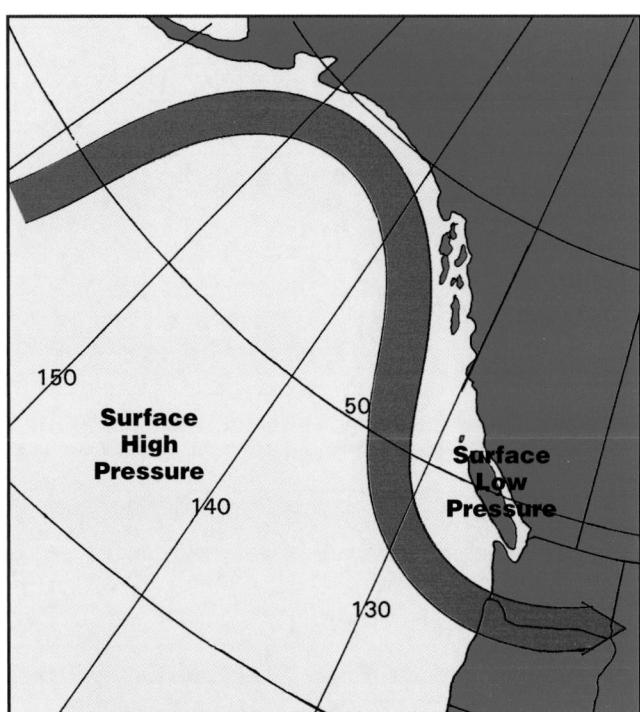

Figure 7.9 The location of jet stream (red) and surface features favorable for heavy snow in the mountains of Washington and Oregon.

that can result in high avalanche hazards. One case in particular was the Wellington disaster early in the morning on March 1, 1910 in the Northern Cascade Mountains of Washington. During the latter part of February 1910, heavy snow continued for several days in the mountains that eventually turned to rain. Avalanches swept two trains, three large locomotives, some electrical motors, a train depot, and a water tank off a ledge and into a canyon 150 feet below. Over 85 people lost their lives. February is often a favorable month for this weather regime to occur.

Lastly, before the subject of snowstorms "melts away," due to warm southwesterly winds, mention is made of the ratio of liquid precipitation to inches of snow. If two feet of snow falls in the mountains, how much liquid precipitation is that? An average figure is a ratio of 10 to 1. That is, for every 0.10 inch of precipitation, there would be a one-inch fall of snow, or one inch of liquid precipitation the equivalent of 10 inches of snow. This ratio can vary considerably with the water content of the snow. For heavy snow with a high water content, one inch of liquid precipitation may only produce five inches of snow since the heavy, wet snow will pack down. For snow that has a low moisture content, the ratio could be as great as 20 to 1 indicating one inch of precipitation would produce 20 inches of snow. The former is the "Cascade concrete" that skiers facetiously refer to and the latter is the light, fluffy, powdery snow that occurs mostly in the areas east of the Cascade Mountains where the moisture content is greatly reduced due to the lower temperature. For this type of snow to occur in the Cascade Mountains, temperatures need to be around 20°F or lower.

In this portion of Chapter 7 we have discussed the various weather patterns that are favorable for causing snow to fall at both low and high elevations in the Pacific Northwest. A few of the major events have been mentioned.

The Snow Spririt

I come from the bosom of yon white cloud
That curtains the saphire sky,
While the winds of the winter, shrill and loud,
Make tunes as they whistle by.
In manifold mediums, writ and unwrit,
God's gospels are given to man,
That all with good heart may perform their part
In our Father's perfect plan.

My beautiful, fast-falling fleecy flakes,
Spread softly my mantle down;
With their delicate aid the Young Spring makes
The garlands that form her crown;
For the harvest fields, and the wood's green growth,
The brooks in the summer's hot glow,
The bright blushing blooms with their sweet perfumes
Are part of my precious snow.

Up there in the far cloud-land is my home,
In brilliant beauty arrayed!
Exquisitely fashioned—its dazzling dome
With sunbeams richly inlaid—
Its columns cloudlets of opaline tint—
Its walls are the ambient air—
Its floor is embossed with fret-work of frost
In rain-bow radiance rare.

Peaceful and noiseless I visit the world,
And cover its drear, bare breast,
With raiment pure as innocence impearled
In smiles of an infant's rest.
I come as a type of that better life,
Where all is perfect and fair,
Which those of the earth in a second birth
In eternal joy shall share.

GMO. L. CURRY
Portland, Oregon, Nov. 26, 1871

There are many others. An arctic outbreak of cold air in December 1879 left most of the Pacific Northwest in a great chill. As conditions in Oregon warmed up prior to the great windstorm of January 9, 1880, most of the snow in Oregon melted. However, in Washington it remained. Snowfall depths were reported to be several inches in the Kalama, Washington area, increasing to two to three feet from Tenino to Winlock. From Tenino north to Tacoma snow depths of three to five feet were reported, and trains were delayed in arriving from northern locations to Portland. Thus, the orientation and track of low-pressure areas and

cold arctic air masses will cause variations in these patterns that will bring heavy snow to one location while another nearby receives only rain or just a few flakes of snow. Certainly not every possibility is covered, but the reader is left with some clues as to what causes significant snow events and why snowfall can be so variable over the states of Washington and Oregon.

Pacific Northwest Hot Spells

The Pacific Ocean is the Pacific Northwest's natural air conditioner. The prevailing westerly winds prevent temperatures from getting too warm, especially west of the Cascade Mountains during the late spring, summer, and early fall. East of the Cascade Mountains, warm temperatures are slightly more frequent, and the effects of the

---

Scorching Heat

"Then, when the sun was hot, God ordered a scorching east wind to blow on Jonah, and the sun beat down upon his head until he grew faint and wished to die."
Jonah 4:8, Life Application Bible

Pacific Ocean lessened. But, like the snowstorms, things sometimes get out of hand. Again, it is one of those special cases. When the flow of air is reversed, or off-shore, and accompanied by a very warm ridge of high pressure aloft in the warm months of the year, temperatures in the Pacific Northwest can rise far above normal values. But what causes this reversal of the wind flow and that ridge of high pressure?

As the sun warms the southwest portion of the United States in the spring, summer, and early fall, heating over this area is extreme. The hottest temperature ever recorded in the United States was 134°F and occurred at Death Valley, California. Remember now, that was in the shade. It is not uncommon for high temperatures in this area to average in the 115- to 125-degree range in the summer. If you have

---

August 1898, near Malheur City, Oregon

Aug 9, "Nearly 100 degrees in shade, 8 pm 82 degrees; Very hot. Hot, hotter, hottest!"; Aug 10, "Very warm these days. Mercury 100 degrees at 1 pm." Aug 11, "2 pm 100 degrees."

Mss2968 Journals of Cyrus Locey,
Oregon Historical Society Archives

---

spent time in Phoenix, Arizona in the summer, you darted from one air-conditioned building to the next to escape the outside heat.

Air that is heated rises. But air over the southwest portion of the United States and northern Mexico in the summer season is very dry with relative humidity values of less than 10 percent. Thus, the air can rise to great heights before it cools enough to form clouds. This rising of very warm air produces a warm ridge of high pressure aloft over this area. The constant pressure surfaces above 700 millibars get pushed upward due to the warm air. Figure 7.10 shows a cross-section of the atmosphere from near Los Angeles, California on the coast to Phoenix, Arizona in the interior and thence to Albuquerque, New Mexico farther inland.

At the surface, where not enough air flows in to take the place of the rising air, an area of low pressure forms. To meteorologists it is known as a "heat low" or "thermal low," meaning that the cause is intense heating of air at the surface from solar radiation. This is a different type of low-pressure area than the one discussed in the chapter on storms. It is thermally induced rather than dynamically induced. Higher in the atmosphere, a warm ridge of high pressure sits on top of the low, since we express air pressure as the weight of a column of air above a point.

This heat low extends into the central valleys of California. Anyone who has been to the San Francisco Bay area in the summer time has been chilled by the prevailing west to northwesterly winds. These winds are blowing from the area of high pressure off the coast into the prevailing low-pressure area over the southwest deserts. It is the same relationship that causes the winds to blow from a north-westerly direction along the coasts of Washington and Oregon in the summer months and even into the valleys west of the Cascade Mountains. Figure 7.11 shows the normal summer isobar pattern and positions of high- and low-pressure centers over the eastern Pacific Ocean and the western portion of the United States.

To get the normal onshore winds to reverse, lower pressure needs to be located along the coast so the wind can blow from the interior of the Pacific Northwest toward the coast. To get this reversal of the pressure gradient, one of two things, or a combination of both, needs to happen. First, the warm ridge of high pressure over the

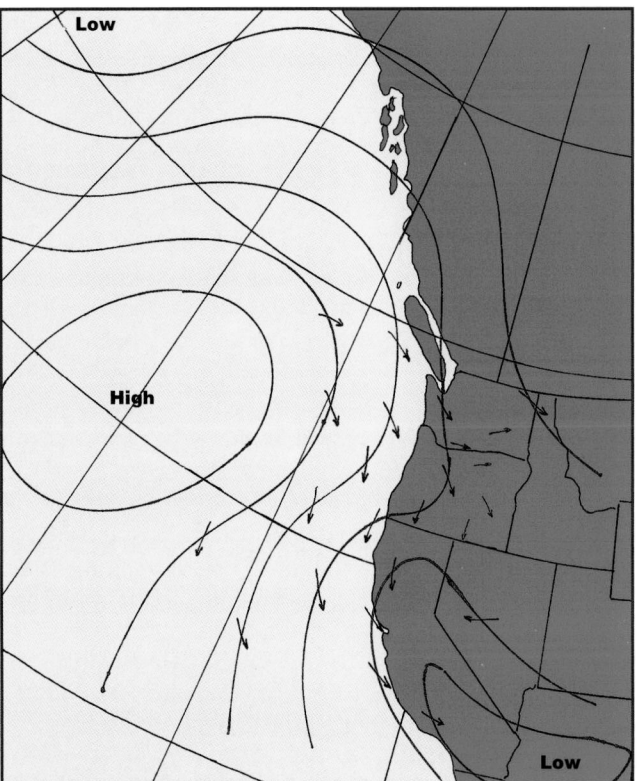

Figure 7.11 A typical weather pattern over the eastern Pacific Ocean and Pacific Northwest in the summer.

southwestern portion of the United States can retrograde, or move in a westerly direction, so it is situated along the coastlines of California, Oregon, and Washington. During the retrogression, it will also show some northward extension. When this happens, the thermal low will travel westward with and underneath the ridge of high pressure. The result is a trough of low pressure (thermal trough) along or just off the coast. Figure 7.12 shows the thermal trough

Figure 7.10 A cross-section through the summer thermal trough over the southwest United States. Solid lines are heights of constant pressure surfaces.

Figure 7.12 A thermal trough that has migrated north to lie just along the coasts of Washington and Oregon. This trough is very narrow, extending just off the coast.

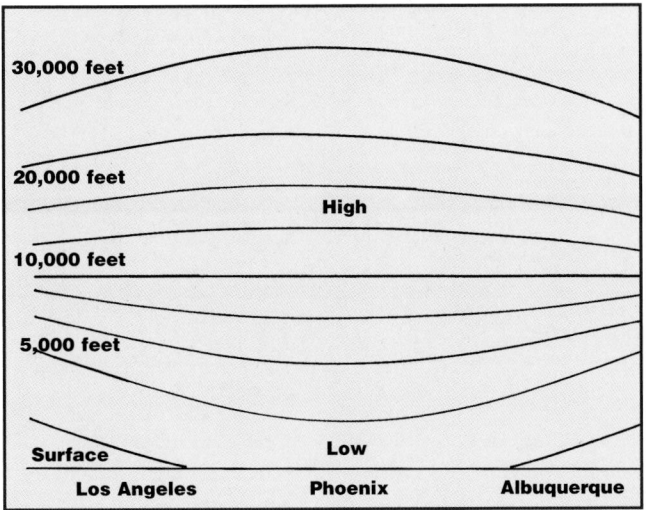

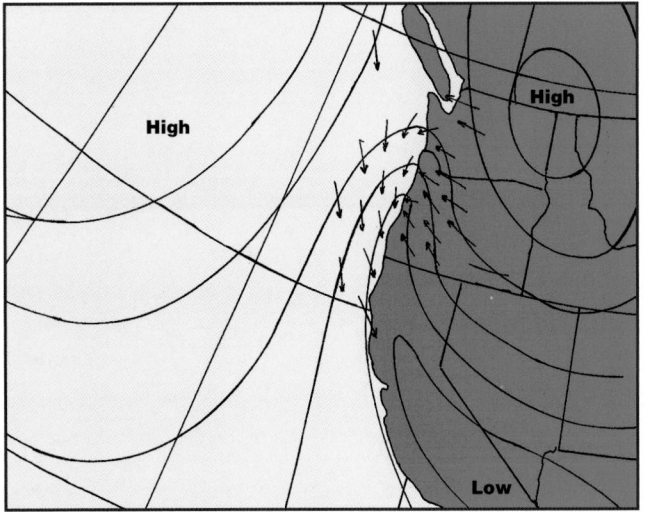

extending north along the coast. This is often referred to as an inverted trough since the apex is pointing north, rather than south.

The ridge of high pressure brings warmer air with it as it advances into the Pacific Northwest. Freezing levels are often above 15,000 feet. General subsidence, or sinking of the air mass in the ridge, continues to warm the air. The wind flow aloft over Washington and Oregon is usually light and can be from a northeasterly direction.

Another scenario can cause very warm temperatures in the Pacific Northwest. In this case a portion of the high-pressure center breaks off from the semi-permanent high-pressure area offshore. This separate high, usually following a weak upper-level trough and surface cold front, moves into British Columbia and then settles south to cover the eastern portions of Washington and Oregon, Idaho, and western Montana. In this case, the thermal trough will respond to the higher pressure east of the Cascade Mountains and expand north along the coast. Now the pressure gradient is reversed and the air flows from higher pressure east of the Cascade Mountains to lower pressure west of the Cascade Mountains, or along the coast. The sequence of events for this pattern is shown in Figure 7.13.

This weather pattern is similar to the cold east wind situation in winter. In this case, the air arriving from the east is much warmer. The trough of low pressure does not extend very far offshore and is very narrow. In most cases this is only a few miles seaward and is elongated along the coastline. The warming over the area west of the Cascade Mountains is enhanced as air flows from the higher desert regions of eastern Oregon and Washington down into the lower valleys west of the Cascade Mountains and near the coast. When dry (unsaturated) air descends, it is warmed through compression at a rate of 5.4°F for every 1,000 feet it lowers in the atmosphere.

Quite often these very warm temperatures will appear first at Brookings on the southern Oregon coast and then move north as the thermal trough expands up the coast.

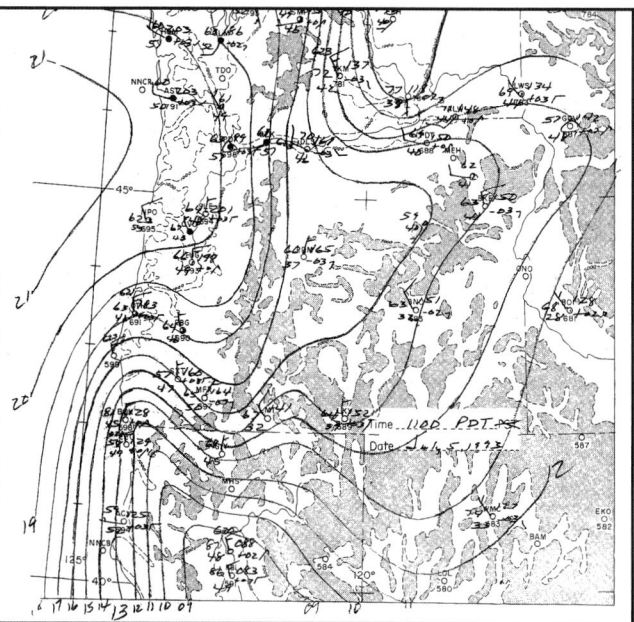

Figure 7.14 A thermal trough extending into extreme southwest Oregon.

Sometimes, however, this is as far north as the thermal trough will extend. Figure 7.14 is a reproduction of a small-scale map drawn by the author for 11 AM, PDT, July 5, 1993. The map is drawn every millibar. Note in this case that the thermal trough only extends into the far southwest corner of Oregon. The temperature at Brookings is already 81 degrees while it is in the 60s elsewhere along the coast. The absence of higher pressure over eastern Washington (not shown) is a clear indication that in this case, the thermal trough will not extend north along the coast, but gradually weaken after it has brought one or two days of very warm temperatures to the Brookings area.

However, if conditions are right and the pressure in eastern Washington is rising, the thermal trough will continue to move and expand north along the coast. Thus, the offshore flow and warm temperatures will spread to North Bend, then northward to Newport, Astoria, and even to the coastal cities of Washington. The interior valleys of western Oregon and Washington will also be quite warm with high temperature readings in the 90- to 100-degree range.

This type of pattern results in very dry, warm easterly winds through the Columbia River Gorge, through mountain passes, and across mountain ridges. It is a very dangerous pattern for forest fire control officials in summer and fall since the relative humidity can lower into the teens and in extreme cases to single-digit values. This results in very high fire danger. Indeed, winds of over 50 miles per hour from the east can occur through mountain passes and over ridges when the location of the thermal trough is just offshore or along the coast. This is especially so along the south coast of Oregon and in areas of northwest California.

Thermal troughs along the coast have been the catalyst for many disastrous forest fires in the Coast Range and

Figure 7.13 A typical sequence of events where a thermal trough moves up the coast, into western valleys, then to eastern sections.

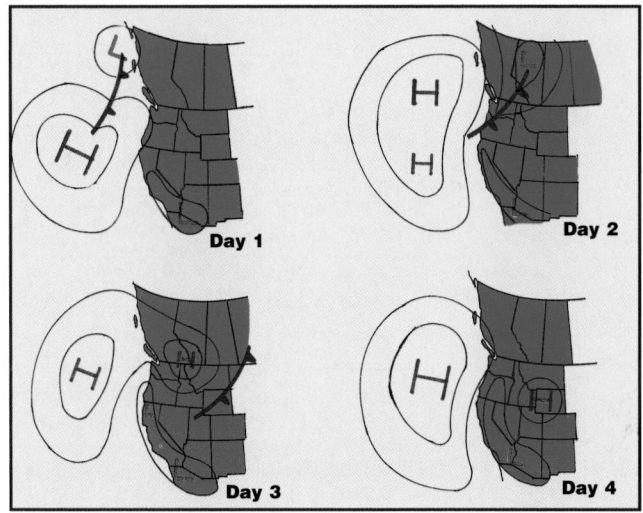

Cascade Mountains. It is this type of pattern that created conditions that sparked the Tillamook Burn fire in the Coast Range Mountains of Oregon in mid to late August 1933. In this case even the flow aloft was from a northeasterly direction causing burning embers from the intense fire to fall on vessels several hundred miles off shore in the Pacific Ocean. It is also the type of pattern responsible for the burning of most of the town of Bandon on the southern Oregon coast in late September 1936.

Offshore flow and very warm temperatures rarely last more than two days along the coast. Usually the thermal trough will move into the interior valleys which will cause an onshore flow along the coast and cooler temperatures. These onshore breezes and cooler temperatures will begin on the southern Oregon coast and then work north. It is not uncommon for Brookings, Oregon to be in the 90s and Astoria, Oregon in the 70s one day, and then have temperatures reversed the next day with 60°F readings and fog at Brookings, while people in Astoria and other locations along the northern Oregon and southwest Washington coasts are basking in 80°F and 90°F readings.

The onslaught of marine air can be quite abrupt along the coast. After a day of hot temperatures, it is not uncommon at the coast for the next day to start out clear and warm with light offshore winds and warm temperatures rising rapidly into the 80s, only to have a strong southwesterly or westerly breeze begin which lowers the temperature very quickly into the 60s accompanied by low stratus clouds and fog much like is shown in Figure 7.15. Satellite pictures vividly display the transition from clear to low clouds and fog along the coast. It is a misnomer, however, to say that the fog and low stratus clouds advect north along the coast. The rapid northward extension shown in satellite pictures indicates that these clouds and fog are forming along the coast as the pressure and wind fields reverse to an onshore component and the cooler air condenses to form the clouds and fog.

As the thermal trough moves into the interior valleys west of the Cascade Mountains and temperatures rise into the 90s and even low 100s, much cooler temperatures will be invading the coastal areas. The old saying, "When it is very hot in the valley, it will be cool along the coast" is right much more often than it is wrong. It is a good rule to follow in the summer months.

If the thermal trough stagnates over the western valleys, very warm temperatures can persist for several days. In Portland, Oregon during one very warm period from August 6-11, 1981, the mercury reached 99, 103, 107, 105, 107, and 97 degrees respectively. This would be the extreme event. The logical sequence is for the thermal trough to continue migrating eastward into the area east of the Cascade Mountains. This will bring cooler ocean air into the valleys west of the Cascade Mountains, and the 100-plus readings will then move into eastern areas of Washington and Oregon. Meteorologists refer to this change as a "marine push" since it is cooler marine air that is pushing into the valleys.

One of the first signs of this cooling or marine air pushing into the Willamette Valley of Oregon is a drop in the temperature at Eugene which is located near a gap in the Coast Range Mountains. Sometimes the cooler air will continue down the Willamette Valley toward Portland and the cooler air will arrive in the Rose City on southwesterly winds. ("Up the valley" and "down the valley" can get confusing. Persons in the northern portion of the Willamette Valley sometimes refer to "down the valley" when they talk about places like Salem, Albany, and Eugene. In reality, that is "up the valley" since it is toward higher terrain.) The air will also flow from Astoria up the Columbia River toward Portland. (We don't seem to have too much trouble with that differentiation!) In Washington, the cooler marine air will spread inland along the Columbia River, through a gap in the Coast Range Mountains east of the Hoquiam/Aberdeen area and through the Strait of Juan de Fuca. Figure 7.16 shows these major gaps and a few others. Undoubtedly there are more.

Once the thermal trough (usually the ridge of high pressure aloft with it) takes up residence east of the Cascade Mountains, the western valleys will be cooler. The hot temperatures have then spread to locations in eastern Washington and Oregon. It is this type of pattern that brought an upward swing in the mercury at Pendleton and Prineville to 119 degrees in 1898, the highest reading ever recorded in Oregon, and 118 degrees at Wahluke in 1928 and Ice Harbor Dam in 1961 in Washington, the highest temperatures recorded in that state. It was this weather pattern that prompted Mr. Locey's comment in his journal that appeared at the opening of this section.

As the thermal trough moves east of the Cascade Mountains it begins to weaken. Very often the progression eastward of this thermal trough is followed by a weak trough of low pressure in the upper atmosphere. In fact, it is the approach of the latter that often sends the thermal trough moving east. The approaching weak upper level trough will cause weak pressure falls at the surface ahead of it which aids in transporting the thermal trough eastward.

Although the warmest temperatures west of the Cascade and Coast Range Mountains occur in the summer

Figure 7.15 A bank of gray stratus clouds (arrow) set to move onshore below some middle and high clouds (white) near Long Beach, Washington.

months, the extension of the thermal trough into these areas can be manifest in the spring and fall months also. Indeed, it is this type of pattern that brings warm, dry weather to the coastal strip of California, Oregon, and Washington in late September, October, and even early November after a period of rain and cloudy weather has initiated the fall rainy season. It is what is often referred to as "Indian Summer" weather, when a warm, dry period follows a rainy period in early fall. This fall extension of the thermal trough along the coast with its offshore flow of air is often the most enjoyable weather coastal locations experience during the year. The cool, gusty northwesterly winds of summer have decreased due to a lowering of the pressure gradient between the high pressure offshore and the lower pressure over the southwest portion of the United States. Additionally, the light offshore winds and warm temperatures may last for two to four days during this time of year. I can recall several occasions when I have enjoyed temperatures in the 80s along the coast in late September and early October.

The Brookings Effect and Downslope Warming

Brookings, Oregon, on the extreme southern Oregon coast has recorded high temperature readings in the 80s during the winter months and over 100 degrees several times during the summer months. It is often referred to as Oregon's "banana belt." What accounts for this warming? We need to go back to our dry adiabatic lapse rate of 5.4 degrees for every thousand feet to understand the "Brookings Effect" and "downslope warming."

The terrain to the east of Brookings in the southern portion of the Coast Range Mountains rises to elevations of 3,000

Figure 7.16 Once the thermal trough moves east of the Cascade Mountains, marine air begins invading the western valleys through several gaps in the Coast Range.

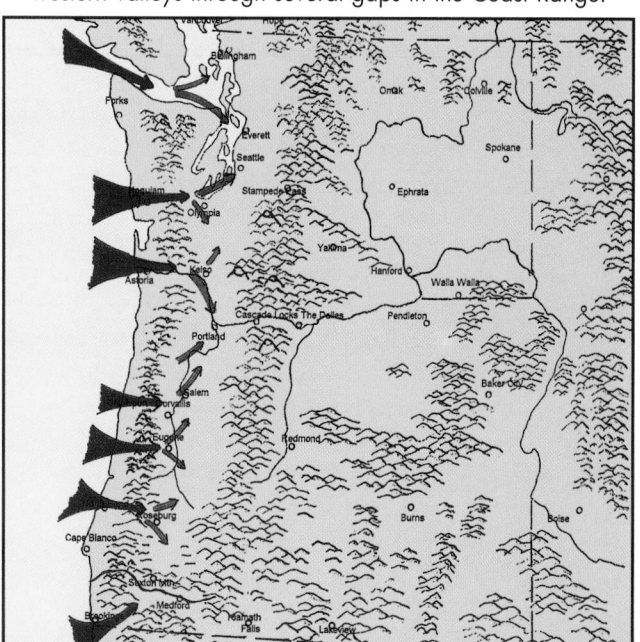

to 4,000 feet. The coastline at Brookings is oriented east-southeast to west-northwest. Any northeasterly component to the wind will thus be blowing offshore at Brookings. Air that descends from 4,000 feet will warm at the dry adiabatic rate as much as 20 degrees from its starting point by the time it reaches the coast line. Figure 7.17 shows this effect as air descends from around Sexton Mountain across the Coast Range Mountains and into the Brookings area.

This warming of the air is due to easterly winds blowing downslope towards the thermal trough that has extended into the southwest corner of the state. Snow Camp, a Forest Service fire lookout just to the east-northeast of Brookings in the Coast Range Mountains, has recorded easterly winds of 75 miles per hour with such conditions. This effect can occur all along the coast when easterly winds blow over the Coast Range Mountains. The rapid downslope warming is similar to the Santa Ana winds that occur along the coastal sections of Southern California.

Above-normal temperatures in the Pacific Northwest result from a combination of thermal trough activity, a very warm ridge of high pressure aloft, and/or air descending downslope to lower elevations. In summer, all three can be involved, but in winter, it is primarily adiabatic warming as air descends to lower elevations. For coastal areas of Washington, Oregon, and California to record temperatures in the 90s and low 100s, it is strictly an offshore component to the wind, enhanced by the warm ridge of high pressure aloft, and aided by adiabatic warming as the air descends from higher elevations. Over interior valleys west of the Cascade Mountains and areas east of those mountains, it is the presence of the thermal trough coupled with a very warm ridge of high pressure aloft that produces the record heat. Sometimes the thermal trough will progress directly north from California valleys into the interior of Oregon, skipping the coastal phase. Additionally, due to the heating in summer in the Columbia Basin of eastern Oregon and Washington, there is a natural heat low or thermal low similar to the one found over the desert southwest, but generally not as strong. The thermal trough from California only enhances this low-pressure area as it extends north.

Figure 7.17 The "Brookings Effect." An offshore component to the wind in extreme southwest Oregon warms dry adiabatically 5.4°F for each 1,000 feet as it descends from 4,000 feet over the interior to sea level.

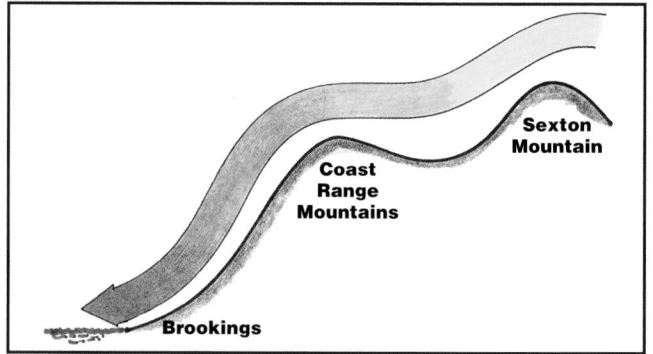

Chapter 8
Severe Weather

We will never know just what Alexander Ross and his companions experienced. We are certain it was not a hurricane. It was a rare event for the Pacific Northwest and obviously has to be put into the category of severe weather. It may have been a strong microburst or even a tornado or both. His Indian guide was so terrified that he fled from the scene. As a dedicated meteorologist, I probably would have stood in awe, wondering why I did not have my camera!

Alexander Ross Crossing the Northern Cascades, August 1813

"Late in the afternoon, however, we were disturbed and greatly agitated, by a fearful and continuous noise in the air, loud as thunder, but with no intervals. Not a breath of wind ruffled the air, but towards the southwest, from whence the noise came, the whole atmosphere was darkened, black, and heavy. Our progress was arrested; we stood and listened in anxious suspense for nearly half an hour, the noise still increasing, and coming, as if nearer and nearer to us. If I could compare it to anything, it would be to the rush of a heavy body of water, falling from a height; but when it came opposite to where we stood, in a moment we beheld the woods before it bending down like grass before the scythe! It was the wind, accompanied with a torrent of rain—a perfect hurricane, such as I had never witnessed before. It reminded me at once of those terrible visitations of the kind peculiar to tropical climates. Sometimes a slight tornado or storm of the kind has been experienced on the Oregon (Territory), but not often. The crash of falling trees, and the dark, heavy cloud, like a volume of condensed smoke, concealed from us at the time the extent of its destructive effects. We remained motionless until the storm was over. It lasted an hour; although it was scarcely a quarter of a mile from us, all we felt of it was a few heavy drops of rain, as cold as ice, with scarcely any wind; but the rolling cloud passed on, carrying destruction before it, as far as the eye could follow. In a short time we perceived the havoc it had made by the avenue it left behind. It had leveled everything in its way to the dust; the very grass was beaten down to the earth for nearly a quarter mile in breadth."

The Fur Hunters of the Far West,
edited by Milo Milton Quaife

When meteorologists talk of severe weather, their reference is usually to massive thunderstorms that spawn strong winds, hailstorms, very heavy rain, and tornadoes. These storms can cause death and destruction and are localized events. Strong middle-latitude storms, that have already been discussed, can also cause damage, injuries and fatalities. The distinction between the two is the extent. Middle-latitude storms can cover thousands of square miles, whereas thunderstorms cover a much smaller area. The conditions that favor middle-latitude storms, however, are very similar to the conditions that are responsible for tornado outbreaks and other severe thunderstorms. Indeed, severe weather is often a product of a middle-latitude storm.

Some thunderstorms produced by these middle-latitude storms contain very strong updrafts that are capable of lifting objects and transporting them sometimes several miles.

The United States has the distinction of having the greatest number of severe thunderstorms and tornadoes, more than any other nation on earth. Wow! What a distinction! But why? What are the primary reasons for this? How is weather in the United States different from weather in other parts of the world? What actually causes this much higher frequency of severe weather events?

For severe weather to occur there must be a certain set of criteria, otherwise every thunderstorm that "popped up" would produce a tornado or large hail stones, or nothing at all. Generally, it is when warm, moist air collides with cool, dry air, or along those fronts we talked about earlier. The area from east of the Rocky Mountains to the eastern seaboard of the United States is by far the best location for these two air masses to do battle. Warm, moist air flowing north from off the Gulf of Mexico meets cool, dry air flowing down from northern latitudes. Add the presence of a strong jet stream and some vertical wind shear and you have the necessary conditions as is shown in Figure 8.1.

Figure 8.1 Warm, moist air from off the Gulf of Mexico often meets cold, dry air from northern latitudes beneath a strong jet stream to produce severe weather in the United States.

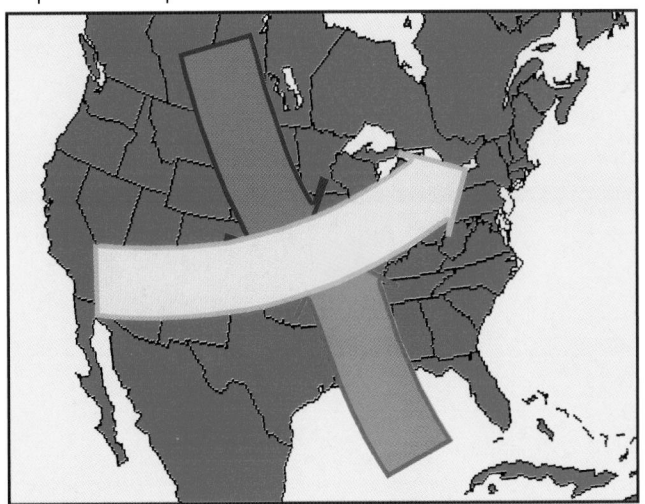

Nowhere else in the world are the geographical features present for the aforementioned to occur with regularity. That is not to say the middle and eastern sections of the country are the only locations on earth where severe weather occurs. China can have its share of severe weather as cool, dry air from its interior meets warm, moist air moving in from the western Pacific Ocean. Severe weather can also occur in areas north of the Mediterranean Sea and in some areas of South America and even Australia. Severe weather has been experienced in the western portion of the United States, and even in the Pacific Northwest.

Stages of Thunderstorm Development

Severe weather is generated from thunderstorms. How do thunderstorms develop and where do they occur? Thunderstorms form when a parcel of air begins rising. If the parcel is warmer than the air surrounding it, it will continue to rise. Thus, thunderstorms are a product of unstable air. Meteorologists have placed the development of a thunderstorm into three stages: Cumulus, mature, and dissipating. Figure 8.2 schematically shows these stages, but identification of each stage is not always that simple. It is often difficult to distinguish one stage from another or when a cumulus cloud with strong updrafts merges into stage two. Indeed, most stage one cumulus clouds never make it to stage two or the mature stage. If a parcel of air reaches a layer of air that is warmer or drier, the updraft ceases, and the cloud will flatten and dissipate.

Stage one, or the cumulus stage is perhaps the easiest to identify. In stage two, downdrafts begin vying with strong updrafts for supremacy within the cloud. Precipitation in the form of rain and sometimes hail begins during the mature stage. It is during this time period that the most severe weather (heavy rain, hail, tornadoes, and strong surface winds) can occur. At this point the anvil at the top of the

cloud begins to form. Stage three, or the dissipating stage, is characterized by this classic anvil shape at the top of the cloud. The anvil indicates the cloud has reached the tropopause and the updrafts have been capped. The cloud is collapsing and downdrafts now predominate and precipitation begins decreasing. Pictures, better than words, can describe the three stages. The cumulus stage shown in both cloud photographs in Figure 8.3 is denoted by the letter A, the mature stage as the letter B, and the dissipating stage by the letter C. In the lower photograph the mature stage is surrounded by the cumulus stage while the anvil from a dissipating thunderstorm looms over these two. Thunderstorms can form and dissipate in time periods of less than an hour, so transition from one stage to the next is often rapid. Minutes can separate one stage from another if the updrafts creating the cloud are strong. Figure 8.4 shows a massive thunderstorm over the Pacific Ocean offshore from Long Beach, Washington. It also shows the three stages of thunderstorm development. The anvil is clearly visible and suggests that the storm was moving from the northwest, which it was.

When we talk of thunderstorms, we need to examine what starts the air rising. There are several ways that air can

Figure 8.3 Two photographs showing the three stages of thunderstorm development. Cumulus, A; mature, B; dissipating, C.

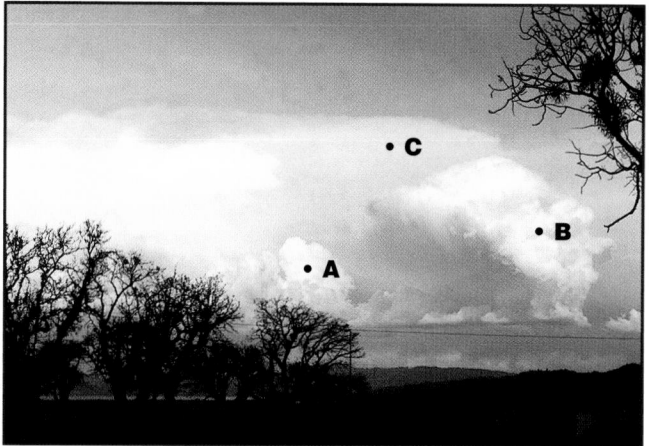

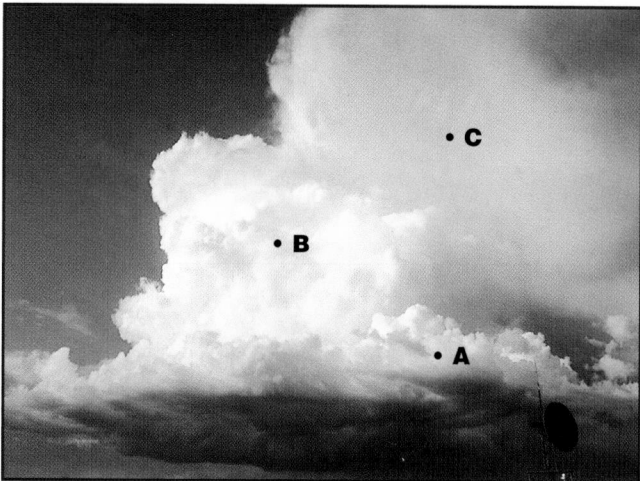

Figure 8.2 Three stages of thunderstorm development.

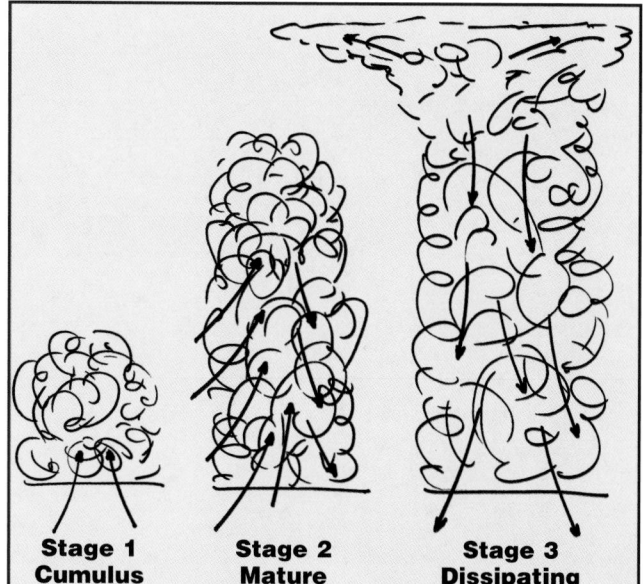

Stage 1 Cumulus   Stage 2 Mature   Stage 3 Dissipating

Figure 8.4 A large thunderstorm over the Pacific Ocean offshore from Long Beach, Washington.

be forced to rise. Warming of the air at the surface or advecting in cooler air aloft creates a more unstable atmosphere (increases the instability) and can set the air near the surface in motion. Frontal systems are another way as air is forced aloft when cold air plunges underneath warm air or warm air overrides cold air. Air is also forced aloft when it must travel over hills and mountains. Air that is forced aloft will cool and eventually condense. The release of heat, as water vapor changes from the gaseous stage to the liquid stage, adds heat to the parcel. It is this addition of heat that makes the parcel of air still warmer than the air around it, which results in a more unstable atmosphere. This release of latent heat carries the formation of a thunderstorm from the cumulus stage where the air is all flowing upward to the mature stage.

Thunderstorms can form singularly, in lines, or in groups. Those that form all by themselves are usually referred to as "air mass" thunderstorms. That is, the primary factor in their development is surface heating. There may be other clouds around. Most thunderstorms that form in the tropics and occur in the mid to late afternoon are "air mass" thunderstorms as a result of surface heating. One could also classify most of the thunderstorms that form west of the Cascade Mountains in winter as air mass thunderstorms, although there could be a squall line or cold front that adds to the instability and forces the air aloft.

Thunderstorms also occur in lines, generally along cold fronts or warm fronts. Figure 8.5 is a picture showing a line

Figure 8.5 A line of cumulus clouds that are well into the mature stage over eastern Oregon. Strong updrafts are actually creating lenticular clouds on top of some of the clouds as the gradient wind is forced aloft over the updraft.

of developing towering cumulus that are well into the mature stage over eastern Oregon. Often thunderstorms form along a line where there is a marked difference in the dewpoint temperature from very moist on one side to very dry on the other side. Such lines are called "dry lines" by meteorologists and appear in the southern Plains States where moist Gulf of Mexico air meets drier air from the West. The ambient air temperature shows very little variation across this "front." The dewpoint variation, however, is enough to cause air to begin rising due to the difference in density between the two air masses.

Thunderstorms can also occur in groups. One thunderstorm can be forming over a location as a dissipating thunderstorm is moving away. It is not unusual to see all three stages of thunderstorm development over a small area as Figures 8.3 and 8.4 show. The strong outflow of cold air from a dissipating thunderstorm can very well act as a small cold front which forces air aloft and starts the entire process again. Severe thunderstorms have been known to occur where outflow lines from two different thunderstorm cells intersect. Figure 8.6 depicts this type of occurrence.

Some thunderstorms reach what is called the "supercell" stage. In this type of thunderstorm complex the entire storm is rotating, usually in a counterclockwise direction in the Northern Hemisphere, much like a miniature, middle-latitude low-pressure area. In fact, the storm will have its localized warm front and cold front. Supercells can persist for several hours and travel hundreds of miles, usually associated with a variety of severe weather including large hail, destructive downdrafts, and/or tornadoes. Some research has shown that these supercells are strongest when they show a slight tendency to turn toward the right. Again, it is in the Midwest where most supercells develop, but such a storm developed over central Oregon near Bend and moved east-northeastward through Condon, Hermiston, and into southeast Washington on July 9, 1995.

Figure 8.6 The intersection of the outflow from two different thunderstorms can start cumulus development which could develop into another thunderstorm.

Tornadoes

By definition a tornado is a violently rotating vortex that is manifest at the surface. A funnel cloud is a vortex suspended from the base of a cloud but having no effect on the ground. Ragged clouds that extend down from the base of a cloud (stratus fractus clouds) are often mistaken for funnel clouds by the untrained observer. Figure 8.7, taken near the author's home, is a classic example of this as the trailing edge of some stratocumulus clouds gives the appearance of a funnel at A in the picture.

The formative stages of a tornado usually show a funnel cloud suspended from the base of a cloud that gradually grows and extends down to the surface. Rising air within the funnel condenses which gives the tornado its gray or dark appearance. Dust, dirt, and sand can be drawn into the funnel which will give it a slightly different appearance depending on the color of the surface over which it is moving. A tornado can be in contact with the ground if a whirling motion in trees and shrubs is noticed. It may cause some damage and show no other visible signs of condensation and/or dust, dirt, and sand. The rotation of small objects drawn into the column is a sign that the funnel has reached the ground and is thus called a tornado. In several incidents that the author investigated, witnesses reported seeing objects aloft rotating and whirling around with shrubs and trees shaking at the surface, yet they did not indicate that a funnel cloud was present.

Often the remark is made, "The funnel did not touch the ground." That is to say the visible portion, or where condensation has occurred or where dust and dirt were seen rotating, did not touch the ground. The inference here is that there was no tornado, only a funnel cloud aloft, but there very well could have been some manifestation at the surface, even in the form of slight damage. Figure 8.8 depicts this.

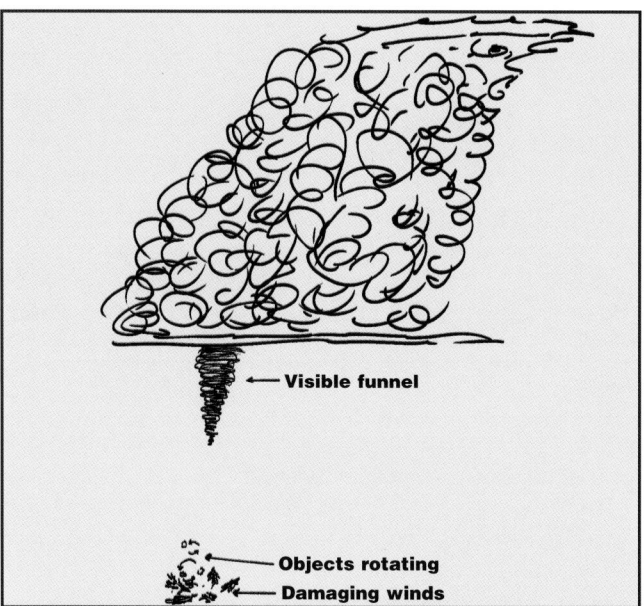

Figure 8.8 The visible portion of a funnel cloud need not touch the ground to be classified as a tornado if damage and destruction occur at the surface below it.

Scientists are not really sure what causes tornadoes but there are several theories. One theory is that in the latter stages of a mature thunderstorm development, very strong updrafts within the cloud are often located next to very strong downdrafts. Two air streams, one going up and one

going down, often create a horizontal vortex at their boundary. It is thought that this horizontal vortex becomes tilted due to other air motions within the cloud, changing its orientation from the horizontal to the vertical, resulting in the formation of a funnel cloud.

Another theory regarding tornado formation is that warm air being drawn into a thunderstorm meets cold air that is flowing out creating a small vortex between the two opposing air streams that can grow into a tornado. This may be the case with a supercell thunderstorm. Tornadoes in the

Figure 8.7 A stratocumulus cloud that gives the appearance of a funnel, A, near the author's home. The cloud was watched for several minutes. No rotation was detected and it dissipated.

laboratory can be created in this manner. Whatever the direct cause, scientists are certain that strong wind shear plays a very important part. Often this wind shear shows up in the vertical. Strong southerly winds in the lower layers of the atmosphere veer to an even stronger westerly direction at higher levels. This strong difference in direction and speed has been noted in many severe weather outbreaks.

Often, a large tornado can be surrounded, so to speak, by a few smaller tornadoes that sometimes look like fingers dropping down from the base of the cloud that are rotating in the same direction as the parent tornado. That is to say, they have their own individual rotation, but are caught up in the air that is flowing around and into the parent tornado. In surveys of major tornado outbreaks in the Midwest, this signature of a spiral-like pattern has been observed on the ground after the storm has passed. This could also be the reason why one house is demolished while the house next to it is only slightly damaged.

Dr. T. Theodore Fujita, formerly with the University of Chicago, spent much of his life, until his death in November 1998, studying these storms. He categorized tornadoes into six different classes from F0 to F5 related to damage and wind speed. In F0 tornadoes, the winds are estimated from between 40 and 72 miles per hour. Light damage occurs, usually in the form of branches broken off trees, some shallow-rooted trees tipped over, and some windows broken. Moderate damage occurs with F1 tornadoes. Here wind speeds are from 73 to 112 miles per hour and mobile homes can be pushed off their foundations, outbuildings demolished, trees snapped or broken, and the surface of roofs peeled off. In the F2 classification of tornadoes considerable damage can occur from wind speeds of 113 to 157 miles per hour. Roofs are torn off frame houses, mobile homes demolished, large trees are snapped off or uprooted, and frame houses with weak foundations lifted or moved. The F3 category brings severe damage caused by winds of 158 to 206 miles per hour. Roofs and some walls are torn off well-constructed houses. In a grouping of trees, most are uprooted. Heavy cars are lifted off the ground and thrown around, and trains can even be overturned. Devastation occurs with the F4 distinction. Well-constructed houses are leveled, structures with weak foundations blown off for some distance, cars thrown and disintegrated, and uprooted trees carried some distance away. This damage is the result of winds estimated at 207 to 260 miles per hour. Only a very few tornadoes reach the F5 category, and in this case, the damage is incredible. Houses and structures are disintegrated and missiles such as automobiles are transported through the air. Trees are debarked and incredible phenomena will occur as wind speeds exceed 260 miles per hour. The scale actually goes higher, but nothing above an F5 has ever been recorded. Most tornadoes fall into the lower categories.

Strong downdrafts from a cloud often produce microbursts which are also classified as severe weather. These downdrafts are the result of a large displacement of air down toward the surface of the earth out of a thunderstorm, perhaps something like Alexander Ross experienced during his journey across the Northern Cascade Mountains. A similar effect can be created by dumping a pail of water on a level surface and watching it flow out in all directions. If you are walking as you do this, the strongest outflow will be in the direction you are moving. Thus, strong downbursts, or microbursts, can create very strong winds at the surface. It is sometimes difficult to distinguish whether the damage and destruction was caused by a tornado or a microburst. Often, a strong microburst can occur with a tornado. Figure 8.9 depicts a microburst. A microburst can be accompanied by heavy rain or in many cases east of the Cascade Mountains, by very little rain.

Microbursts have been the cause of several airplane disasters. An airplane flying through a microburst near the ground will first encounter a strong head wind. As transit is made through the microburst to the other side, the head wind will suddenly change to a tail wind resulting in a sudden loss of air speed which can cause an airplane to stall. Thunderstorms with strong downdrafts have caused massive blow-downs of large sections of forested areas in eastern Oregon. Such was probably the case on May 21, 1971. A large thunderstorm blew down an estimated 100 million board feet of timber in a path that stretched for 10 to 12 miles through the Ochoco and Malheur national forests.

Hail

Hail is a product of convective clouds but it does not have to be a thunderstorm that produces hail. Small hail, or hail showing a diameter of less than one-quarter of an inch, can occur with clouds of less vertical extent than thunderstorms.

Figure 8.9 A microburst as seen from the side and looking down on the wind pattern at the surface.

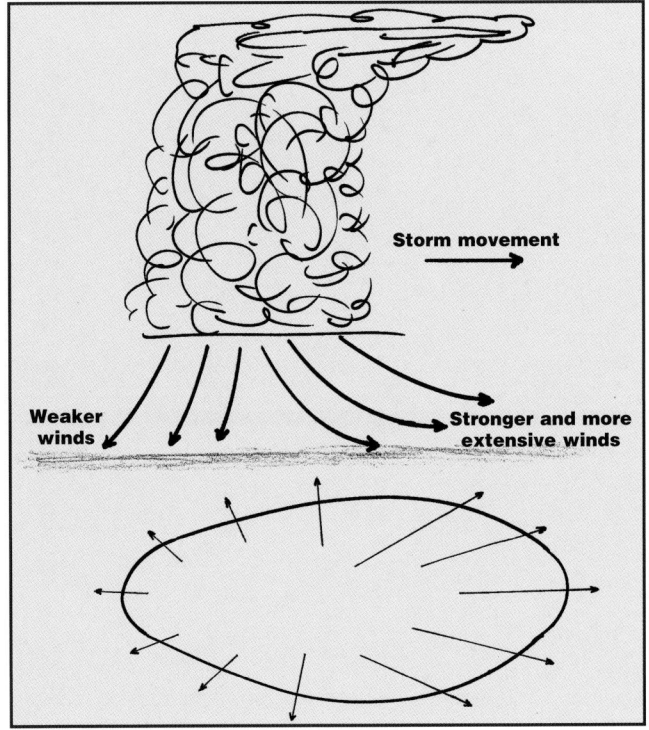

Indeed, small hail occurs frequently in the Pacific Northwest and is often referred to as ice pellets. Larger hailstones are more often noted in those areas east of the Rocky Mountains where the incidence of severe weather is greater than it is in the Pacific Northwest. Hail three-quarters of an inch and larger is considered by the National Weather Service as part of the criteria for a severe thunderstorm.

> ### Hail?
> *"Where do you hail from?" queried a tall Yankee of a traveler. "Where did you rain from?" was the reply. "Don't rain at all," said the astonished Jonathan. "Neither do I hail–so mind your own business."*
>
> *Daily Oregonian*, November 11, 1861

Strong updrafts and downdrafts within a thunderstorm propel hailstones through areas containing supercooled droplets of water. The water freezes on the hailstone increasing the size, often giving a layered effect. The larger the hailstone, the larger the updraft must be to keep it from falling.

Lightning

Another product of thunderstorms is lightning. Lightning comes very close to being the greatest cause of deaths per year from a natural phenomena. (Floods are number one.) Lightning results when two areas of a cloud, or two different clouds, or the cloud and the earth have different charges of electricity, one positively charged and the other negatively charged. In the majority of cases, the ground has a positive charge and the base of the cloud a negative charge, Figure 8.10. A leader stroke will begin its earthward migration from the base of the cloud, and if it encounters a secondary leader from the ground, the two will meet to form a path for the flow of electricity. These two leader strokes can move along with the cloud and never meet, or the formation can be very quick. I can remember golfing in Utah one day when there were thunderstorms present. (I was young and foolish at the time!) The foursome that I was in was on a large green getting ready to putt. Two of us were on one side of the green and two on the other side. Suddenly the fellow next to me turned and said, "Did you feel that?" I said, "Yeah, I felt it!" The sensation we experienced was almost certainly the beginning of that leader stroke from the ground. The two people on the other side of the green felt nothing, although they were merely yards away. The lightning did not occur for many minutes after that and quite a distance from where we were standing. I have thought back to that moment many times. Metal golf shaft, metal cleats! I was very lucky. But the experience reveals that the two leading strokes can cover a very small area.

Lightning not only travels from the ground to the cloud (which is primarily the direction it goes), but also from the cloud to the ground, from one cloud to another cloud, and from one area in the cloud to another area in the cloud. The direction the stroke moves depends on where the negative and positive charges are. Lightning heats the air in proxim-

Figure 8.10 Lightning normally travels from the positively charged ground to the negatively charged base of the cloud, but can occur within a cloud or from one cloud to another.

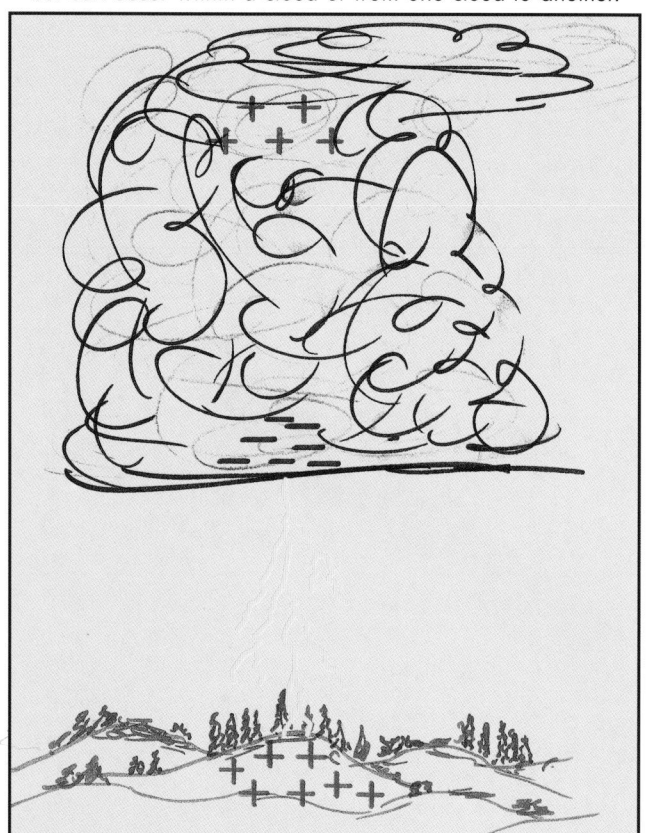

> ### Navajo Indians and Lightning
> *No Navajo Indian will ever make a campfire of wood from a tree that was struck by lightning or that might have been. If such a fire is made by an irreverent white man, the Indians will retire to a distance where they cannot feel the heat or smell the smoke, and they will go to sleep in their blankets, fireless and supperless, rather than eat the food prepared on that kind of fire. The Navajo believes that if he comes within the influence of the flame he will absorb some of the essence of the lightning which will thereafter be attracted to him and sooner or later will kill him.*
>
> USDA, *Climate and Crops: Oregon Section*, June 1903

ity to it, to thousands of degrees Fahrenheit and causes incandescence. That heated air rapidly expands, and it is this expansion that causes thunder. The rumbling sound that thunder makes is due to the sound arriving at your location having bounced off surrounding obstacles. If you are very close to the lightning bolt, the sound will resemble a loud bang.

I can remember my mother referring to "heat lightning" on a warm summer evening when we could see lightning but hear no thunder. Sorry, mom! You were right most of the time, but there is no such thing as heat lightning. Heat lightning is a misnomer. Well, the thunderstorm that caused the lightning may have resulted from surface heating earlier in the day, but it is merely the reflection of lightning off clouds, when the actual stroke is hidden. It obviously originated in the Midwest on warm summer evenings. The flat ground made the reflection of lightning from distant thunderstorms visible, but the actual thunderstorms were too far away for the thunder to be heard.

This section has very briefly covered severe weather, its definition and causes. Severe weather is the product of colliding air masses with drastically different qualities. Wind shear and the presence of a strong jet stream are definite factors in the creation of severe weather. Thousands of thunderstorms are occurring over the surface of the earth every minute. In most cases, these thunderstorms do not cause damage. They do not generate severe weather. There is the flash of lightning, the rumble of thunder, perhaps two or three times, and the scene is over. However, as we have seen, many thunderstorms reach the severe category and can cause damage. The Pacific Northwest is not devoid of these.

Thunderstorms and Severe Weather in the Pacific Northwest

Early settlers spoke of the benign climate in the Pacific Northwest. But this section of the country is not without its thunderstorms. Some can be severe enough to cause flash floods, hail, strong downdrafts, and tornadoes. The quote from the *Long Creek Eagle* only partially describes the destruction that this tornado caused to a small town in eastern Oregon over 100 years ago. Granted, not as many thunderstorms occur in the Pacific Northwest as in other parts of the country, but they do occur. In the Pacific Northwest the distribution of thunderstorms is somewhat even with

---

Long Creek, Oregon Tornado June 3, 1894
"A heavy growth of timber on the mountainside one-half mile in width fell before it as readily as grain before a sickle, and in but very few seconds the entire Eastern portion of Long Creek was at its mercy. Dwellings, barns and store buildings were lifted into the air as if but the weight of a feather, and torn into atoms, portions of which was carried for miles distant. For a moment the air was a thickened mass of missiles, flying in every direction."

Long Creek Eagle, June 8, 1894,

---

more occurring east of the Cascade Mountains during the spring, summer, and early fall, and west of these mountains during the late fall, winter, and early spring.

Strong thunderstorms can occur during any month in the Pacific Northwest. Wintertime thunderstorms are usually associated with the passage of a cold front, cold

occlusion, or squall line. They can also occur as very cold air replaces warmer air at higher elevations in the atmosphere associated with the trough of low pressure following a surface front. Generally, one or two claps of thunder are heard, and that is the extent of the thunderstorm. Lightning may not even be observed.

Springtime thunderstorms, or those that occur during what is the peak season, are perhaps the strongest and most severe. In spring, the air aloft associated with migrating troughs of low pressure can still be very cold. Yet the sun, now much higher in the sky, is capable of providing intense surface heating. The result is an atmosphere that is very unstable. It is during this period, April into July, that the Pacific Northwest has experienced some its most severe weather caused by thunderstorms.

Flash Floods

Flash floods are included in this category of severe weather. A flash flood results from heavy rain in a short period of time over a small area. The rain descends from a large thundershower (cumulonimbus cloud) or from several of these clouds, over a small drainage area. The rainfall is intense with one or two inches falling in less than one hour. The creeks and streams that are affected will show a rapid rise as the water cascades down the hillsides and congregates in the canyons and draws. The rush of the water down the canyon in many cases has been described as a "wall of water" several feet high. Flash floods occur east of the Cascades during the months from April through September. The month of June probably holds the distinction of having the greatest number of flash floods.

Heppner, Oregon Flash Flood June 14, 1903
"The crest of the flood wave is said to have been almost simultaneous with the first water as far down the creek as Lexington; so that if a person had been standing on a structure 40 feet in height above the center of the creek bed at Heppner he would have seen flowing down the creek a bank of water 20 to 25 feet in height and having a face slope of about 30° with the horizontal."

Destructive Floods in 1903,
USGS Water Supply Paper No. 96

West of the Cascade Mountains, excluding the southwest portion of Oregon, flash floods resulting from thunderstorms are uncommon. In fact, in this area they are a rarity. Several conditions factor into this far greater occurrence of flash floods east of the Cascade Mountains. First is the absence of vegetation. The lush forests on the western slopes intercept much of the heavy rain and dispense it more slowly. This is usually not the case east of the Cascade Mountains where vegetation is less dense. Second, thunderstorms in eastern Washington and Oregon often reach greater heights in the atmosphere than their counterparts on the west side, allowing for a greater thickness from top of the cloud to the bottom.

An additional factor is the type of soil. Much of the area in eastern Washington and Oregon is of the lava variety. Water has a tendency to run off quickly and not soak into the soil. Steepness of the slope is also a contributing factor. On steep slopes, the rainfall does not penetrate into the soil and runs off quickly. Thus, the main reason for flash floods in eastern Washington and Oregon is a large amount of rain in a short time span, over a very small area, devoid of most vegetation, with relatively steep slopes, and due to an intense thunderstorm. Figure 8.11 is an example of the terrain around Heppner, Oregon which is typical of the terrain in eastern Washington and Oregon, comprised of relatively flat valleys broken up by hills with sparse vegetation.

There have been many historic flash floods in the United States. The Big Thompson Canyon flash flood of July 1976 in Colorado, the South Dakota Black Hills flash flood in July 1972, and the Johnstown, Pennsylvania flash flood in May 1889 are but three. Eastern Oregon and Washington have had their share also. On September 5, 1925, fourteen persons were killed in a flash flood that descended down Squillchuck Canyon near Wenatchee, Washington. The town of Heppner, Oregon has been partially destroyed several times by flash floods. The most severe was in June 14, 1903 when over half the town was destroyed and around 265 people lost their lives.

Heppner sits at the confluence of four small streams: Hinton Creek, Balm Fork, Shobe Creek, and Willow Creek. Willow Creek continues to flow north and eventually empties into the Columbia River. The terrain surrounding the town is virtually void of any trees. Torrential rains above the town, in the small watersheds of primarily Willow Creek and Balm Fork, flowed down the canyons into this small town. Figure 8.12 is a map of the local area. The storm moved north from off the foothills of the Blue Mountains located to the south accompanied by heavy rain and hail. A person standing above the town would have observed a bank of water 20 to 25 feet high descending on the small town. They would have observed the event, that is, but probably would have been driven to shelter by heavy hail that measured over an inch in diameter. So intense and deep was the hail that five days after the storm

Figure 8.11 The terrain around Heppner, Oregon which is typical of areas in eastern Washington and eastern Oregon.

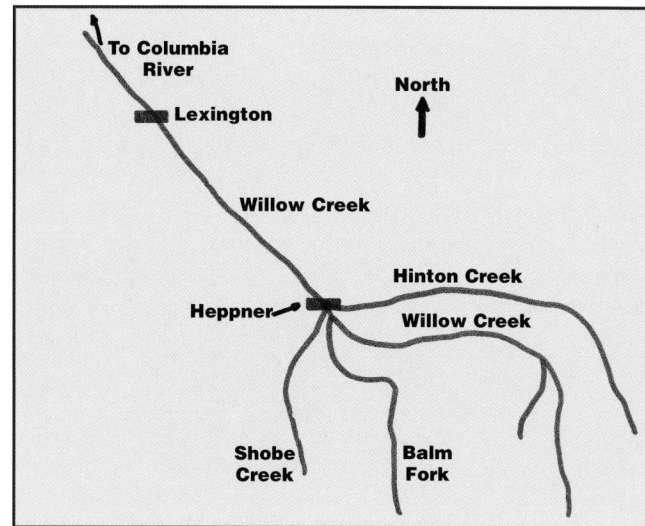

Figure 8.12 A map of Heppner, Oregon area showing the four small creeks that meet near the town.

some bodies were found in drifts of hail in a nearly perfect state of preservation. The flash flood continued down Willow Creek to the community of Lexington, eventually finding its way into the Columbia River. Perhaps others would have been killed in the town of Lexington and other places along Willow Creek had they not been warned by a Leslie Matlock who rode horseback down the creek warning residents of the impending disaster. Today a dam below the confluence of Willow Creek and Balm Fork protects Heppner from these devastating events.

Many other towns east of the Cascade Mountains such as Mitchell and Mt. Vernon that sit at the mouth of a small canyon, or the confluence of two canyons, have had similar occurrences. A drive along the John Day River in eastern Oregon will reveal rocks and debris, much of it deposited by previous flash floods from the canyons above. Some of the debris can extend a long distance from the mouth of a canyon. I have driven roads in eastern Oregon and seen rocks and mud from a flash flood along the roadway when the canyon from which it came was at least two miles away.

I remember an experience I had with my family in the Uinta Mountains in northeast Utah. We set up camp by a small gurgling brook and pitched our tent. Thunderstorms had been occurring during the day. They continued well into the night, and although the spot where we were located experienced very little rainfall, I kept looking up the canyon to where the thunderstorms were occurring. Around 2 a.m., I woke everyone up, and we got into the truck and drove fifty yards to a higher spot. The next morning, the tent was still there alongside the creek, but I could see where the water had risen to almost its opening. The lesson: It does not have to rain very hard where you are for a flash flood to occur. Some of the folks far downstream in Big Thompson Canyon in Colorado experienced very little rain.

Early settlers to eastern Oregon and Washington referred to these very heavy downpours of rain from large thunderstorms as "waterspouts." (Cloudburst is the popular term today, and we think of a waterspout as a small tornado over water.) These early residents were concerned about crossing dry creek beds when thunderstorms were present. The dangers today are more apparent as many roads are paved through small canyons and dry creek beds in desert areas. Surprisingly, it takes very little water for an automobile to become buoyant and begin to move sideways. Thus, it is never a good idea to drive through water covering the road in low spots along the highway. A good rule is that if you cannot see the roadway or the white or yellow lines beneath the water, the water is too high to cross. Figure 8.13 a heavy shower (cloudburst) over the distant hills (A) and what could be a funnel cloud trailing on the back edge of the thunderstorm at B.

Virga

Not all thunderstorms, however, produce heavy precipitation. Frequently, thunderstorms in the Pacific Northwest, particularly east of the Cascade Mountains in summer, form at very high levels in the atmosphere. The bases of these cumulonimbus clouds, or the lifting condensation level (LCL), can be greater than 10,000 to 15,000 feet above the terrain. This is due to large differences between the temperature and dewpoint temperature that allows the air to rise to great heights before condensation occurs. As the rain begins falling, it evaporates before reaching the ground, leaving streaks of precipitation. These streaks of precipitation are called virga from the Latin word meaning branch, streak, or rod. Figure 8.14 shows two examples of virga. In the top photo, ice crystals are falling from a cumulus cloud and evaporating before reaching the ground. The bottom picture shows gray streaks of precipitation (rain) that is also evaporating as it descends into drier air.

Virga is often the sign of a downburst or a microburst. Downbursts from these thunderstorms are particularly dangerous in areas east of the Cascade Mountains since only the cold air reaches the ground resulting in strong, gusty winds. These events are feared by fire control officials since the strong winds can quickly spread a forest fire out of control. Frequent lightning occurs with such storms and generally

Figure 8.14 Virga, falling as ice crystals in the upper photograph, and as rain drops in the lower evaporating before reaching the ground.

only drops of rain at the surface. The storms are referred to as "dry lightning" storms or "dry thunderstorms." The scant amounts of rain with these storms has facetiously been referred to as a "two-inch" rain, meaning that there was a drop every two inches at the surface.

Pacific Northwest Tornadoes

The Pacific Northwest also experiences tornadoes and some have even caused death. Two tornadoes east of the Cascade Mountains in Oregon, one on June 14, 1888, in the small community of Lexington killed three people, and one on June 3, 1894, in the small village of Long Creek, also killed three people. There have been no recorded deaths this century in Oregon, although a small tornado that occurred on Interstate 5 between Salem and Portland on March 22, 1967, is suspected by the author and a local newspaper to have been a factor in a fatal one-car crash just south of Wilsonville, Oregon. The light foreign vehicle went into the median strip and rolled over several times for no apparent reason. The woman was thrown from the car. Several minutes later a small tornado struck a nursery near the freeway and caused some damage. Tornadoes have caused at least eight deaths in Washington. The total number of occurrences is shown in Figure 8.15. Although the figure for Oregon is greater

Figure 8.13 A thunderstorm producing a cloudburst over the distant hills at A and what could be a small funnel cloud trailing the cloud at B.

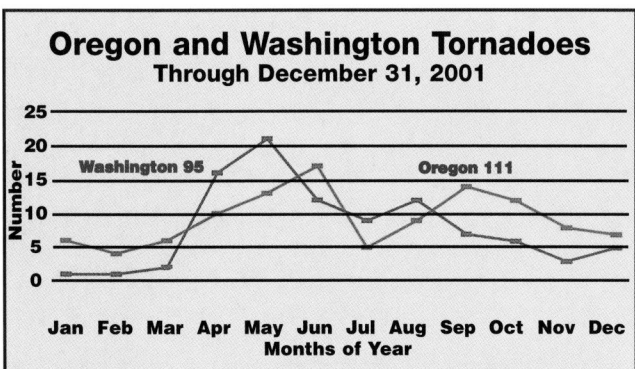

Figure 8.15 Most Washington and Oregon tornadoes occur during the spring. A secondary maximum occurs in late summer or early fall as the jet stream begins to migrate south.

than for Washington, the author has done far more research into Oregon tornadoes than Washington events. Data for this graph was obtained from local historical records, weather documents, newspapers, climatological reports, local storm reports, data bases from Seattle, Portland, and the National Climatic Data Center in Asheville, North Carolina. It is incomplete as additional historical records are continuously being found that

Tornado Myths

MYTH: Areas near rivers, lakes, and mountains are safe from tornadoes.

FACT: No place is safe from tornadoes. In the late 1980's, a tornado swept through Yellowstone National Park leaving a path of destruction up and down a 10,000-foot mountain.

MYTH: The low pressure with a tornado causes buildings to "explode" as the tornado passes overhead.

FACT: Violent winds and debris slamming into buildings cause most structural damage.

MYTH: Windows should be opened before a tornado approaches to equalize pressure and minimize damage.

FACT: Opening windows allows damaging winds to enter the structure. Leave the windows alone; instead, immediately go to a safe place.

Tornadoes...Nature's Most Violent Storms
NOAA/PA 92052 or ARC 5002

strongly suggest other occurrences. It was only in 1950 that the National Severe Storms Laboratory, then in Kansas City, started compiling statistics about tornadoes.

Tornadoes in the Pacific Northwest are usually in the F0 and F1 class. Some more devastating ones have occurred, such as the Vancouver, Washington tornado in April 1972, that first touched down near Northeast 33rd and Marine Drive in Portland and then moved across the

Columbia River into Washington destroying a shopping mall and heavily damaging an elementary school. This tornado killed six people while injuring hundreds more and reached the F3 classification. Another tornado occurred in the St. Paul-Newberg area in Oregon during December 1993 that moved through a sparsely populated area and reached the F2 classification.

As in the Midwest, the greatest frequency of tornadoes in the Pacific Northwest is in the spring months when there are contrasting air masses. A secondary peak occurs in late summer and early fall as the jet stream is strengthening over the area and air masses at middle latitudes are beginning to display more contrast. Tornadoes have occurred in Oregon and Washington every month of the year, confined primarily to the area west of the Cascade Mountains during December, January and February.

For many years there seemed to be a general reluctance on the part of meteorologists and Weather Bureau officials in the Pacific Northwest to actually classify an event as a tornado. Some Pacific Northwest climatological documents actually make the statement, "Tornadoes are unknown." Descriptions such as "tornado-like winds," "whirling winds," "freak windstorm," "unusual winds," "wind rush," and other descriptive terms have been used to describe events that the author believes are genuine tornadoes. Even today, government officials have used a statement, "...radar data ruled out the likelihood of a tornado..." Radar cannot verify whether a tornado did or did not occur. Often the remark is made, "The funnel did not touch the ground." When viewed from a distance, however, it is unlikely that the observer could see whether or not the whirling column of air was disturbing trees and objects at the surface. Thus, the author has included several of these occurrences as tornadoes after extensive examination of newspaper references and personal notes revealed damage at the surface.

Lately, however, sightings of tornadoes have increased in Washington and Oregon. This is probably due to two causes: (1) The realization that tornadoes, albeit most of them small, do occur with some regularity in the Pacific Northwest, and (2) The influx of people from tornado-prone areas in other parts of the country who have experienced the event in the locality from which they came and then witnessed the occurrence in the Pacific Northwest. An increase in populace will undoubtedly cause an increase in sightings, especially in densely populated areas.

The Willamette Valley seems to be a favored location for tornadoes to develop, especially during the cooler months of the year, October through April. This could be due to the increased populace in this area, but the author believes there may be other reasons for the increase. Quite often the winds are southerly at the surface in the valley, being channeled north by the Cascade Mountains to the east and the Coast Range Mountains to the west, toward a surface low-pressure area somewhere near Vancouver

Island. At elevations above 4,000 to 5,000 feet, the winds are often blowing west-southwesterly and somewhat stronger. This seems to create sufficient vertical wind shear in both direction and speed that contributes to weak tornado development when the air mass moving in off the Pacific Ocean is very unstable. Figure 8.16 depicts this change in direction.

The conditions necessary for severe thunderstorms to develop in the Pacific Northwest are similar to the conditions necessary elsewhere: A warm, moist unstable air mass, a strong cold front, diverging air aloft that supports strong vertical motion, a strong jet stream and vertical wind shear. Quite often, east of the Cascade Mountains in summer, the source of this moisture is the Gulf of California or even the Gulf of Mexico. The approach of an upper level trough of low pressure with its diverging air streams is a strong factor when warm moist air is present at the surface. Generally, east of the Cascade Mountains, dewpoint temperatures during the warm summer months are mostly in the 40° to 50°F range. When those values creep into the 50s and even low 60s the possibility of thunderstorms is greatly increased.

Thunderstorms in the Pacific Northwest occur more frequently over mountains and ridges than over valleys. Figure 8.17 depicts this.

Mountains and ridges act as barriers to the wind and the air is forced to rise as it approaches these obstacles. Also, air along a mountain slope or ridge heats up much

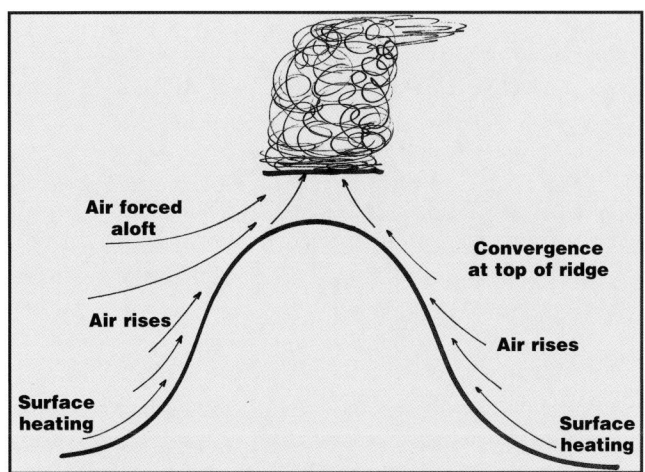

Figure 8.17 Thunderstorms are more likely to form over ridges where the air is forced aloft and surface heating brings converging air streams.

faster than a large volume of air in a valley. It is not uncommon to have thunderstorms develop over the Cascade Mountains and then drift slowly out over valleys to the west and east, depending on the direction of the upper level winds. Thunderstorms at coastal locations during the summer months in the Pacific Northwest generally arrive from the east or off the Coast Range Mountains.

Hailstones, some very large, can also occur with Pacific Northwest thunderstorms. Small hail of the pea-sized variety, often referred to as ice pellets, occurs frequently in Washington and Oregon, especially during the spring months of the year. Larger hailstones have also been reported. The severe thunderstorm mentioned earlier that swept east-northeast through eastern Oregon into southeast Washington in July 1995 caused millions of dollars in damage to agricultural interests as well as to a car dealership. Some of the hailstones were reported to be the size of golf balls and baseballs. The area west of the Cascade Mountains is not exempt from large hailstones. Near Mapleton, Oregon on June 6, 1948, hailstones very nearly

Figure 8.16 Strong southerly winds (gold) blowing in the Willamette Valley often occur below strong westerly winds (blue) at 5,000 feet creating wind shear conditions.

Figure 8.18 Hailstones 3/4 inch in diameter that fell at author's home.

the size of hen's eggs, and some probably as large as base-balls, fell from a severe thunderstorm. Chickens were reported to have been killed and, when striking the Siletz River, the hailstones caused water to splash up three or four feet. Figure 8.18 shows hailstones as large as pennies that fell in Gresham, Oregon at the author's home. The storm that deposited the hailstones moved east and a weak rotation was observed for a very brief period at the base of the cloud but no funnel was observed. The cloud continued moving east and began dissipating.

Waterspouts and Dust Devils

The coastal areas of the Pacific Northwest have experienced several waterspouts. Contrary to early settler definition, a waterspout is a small tornado that forms over water. Several have been observed over the Pacific Ocean with unstable atmospheric conditions. Occasionally these waterspouts move onshore and would then be classified as a tornado. They can cause damage.

Dust devils, or those small rotating columns of dusty air that a person observes scooting across a plowed field or over sage brush-covered terrain east of the Cascade Mountains, are only related to tornadoes in their rotation.

There, the kinship stops. Dust devils are small perturbations in the low-level flow next to the surface, caused by air flowing around an obstacle, induced by an automobile or truck, or as some believe, simply by rabbits and other animals. Whatever their cause, large ones can reach several hundred feet into the atmosphere. They have been strong enough to move parked cars several feet from their initial location. A large dust devil is shown in Figure 8.19 moving north-northeast next to the I-5 just north of Eugene, Oregon in September 1994. Dust devils can rotate either clockwise or counter-clockwise and often extend for at least several hundred feet into the air. As with tornadoes, large dust devils that are several yards in diameter may have very small vortices rotating around the main vortex. Dust devils are usually moving with the speed of the wind. Instantaneous wind speeds are usually less than 25 miles per hour, but higher speeds with these phenomena have been known to shift cars around.

Although certainly not as apparent as in the central and eastern portions of the United States, thunderstorms and severe weather do occur in the Pacific Northwest. Many of these events have caused death and destruction and will likely do so in the future.

Figure 8.19 A large dust devil rotating in a clockwise direction along the Interstate-5 north of Eugene, Oregon.

Chapter 9
Small-Scale and Local Effects

Global circulation was discussed in Chapter 3, and the topic was then scaled down to individual storms and air masses. In this chapter we carry this concept down another step. Weather on a small scale operates very much like weather on a large scale, driven by differential heating of various earth surfaces. An excellent example is land and water. Water heats up much more slowly than land surfaces. However, it also retains its heat much longer than land surfaces. This differential heating produces local winds called land and sea breezes or lake breezes that are similar to the large-scale weather features. Land and sea (lake) breezes can have various effects on the weather, from causing thundershowers, to marked cooling inland, to very small-scale effects such as which way the smoke from your campfire blows. The winds that prevail in canyons and around cities also fall into this category of small-scale effects.

Land and Sea Breezes

A sea breeze or, if the body of water is large enough, a lake breeze is simply a response to differential heating. During the day, land surfaces heat up much more quickly than water surfaces because heat on land is concentrated at the surface. Radiation does not penetrate beyond the surface and any heating of the soil or rocks below is done by conduction. In water, however, the sun's light rays can penetrate much farther into the liquid than they can the solid surface of land. Water is generally turbulent with convective currents that transport the heat from one location to another.

Air over land, heated by conduction from the surface, will begin rising during the day. Air molecules will rise and leave creating an area of relatively low pressure. Other air molecules will begin moving in to take the place of those that left. This starts a circulation from the higher pressure over the water where surface air is cooler to the lower pressure over land. The effect is called a sea breeze, shown in Figure 9.1. If the gradient winds are light, the air that rises over the land will then move, at a higher elevation, out over the water surface and begin to descend. The result is the formation of what could be called a small Hadley-type cell, or as some say, a convective cell. The descending air will contribute to the higher pressure over the water.

At night the reverse occurs. Land surfaces radiate heat back to space more quickly than an area covered with water. Thus, air over a solid surface, in direct contact with the surface, cools much faster than air over water. The cooler, more dense air creates a region of higher pressure over the land surface as opposed to the water surface where there is a shallow area of low pressure. Flow, then, is from the land to the water — a land breeze. Again, if the gradient winds aloft are light, a return flow could exist with air descending over the land and rising over the water. Figure 9.2 illustrates a land breeze. Generally speaking, those breezes blowing from the land to the water, land breezes, will be weaker than their counterparts that blow from the water to the land, sea breezes.

Land and sea breezes occur in the tropics but are much more prevalent in the sub-tropics and middle latitudes. In the tropics, land and ocean are nearly the same temperature which inhibits the formation of any pressure gradient between land and sea. In this area the water content of the air is usually high which inhibits longwave radiation from

Figure 9.1 A sea breeze. Air, heated at the surface over land, rises. Cooler air off the water begins flowing in to take the place of air that has risen.

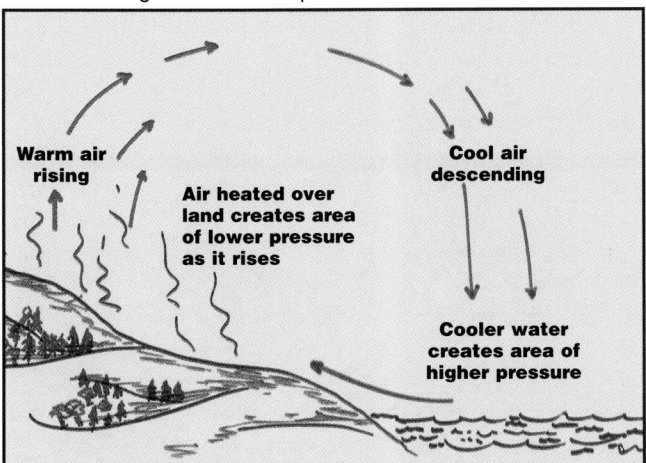

Figure 9.2 A land breeze. Radiation cooling at night causes an area of high pressure over land. Air flows toward the lower pressure over water.

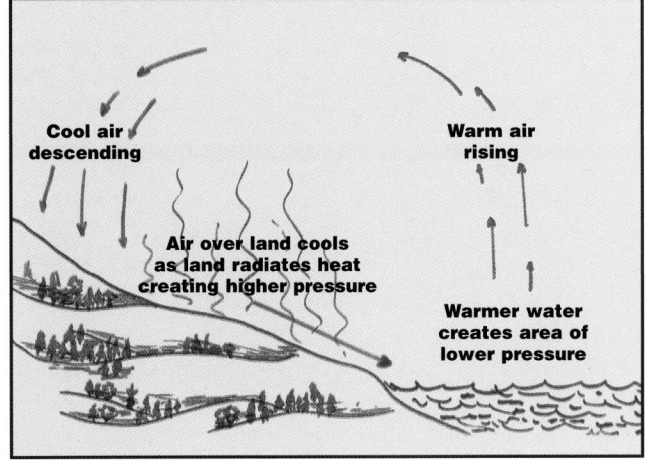

escaping from the earth into space that would have resulted in cooling of the land surface. In the polar regions there is usually insufficient heating of the land surface to start a land-sea circulation, although they can occur during the summer months. In the subtropics and middle latitudes, however, the sea breeze can be of such strength that it acts like a cool front with forced ascent sometimes causing thunderstorms and showers along its leading edge. The Florida peninsula is an excellent location to observe sea breezes. Areas around the Great Lakes experience well-defined lake breezes in warm summer months. The marine push into valleys west of the Cascade Mountains can be thought of as a sea breeze, but it is responding more to larger-scale pressure differences.

Sea breezes are not as well defined along the Pacific Northwest coast as some areas, although the summer northwesterly winds that prevail along the coast are certainly a type of sea breeze. The primary reason for these winds is the location of the Pacific high-pressure area offshore and the thermal low-pressure area that has formed over the Southwest deserts. The fact that the winds increase during the day along the coast and then decrease after sunset is in response to local heating of the land during the day and cooling at night. Large bodies of water such as reservoirs behind dams can generate weak areas of relatively higher pressure during the day over their surfaces as opposed to slightly lower pressure over the surrounding terrain, which may be devoid of trees. The result is a lake breeze.

It does not take a very large body of water to create these winds, although a larger body of water will normally create a greater temperature difference between land and water and thus, a stronger wind. The surrounding terrain will also have some effect on the strength of the land or lake breeze, especially if it is devoid of trees and vegetation. Forested areas would heat slower than areas devoid of trees, but the treeless areas would radiate their heat more rapidly at night resulting in a higher pressure. Smaller and shallower bodies of water might heat at a rate that is similar to the adjacent land surfaces and thus a weaker gradient would be created. I have camped around small mountain lakes in the summer time and noticed a weak breeze from the lake to the land during the day and then watched the smoke from my campfire blow slowly toward the lake after dark. This is an excellent example of the local wind responding to minor differences in air pressure. Cooling over the land creates a weak area of high pressure with winds that blow toward the weak low pressure over the warmer water. (And all the while you thought there was something to the saying, "Smoke follows beauty!" Now you know that at night around the campfire, you do not sit between the fire and the lake.)

Occasionally in the Columbia River Gorge, when the winds are light (a somewhat rare occurrence), there will be clouds and showers on both sides of the river and a clear area directly over the river as depicted in Figure 9.3. This is due to heating of the land surfaces on both sides of the river

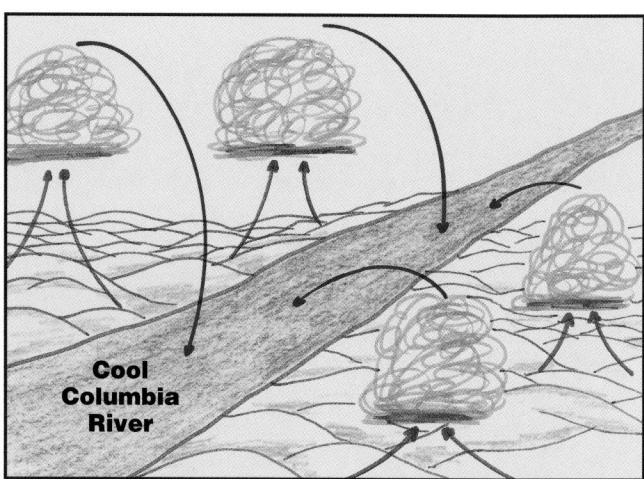

Figure 9.3 Often in spring with light winds, the cool Columbia River water will create a weak high-pressure area as opposed to lower pressure over land.

and air that is descending over the river. This is often apparent in the spring when the water in the Columbia River is still very cold but the surrounding hillsides are heated by the warm spring sun. The air over the cooler water creates an area of higher pressure relative to the lower pressure created over the land surfaces due to heating. Weak pressure differences between the areas west and east of the Cascade Mountains along with a weak gradient wind contribute to this event.

The strength of land and sea breezes is affected by the gradient wind. As an example, a light westerly gradient wind blowing toward the eastern shores of the Florida peninsula would weaken the onshore wind from the Atlantic Ocean and perhaps increase the evening offshore component. Conversely, given the same conditions, on the Gulf of Mexico side of the Florida peninsula the opposite effect would be manifest. The result of both would be some disruption in the weak Hadley-type cell that may have been formed between the ocean and the coastal areas. Thus, to totally understand the effect of a gradient wind or a wind generated by pressure differences, one should know from which direction the gradient wind is blowing and where the major pressure centers are located.

Showers may also be affected by land and sea breezes. One mechanism for causing air to rise (heating of the surface) could be complemented by the advection of slightly more moist air into the area by gradient winds. This addition of moisture could lower the lifting condensation level (the level at which most clouds, especially cumulus clouds, begin forming) which then would enhance the shower activity in the afternoon and in some cases, cause thunderstorm development.

The reverse effect can occur at night with light winds aloft as is depicted in Figure 9.4. Clouds caused by convective activity, and that result in showers, have a tendency to dissipate over land surfaces after sunset due to the lack of surface heating. Air that is rising over the water surface

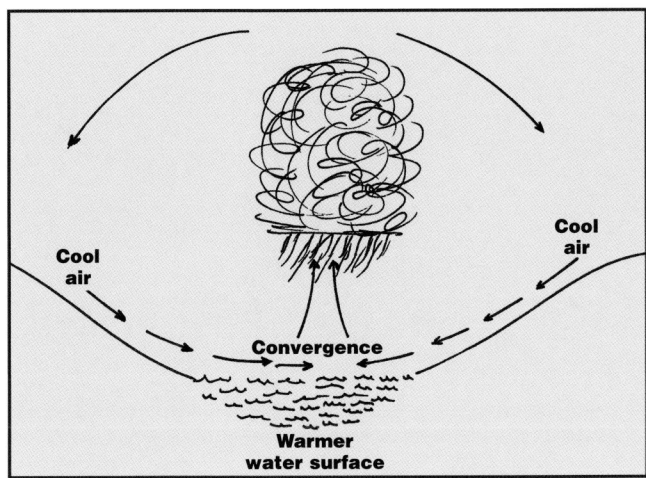

Figure 9.4 At night, cooler air over land converging over warmer water could continue the day's shower activity into the evening hours over water.

could maintain shower activity over the water after the showers have dissipated over land due simply to the upward convection of air occurring over the warmer body of water. Again, this assumes that the air mass undergoes no changes and that gradient winds are light or non-existent.

Differential heating, then, is the reason for land and sea (lake) breezes. On cloudy days this differential heating will be inhibited and the breezes will be lighter or even non-existent. A cloudy day with no sea (lake) breeze might clear in the evening, causing the land surface to radiate and thus produce a moderate land breeze; whereas during the day the sea or lake breeze may have been absent. Wind caused by a strong pressure gradient will have a profound effect on these winds and even reverse the flow as the air responds to a greater pressure difference. This could be due to an active low-pressure system moving through the area with strong gradient winds.

Canyon and Valley Breezes

Canyon and valley breezes are an important part of meteorology, especially in the Pacific Northwest where there are many mountains, ridges, and valleys. These winds can be quite strong at times and have a profound effect on forest fires. They can enhance or inhibit the formation of lake and land breezes. The discussion regarding canyon and valley winds, as with land and sea breezes, assumes clear skies and a light or non-existent gradient wind.

Differential heating! It has been talked about from the beginning. It causes major circulations, land and sea breezes, and it is also the driving force behind canyon breezes. First of all, there needs to be clarification between what is meant by valley and canyon. It is impossible to attach a qualification regarding actual size such as length, width, and depth. Thus, in this text, the valley will be the larger geographical area and the canyon the smaller one. This can be kept in mind if a person remembers the Willamette Valley and the canyons on either side of it.

However, side canyons like the McKenzie River or Santiam River are often called "valleys" and the small creeks feeding into them referred to as "canyons." In Washington, the Snoqualmie, Cowlitz, Yakima, and other rivers are often called valleys and the smaller streams feeding into them referred to as canyons.

Air is a poor conductor of the sun's radiation, but land surfaces will absorb this insolation. Thus the sun, in the early morning hours, will begin heating the west side of a north-south orientated canyon. This heat is transferred to the air by conduction. Heated air, as we know, rises. It will begin moving slowly up the slope. Hence the term "upslope" winds. This movement of air begins first in the very small side canyons heated by the sun and would be enhanced on east-facing slopes in the early morning hours. Movement of air from one area into another leaves a slight void. The result is for other air molecules to move in and fill that void. Air is then brought up from the lower regions of the canyon or valley where it is cooler (higher pressure) to fill the void. The sequence can be followed in Figure 9.5.

The amount and type of vegetation and steepness of the slope all factor into the strength of an upslope wind. A slope that is gentle will likely have weaker upslope winds than a slope with some steepness to it, but too steep and the process is interrupted. An area devoid of trees, a clear cut area for instance, will experience stronger upslope winds than an area that is covered with trees. Exposure to the sun is also a strong factor. South-facing slopes will have much stronger upslope winds than north-facing slopes. East-facing slopes will have stronger upslope winds in the morning hours than west-facing slopes with the opposite true in the afternoon.

Air that is moving upslope is being replaced by air below it, eventually leading to an upvalley wind or upcanyon breeze. If the gradient wind is weak, the upslope or even upcanyon winds will continue rising at the top of the ridge, and in some cases begin descending over the center of

Figure 9.5 An upcanyon or upvalley breeze. The flow begins as weak upslope in early morning (left) as the land surface heats. Winds increase during the day and become more upcanyon (right) by afternoon.

the valley. Once again, a weak Hadley-type cell has been developed by differential heating, with air rising over the ridges and descending over the center of the valley. However, because a gradient wind is often present in the Pacific Northwest, this phenomenon of a return flow over the valley is not often observed.

One effect of upslope winds can be observed by watching birds that soar along the edges of steep slopes where these winds converge and become convective currents of air, Figure 9.6. Hang-gliders will use this upslope breeze to launch themselves from a ridge top. Ridges are also favorable locations for showers to form as the rising currents of air converge at the top, enhancing the upward motion, eventually leading to condensation and cloud development, if sufficient moisture is present.

But, as the saying goes, "Everything that goes up must come down!" During late afternoon, those slopes facing east, and now in the shadows as the sun begins to set, will begin radiating the heat they have accumulated during the day. Here, more radiation is escaping than is being received. The result is evident. Air next to those slopes is cooled by contact with the ground. This air, now cooler than the air above it, will begin moving slowly down the slope. As the sun sinks lower in the west, more of the canyon falls into the shadows. More radiation cooling takes place and the downslope winds strengthen. Figure 9.7 illustrates this. Downslope or downcanyon winds are more laminar, or tending to follow the terrain, because the air is cool and stable. Upvalley or upcanyon winds are of a more unstable character due to the heating near the surface.

The effect of downslope winds coming together at the bottom of the valley can create a weak area of convergence at this location resulting in slight upward motion of the air, or a weak Hadley-type cell in reverse of the upslope winds discussed earlier. The effect is likely short-lived, however, since continued cooling due to loss of heat will cause the winds to begin blowing down the canyon or valley.

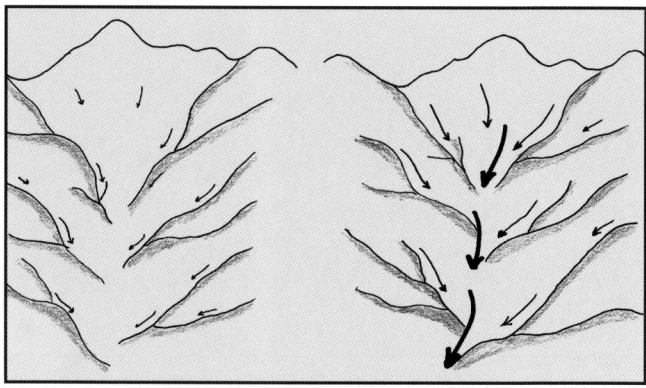

Figure 9.7 Downcanyon or downvalley breezes. Flow begins as weak downslope in early evening (left) as land surfaces begin cooling. Winds increase during late evening and become downcanyon at night.

It is not unusual for a canyon open to the south or north to have upslope winds on one side and downslope winds on the other side. As a fire weather meteorologist stationed at Medford, Oregon, I was dispatched to forest fires to give weather advice to fire-control officials. I would often observe smoke rising on east-facing slopes in the early morning hours as the sun warmed them, while on the west-facing slopes in the shadows, light downslope winds were still occurring as cool air was still draining to lower elevations. The reversal would occur in the late afternoon as east-facing slopes cooled, producing downslope winds. West-facing slopes were still being heated causing upslope winds. Figures 9.8 and 9.9 depict both upslope and downslope winds occurring at the same time.

Pressure gradients affect canyon winds. The summer pattern of higher pressure west of the Cascade Mountains and lower pressure east of these mountains normally causes an increase in the upcanyon breezes in the afternoon in those canyons on the west slopes of the Cascade Mountains that are oriented east-west. The effect of this pressure gradient, however, is often negated, or even reversed, on the

Figure 9.6 Heated air that is rising up the slopes of a ridge will converge at the top creating an updraft.

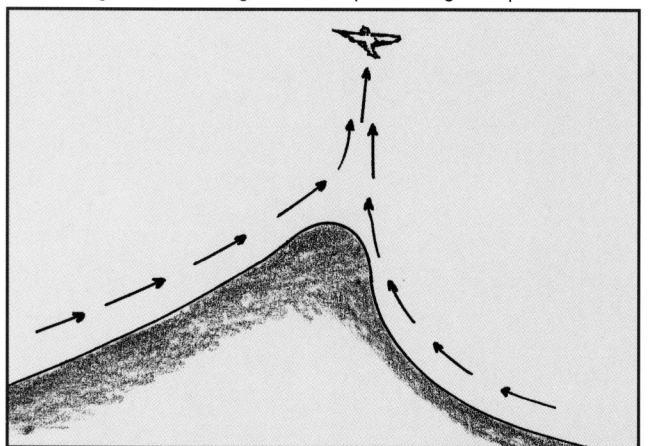

Figure 9.8 Upslope and downslope winds occurring at the same time in early morning.

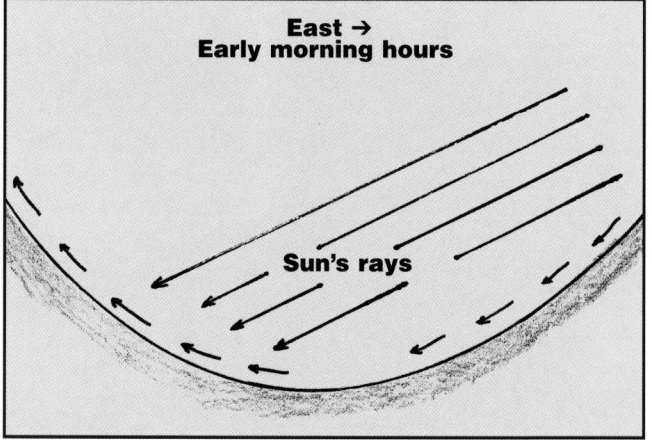

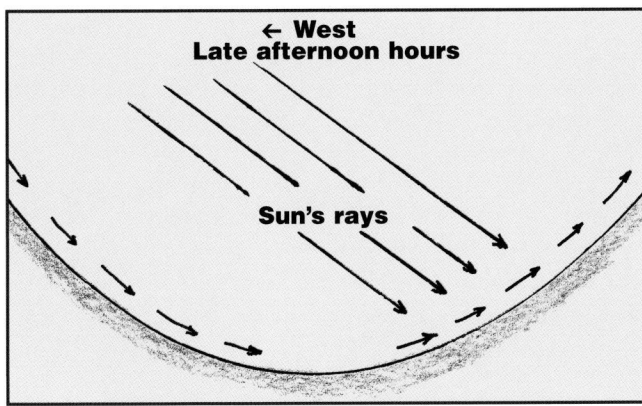

Figure 9.9 Downslope and upslope winds occurring at the same time in the late afternoon.

east side of these mountains and on the east-facing slopes of the Coast Range Mountains. The upcanyon breezes in these locations, now blowing from the east, would be weaker than their counterparts on the western slopes of these mountains and sometimes, as mentioned, even reversed.

A gradient wind can also have a pronounced effect on canyon winds that is very similar to the pressure gradient effect. A southwesterly gradient wind, for example, could enhance the winds on the westerly and southwesterly facing slopes of one side of the valley while causing a decrease or even a reversal of the wind on the other side of the valley. Eddies and often turbulent conditions will exist on the lee side of the valley where the normal upslope winds encounter the effects of the gradient wind. This is shown in Figure 9.10. Notice the stronger arrows in the same direction that the gradient wind is blowing.

Figure 9.10 A strong gradient wind can enhance the wind on the windward side of a canyon and decrease it, or even reverse the wind, on the lee side of the same canyon.

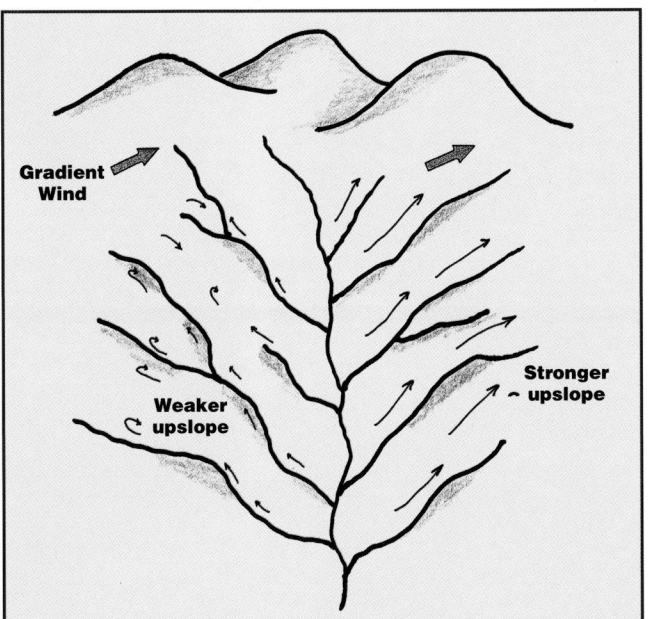

The effect of a strong gradient wind occurred several years ago when a number of firefighters lost their lives battling a blaze in western Colorado. The canyon was oriented north-south with the lower elevation to the south. The gradient wind was southerly ahead of an approaching cold front. A weak inversion (an increase in temperature with elevation) was present at the base of the canyon during the early morning hours. The inversion "broke," allowing the air to become unstable and rush up the canyon aided by the gradient wind. Tragedy was the result.

Normally, upcanyon winds are stronger than downcanyon winds but there are exceptions. Steep, east-facing slopes that cool rapidly in the late afternoon and early evening can experience downcanyon winds of 20 mph or more. This is especially true on the east slopes of the Steens Mountain in southeast Oregon and on the east slopes of Winter Ridge located north-northwest of Lakeview, Oregon. Other areas that could experience strong downcanyon winds include most east-facing slopes of the Cascade Mountains in Washington and Oregon where there is some steepness to the terrain. Weak downslope and downcanyon breezes have been noted on the northeast side of the West Hills in Portland after the sun has set. Homeowners and apartment dwellers are normally aware of this cool, summer breeze that is often slightly enhanced by the normal afternoon northwesterly wind that occurs in the Portland area. In Salt Lake City, our home was about a mile from the mouth of Big Cottonwood Canyon to the east. In the evening, all we had to do after a warm day was to open the windows and let the canyon breeze (this time blowing down the canyon from the east) cool the house.

On one summer camping trip to Leigh Lake in the Grand Tetons in Wyoming, I experienced a strong downcanyon wind. Leigh Lake and the surrounding terrain are depicted in Figure 9.11. Late one afternoon I started out in my canoe from our campsite on the southwest shore of the lake to a point on the northwest corner of the lake. When I left the camp, the winds were light but shadows were beginning to lengthen. Rounding the point where the lake curves in toward the west, the winds began increasing. As I continued across the inlet toward the northwest shore, the wind became stronger, and the waves higher, lapping over the side of the canoe. I barely made it to the north shore, being encouraged (or laughed at) by an osprey nesting in a tall tree on the north side of the lake. However, I landed far to the east of my destination.

The setting sun had cooled the air on the east-facing slopes of the Grand Tetons. The air was rushing down the steep canyon toward the inlet and then out across the lake. It was, perhaps, one of the strongest downcanyon winds that I had ever experienced, and I estimated the speed to be at least 15-25 miles per hour. It was aided by a strong westerly gradient wind which I noticed later while looking at the weather map for that day.

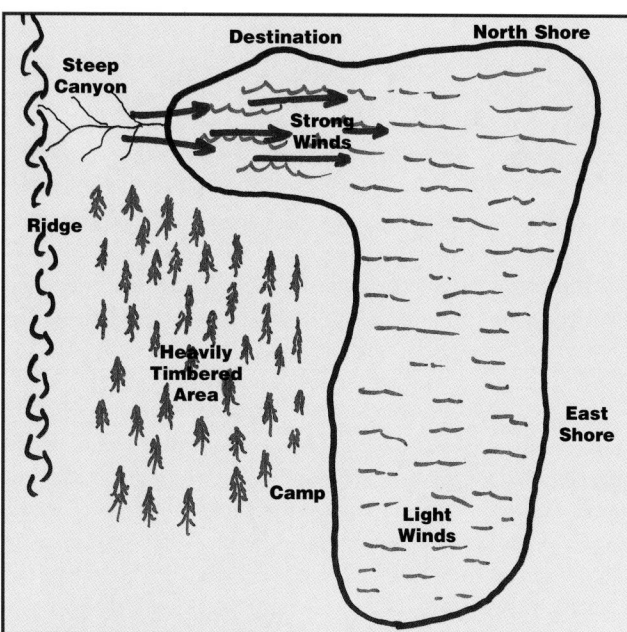

Figure 9.11 Rapid cooling on the eastern slopes of the Grand Tetons in Wyoming, together with a westerly gradient wind, produced a strong downcanyon wind.

Chinook Winds

The term Chinook wind is currently, by definition, a warm, dry wind that descends the slopes of a mountain range. Somehow, the term over the last 150 years has taken on a different meaning from what it was originally referred to, but the Indian legend mentioned in Chapter 6 may have had some-

thing to do with it. Early settlers in the Portland, Oregon area during the mid-1800s referred to a Chinook wind as a wind blowing up the Columbia River from the Pacific Ocean. At the mouth of the river lived a tribe of Native Americans called the Chinook. In winter this wind was a warmer wind than the cold east wind blowing out of the Columbia River Gorge. As fur traders and settlers moved throughout the Pacific Northwest, especially to areas east of the Cascade Mountains, they took the term with them. When a warm spell was then observed, they came to refer to it as a "Chinook" wind. Now the definition applies to any warm, downslope wind that descends on

the lee slopes of mountains throughout the United States and Canada and brings an increase in temperature along with a decrease in relative humidity. Indeed, the winds that occur on the eastern slopes of the Rocky Mountains and the Black Hills are now considered Chinook winds.

The Santa Ana winds that blow from the northeast and cause the devastating fires in Southern California, and that transport all the smog in Los Angeles out into the ocean, are a type of Chinook wind. Several areas in the world experience this. In Europe they are called foehn (pronounced "fern") winds.

Winds that blow downslope are warmed at the dry adiabatic lapse rate of 5.4°F per 1,000 feet. These winds are warmed by compression as the air descends from lower pressure to higher pressure. Thus, one can see why there can be such abrupt warming on the eastern slopes of the Rocky Mountains. This effect is often noted in southeast Washington and northeast Oregon on the leeward north and northwestern slopes of the Blue Mountains in these areas. It is depicted in Figure 9.12. If air at 20°F descends from 8 to 10 thousand feet down to 4, 3, or even 2 thousand feet, it can warm as much as 50°F. The warm air does not always scour out the cold air but frequently overrides it and forms an inversion. When it does reach the surface, abrupt temperature increases of 30 to 40 degrees are not uncommon, along with some very mild winter temperatures.

There are many other local winds known by a variety of names that occur around the world. Large glaciers can even create winds due to the cool air above them causing an area of high pressure. Air, then, would be blowing from off the glacier or large snowfield to surrounding areas free of ice and snow. Additionally, even in small areas such as an asphalt parking lot adjacent to a grassy area, weak local winds can occur if other pressure gradient forces are minor or non-existent. In this case, the heating of the asphalt creates an area of low pressure, while the cool, grassy area may have a slightly higher pressure.

Weather has been discussed on a global scale in previous chapters. In this part of Chapter 9 concentration continues on a smaller scale, perhaps one step below the sea,

Figure 9.12 A south-southeasterly flow of air over the Blue Mountains in northeast Oregon can descend on the leeward side warming at 5.4°F per 1,000 feet, bringing record temperatures in winter to valleys and lower elevations in northeast Oregon and southeast Washington.

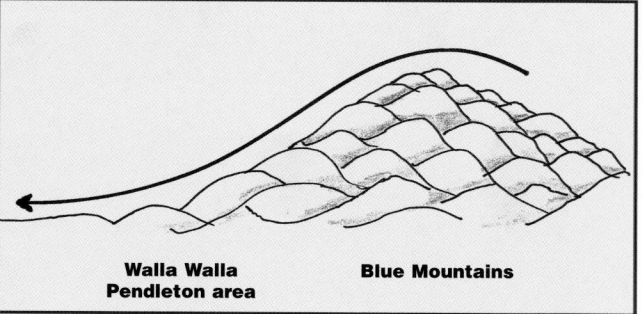

land, and canyon breezes. Once again, these meteorological phenomena are due to differential heating and cooling plus the effects of wind.

Cold Temperatures in High Mountain Valleys

The coldest temperature ever recorded in Oregon is -54°F at Ukiah, Seneca, and Bates, and probably several other locations where there are no thermometers in eastern Oregon. In Washington the coldest recorded temperature is -48°F at both Mazama and Winthrop located in the north-central portion of the state. One might wonder why Oregon has a colder recorded minimum temperature than Washington when Oregon is farther south. Most of eastern Washington, except the northern part, is lower in elevation than Oregon. An examination of a topographical map of Oregon reveals several mountain ranges, divided by high mountain valleys. It is in these high mountain valleys like the one shown in Figure 9.13 that extremely low temperatures can occur. Similar conditions exist in the north-central section of Washington. But what makes temperatures at night in these valleys so cold?

For the record-breaking temperatures like those in the -30 to -50°F categories, an arctic air mass must be present. Normal fluctuations of temperature throughout the year will not produce these extreme temperatures. One of those "special" types of weather situations is needed, since arctic air contributes greatly to record low temperatures. Once the area is covered with a very cold air mass, any precipitation that falls will be as snow. Actually the snow could be on the ground before the invasion of very cold arctic air. Snow has a high albedo. During the winter months, the angle of the sun is low. The snow does not absorb much heat. Snow also has excellent insulating qualities, and it prevents heat from the earth warming the air that is in contact with the surface. Thus, two characteristics are already present for very cold temperatures, the air mass and snow cover.

But even in the absence of arctic air, temperatures in these high mountain valleys can still get very cold. Close examination of many of the high mountain valleys east of the Cascade Mountains reveals they do not have large openings at their lowest elevations. During nighttime hours, the slopes of the valley, and the valley itself, radiate what heat they have absorbed during the day back into space. Clear skies and dry air do not stop this radiation. The air along the slopes, now cooler than the air above it because of contact with the ground, begins draining down into the valley. It is a weak downslope wind that is laminar in nature. The result is a valley that becomes filled with cold air that will continue to radiate what heat it has back to space. This is shown in Figure 9.14.

The air draining down into the valley may warm very slightly as it descends at the dry adiabatic lapse rate, but this warming does not compensate for the radiational cooling. Also, the difference in elevation is relatively small, usually 1,000 feet or even less. Another contributing factor is the absence of moisture. Water vapor absorbs longwave radiation emitted by the earth and then retransmits it back to the earth, keeping the surface warm. In the absence of moisture, this radiation is allowed to escape into space. Air is normally much drier east of the Cascade Mountains than on the west side of these mountains.

Wind is also a factor. A strong gradient wind, or a wind due to a strong pressure difference, will create turbulent conditions that result in bringing warmer air aloft down to the surface. Air movement keeps mixing the air, preventing it from remaining in contact with the ground that is continually radiating heat. Light or calm winds are favorable for large temperature extremes in these high mountain valleys.

Since these valleys are quite shallow, they are susceptible to large temperature variations from afternoon high temperatures to overnight low temperatures. In late summer, it is not unusual for these locations to experience a 50-degree temperature change from the morning low, which could be in the 30s or even the 20s, to the afternoon high which will soar into the 70s or even the 80s. Just as the air at night cooled because of contact with the ground, the air during the day warmed by contact with the ground. The above factors make growing plants susceptible to freezing temperatures a challenge in these areas. This is not because of the rapid fluctuation, but because of the cold temperatures at night. It has been facetiously stated that the growing season in these high mountain valleys is often just one day—from June 30 to July 1.

Figure 9.13 High mountain valleys, like this one around Long Creek, Oregon, are susceptible to very cold temperatures at night as cold air drains down off the hills into the valley and clear skies allow for strong radiation.

Figure 9.14 Cold overnight temperatures in high mountain valleys east of the Cascade Mountains result from cold air draining down into the valley from surrounding slopes that have lost their heat due to radiation.

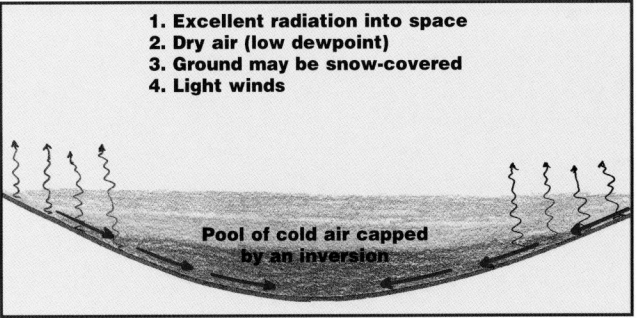

1. **Excellent radiation into space**
2. **Dry air (low dewpoint)**
3. **Ground may be snow-covered**
4. **Light winds**

Pool of cold air capped by an inversion

Thermal Belt

The floor or bottom of a valley is not the warmest place to pitch a tent and spend the night. Native Americans knew this very well and placed their camps on the side of valleys in what has been called the thermal belt. The thermal belt is located mid-way up the slope. It is in this area that the overall average temperature is the highest. The air at the floor of the valley will respond to heating of the ground during the day. It will also cool rapidly at night as the heat energy is radiated into space and colder air from surrounding slopes drains down onto the valley floor. The result is a large temperature variation as shown in Figure 9.15.

In Zone A, the thermal belt, warmer nighttime temperatures will result in a slightly higher average daily temperature that often enhances growth and minimizes damage due to frosts. In Zone B, plant development is often inhibited by cooler temperatures at night that could very well drop to below freezing in spring and fall and even during summer in areas east of the Cascade Mountains. In Zone C, afternoon high temperatures will be cooler than at the valley floor depending, of course, on the depth of the valley. Thermal belts are more apparent with clear skies and light winds.

The effect of cool air draining to lower elevations can be found on even small lots of less than an acre in size where there is just a slight difference in elevation from the highest point to the lowest point. Vegetables planted at the lower elevation will often show frost damage in late spring and early fall while those higher up the slope are not affected. The result is a slightly longer growing season at the higher elevation which may be only 10 to 15 feet. A slope such as that shown in Figure 9.16 may have two zones of cooler temperatures. Note that in this figure the temperature at Point A is freezing or 32°F while at Point B the temperature is 35°F. At Point C, near the bottom of the valley or depression, the temperature is well below freezing. Meanwhile at Point D, which is midway between C and B, the temperature is still above freezing.

Vegetation and other obstacles could have a pronounced effect on the above discussions regarding thermal belts and cool air draining down into the bottom of the valley. A thick hedge, for instance, as well as a rock wall, could act as Point B in Figure 9.16, damming the cool air behind them. Even row crops, such as grapes, planted in horizontal rows rather than vertical rows might inhibit the drainage of cool air down the slope.

Vineyards and orchards that may be susceptible to late-spring frosts or early-fall frosts are planted mostly around mid-slope rather than in the valley bottoms. There is usually more air circulation at mid-slope to keep mixing the air, preventing it from reaching the freezing point at night. Thermal belts are most often found where elevation changes are 500 to 1,500 feet.

Urban Effects

Wind that flows from high pressure to low pressure takes the path of least resistance. When something gets in its way, however, the flow is disrupted. Anyone who has walked among buildings in a large city on a breezy day has experienced gusty, changing winds. The height of buildings, their spacing, their orientation, their proximity to other buildings, stability of the air, pressure gradient—all are factors. A tall building will force the air around it, or if it is large enough, up and over it. This produces eddies on the lee side of the buildings where the wind may actually be blowing contrary to what it should be given the current pressure gradient. Where two of these eddies come in contact, the wind could actually be increased and blowing from the opposite direction on the leeward side of the building. On the windward side there might even be a minor reversal of the wind as it accumulates on this side.

Figure 9.17 gives some examples of how buildings affect wind flow. Notice how the flow can be reversed. If the buildings are closely spaced, the wind caused by a pressure gradient force may actually flow over the top and have little effect. In addition to reversals of the wind on the lee side of buildings, the wind can even reverse direction on the windward side as its volume increases and air flows up and over the obstacle.

Acceleration of the wind can occur where two streamlines come together. If two buildings are closely spaced, the

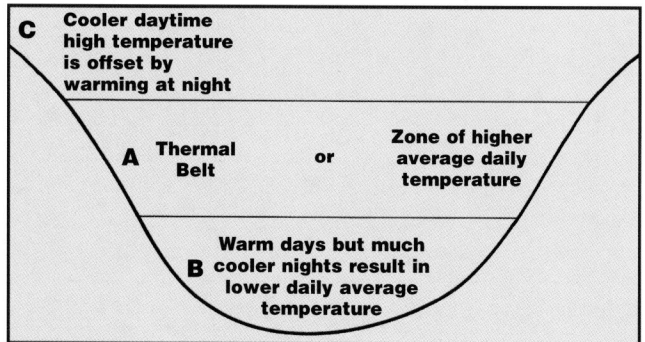

Figure 9.15 A schematic showing the thermal belt found on a slope.

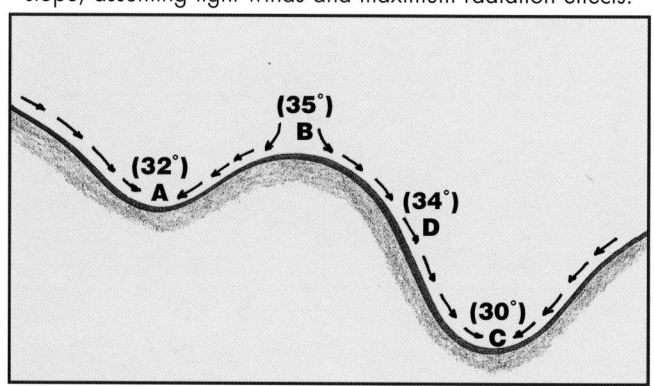

Figure 9.16 Possible minimum temperatures along a slope, assuming light winds and maximum radiation effects.

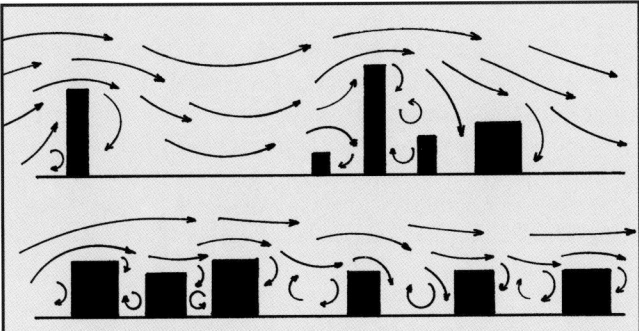

Figure 9.17 Building height, spacing, closeness, orientation, shape, air stability, and general wind speed all affect movement of air in and around buildings. (Diagram does not attempt to show all the possibilities.)

wind caused by a pressure gradient force will accelerate as it moves between the buildings toward lower pressure. Eddies are created at many locations as shown in Figure 9.18.

The speed of the wind caused by the pressure gradient is a definite factor in the gustiness of the wind as it passes around and over obstacles. A gust of wind is caused by the wind actually piling the air up on the windward side of an obstruction. The pressure becomes too intense, and the "pile" of air is released as a gust. Gusts of wind likely do much more damage than steady, strong winds.

Urban Heat Island

It has been known for many years that one of the effects an urban location can have on the weather is the manifestation of what is termed a "heat island" within a city. This

Figure 9.18 When wind flows over and around buildings, the possibilities of speed and direction are unlimited. The flow is often reversed. Where streamlines converge, air may accelerate; where two opposite directions meet, there is usually an eddy.

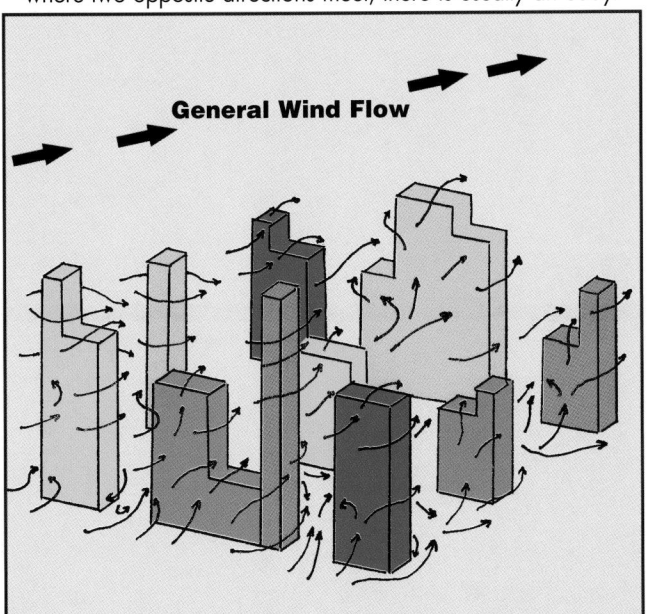

General Wind Flow

is readily apparent in large cities with vast quantities of cement, asphalt, and stone that absorb radiation from the sun during the day and then emit longwave radiation at night in all directions. The result is that minimum temperatures within cities will be higher than minimum temperatures in the surrounding countryside. Forecasters often refer to this difference with a forecast of, "Low temperatures tonight near 40 but in the low 30s in outlying (rural) areas."

Maximum temperatures do not seem to be affected as much as minimum temperatures. A graph of 24-hour average temperatures, showing rural and urban values, is shown in Figure 9.19 with temperature increasing upward. The afternoon high temperature within a city will be very nearly the same, or maybe a degree or two higher, than the high temperature recorded in the nearby rural area for that day. Rural and urban areas may reach their highest readings about the same time of day, but temperatures in rural areas will drop off more rapidly than in urban areas as solar insolation decreases in the afternoon. In the cities, however, the maximum temperature for the day remains at or near that value longer in the afternoon than rural high temperature readings. In urban areas, radiant heat absorbed by buildings and roads is enough to offset the loss due to a decrease in solar radiation. Rural areas experience heat loss at night through radiation while in the cities, buildings, asphalt, cement and automobiles are still radiating heat, maintaining higher readings than in the country. This radiation keeps the minimum temperatures within an urban area higher than minimum temperatures recorded in rural areas. In urban areas higher minimum temperatures, together with maximum temperatures that are nearly the same or slightly higher but last longer, will produce a higher average temperature for the day between the two locations. The urban heat island effect is greatest with clear skies and light winds. Often with strong winds and thorough mixing of the atmosphere there is little difference between urban and rural locations.

Parks and green areas are definitely a controlling factor regarding minimum temperatures within an urban area. A

Figure 9.19 Urban and rural maximum temperatures only vary by a degree or so. It is the higher minimum temperatures that occur in urban areas that cause higher average daily temperatures here than in rural settings.

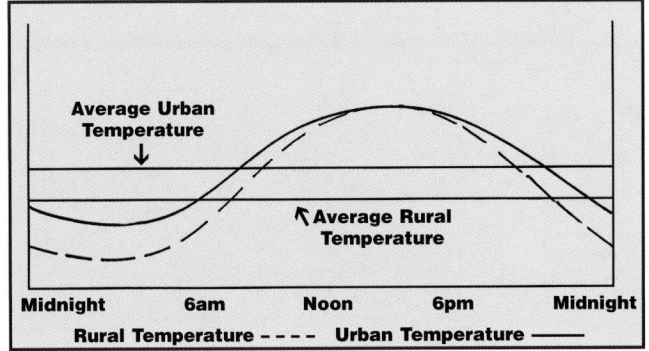

Average Urban Temperature

Average Rural Temperature

| Midnight | 6am | Noon | 6pm | Midnight |

Rural Temperature - - - - Urban Temperature ———

park located within a city can reduce the average difference in minimum temperature between the urban and rural locations by as much as 4 degrees, making it similar to the rural area. This difference in average minimum temperature values is shown graphically in Figure 9.20. Notice how the difference between the city and the rural area minimum temperatures can be as much as 10 degrees or more, assuming clear skies and light winds.

The urban heat island has a pronounced effect on the growing season between the two locations. I have observed this variance in temperature between rural and urban areas many times in downtown Portland, especially when comparing the growth rate of vegetation between that location and my home in Gresham, Oregon. Roses are a prime example. They bud out and are much more developed in the urban setting than my roses at home in the suburbs which, in turn, are more advanced than the roses in a more rural setting. Spring bulbs will normally bloom earlier in the city since soil temperatures are usually warmer there.

Effects of Wind on Temperature

Wind, even when it is not advecting in warmer or colder air, can have a pronounced effect on the temperature. Wind causes mixing of the air mass. As the air is heated near the surface, wind will transport the heated air away and replace it with cooler air that in turn must be heated by contact with the ground. The result is a much slower rise in temperature on days when the wind is blowing and the air mass is not changing.

This phenomenon is quite apparent when cool, east winds are blowing out of the Columbia River Gorge. On a clear, sunny day in the cooler months of the year, high temperatures in Gresham and Troutdale, Oregon and Washougal and Camas, Washington will often be 6 to even 10 degrees cooler than locations in Lake Oswego, Oregon City, or Beaverton, Oregon and Vancouver or Battle Ground, Washington. Here, the wind is much less and solar radiation is allowed to heat the ground and thus there is more time for that air to remain in contact with the ground making it warmer. The same effect is likely near the opening of any east-west passage through the Cascade Mountains when cool east winds are blowing through those passages.

The reverse is true at night. As the earth radiates heat into space, it cools the air directly over it. However, mixing of the air due to wind prevents the temperature from dropping as the air next to the surface is mixed with warmer air. Thus, on windy nights the temperature will likely fall to lower values in areas not exposed to the wind, or the towns mentioned above, as opposed to towns where the east wind is blowing. The same 6 to 10 degree variance above is now manifest in warmer temperatures in windy areas.

Orchardists use this movement of air to keep minimum temperatures in an orchard from lowering to below critical values by using large fans, or in some cases helicopters. Fans bring warmer air from elevations a few hundred feet above the orchard down into the area surrounding the trees. Such a fan is shown in Figure 9.21. This is exactly what a ceiling fan in a home does. It brings warm air down from near the ceiling and mixes it with other air in the room.

Figure 9.21 Large fans keep orchard minimum temperatures slightly above the critical point, circulating warmer air aloft down to the surface.

Figure 9.20 The potential difference between rural and urban minimum temperatures (F°) assuming clear skies and light winds.

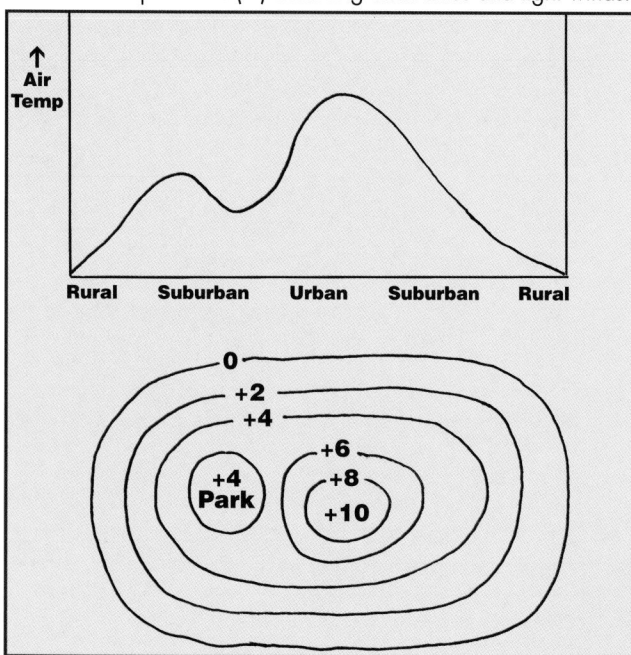

Micro climates can also be found on small city lots. Plants that do well in the shade and cool temperatures are planted on the north side of a house. My tomato plants are nearly always grown on the south side of my home, a short distance from the south wall. This ground heats up faster in the spring since it is exposed to radiation from the sun and radiation off the side of the house. This same area remains warmer longer into the fall and at night. I have observed slight frost damage on the open side of the tomato plants while the side next to the house showed no signs of freezing.

Fog and Inversions

Fog and inversions are somewhat related. Often with one, comes the other. It might seem that there can only be one type of inversion, and by definition that is correct. Basically, an inversion is an increase in temperature with elevation. But there are several different atmospheric phenomena that can cause inversions. Fog also might just seem like, well, fog. Yet there are different ways that fog is formed that result in the various names. Although fog and inversions are included in the discussion on small scale features, their extent can be manifest over several hundred square miles.

Inversions

An inversion results when the normal decrease in temperature with elevation is interrupted, Figure 9.22. The result is an increase in temperature with elevation to the top of the inversion, or the cap. The tropopause is a good example of an inversion, because at this level the temperature stops decreasing with elevation and begins increasing or remains the same.

Most inversions are of the radiation type and occur overnight with light wind conditions as the earth radiates its heat back to space. The air next to the ground cools faster than the air immediately above it because of contact with the cool ground. The result is that vertically in the atmosphere the temperature increases with elevation.

With cooler or colder air next to the ground the vertical movement of air is restricted. If an air parcel is pushed upward when an inversion is present, it immediately becomes cooler than the air around it, and it will sink. The warmer air acts as a lid. Thus, there is very little mixing in the inversion layer which causes a build-up of pollutants. Visibility is usually reduced when an inversion is present. Fog readily forms in an inversion due to the additional nuclei present and the stable conditions with light winds.

In addition to a radiation inversion, there are other types of inversions. One already discussed is the "frontal inversion." As the advancing cold air pushes the warm air aloft, an inversion can occur at the frontal boundary. The inversion moves along with the front and is only momentarily experienced. The warm front inversion is more easily discernable than the cold front inversion. As warm air is lifted over the cold air, an inversion is created. A warm frontal inversion can exist for long periods, especially if the warm front is moving very slowly and the air being replaced is cold, preventing mixing of the air and subsequent dissipation of the inversion. The condition of cool air in the Portland area resulting from easterly winds out of the Columbia River Gorge, and warm air advecting in from the southwest at slightly higher elevations, is a prime example of this type of inversion. A depiction of the frontal inversion is shown in Figure 9.23.

One other type of inversion is called the "subsidence" inversion. We know that air is sinking, or subsiding, on the eastern edge of those semi-permanent high-pressure areas over the ocean and is warmed by compression due to the higher pressure as it is brought to the surface. This type of inversion is especially predominant off the Pacific coast in the summertime. Because of the cool ocean, the warm air

Figure 9.22 An inversion is an increase in temperature with elevation, as opposed to the normal decrease in temperature with elevation.

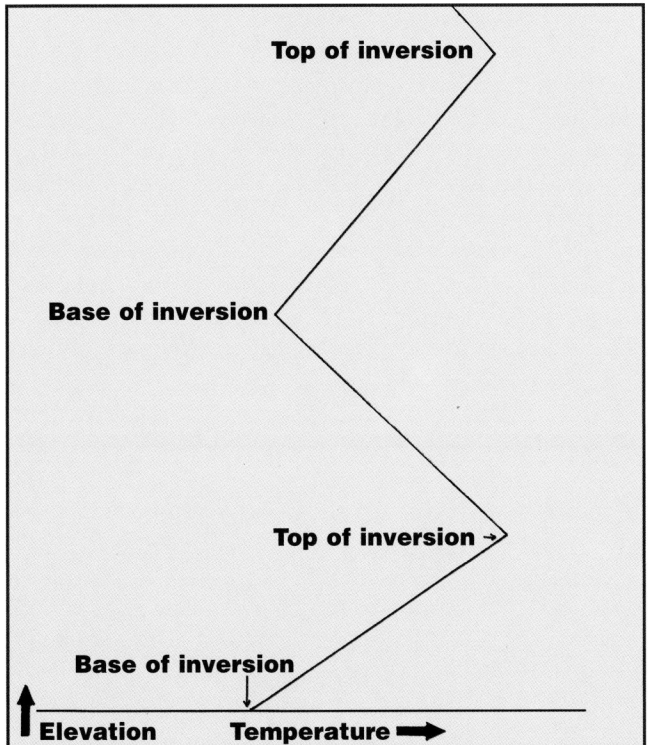

Figure 9.23 Inversions can occur near cold or warm fronts as warm air overrides cold air, and are usually of short duration unless the front is stationary.

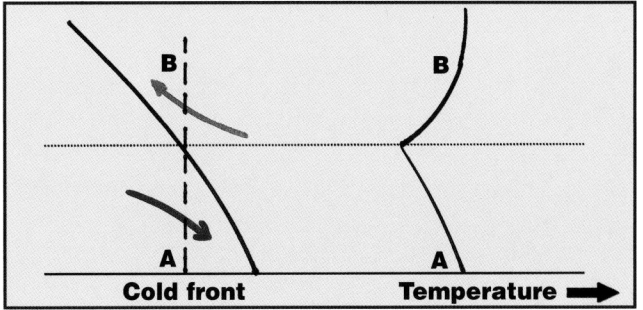

does not extend down to the ocean surface, Figure 9.24. In this case the inversion can be attributed to two causes: the subsiding air, and air near the surface being cooled by contact with the cooler water.

Sometimes over land a subsidence inversion will occur as very warm temperatures aloft, accompanied by much lower dewpoint temperatures, first appear at higher elevations, and then in the valleys below. A subsidence inversion that happens over a forest fire can cause a "blow-up" of the fire due to the very warm temperatures and low dewpoints that are brought to the surface.

A radiation inversion is dissipated usually by the sun heating the ground which heats the air beneath the top of the inversion. Figure 9.25 depicts this. The base of the inversion starts out at the surface and then gradually lifts to slightly higher elevations as the day progresses. This is shown as T+1, T+2, and so on in Figure 9.25. This is the normal sequence of events especially during a clear summer day. If fog is present, the time of dissipation will be delayed since a portion of the sun's rays are being reflected off the fog. The fog, however, will often "lift" off the ground into low stratus clouds as the base of the inversion lifts. Radiation inversions can also be dissipated by wind mixing the warmer air aloft with the cooler air below. Ground surfaces that may lie above the top of the fog, such as the side of a valley, will warm faster than surfaces below the fog as the sun rises higher. Thus, weak areas of low pressure can form in the fog-free, heated areas as opposed to cooler air and weak high pressure beneath the fog. This

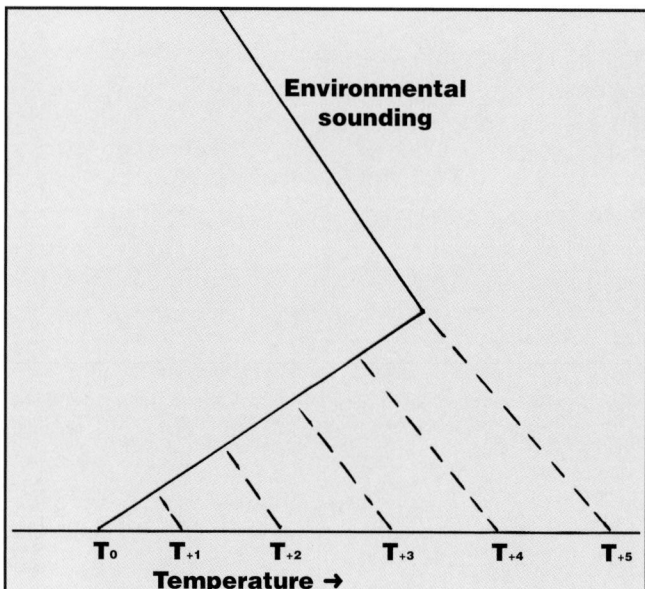

Figure 9.25 As the sun warms the surface, the base of the radiation inversion lifts, eventually breaking. "T" is increments of time.

weak circulation, from the foggy area to the clear area, also acts to dissipate the fog.

Fog

Fog is merely a cloud that surrounds you. The temperature has been lowered to the dewpoint temperature and condensation has resulted in the formation of tiny droplets of water. If the temperature is below the freezing mark, the water droplets are supercooled, meaning they exist as a liquid in an environment that is below freezing. There are different weather situations that produce fog.

Perhaps the most prevalent fog in the Pacific Northwest is radiation fog as shown in Figure 9.26. Loss of the earth's heat at night results in the temperature of air close to the surface of the earth being lowered to the dewpoint temperature. Favored locations for fog formation are low valleys where there may be a source of condensation nuclei, such as around mills and factories or some other source that is placing these nuclei into the atmosphere. A source of moisture such as a lake or river could also aid in the formation of fog. If the radiation fog becomes thick enough in winter and persists for several days, it can become a valley fog. Radiation fog forms beneath the top of an inversion where the temperature of the air increases with elevation. Figure 9.27 shows fog that has filled up the lower Columbia River Valley near St. Helens, Oregon.

The Rogue River Valley in southwest Oregon is a prime location for radiation fog to form as are many of the valleys west of the Cascade Mountains and occasionally east of those mountains. Often the hills above a radiation fog will be in the sunshine, while valley locations are in the fog. Medford, in the Rogue River Valley, is located around 1,300 feet above sea level. Ashland to the south-southeast is at

Figure 9.24 An example of a subsidence inversion along the Pacific Northwest coast. Warm air from above lies on top of air being cooled by contact with the ocean.

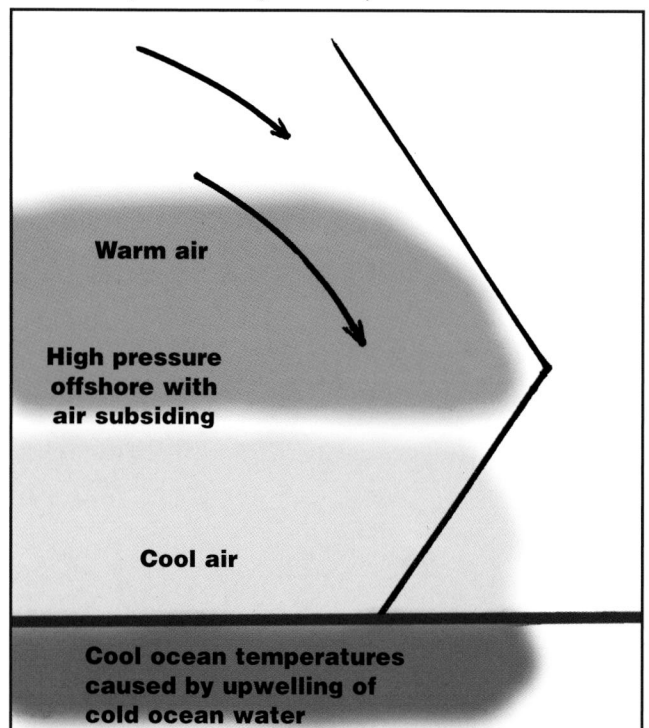

Figure 9.28 A fog bank along the Oregon coast about to move onshore.

Figure 9.26 Radiation fog near Portland International Airport (top), and near Klamath Falls, Oregon (bottom).

1,900 feet. Many times the town of Ashland will be in the sun with southeast winds while residents of Medford are driving around at mid-day with their car lights on in poor visibility due to fog.

Advection fog is not as apparent in the Pacific Northwest as it is in the flatter areas of the country such as in the Midwest or the Great Plains. It occurs when warm, moist air is advected over a colder surface. The air is cooled to the dewpoint temperature allowing condensation to occur. The coastal fog that occurs along the coasts of Washington and Oregon can be classified as an advection fog as it moves onshore in the evening, sometimes being transported along by a stiff ocean breeze. Figure

9.28 shows a fog bank along the Oregon coast that is being advected onshore.

Upslope fog is not as apparent west of the Cascade Mountains as it is on the eastern slopes of these mountains in the wintertime. However, one could certainly make a case for the fog (clouds) that obscure the western slopes with a westerly wind as upslope fog. In the Columbia Basin during the cool winter nights with clear conditions, a radiation fog will begin forming. Usually the weather regime that accounts for stagnant conditions in this area consists of an area of high pressure over eastern Washington, eastern Oregon, and Idaho with a low-pressure area off the Pacific Northwest coast. The wind flow associated with this weather pattern, although weak, would be from an easterly direction, or upslope on the east side of the Cascade Mountains.

The terrain rises gently from Pendleton to places like Redmond and Bend, Oregon or from the Tri-Cities area into Yakima and Ellensburg, Washington. As this air flows upslope towards these locations, it cools adiabatically until the temperature and the dewpoint temperature are the same. Condensation takes place. In winter when an easterly flow

Figure 9.27 Radiation fog that did not dissipate during the day and after several days filled up the lower Columbia River Valley near St. Helens, Oregon.

is present, motorists driving Highway 26 in Oregon or Highway 12 in Washington will often leave clear skies in the western valleys and then encounter cloudy, foggy, upslope conditions on the east side of the Cascade Mountains. Figure 9.29 is an illustration of the formation of upslope fog. Quite often the temperature in this fog is below freezing, but the water droplets within the fog are still in a liquid state, or supercooled. The result is a clear ice that forms on trees and often collects on roadways causing the condition known as "black ice" on highways. This fog will stack up to the crest of the Cascade Mountains, and begin spilling over the top as in Figure 9.30. In this case, the easterly winds, blowing downslope on the western side of the mountains, soon dissipate the fog. It is one of those rare occurrences when a person will not want to go east of the mountains to find sunny weather because there it will cloudy, foggy and dreary due to upslope conditions.

Steam fog is a phenomena that is readily observed over rivers and lakes in the early fall months. The temperature of the water at this time of year is often higher than the temperature of the air immediately above it, especially in the early morning hours. Having a higher vapor pressure, the water molecules escape from the surface of the water, cool, and condense in the air above. This produces small columns of steam that are visible over rivers and lakes extending sometimes several feet into the air. This fog dissipates rapidly as the day progresses and ceases to occur once the temperature of the water lowers during the cooler season of the year. Two examples of steam fog are shown in Figure 9.31, on a small pond in Gresham, Oregon and along the McKenzie River on the west slopes of the Cascade Mountains in Oregon.

Often, during the "breaking up" of a cold spell, areas in the Pacific Northwest will experience precipitation fog. This light fog forms as warm rain falls through cooler temperatures. The added moisture due to some of the rain evaporating can raise the dewpoint to near the temperature causing condensation and fog.

Small-scale and local effects respond to temperature and pressure changes much like large-scale weather features discussed in earlier chapters. Land and sea breezes, canyon

Figure 9.30 Upslope fog from easterly winds spilling over the crest of the Cascade Mountains, then dissipating as the air descends the western slopes.

winds, valley temperatures, all are affected by differences in temperature and pressure. Often, however, these weak circulations are disrupted by gradient winds that are responding to larger-scale pressure differences. This can cause these local winds to decrease, increase, or even reverse. Adiabatic warming as air descends barriers produces local effects that are manifest as very warm temperatures. Adiabatic cooling as air ascends these barriers can produce condensation that has local significance. Cooling of the air by radiation from the earth's surface results in areas where temperature differences produce small-scale effects. Here, inversions are created where stable conditions are present. Small scale and local effects are an important part of any area's weather.

Figure 9.31 Steam fog on a pond near Gresham, Oregon (top) and along the McKenzie River in Oregon (bottom).

Figure 9.29 Upslope fog along the eastern slopes of the Cascade Mountains in Oregon.

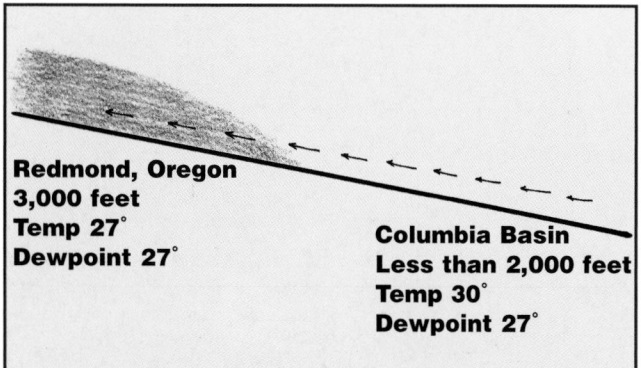

**Redmond, Oregon
3,000 feet
Temp 27°
Dewpoint 27°**

**Columbia Basin
Less than 2,000 feet
Temp 30°
Dewpoint 27°**

Chapter 10
Rivers and Flooding

Measuring the Height of a River and What Causes Floods

Lying in the belt of westerlies, the Pacific Northwest is definitely susceptible to heavy amounts of rain and snow, two ingredients that contribute to flooding. Captain Pease had taken his vessel from Canema, above the Falls of the Willamette upriver during the height of the December 1861 Flood. This flood is considered by many to be the

> **December 1861 Flood on the Willamette River**
> *"When we got to Salem," said Capt. Pease, "we found things booming. The bridge spanning Mill Creek had been swept away, and I could have easily taken the Onward clear around to the courthouse if I had wished."*
>
> *The Sunday Oregonian,* February 12, 1888,

greatest flood on that river since the arrival of the earliest settlers. (Native Americans have suggested an even greater event, but there is no confirmation.) But before we get inundated (no pun intended) by the topic of flooding, it is necessary that we understand the earth's complete hydrologic cycle.

Basically, all rivers run to the sea. There are a few places in the Pacific Northwest and other areas of the world where some rivers do not find their way to the ocean. In Oregon, the Silvies in the southeast portion of Oregon ends up in Malheur Lake. But for the most part, all rivers flow into the ocean, but the ocean never fills up. Why? Water evaporates from the oceans in tremendous quantities, is carried thousands of miles, and then deposited as rain, snow, and other forms of precipitation on land. The moisture is then carried by the rivers back to the oceans where the process starts again. It is depicted in Figure 10.1. Of course, some of the moisture never returns to the ocean and is locked up in glaciers and underground aquifers, but a balance is maintained.

Sometimes, however, there is more moisture that falls than a river can contain. The river rises, gets out of control, and the result is a flood. But what exactly is a flood, and how can we tell if a river is flooding, or even close to flooding? The answer to that question is obvious: we need to know the height of the river and how much water it contains.

Measuring the height of rivers is likely as old as the earliest inhabitants that lived along them. They observed that there were fluctuations in the height of the water. One of the earliest records of how the height of a river was measured is almost exactly one of the methods we still use today. The

Egyptians, thousands of years ago, would make marks on the side of structures to keep track of the height of the Nile River when it was flooding in the late spring and summer months. Some of these marks are still present today north of the Aswan Dam. A similar method is used today, we call it a staff gauge.

A staff gauge, Figure 10.2, is marked off in feet and tenths of feet. It is usually put on a bridge support, on a tree that is close to the river, or occasionally cemented to the bank of the river. For easy viewing, a staff gauge is located directly under the Morrison Bridge that spans the Willamette River in downtown Portland. It is on the west side of the river and is easily seen from the sea wall underneath the bridge. Figure 10.3 shows the same gauge at the height of the February 1996 flood when it reached 28.6 feet.

Other gauges involve the use of a float that is located inside an enclosure and connected through an opening to the river. As the river rises and falls, water in the enclosure rises and falls, moving the float up and down. This can be recorded on a chart for later reference, or it can be accessed in "real time" through the use of a telephone line and modem. Many of these recording devices are now accessible through satellite communications and can be placed in remote locations. They are powered by solar batteries. This ensures that data can be retrieved during storms that might cause interruptions in telephone or power service.

When the height of a river is mentioned, it is usually in reference to feet. What actually does that reading in feet mean? Feet above what? The height is actually above a reference point that is called a datum plane. A datum plane is merely a reference point. Sometimes it may be in reference

Figure 10.1 The hydrologic cycle. Water evaporates from the ocean, is carried thousands of miles, condenses and forms clouds. Precipitation falls as snow or rain on land to be carried by rivers back to the ocean.

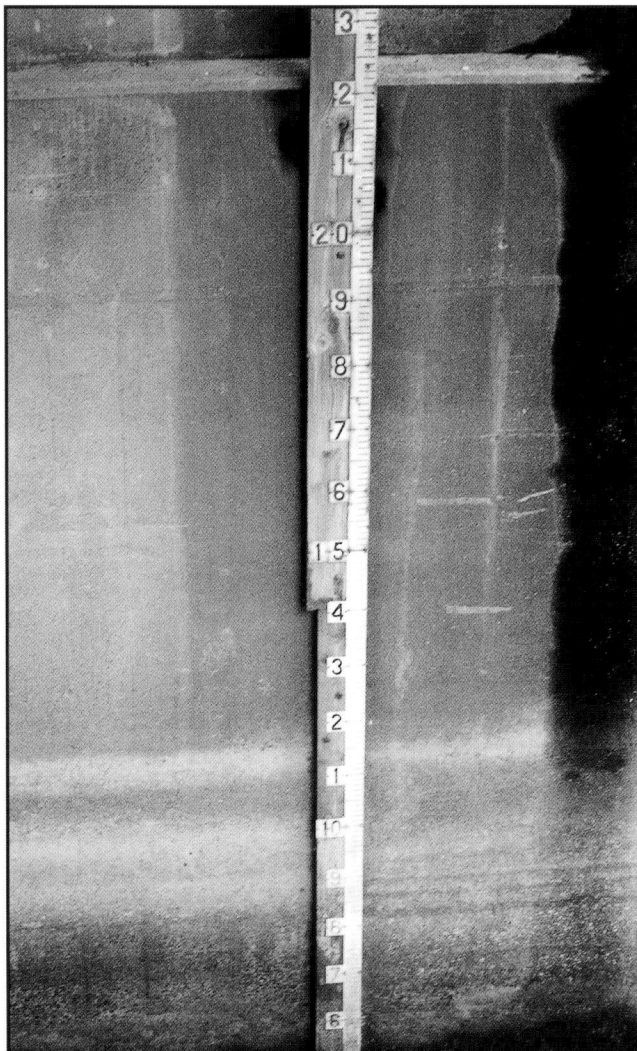

Figure 10.2 A staff gauge located on the Morrison Bridge spanning the Willamette River in Portland, Oregon.

Figure 10.3 The Morrison Bridge staff gauge at the height of the February 1996 flood at 28.6 feet.

There are various locations along a river that are designated as "forecast points" by hydrologists. At each of these forecast points, the actual flow of the river is measured in total cubic feet per second, or CFS. (A cubic foot is a cube one foot high, one foot long, and one foot wide.) If the geography of the river bottom is known, actual values of the flow at various depths and distances from shore can be measured with a flow meter. The result is a cross-section similar to that shown in Figure 10.5. The number of measurements is limited if the river height is changing rapidly.

Once the cross-section of a river at a certain point and at various depths and distances from shore is known, the actual flow can be well estimated in CFS. Thus, there is a relationship between the height of a river and the CFS flowing by a point. The higher the river at a location, the greater will be the CFS flowing by that location. The relationship between the two is expressed as a rating table. Figure 10.6 is a rating table for the Foss gauge on the Nehalem River in Oregon. If a hydrologist knows the height of a river, he or she can go to a rating table and find the flow of the river. Also, if a hydrologist knows how much flow in CFS is being added to the stream by way of runoff or discharge from a control dam, a prediction

to mean sea level for rivers close to the coast. At other times it is from the lowest level, or bottom of a river. In most cases, however, the datum plane is the average of all the lowest levels recorded in a river over a period of time at that particular location. This means that water is still flowing in the river, but at a very low level.

In the last example, if a river reading or level is measured at a very low point, say during a period of below normal rainfall in late summer or early fall, there could be readings with minus values. That does not mean that the river is dry. It only means that the flow is below the reference point, or in this case, very low. On rare occasions during the late summer and very early fall, before the rainy season has set in, the Columbia River has experienced minus readings at the Vancouver, Washington gauge. The river is not dry, but the flow is so low that the river has fallen below the reference point, or datum plane. Figure 10.4 is a theoretical cross-section of a river showing the relative position of the datum plane and positions of two other terms, bankfull and flood stage, which are discussed later.

Figure 10.4 A theoretical cross-section of a river showing relative positions of datum plane, bankfull, flood stage and the highest recorded stage or greatest flood on record.

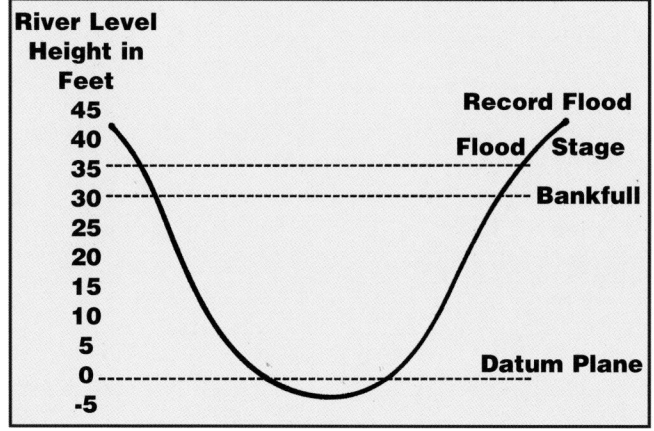

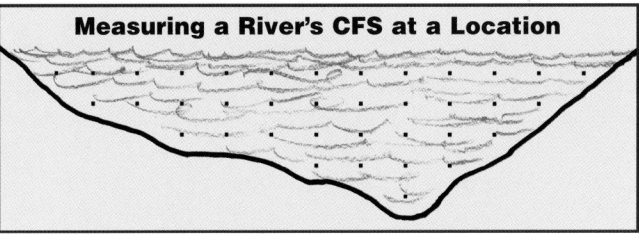

Measuring a River's CFS at a Location

Figure 10.5 The discharge of a river at a point on the river is computed by multiplying the area by the average flow at that point. Example: Area 150 square feet times 5 feet per second equals 750 CFS.

can be made as to how high the water will rise at a particular location or forecast point downstream.

The stage/flow relationship is constantly changing, however, as the geography of the river bottom changes. This is especially so during flood episodes when large deposits of silt and sand are deposited in the main channel of a river and thus raise the river bottom. This would change the cross-section area. The United States Geological Survey has been tasked with the responsibility of monitoring rivers to see if their shape has changed. During and after the eruption of Mt. St. Helens in Washington, immense quantities of ash

Figure 10.6 A rating table for the Foss gauge on the Nehalem River in northwest Oregon. Height in feet along the left; tenths of feet across the top. Example: Gauge height 10.5 feet; CFS 12,000.

Gauge Height (Feet)	Discharge in CFS									
	.0	.1	.2	.3	.4	.5	.6	.7	.8	.9
1							40	60	97	120
2	156	195	238	283	332	383	437	494	559	626
3	693	764	836	916	1,004	1,095	1,190	1,284	1,381	1,481
4	1,584	1,693	1,813	1,937	2,057	2,173	2,292	2,414	2,537	2,663
5	2,790	2,921	3,053	3,186	3,321	3,458	3,593	3,727	3,863	4,000
6	4,139	4,280	4,423	4,567	4,713	4,861	5,010	5,161	5,313	5,467
7	5,623	5,780	5,939	6,101	6,263	6,427	6,593	6,769	6,929	7,099
8	7,270	7,444	7,618	7,794	7,972	8,151	8,331	8,513	8,696	8,881
9	9,067	9,254	9,443	9,633	9,824	10,000	10,200	10,400	10,600	10,800
10	11,000	11,200	11,400	11,600	11,800	12,000	12,200	12,400	12,600	12,900
11	13,100	13,300	13,500	13,700	13,900	14,100	14,400	14,600	14,800	15,000
12	15,300	15,500	15,700	15,900	16,200	16,400	16,600	16,900	17,100	17,300
13	17,600	17,800	18,000	18,300	18,500	18,800	19,000	19,300	19,500	19,800
14	20,000	20,200	20,500	20,800	21,000	21,300	21,500	21,800	22,000	22,300
15	22,500	22,800	23,100	23,300	23,600	23,900	24,100	24,400	24,700	24,900
16	25,200	25,500	25,700	26,000	26,300	26,600	26,800	27,100	27,400	27,700
17	28,000	28,200	28,500	28,800	29,100	29,400	29,700	29,900	30,200	30,500
18	30,800	31,100	31,400	31,700	32,000	32,300	32,600	32,900	33,200	33,500
19	33,800	34,100	34,400	34,700	35,000	35,300	35,600	35,900	36,200	36,500
20	36,800	37,100	37,500	37,800	38,100	38,400	38,700	39,000	39,400	39,700
21	40,000	40,300	40,600	41,000	41,300	41,600	41,900	42,300	42,600	42,900
22	43,200	43,600	43,900	44,200	44,600	44,900	45,200	45,600	45,900	46,200
23	46,600	46,900	47,300	47,600	47,900	48,300	48,600	49,000	49,300	49,700
24	50,000	50,300	50,600	51,000	51,300	51,600	51,900	52,200	52,600	52,900
25	53,200	53,500	53,900	54,200	54,500	54,800	55,200	55,500	55,800	56,100
26	56,500	56,800	57,100	57,500	57,800	58,200	58,400	58,900	59,400	59,800
27	60,400	61,100	62,000	63,000	64,000	65,000				

Bankfull 12.0 feet, 15,300 CFS; Flood Stage 14.0 feet, 20,000 CFS; Maximum flow: 63,000 CFS (estimated), gauge height 27.4 at 11:00 p.m., 2/8/96; previous record flood 53,000 CFS, 24.9 feet, 1/9/90

and silt changed the geography of the Toutle River, Cowlitz River and even the Columbia River. Dredging had to be done to remove the silt and ash from the bottom of these rivers. This was especially important in the Columbia River, making it safe for ocean-going vessels.

A rating table will show other information in addition to a conversion of river flow to river height and river height to river flow. Among these are bankfull and flood stage. The term bankfull is self-explanatory. When the river holds all the water it can hold without overflowing its banks, that is bankfull. Rating tables will also indicate the greatest height the river has reached at that location over the years records have been kept. This is helpful in comparing flood events.

Flood stage is a slightly higher stage than bankfull and slightly more difficult to determine. It is the point at which some damage begins to occur or inundation of some key locations begins. This level is determined through information received from local, county and state officials as well as input from the National Weather Service. The demographics of an area is an important factor in determining flood stage and can even cause a change in the flood stage at a location. For example, flood stage at the Morrison Bridge measuring point is 18.0 feet. Very little damage results, however, when the river reaches this stage, but there can be some minor inundation. Rating tables for various rivers in Washington and Oregon can be obtained from the nearest National Weather Service Office that is responsible for forecasting the height of the river at that particular river gauge.

> **An Account of the December 1861 Flood**
> *"For awhile we lingered by the windows watching houses, still with lights burning in them floating slowly off down the river. We could hear people shouting as they passed by."*
>
> "True Story of a Flood as Told by Mary Higley Hopkins"
> Mss1509, Oregon Historical Society Archives

The CFS or the amount of water flowing past a point can be awesome. During the February 1996 flood, the Willamette River at the Morrison Bridge gauge reached a height of 28.6 feet with a flow of 365,000 CFS. That meant that every second 365,000 cubes of water one foot, by one foot, by one foot were flowing past the gauge. Estimates put the flow past Oregon City in the December 1861 flood at 590,000 CFS. This flood on the Willamette River completely destroyed the town of Orleans across from Corvallis and most of Linn City near the present-day town of West Linn. It also destroyed the town of Champoeg, the birthplace of the State of Oregon, located between Portland and Salem. The insert is a true account of a person who escaped the flood at Champoeg by moving to higher ground during the middle of the night. The falls at Oregon City had become just ripples in the flow much as Figure 10.7 from the Oregon Historical Society's photo archives shows of the February 1890 flood on the Willamette River.

Figure 10.7 February 1890 flood at Oregon City Power Plant. (Oregon Historical Society neg., cn#000651

Reasons for Flooding

But what actually are the factors that contribute to flooding? A flood can be caused by one of six things: (1) Heavy rain; (2) Snowmelt; (3) A combination of heavy rain and snowmelt; (4) Rain on frozen ground, (5) Ice jam; (6) A dam break. Since our topic is weather, we will leave the last cause to the engineers and focus on the first five, although these could certainly contribute to number six.

Heavy Rain

The earth and its vegetation are capable of containing large amounts of water. When rain falls, some of the precipitation runs off into the streams and rivers, some permeates into the soil, and some is intercepted by vegetation. When the capability of the ground to hold water is exceeded, more of the water begins to run off. It fills the streams and rivers to a point at which they can hold no more water. The river overflows its banks and begins causing destruction. If the rainfall rate exceeds the runoff rate, flooding can occur. This is especially the case with flash floods east of the Cascade Mountains that were discussed earlier when severe weather was the topic.

Most floods resulting strictly from heavy rain, at least west of the Cascade Mountains, occur during the months of October and November. If, however, snowpack in the mountains is meager, floods caused by heavy rain can occur during the colder months of the year. Minor flooding due to heavy rain in tributaries west of the Cascade Mountains can occur in April, May and even into June, but the amounts of precipitation are usually not as great or prolonged. The reason for the fall occurrence is that during this period, snow has usually not accumulated in the mountains to depths that, even if it melted, the additional water would not be a large contributing factor.

A strong southwesterly jet stream, with a succession of storms and their occlusions striking the Pacific Northwest, is a likely beginning to flooding due to heavy rain. However, even in this weather regime, there is often a break between storms of long enough duration to allow the streams and rivers to fall before the onset of the next storm. If the time between storms is small, the rivers do not have an opportunity to recede. Such is the case when the Pacific Northwest is affected by the subtropical jet stream. When this weather regime is present as shown in Figure 10.8, it transports storms with large amounts of moisture from lower latitudes northeastward into the Pacific Northwest. It has been given the name "Pineapple Express" because it sometimes originates near the Hawaiian Islands or even beyond. This was the case in November 1993 in western Washington and in November 1996 in southwest Oregon when rivers in these areas overflowed their banks and caused millions of dollars in damage. In both cases little snow had accumulated in the mountains to augment stream flow. The flooding was primarily a result of heavy rain over an extended period of time. In situations such as this, the rain continues without any, or very little, break between storms and the ground soon becomes saturated. Once that happens, rainfall does not penetrate into the soil, but begins to run off. The air is also quite warm during this time of year, arriving from lower latitudes. Warm air can hold copious amounts of moisture. Heavy rain that contributes to fall, winter and spring flooding causes the rivers to rise at rates that usually allow for some advance warning and protective measures can be taken.

Snowmelt

Snow is great for skiing, sledding and making snowmen. It can accumulate very rapidly in the mountains of the Pacific Northwest given the right meteorological conditions. Then in the springtime it melts. A warm ridge of high pressure with its attendant above-normal temperatures can enhance the melting. When that happens, flooding is the result.

Floods due strictly to snowmelt occur mostly in the springtime. A heavy mountain snowpack that has accumulated over the winter and into the spring can suddenly melt, bringing large quantities of water downstream. These floods are mostly confined to the Columbia River and its major tributaries. The melting is in the upper reaches of the Columbia River watershed in Idaho, Montana, and Canada. A flood in the spring of 1948 destroyed the settlement of Vanport, Oregon, where the Portland International Raceway and the Portland Exposition Center are now

Figure 10.8 Location of jet stream favorable for heavy rain during October and November in the Pacific Northwest. The flow could be slightly anticyclonic.

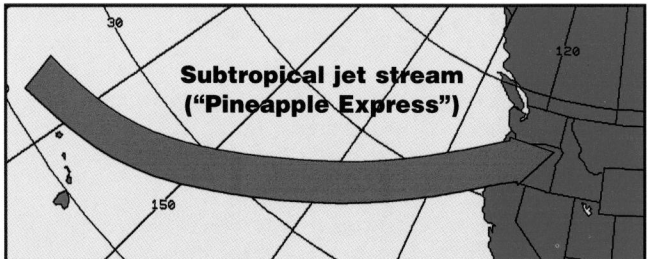

located. It was caused by very high water levels in the Columbia River due primarily to a rapid melting of the snowpack in its headwaters. The failure of a dike contributed to the disaster.

Spring snowmelt flooding can also occur on tributaries of the Columbia and Snake rivers in eastern Washington and Oregon. In these cases a warm period in the spring causes rapid melting of a major winter snowpack. This occurs over a few days or weeks and produces rises in streams flowing from such areas as the Blue Mountains in northeast Oregon. Rises in streams and rivers resulting from snowmelt flooding are generally slow which gives time for adequate preparation by emergency management and local and county disaster officials.

A large flow of water in the Columbia River can back up other streams flowing into it. The highest level ever reached on the Willamette River in Portland at the Morrison Bridge gauge since records have been kept was 33.0 feet in June 1894. A large portion of the business section of downtown Portland was under water, extending eleven blocks back from the river. Row boats and canoes were the method of travel, not horse and buggy as is depicted in Figure 10.9. This flood was a result of very high water levels in the main stem Columbia River that backed up the flow of the Willamette River. The water remained above 30 feet for 13 days and above flood stage for many more days. Flooding was extensive all along the Columbia River and several of its tributaries even east of the Cascade Mountains. With this type of flood the rise of the water is slow, except in cases like Vanport where the failure of a dike contributed to the event.

Today the flow of the Columbia River is highly regulated by a series of dams on its main stem and a majority of its tributaries. Water behind these dams is stored for use later in the summer season for agriculture and recreation. This mitigates the threat of extreme flows in the spring from melting of an abundant snowpack. The Willamette River is not as susceptible to flooding from snowmelt in the spring, nor are the rivers in Washington west of the Cascade Mountains. The

area covered by the watershed of the Willamette River is not as high in elevation as the upper reaches of the Columbia River, nor is it as large. Snowmelt over this watershed is much slower. In Washington rivers also rise in the spring, but the watersheds are smaller and the rise is usually slow and spread out over several months. The main flood threat to the Portland area in spring is high water in the Columbia River restricting the flow of the Willamette River.

Snowmelt and Heavy Rain Combined

The type of flood that probably causes the most damage in the Pacific Northwest is due to a combination of snowmelt and heavy rain. Many have occurred over the years that settlers have been in the area and probably many more before their arrival. The most recent was February 1996 when the Willamette River at Portland reached a height of 28.6 feet. A temporary "sea wall" was constructed along Waterfront Park in Portland, Oregon (Figure 10.10) to protect downtown businesses in case the water rose above the permanent wall, which it did not. Another disastrous flood that was due to snowmelt and heavy rain occurred around Christmas in 1964 throughout the Pacific Northwest and northern California. December, January, and February are months when a combination of snowmelt and heavy rain are common.

Perhaps the greatest flood along the Willamette River was the flood in December 1861 that was mentioned earlier. Warm rains of late October and early November were followed by a cold rain through most of November. The latter deposited heavy amounts of snow in the mountains and foothills. The soils had become saturated. Then, during the last few days of November and the first few days of December, the weather regime changed. A very warm period followed that some reports have termed as "tropical" in nature. It was accompanied by a very heavy rain. The Willamette River at many points reached unprecedented heights. A marker on the pavilion at Champoeg Park (Figure 10.11) attests to the height of the river. Many businesses in

Figure 10.9 Downtown Portland, Oregon at 3rd Street on June 8, 1894 during the record setting flood. Floods in early Portland were often referred to as "cellar" floods since they would fill cellars in downtown Portland businesses.
Oregon Historical Society, #cn018594

Figure 10.10 During the February 1996 flood on the Willamette River a temporary "sea wall" was constructed along Waterfront Park in Portland.

Figure 10.11 The location of the arrow left on the pavilion at Champoeg Park shows the calculated height of the December 1861 flood. The Willamette River today is shown at right.

Oregon City and all along the Willamette River were destroyed or simply floated away. One was found many days later 12 miles upriver from Astoria, Oregon! This flood not only affected the Pacific Northwest, but was general throughout California, Nevada, Utah, and Arizona.

All of the above floods—1861, 1890, 1964, and 1996—followed the same pattern. In each of these cases, heavy snow accumulated in the mountains and at low elevations. Then, a warm southwesterly wind laden with moisture, the Pineapple Express, followed. A typical weather map favorable for heavy snowfall but then switching quickly to heavy rainfall in the Pacific Northwest is shown in Figure 10.12. Note in this case how close the two jet streams are to each other over the Pacific Northwest. This allows for rapid fluctuations from a cold regime to a warm regime. During cold episodes, when the northern branch of the jet stream prevails, substantial snow can be deposited, often at low elevations. Then, with a retreat of the northern branch of the jet stream and advance of the southern branch, this snow can melt quickly accompanied by warm, heavy rain resulting in rapid rises of streams and rivers.

Figure 10.12 Location of subtropical and polar jet streams favorable for alternating periods of heavy snow and then heavy rain in the Pacific Northwest.

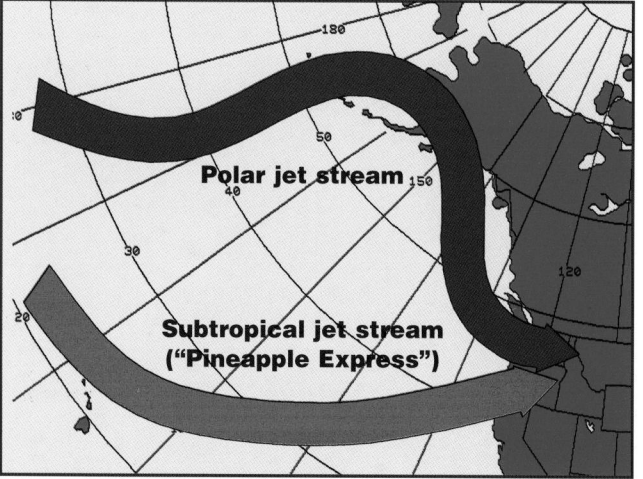

Warm Rain on Frozen Ground
This type of flooding occurs almost exclusively east of the Cascade Mountains. During cold arctic outbreaks the ground in this area can freeze to great depths. A sudden surge of warm moist air produces heavy rain that cannot penetrate the frozen soil, and the water runs off into the creeks and rivers. Some melting of any accumulated snow also can contribute to this type of flooding.

Ice Jam
Flooding due to an ice jam usually occurs east of the Cascade Mountains, but in very rare instances could occur briefly west of these mountains following a long cold spell. Very cold temperatures followed by warming are usually the cause. Early spring is a favored time for this type of flooding. The ice breaks up, but does not melt as fast as snow, and creates ice jams. Thus, a warm rain on snow with temperatures near or slightly above freezing will create this situation.

Forecasting the Height of a River
The reasons for flooding have been discussed, as well as how the flow in a river or stream is measured. But how are the levels forecast? What clues help hydrologists determine the river height or CFS? Certainly the depth of snow in the mountains is a prime factor with the snowmelt, and heavy rain/snowmelt combination. Estimates of the maximum springtime flow in the Columbia River incorporate snow depth in the headwaters of that river and its major tributaries as compiled by the Natural Resource Conservation Service. Rainfall is another prime ingredient in determining how high a river will rise. Rainfall can be correlated well with runoff. A series of precipitation gauges over a watershed will give an approximation of the

Factors Contributing to Runoff:
1. **Amount of precipitation.**
2. **Duration of precipitation.**
3. **Type of surface.**
4. **Condition of the soil.**
5. **Slope of the surface.**

amount of rain that has fallen over the entire watershed. From these data hydrologists can determine just how much will run off into the streams to find its way back to the ocean.

Runoff, however, is affected by several conditions. Those include (1) Amount of precipitation, (2) Duration of precipitation, (3) Type of surface on which the precipitation is falling, (4) Condition of the soil, and (5) Slope of the surface on which the precipitation is falling. It is easy to see that the greater the amount of precipitation, the greater will be the runoff. Small amounts of precipitation have a tendency to seep into the ground leaving very little to run off into the streams. The duration of precipitation is a contributing factor regarding how much precipitation will find its way into a stream. One inch of rain falling over a 24-hour period over a watershed will not produce as much runoff as one inch of rain falling in one hour over the same area.

The type of surface affects the amount of runoff. Given the same amount of rainfall, there will be much more runoff if the area is rocky than if there is lush vegetation. The thick redwood forests in northwest California intercept some of the precipitation that falls, especially in the summer months when the precipitation is of a fine mist or drizzle. This fact is easily observed when it first starts to rain, since it will remain dry under a thick tree for several minutes, sometimes hours if the precipitation is light. In summer I have measured over 0.25 inch precipitation falling slowly over several hours in my rain gauge, yet areas nearby under large fir trees and deciduous trees remained totally dry. An area where all the trees have been cut will experience more runoff than a heavily forested area next to it. The condition of the soil is also a strong contributing factor to runoff. Repeated rains over a prolonged period of time will cause the moisture value in the soil to increase. Soils with high moisture values will produce more runoff than those with lower values simply because the water cannot penetrate into the soil. This is the situation that causes mud slides. The soil becomes saturated and is the consistency of jelly in some instances. Finally, there is the steepness of the slope. The steeper the slope, the greater will be the runoff. All of the above factors are taken into consideration when a hydrologist is making a forecast of how high a river will rise.

Factors Contributing to the Amount of Precipitation

There are several factors that affect the amount of rainfall over an area. The first is topography. Mountains have a pronounced effect on the amount of precipitation falling over an area. Air that flows up and over the Cascade Mountains arrives at eastern locations much drier than when it started out on the west side, the excess having been deposited as rain on the western slopes.

Another factor contributing to the amount of rainfall is the origin of the air mass. Those maritime tropical air masses with their warm temperatures contain much more moisture than the maritime polar air masses. This is why southern California receives so much rain when it finally does rain there. The air arriving is usually in the 50s and even the 60s. Air at that temperature has the ability to hold much more moisture than air in the 40s.

The direction of the wind can also have an effect on the amount of rainfall. This relationship is shown in Figure 10.13. Wind flow that is perpendicular to a mountain range will deposit much more rain on the windward slopes than a flow that is parallel to the mountain range. Air that is flowing parallel to a barrier will not be forced aloft. Studies have been done correlating the precipitation at Seattle, Washington, to that at Stampede Pass located east of Seattle in the Cascade Mountains. A southerly flow of air aloft will

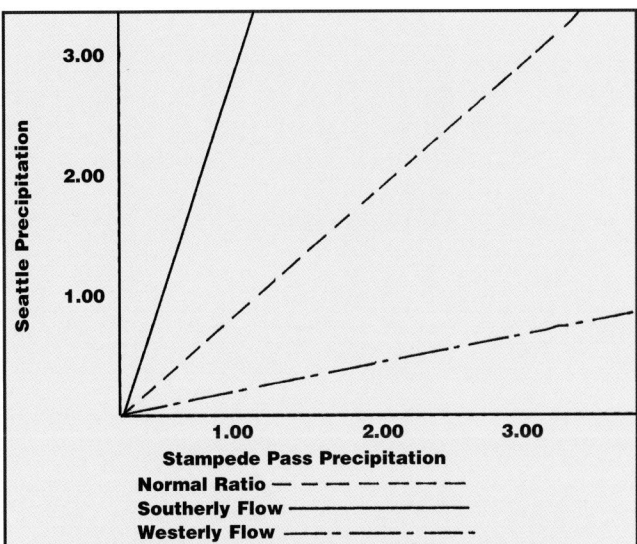

Figure 10.13 A schematic showing the relationship of the amount of precipitation in inches recorded at Stampede Pass in the Cascade Mountains with that of Seattle, Washington with wind direction as a factor.

often bring more precipitation to the Seattle area than what is recorded at Stampede Pass, which is at an elevation of around 4,000 feet. A westerly flow can often bring four to as much as ten times as much rain to Stampede Pass compared to what might fall in Seattle.

The last effect on the amount of rainfall is the speed of the frontal system or the speed of the air mass. A rapidly moving frontal system will not deposit as much precipitation as one that is moving slowly. This is somewhat manifest when we compare annual precipitation values at Eugene, Oregon to that at Portland, Oregon. Eugene receives about ten inches more on an annual basis. Some of this difference is due to Eugene's slightly higher elevation, but a portion of the difference is due to frontal systems that will often slow down and even stall as they approach the higher terrain south of Eugene. A frontal system moving southward might deposit one-half inch in the Portland area, but might cause nearly an inch in the Eugene area as the front stalls moving through the mountains.

Precipitation and River Height

It is easy to see how some of these factors are related to stream flow. This is especially so when rainfall is the only contributing factor. Figure 10.14 is the plot of a hydrograph of the Foss river gauge on the Nehalem River in Oregon from January 27 to 31, 1992. The precipitation record is from Lees Camp in the northern Coast Range Mountains and is a good representation of the rainfall over the Nehalem River watershed. Note that rainfall amounts of one to two inches caused a sharp rise in the river at the Foss gauge. The height of the river then leveled off, but began rising again as the rain increased. In Figure 10.14 the height of the river is labeled every two feet, and the precipitation is in inches. Flood stage on the river is at 13 feet. The numbers at the bottom represent six-hour intervals using the 24-hour

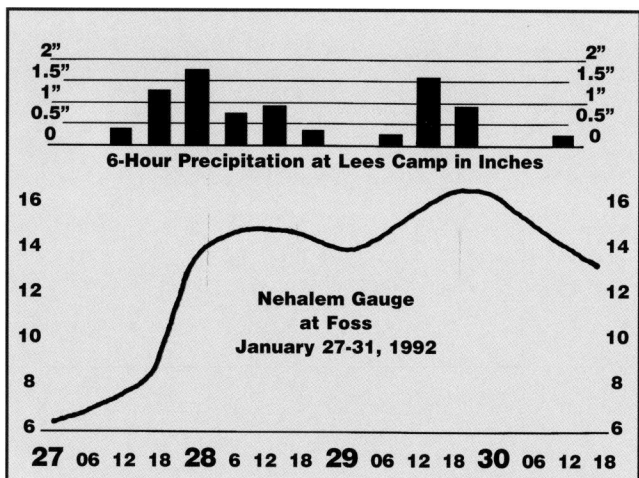

Figure 10.14 The relationship showing how rainfall affects a river gauge. Heavy rain in the headwaters of the Nehalem River caused the river at Foss to rise rapidly, then level off, only to rise again with additional rainfall.

clock. This hydrograph is typical of a plot of river height vs. time. Hydrographs are also constructed using CFS.

The 100-Year Flood

The term "100-year" flood is often mentioned and often misinterpreted. It does not mean that this type of flood occurs once every one hundred years. Rather, the term means there is a one percent chance that the river in question will reach that value in any given year. Theoretically, a 100-year flood could occur one year and then occur again the next year. The 10-year, 50-year, 100-year, 500-year, etc., floods are statistically determined from the brief historical data for that river. River levels have been recorded for slightly over 100 years on several Pacific Northwest streams and rivers, but less on others. Yet, 100-year floods can statistically be derived from the data. Most building codes and insurance rates are based on the 100-year occurrence.

There is a formula for computing the likelihood of a flood with a certain return frequency. For instance, if an individual lives in a 100-year flood plain for 25 years, there is a 22 percent chance that the event will be experienced; residing there for 50 years increases the risk to 40 percent; and for 100 years 68 percent. Note that even if a person is in the 100-year flood plain for 100 years, there still is not a 100 percent chance the event will happen.

The Bretz Floods

Before the topic of floods recedes, we should mention what were perhaps the worst floods to ever occur on the Columbia River. Fortunately, there were not many individuals around at the time of the floods, although I am wondering if the "Kennewick Man" who was found along the Columbia River near Kennewick, Washington several years ago may have been a victim of one of the very last of these great floods, of which there were several.

At the end of the last ice age, 10,000 to 15,000 years ago, there was a large lake in what is now western Montana and northern Idaho called Lake Missoula. It was held back by an ice jam. As the climate slowly warmed at the end of the ice age, the ice jam holding back Lake Missoula would temporarily break, sending large volumes of water down the Columbia River. It is believed that there was not just one breakage of the ice jam, but several that resulted in horrendous floods along the Columbia River. The ice jam would break, then refreeze for several hundred years, and then break again.

It is estimated that the height of the Columbia River at Crown Point, Figure 10.15, during one of these floods was 700 feet, 500 feet at Troutdale, 400 feet in the Portland area, and 380 feet as far south as Eugene. If the US Bank building in downtown Portland had been around, only the top of it would have been above the water. Huge rocks contained in glacial ice were transported downstream. Many of these rocks can still be seen around the Portland area today. The area south of McMinnville contains sandstone that is not indigenous to the Willamette Valley. Those rocks were brought down from the northeastern Washington area during the Bretz Floods. Some even speculate that the great Willamette Meteorite found south of Oregon City many years ago may have been brought down the Columbia River from somewhere upstream by the Bretz Floods, sometimes called the Missoula Floods.

Flooding is a regular occurrence in the Pacific Northwest. It is the result of a number of factors including rain, rain and snow, snowmelt, and ice jam. Each of these have caused rivers to rise bringing devastation and death. Various weather regimes as well as antecedent conditions such as amount and duration of precipitation, type of soil, origin of a particular air mass and movement contribute to rivers rising to these dangerous levels. Hydrologists, however, are aware of these conditions. Thus, the height of a river or its CFS can be forecast minimizing the damage.

Figure 10.15 During the Bretz Floods, a person standing at Crown Point, elevation 650 feet would have been swept downstream. Estimated height here reached 700 feet.

Chapter 11
Global and Pacific Northwest Climatology

If you have lived in or visited various parts of the world, United States, or even the Pacific Northwest, you have experienced different climates. Climatology is a topic all its own, but the factors that govern climate on a global scale also govern the climate of the Pacific Northwest. This overview will allow a person to see how the topics discussed earlier that include the major wind belts, surface heating, subsidence, convergence, terrain, and other controls all come together to form a particular climate.

Factors That Control Climate

When we speak of climate, what are we referring to? Is climate different than weather? In a way, yes. We usually think of weather as what we experience on a daily basis. Weather is what is occurring right now, or tomorrow. Climate is an average, over a long period of time, of the weather at a location. And just as there are controlling features to weather, there are controlling features to climate. Those features, or factors, are: (1) Oceans and Ocean Currents, (2) Latitude, (3) Mountains, (4) Pressure and Wind Systems, (5) Geographic Position on a Land Mass, and (6) Land and Water Distribution.

Oceans and Ocean Currents

Roughly 70 percent of the earth's surface is covered by water. We can only speculate what type of climate the earth would have if that figure were 50 percent. The earth would probably be much drier, and probably hotter. The oceans control the amount of moisture in the air. Not only are the oceans a source of moisture, but they have the ability to store large quantities of heat. They are often referred to as large "heat sinks" because of the heat stored in them. Not only can oceans store heat, they can move it around. The Gulf Stream moves large quantities of warm water northward in the Atlantic Ocean, and is of primary importance in keeping the climate of England relatively mild. Ocean currents can act as both a warming and cooling factor in producing a type of climate. A cooler body of water will not heat the air above it as readily as a warmer one. The Pacific Ocean off the coasts of Washington and Oregon has a profound effect on the climate of the Pacific Northwest.

Ocean currents like those shown in Figure 11.1 for the North Pacific Ocean basically follow the surface wind around the major high and low pressure areas. The Kuroshio Current, a warm current, flows northeastward off Japan and becomes the North Pacific Drift across the North Pacific Ocean, also a basically warm current. Near the coast of North America around 50 degrees North Latitude, it splits with a portion flowing north into the Gulf of Alaska and a portion flowing south off the coast of the

Pacific Northwest, often referred to as the California Current. Here it becomes basically a cold current, especially in the warmer months of the year. During these months, May into September, the Pacific high pressure area is farther north, strongest, and northwesterly winds along the coast have reached their greatest intensity. This current, however, often reverses in winter to a slight southerly current as the Pacific high pressure area weakens and retreats south, and the Gulf of Alaska low pressure area expands and strengthens, which results in a more southerly flow of air along the coast.

Evidence is now being gathered on another current that flows counter to the Gulf Stream at great depths in the Atlantic Ocean. This current then flows south around Africa into the Indian Ocean and eventually finds its way into the Pacific Ocean. Some scientists believe that it is one of the driving forces behind the short-term (less than 100 years) variations in climate.

Latitude

Latitude has a profound effect on climate. Tropical regions receive much more heat from the sun than polar regions. Thus, tropical regions will be warmer than polar regions. Where it is warmer, there will generally be more precipitation if in proximity to an ocean due to the air's capacity to contain moisture, especially if the air streams are converging in that area.

Mountains and Highlands

Mountains can produce their own climate systems. This fact is evident to people in the Pacific Northwest as they drive across the Cascade Mountains. The Columbia River Gorge

Figure 11.1 Major currents in the North Pacific Ocean: (1) Kuroshio, (2) North Pacific Drift, (3) Alaska, (4) California, (5) North Equatorial, (6) Oyashio

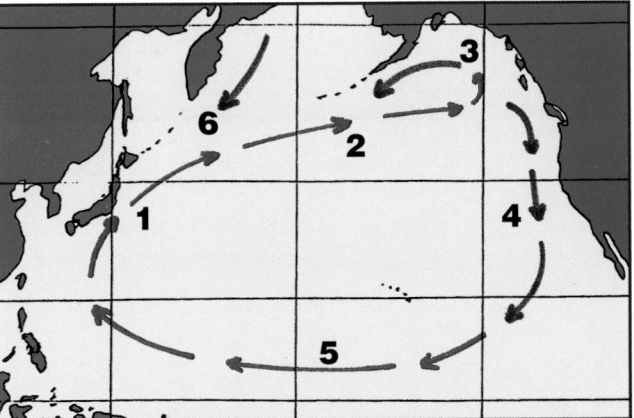

Figure 11.2 Steens Mountain in southeast Oregon. Several climate zones exist from desert to alpine forest.

is an excellent place to observe a change in climate caused by the Cascade Mountains. Thus, if any type of climate classification is to be done, a factor called mountains and some of the areas within them called highlands must be included. Figure 11.2 shows Steens Mountain in southeast Oregon which rise from the desert floor to nearly 10,000 feet. Several climatic zones exist from desert to alpine forest.

Pressure and Wind Systems

The earth's major wind belts and the areas of high and low pressure around the earth play important roles in determining climate. A station located on the western side of one of the sub-tropical high pressure areas will have a different climate than a station located on the eastern side, even though they may be at the same latitude. Tokyo, Japan and San Francisco, California are prime examples of this. Virtually no rain falls at San Francisco in the summer months, while Tokyo records more precipitation in the period May through October than from November through April, just the opposite of San Francisco, Figure 11.3. Summer winds at San Francisco are off the cold ocean to the west and subsiding, while summer winds at Tokyo are southeast off the warm, western Pacific Ocean and generally rising. A cold ocean results in a more stable atmosphere near the surface

while a warm ocean enhances convective activity resulting in showers and thundershowers. Locations that are affected by the jet stream will show a maximum of precipitation when that feature is in proximity to them. These locations will also show a decrease in precipitation as the jet stream migrates north of their area during the Northern Hemisphere summer.

Geographic Position on a Land Mass

The location on a continent is a definite climate factor. A predominant westerly flow of air across North America produces some large variations in climate. Portland, Oregon, has a different climate than Minneapolis, Minnesota, which is different than Boston, Massachusetts, even though all three locations are at roughly the same latitude, but at different locations on the North American continent. The prevailing westerlies keep Portland's climate modified with a winter maximum of precipitation. Minneapolis is often engulfed during the winter months by invasions of arctic air masses that do not have much available moisture. Here, also, average winter temperatures are much lower than those in Portland and the summers are warm and humid in Minnesota. Boston, in a prevailing westerly flow, receives roughly the same amount of yearly precipitation as Portland, yet the total yearly value at Boston is spread almost evenly over the 12-month period. The total for the year is shared by winter storms moving in the westerly jet stream with convective showers and thundershowers responsible for summer's precipitation. Comparisons of monthly temperature and monthly precipitation for Portland, Minneapolis, and Boston are shown in Figure 11.4 and Figure 11.5. Yearly snowfall totals also show a great variation from only slightly over 6 inches at Portland to over 57 inches at Minneapolis. Boston's average annual snowfall is around 42 inches.

Land and Water Distribution

Land surfaces heat much more rapidly than water surfaces. They also cool much more rapidly. Consequently, temperature variations will be least for those areas that are in proximity to a water source. In the discussion on air masses, it was

Figure 11.3 Located on opposite sides of the north Pacific high pressure center and at relatively the same latitude, the annual march of precipitation is reversed from Tokyo, Japan to San Fransisco, California.

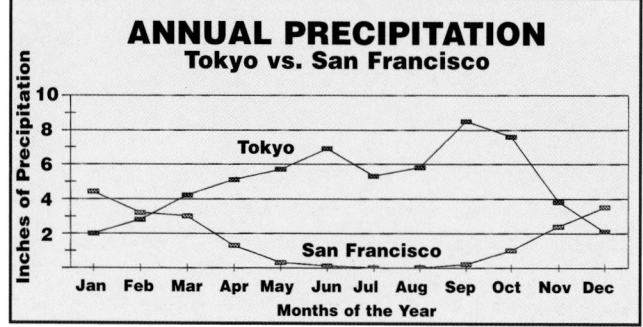

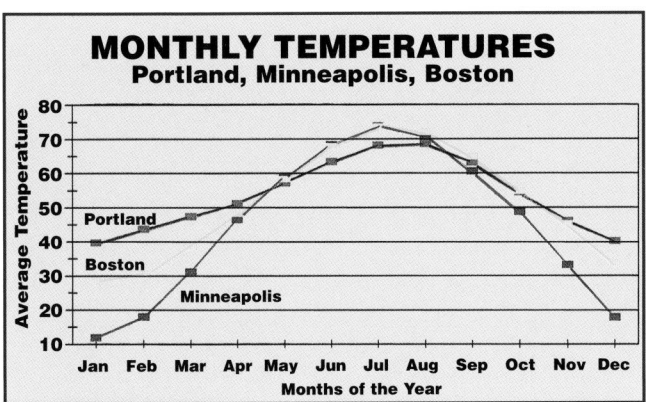

Figure 11.4 Average monthly temperature at Portland, Minneapolis, and Boston. Marine influence is greatest at Portland, least at Minneapolis.

Figure 11.6 The Painted Hills area of eastern Oregon receives around 10 inches of precipitation annually, located far inland from the Pacific Ocean.

noted that continental air does not contain as much moisture as maritime air. Figure 11.6 shows the semi-arid region of eastern Oregon, separated from the Pacific Ocean by a range of mountains. Heating of land surfaces will affect the seasonal distribution of precipitation in proximity to a water source and even in areas somewhat removed from a moisture source. An example is the area near the "heat low" over the southwest deserts in the summer. Here the air is very warm and dry but the lower pressure eventually draws in moisture from the Gulf of Mexico and the Gulf of California that accounts for a weak maximum of precipitation in mid to late summer in southwestern United States. Some of this moisture can even creep as far north as eastern Oregon in the summer.

Köppen Classification of Climate

There have been several attempts to classify the world's climates over the last 100 years. Perhaps the most widely accepted is that by Wladimir Köppen. His classification is based on the distribution of vegetation. He recognized six major climate types: The humid tropical which he called A; the dry, or desert areas, which he gave a B; humid middle latitude where the winters are mild was called C; humid middle latitude in which the winters are cold D; the Polar or E classification; and H or highlands.

Köppen went even further and divided each with regard to temperature and precipitation. The tropics were divided into a tropical wet, tropical wet-and-dry, and a tropical monsoon. The deserts were divided into two categories called steppe and desert. The C category was divided into a Mediterranean, a middle latitude wet-and-dry with a mild winter, and a middle latitude rainy with a mild winter. The D classification was given two subtitles, middle latitude wet-and-dry with a cold winter, and a middle latitude rainy with a cold winter. The Polar climate was divided into two sub-classifications called the tundra and the ice cap. There are no sub-divisions to the highlands type of climate.

The Pacific Northwest has several of the above classifications. The extreme southwest portion of Oregon could certainly be called a Mediterranean type climate, which is how the coastal areas of California are classified. Most of the area west of the Cascade Mountains falls into a middle latitude wet-and-dry, meaning most of the precipitation falls in the October through mid-May period with dry summers. At times, however, when the Pacific Northwest suffers through a soggy summer, it could be classified as a middle latitude rainy with a mild winter, meaning that significant precipitation still falls in the summer months. This type of climate is found along the British Columbia and southeast Alaska coasts. Alpine or highland climates exist in the higher elevations of the Cascade Mountains, the Olympic Mountains in Washington and the Blue Mountains of eastern Oregon. East of the Cascade Mountains the climate classification under Köppen is mostly a middle latitude steppe with some years approaching the middle latitude wet-and-dry with a cold winter.

With that, the general discussion about climate ends. Much has been written about each one. It suffices to say that the boundary between one type of climate and another is certainly not a fixed line but can oscillate many miles over several years or within a year. Sometimes the summers west of the Cascade Mountains bring copious amounts of rain, and some winters have been bitterly cold. These local fluctuations

Figure 11.5 Monthly precipitation for Portland, Minneapolis, and Boston. Note the reversed curves for Portland and Minneapolis; relatively even distribution for Boston.

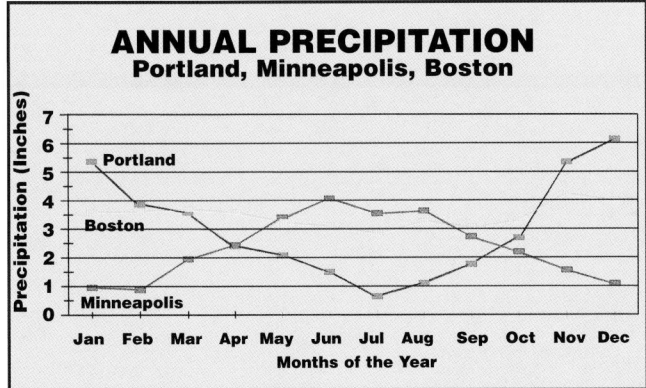

might seem as though the climate is changing, when probably it is only a slight fluctuation in the location of the broad line that separates one climate type from another.

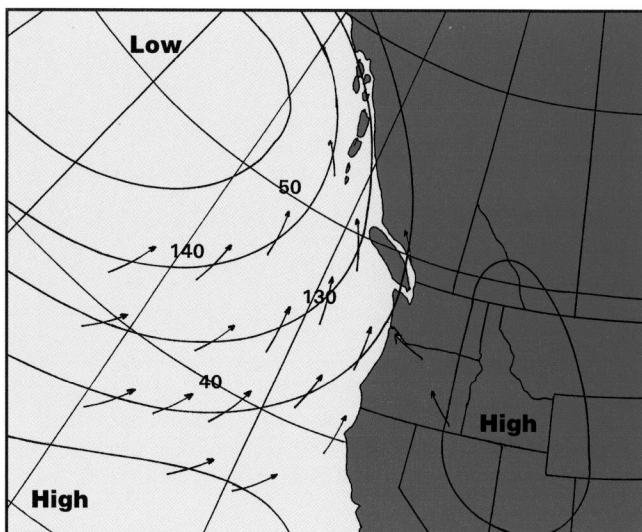

Figure 11.7 The normal surface pressure pattern and winds over the eastern Pacific Ocean during the winter months.

Pacific Northwest Climates

As mentioned the Pacific Northwest contains several of the climates in the Köppen classification including some in the B category, some in the C category, and some in the H category. There are four basic factors that control the climate in the Pacific Northwest: The Pacific Ocean, the Cascade Mountains, the movement of the high and low pressure areas offshore, and to some extent ocean currents.

General Circulation

With a prevailing westerly flow of air aloft there is a moderating effect by the Pacific Ocean to temperature throughout the Pacific Northwest, especially west of the Cascade Mountains. Here this flow changes at the surface from a general southerly direction in winter to a general northerly direction in summer, but the moderating effect of the ocean occurs in all seasons.

During the winter months the prevailing surface low pressure in the Gulf of Alaska and the Pacific high pressure center east-northeast of the Hawaiian Islands create a southwesterly flow of air at the surface into the Pacific Northwest, Figure 11.7. At coastal locations and inland valley locations west of the Cascade Mountains the prevailing flow of air at the surface is south to southwesterly in the winter because of orographic features. There are disruptions to this general flow of air, however. A weak high pressure area prevails over the Plateau area of Utah, Nevada, and Idaho and extends into eastern Washington and eastern Oregon. The high pressure area is due to colder surface temperatures in this area during the winter. This weak high pressure area affects the wind flow. At Portland, Oregon, for instance, the prevailing direction of the wind in winter is from the southeast, as a result of a strong easterly flow of air out of the Columbia River Gorge. At some coastal locations, the prevailing flow of air can also be southeasterly due to geographic features such as at the mouth of the Columbia

River. East of the Cascade Mountains the surface wind direction is primarily south or southeasterly in winter. Wind flow is also lighter east of these mountains in the winter, and geographic features cause many local variations that can enhance the wind speed as well as decrease it.

During the spring, the average pressure pattern over the eastern Pacific Ocean begins to change. As the warmer summer months approach, the area of high pressure over the ocean expands and moves north. The area of low pressure in the Gulf of Alaska begins to weaken and retreat into the Bering Sea. Warmer temperatures over the Plateau eliminate the high pressure of winter. Intense heating over the southwest portion of the United States forms a heat low over that area. A similar weak heat low forms over the Columbia Basin. Figure 11.8 shows these changes.

West of the Cascade Mountains, the prevailing wind along the coastal strip and most inland valleys is now northerly to northwesterly. The sand dunes along the Oregon coast have often been called the "traveling sand dunes," meaning they migrate slightly north in winter due to the prevailing southerly winds and then south in the summer due to the prevailing northwesterly winds.

From an easterly flow in winter, the prevailing flow through the Columbia River Gorge switches to westerly in summer. Now, air is flowing through the one main gap in the Cascade Mountains from high pressure offshore to a low pressure over the interior. These two prevailing wind flows (easterly in winter and westerly in summer) are clearly shown in Figure 11.9. This photograph was taken several years ago near the top of Beacon Rock in the middle portion of the Columbia River Gorge. It shows two fir trees with distinct features. The tree on the right has only short stubby branches on its east side, showing a prevailing strong easterly flow. The tree on the left has very few branches on the west, or left, side indicating a

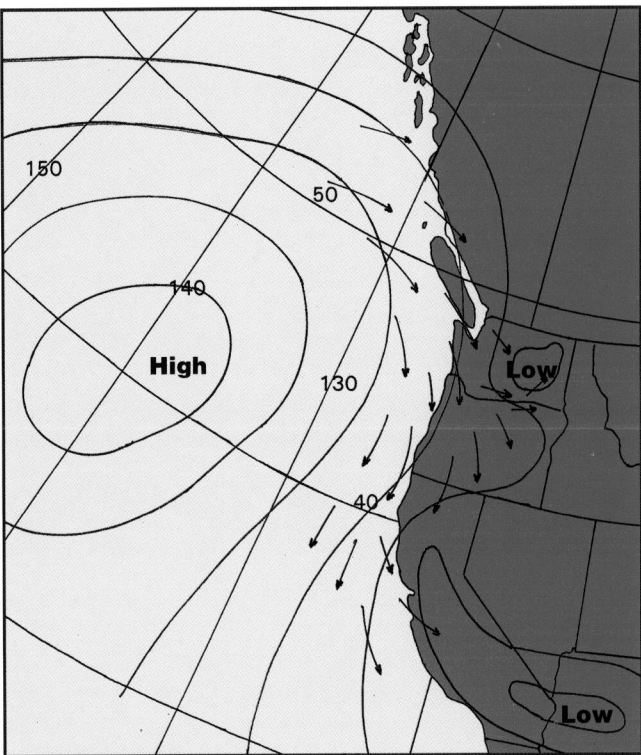

Figure 11.8 Normal pressure and wind pattern over the eastern Pacific Ocean and Pacific Northwest in summer.

prevailing westerly flow. The leeward side of each tree is protected by the other tree.

Surface wind flow east of the Cascade Mountains in summer is primarily northwesterly. This is especially so immediately east of these mountains and other mountains. There are exceptions to this, however. Locations directly to the east of a gap in the Cascade Mountains will have a pre-

Figure 11.9 Embracing fir trees near the center of the Columbia River Gorge that show prevailing westerly flow during summer (left) and prevailing easterly flow during the winter (right)

vailing wind flow that reflects the orientation of the mountain pass. This could result in the flow becoming westerly or even southwesterly. Locations in proximity to the weak heat low in the Columbia Basin will show prevailing wind that is flowing around and into that weak area of low pressure. Elevation also becomes a factor in these prevailing winds. Spokane, in northeastern Washington, exhibits a somewhat prevailing southwesterly flow in summer as winds react to increasing elevation.

Terrain Features

If there were no Cascade Mountains, there would perhaps be one, maybe as many as two, climates in the Pacific Northwest. This range of mountains, located perpendicular to the prevailing westerly flow of wind, greatly affects the temperature and precipitation regime in the Pacific Northwest.

Air that is forced aloft cools, condenses, and deposits excess moisture as precipitation on the windward side of mountain ranges. A map showing isohyets (lines of equal precipitation) in Oregon and Washington is shown in Figure 11.10. The map is generalized and smoothed but the intent is to show the difference in precipitation across the states. Oregon and Washington are unique in that not many places can boast of such a difference in precipitation from west to east. Precipitation approaches 200 inches yearly in many locations in the Coast Range and Olympic Mountains. It decreases abruptly to values less than ten inches annually in many areas in eastern Washington and

Figure 11.10 An isohyetal map of Washington and Oregon that shows average annual precipitation in inches. The map does not show every terrain feature.

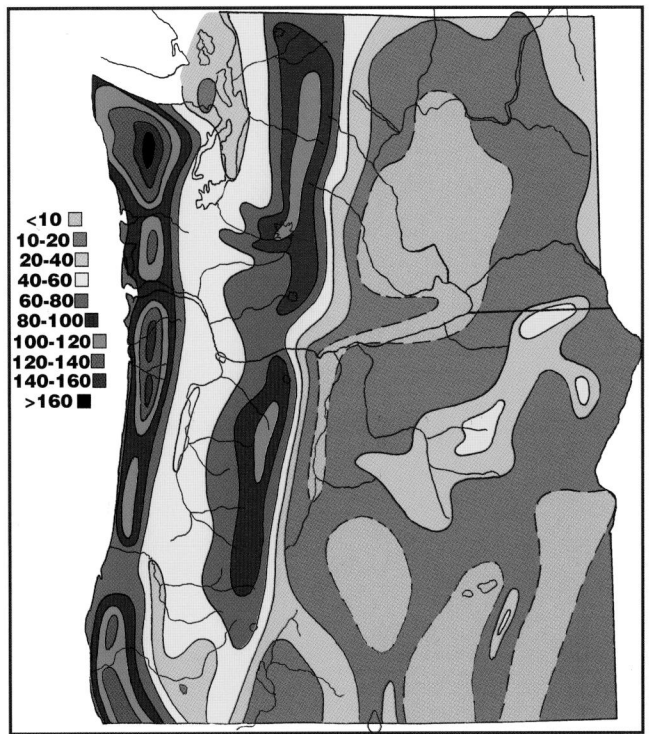

eastern Oregon. In fact, most of the Columbia Basin in east-central Washington falls inside the 10-inch isohyet. Many areas in eastern Oregon also receive less than 10 inches of precipitation annually especially directly east of north-south oriented mountain ranges as Figure 11.10 shows.

Figure 11.11 illustrates what happens when air is forced over the Coast Range Mountains, descends into the Willamette Valley and is forced aloft again crossing the Cascade Mountains and descends into eastern Oregon. It is then forced aloft once more in crossing the Blue Mountains in northeast Oregon, or Steens Mountain in southeast Oregon or any other north-south oriented range of mountains or hills. Roughly the same situation exists in Washington. Here air is forced over the Olympic Mountains, descends into Puget Sound, is forced aloft over the Cascade Mountains, descends into eastern Washington and then gradually ascends in northeast Washington, Figure 11.12. Over each area where the air is forced to rise, there will be an increase in precipitation on the windward side of any mountain barrier and a decrease on the leeward side as the air descends. The result over the eastern sections of both states is a strong decrease in clouds and precipitation over these semi-arid regions.

Ocean Temperatures

The Pacific Ocean is the natural air conditioner for the Pacific Northwest in summer and the moderator of cold temperatures in winter. Visitors from locations on the eastern seaboard of the United States often rush to the Pacific Ocean, only to run away screaming, "But it is soooo cold!" What makes the ocean water off northern California, Oregon, and Washington colder than the Atlantic Ocean at the same latitude? What climatic feature is this? The answer is upwelling.

To understand this phenomenon we go back to the basic air circulation at the surface off the coast of the Pacific Northwest and the forces acting on that flow. During the months from April to October, that flow is predominantly from a northwesterly direction. It is flowing clockwise and outward around the large area of high pressure off the coast

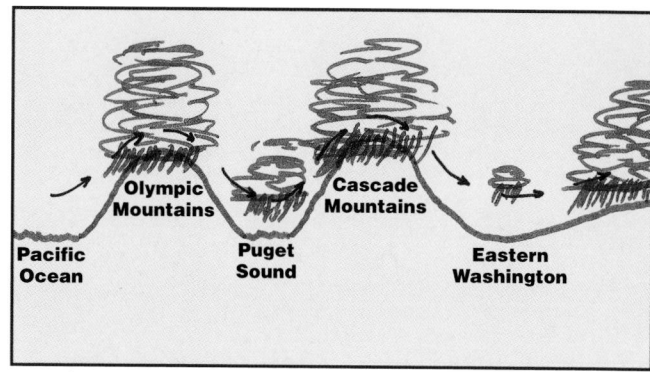

Figure 11.12 The Olympic and Cascade Mountains intercept much of the moisture in a prevailing westerly flow.

into the area of low pressure over the southwest portion of the United States. The Coriolis effect is acting on this northwesterly flow. The earth's rotation causes particles in motion to curve to the right in the Northern Hemisphere. This effect acting on the wind and ocean currents causes the warm surface water that the sun has heated to be pushed offshore by this offshore component of the wind and current. The warm water that is displaced offshore is replaced by colder water that is brought up from greater depths in the ocean. This process is called upwelling. It is shown in Figure 11.13. The stronger the pressure gradient, the stronger the wind. The stronger the wind, the greater is the Coriolis effect and thus the greater the upwelling.

Temperatures off the Washington and Oregon coasts are normally in the low 50s on the Fahrenheit scale in the summer months as a direct result of the upwelling that is occurring. In extreme cases, the temperature of the ocean falls into the upper 40s. Meanwhile, ocean temperatures several hundred miles west of the coastline will rise into the 60s by early September. This is a result of two factors. First, insolation from the sun is heating the ocean and second, to a lesser degree, warm water is being pushed westward into this area. Any effect of the sun's insolation near shore is usually negated by upwelling.

Figure 11.11 When air is forced aloft over mountain ranges it cools. The water vapor condenses into clouds and precipitation.

Figure 11.13 Upwelling. Warm surface water is pushed offshore by the Coriolis effect acting on northwesterly surface winds and ocean currents. It is replaced by colder water from greater depths.

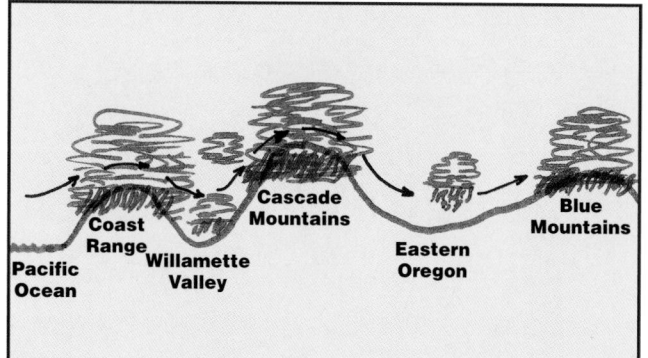

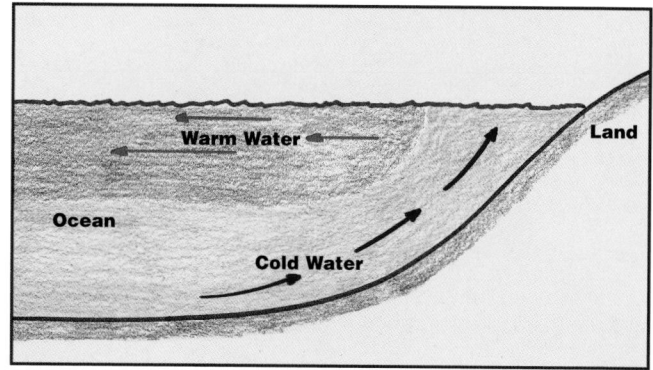

Figure 11.14 shows average ocean surface temperatures for the eastern Pacific during the month of August. The narrow area of 55°F and below near the coast is a result of upwelling. Often, there is a distinct boundary between the warmer water offshore and the cold water in proximity to the coastline. This boundary is easily detected by infrared satellite observations, and it is important to the fishing industry since it is a prime location for fish to congregate.

By February Figure 11.15 temperatures over the north Pacific Ocean have changed markedly. Near the coastlines of Washington and Oregon, however, changes have not been as great. In this area, especially near the coastline of Oregon, very little change has occurred in ocean temperatures from the cold readings measured in August. Farther north along the Washington coast, some cooling has occurred from summer to winter, but considerable cooling has occurred several hundred miles offshore. The ocean in this area is losing far more heat than it is gaining.

As the Aleutian low pressure area begins to dominate the eastern Pacific weather regime in the fall, the north to northwesterly flow of air weakens and becomes southerly or southwesterly. A southerly flow along the coast is not conducive to upwelling since the Coriolis effect is applying a force that is directed toward the coast instead of away from it. Thus, ocean temperatures immediately off the Pacific Northwest coast show very little change from summer to winter and quite often they are colder in the late summer months than during the winter months because of strong upwelling that is occurring.

Upwelling produces the fog and low clouds that are prevalent along the coasts of California, Oregon and Washington in the summer months. As air comes in contact with the cool, or cold, ocean, it is cooled by conduction. The result is often a bank of fog or low clouds that appear to be concentrated just offshore. These clouds and fog will usually drift offshore during the day and often dissipate as the north to northwesterly winds increase, then move back onshore during the late afternoon and early evening as the winds decrease and the Coriolis effect is weakened. Figure 11.16 shows low stratus clouds forming along the immediate coast off the Long Beach Peninsula in Washington. Upwelling is not just a phenomenon along the west coast of the United States. Any location where the prevailing winds are parallel to the coastline and the Coriolis effect pushes the surface water away from land will experience some upwelling.

Figure 11.14 Average sea surface temperatures (°F) over eastern Pacific Ocean during August.

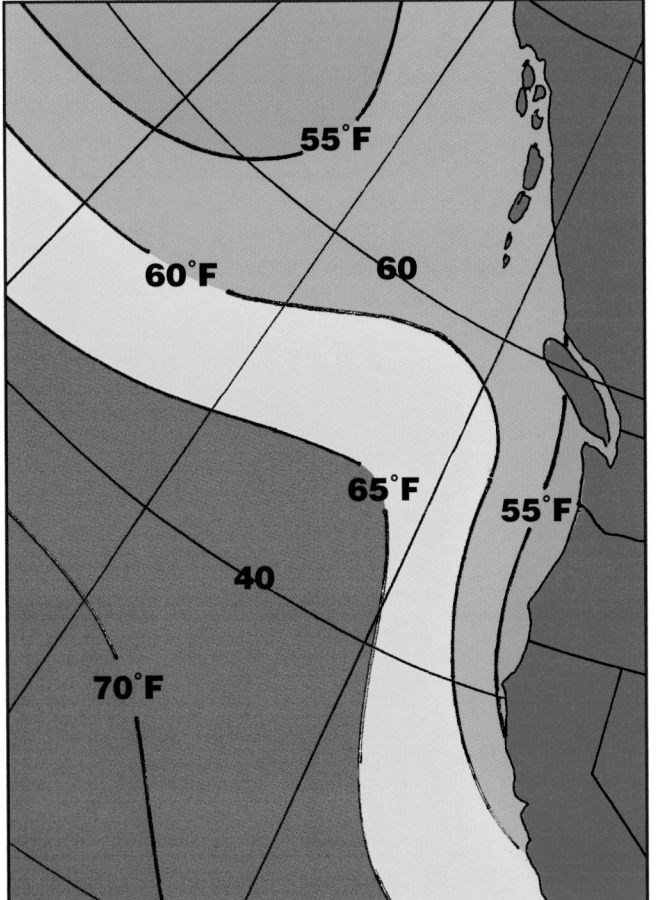

Figure 11.15 Average sea surface temperatures (°F) over eastern Pacific Ocean during February.

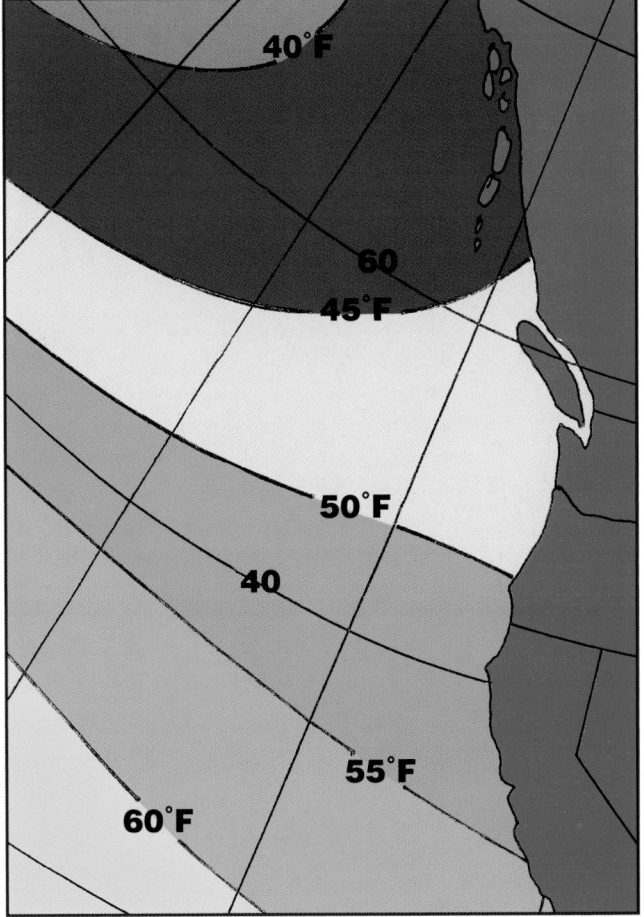

Figure 11.16 Stratus clouds forming just offshore near Long Beach, WA.

Some years, however, upwelling is not as strong along the coast as it is in other years. Such was the case in the summer of 1997 when fish such as marlin and turtles, as well as other species of warm aquatic life that normally inhabit warm waters, strayed north with the warmer ocean waters. This warm ocean water did not arrive off the Pacific Northwest coast from tropical waters off northern South America. Rather, it was more the result of the lack of north to northwesterly winds that produce the upwelling. It is very simple. When the north to northwesterly winds are absent, there is no upwelling. Many times during visits to the southwest Washington coast during the summer of 1997, I was greeted with light south to southwesterly winds and warm temperatures. During most of that summer the Gulf of Alaska low pressure area was slightly stronger than normal.

The temperature of the North Pacific Ocean reaches its peak in mid-September. Meanwhile, air temperatures are beginning to cool, especially at high latitudes. This sharp contrast is a good spawning ground for intense middle latitude storms. The antithesis is that the coolest ocean temperatures are reached in late winter or early spring, when the earth is beginning to warm.

Climate Zones in Washington and Oregon

In the Köppen classification of C climates, there is a winter maximum and a summer minimum of precipitation. So it is with most areas in the Pacific Northwest. Most precipitation falls from November into mid May in this climate classification. East of the Cascade Mountains the regime is similar, although amounts are lighter and somewhat evenly distributed throughout the year.

For weather forecasting purposes, Washington and Oregon have been broken up into fairly homogenous forecasting regions that are called climatic zones. These include coastal zones located in proximity to the Pacific Ocean; valley zones that encompass the valleys west of the Cascade Mountains; mountain zones that include the Olympic Mountains in northwest Washington; the Cascade Mountains that stretch from the Canadian border to the California border; the Blue Mountains of northeast Oregon; the steppe regions of eastern Oregon and Washington; the

Columbia Basin; and the Columbia River Gorge. Even smaller divisions were realized with the reorganization of the National Weather Service in the year 2000. This was to reflect the variances that can exist in these aforementioned zones.

The coastal regions of Washington and Oregon are a prime example of these variations. Yearly values can vary from around 60 inches of precipitation at locations in proximity to the ocean to values that approach 200 inches at the crest of the Coast Range and Olympic Mountains. Annual precipitation values for Aberdeen and Aberdeen 20NNE in Washington and Seaside and Nehalem 9NE in Oregon are shown in Figure 11.17. Both Aberdeen and Seaside are very close to sea level while the other two stations are 435 feet and 140 feet in elevation respectively. In the former case the difference in annual precipitation is over 50 inches, yet the two stations are only 20 miles apart and slightly over 400 feet different in elevation. Between Seaside and Nehalem 9NE there is also a difference of around 50 inches of precipitation annually over a distance of only 15 miles and 140 feet change in elevation. This variation of precipitation with elevation can be found along the entire coasts of Washington and Oregon.

When precipitation values were recorded at the Tillamook Rock Lighthouse one mile offshore from Tillamook Head on the northwest Oregon coast in the late 1800s, they revealed precipitation amounts even lower than nearby coastal locations. Part of this reduction may have been due to exposure and wind but the fact remains: topography definitely enhances precipitation and this effect begins at the immediate coastline as the air is forced aloft over the Coast Range Mountains. When only light rain is falling along the coast, heavy rain could well be falling at higher elevations in the Coast Range Mountains.

The effect is also displayed in a showery weather regime as shown in Figure 11.18. The immediate coastline can be clear or partly cloudy, but showers will be visible just a few miles inland as the air rises up over the Coast Range Mountains. A traveler headed to the coast from interior valleys should not be discouraged driving through showers

Figure 11.17 Precipitation at coastal locations in the Pacific Northwest shows a winter maximum and summer minimum. Annual values, however, increase markedly due to increase in elevation from sea level locations.

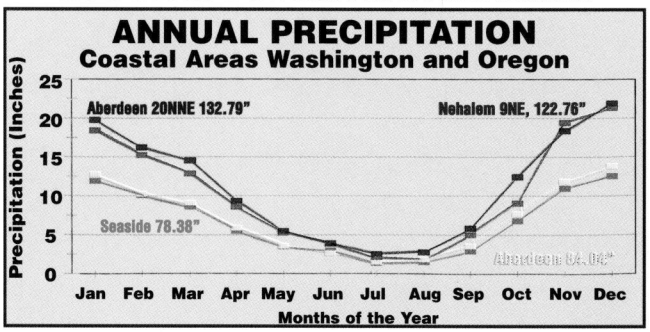

Figure 11.18 Often during unstable atmospheric conditions showers will form as air crosses the Coast Range Mountains leaving the coast in sunny skies as shown in this photograph taken near the mouth of the Columbia River looking east.

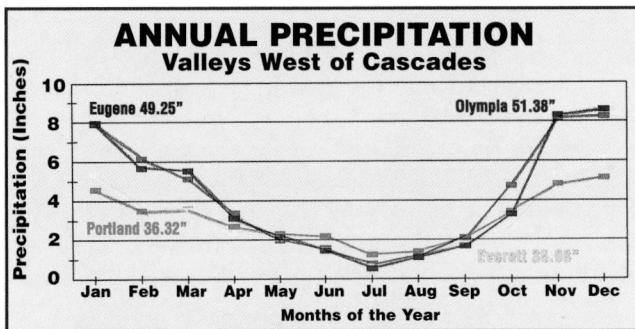

Figure 11.19 Stations within the interior valleys west of the Cascade Mountains display a distinct winter maximum and summer minimum.

while crossing the Coast Range Mountains. Frequently, they will be greeted with partly to mostly sunny skies that are free of showers when they arrive at the beach. In Figure 11.18 showers have formed over the mountains to the east but the mouth of the Columbia River remains clear.

In the valleys between the Coast Range and Cascade Mountains in both Washington and Oregon, elevation ranges from near mean sea level to near 400 feet at the southern end of the Willamette Valley in Oregon. Precipitation in this area ranges from a low of near 36 inches at Portland, Oregon Airport to slightly over 50 inches at Olympia, Washington. A cross-section east and west, however, would show annual precipitation figures of over 100 inches along the eastern slopes of the Coast Range Mountains, dropping to 35 to 50 inches through the Valley, and rising again to near 100 inches along the western slopes of the Cascade Mountains. The reader is referred again to Figure 11.10.

The annual precipitation at four locations in the inland valleys west of the Cascade Mountains is shown in Figure 11.19. As with coastal locations, the predominant winter maximum and summer minimum shows up at all four stations. The precipitation at Everett, although less in the winter months, is slightly above the others during the summer months.

On an even smaller scale within this zone, Figure 11.20, there can be large variations. Precipitation within the Portland Metropolitan area can vary by as much as 15 inches from values over 50 inches annually in the West Hills to values near 35 inches in the vicinity of Beaverton, Hillsboro, and the Portland Airport. This variance is due to elevation. Portland's West Hills rise to elevations of over 1,000 feet

within the city where annual precipitation values exceed 50 inches. The airport location is roughly 30 feet above mean sea level and the annual value is around 36 inches, making it one of the driest areas in the Portland Metropolitan area.

Official precipitation measurements began in downtown Portland in 1871 and were taken continuously in that general area for nearly 100 years. Portland airport observations began in 1940. Downtown Portland receives about seven inches more precipitation on the average each year

Figure 11.20 Annual precipitation within the Portland metropolitan area can vary by as much as 15 inches. Map is drawn from BPA and other data.

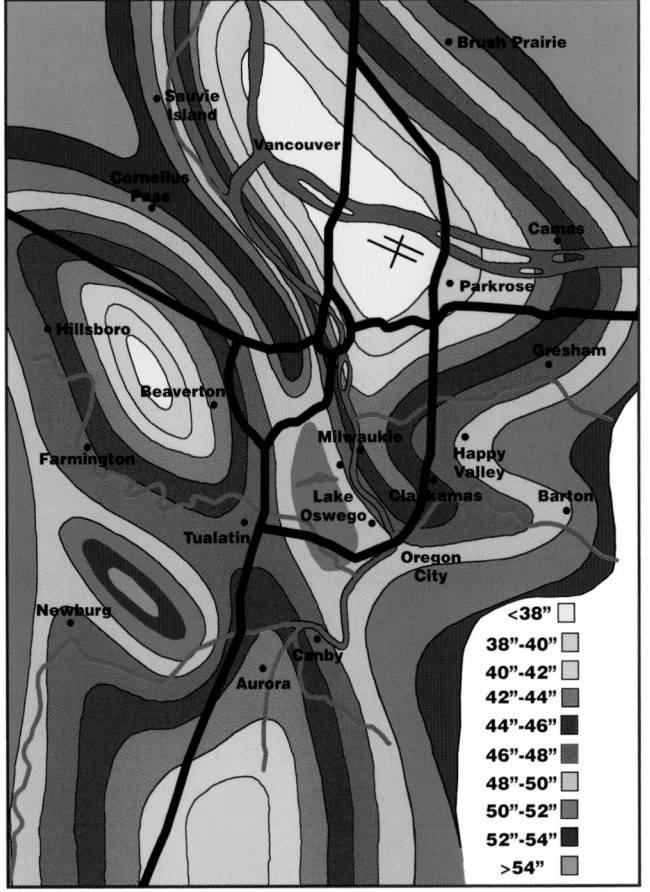

than the airport location because of its proximity to the effect of the West Hills.

Meteorologists with the Bonneville Power Administration (BPA) have been recording Portland area precipitation from faithful observers for many years. Figure 11.20 is a map of precipitation for the Portland metropolitan area drawn from these data and several other observations. The effect of the West Hills is very clear in the close spacing of the isohyets both on the southwest side and especially on the northeast side of these hills along the Willamette River. The effect of the Chehalem Mountains southwest of Beaverton is clearly apparent. Here values exceed 50 inches annually while yearly totals in the area northeast of these mountains are again reduced to around 35 inches. The map does not account for every small hill, thus there will be variations within this local variation.

The lee effect of air descending a mountain range is also very evident in the area northeast of the Olympic Mountains in Washington, stretching northeast across Puget Sound. Annual precipitation values on the windward side of the mountains facing the Pacific Ocean approach 200 inches annually while at Sequim, Washington on the northeast side, the annual total is less than 20 inches. This downslope effect of drying the air as it descends the north and east sides of the Olympic Mountains creates a "rain shadow" all across Puget Sound. Seattle's annual precipitation of around 35 inches is very close to the value for Portland because of this rain shadow effect, even though Seattle is farther north, subject to more Pacific storms. Figure 11.21 shows this variation and

the rain shadow effect. This decrease in precipitation shows a triangular shape as a result in variations of the prevailing flow of air aloft from a more westerly component to a more southerly component. Even on islands within Puget Sound there will be variations in annual precipitation due to this rain shadow effect and also because of elevation changes on individual islands.

The area in southwest Oregon is unique from a climatological viewpoint. Here, the mountain range is not north-south, but covers a wide area, broken up by the Rogue River, Umpqua River, and several other valleys. Precipitation in the foothills of the surrounding Coast Range and Cascade Mountains will average 40 to 60 inches annually. Grants Pass in the western portion of the Rogue River Valley receives slightly over 30 inches annually, compared to slightly less than 20 inches annually at Medford. Roseburg (near 30 inches annually) is included in this area. It is separated from the Willamette Valley to the north by the Calapooya Divide. Within this zone, there are many variations in annual precipitation that are accentuated by elevation.

Both Washington and Oregon have a mountainous zone along the Cascade Mountains. Precipitation within this zone ranges from 60 to 100 inches annually with a substantial amount falling as snow in late fall through mid-spring. Figure 11.22 shows the monthly values for Stampede Pass in Washington and Government Camp and Crater Lake in Oregon. Even at mountain locations in the Pacific Northwest the winter maximum, summer minimum of precipitation is apparent.

The Columbia River Gorge is a beautiful lesson in climatology as temperature and precipitation values show great variation. The Corps of Discovery on their journey to the Pacific Ocean and during the return trip noted this variation. Precipitation values are plotted in Figure 11.23. At the west end of the Columbia River Gorge the precipitation value of near 40 inches annually increases rapidly to almost 80 inches at Bonneville Dam, a distance of only 25 miles, even though the elevation change is minimal. The increase is due to air being forced aloft as it crosses the Cascade Mountains and also convergence as air enters the narrow opening of the Gorge. This passage that the Columbia River

Figure 11.21 Annual rainfall amounts in the Puget Sound area show the rain shadow effect of the Olympic Mountains located to the southeast.

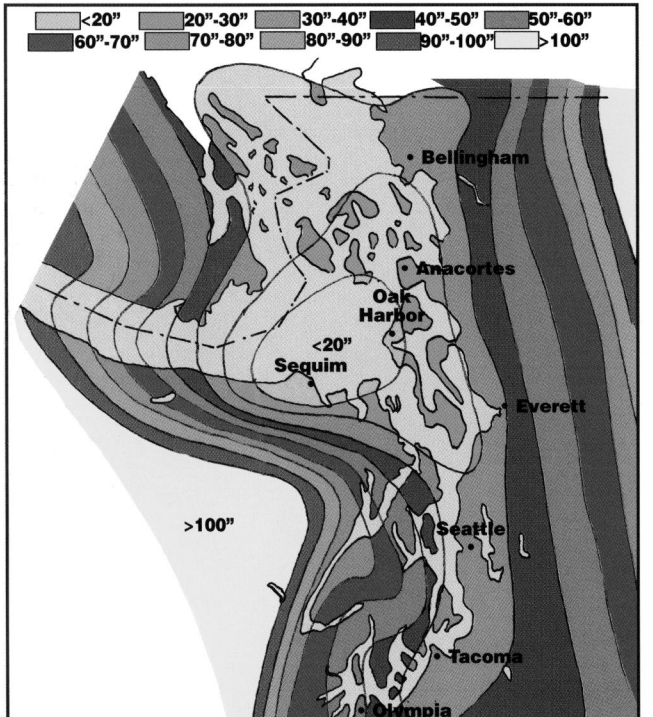

Figure 11.22 Annual precipitation at three stations within the Cascade Mountains.

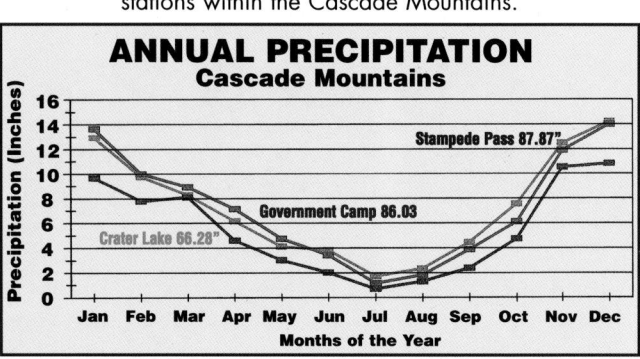

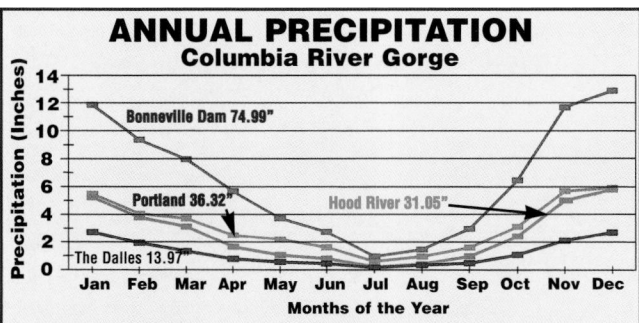

Figure 11.23 Annual precipitation within the Columbia River Gorge varies from almost 80 inches around Bonneville Dam to less than 15 inches at The Dalles

has carved through the mountains over the years does not serve to decrease precipitation. (Actually, the Columbia River was in existence before the Cascade Mountains were formed, and the river has continued its march to the ocean despite mountains building around it.) At Hood River the annual precipitation drops to near 40 inches annually and the vegetation begins to change to more pine and oak. The value drops off dramatically to around 10 inches annually just east of The Dalles.

This sometimes presents a confusing picture to pilots wanting to fly using visual flight rules through the only east-west gap in the Cascade Mountains. Cloud heights at Portland which allow visual flying can be very misleading and quickly lower to values of near zero ceiling height and zero visibility in the narrow Gorge. Clouds decrease rapidly from Hood River east with a westerly flow as shown in Figure 11.24. The top photograph allows for visual flying near Crown Point at the west end, but off in the distance showers are obscuring the terrain. As air descends the eastern slopes of the Cascade Mountains the clouds will often have a scattered appearance at Hood River as in the lower photograph.

The antithesis to the above is often noted in winter months with an easterly flow of air. If the Columbia Basin is shrouded in low clouds and fog due to radiation and upslope flow, these clouds will often dissipate west of Hood River with clear conditions from there to Portland. The adiabatic warming due to air flowing down to a slightly lower elevation will raise the temperature and lower the dewpoint temperature enough to eliminate the condensation that was occurring on the eastern slopes. This feature can often be observed when the Portland area is experiencing strong east winds in winter. Clouds may be seen just at the top of the Cascade crest, but dissipating on the leeward side (in this case the west side) as the easterly flow descends the mountains. This was shown in Figure 9.30.

East of the Cascade Mountains across the flat lower elevations, one relatively homogeneous climatic zone exists. This climate is classified mostly as a semi-arid steppe in the Köppen classification. Here sagebrush, native grasses, juniper trees and scrub brush prevail. Again, precipitation is highly dictated by elevation and quickly changes with an increase in elevation to a more highland type of climate with mixed forests of

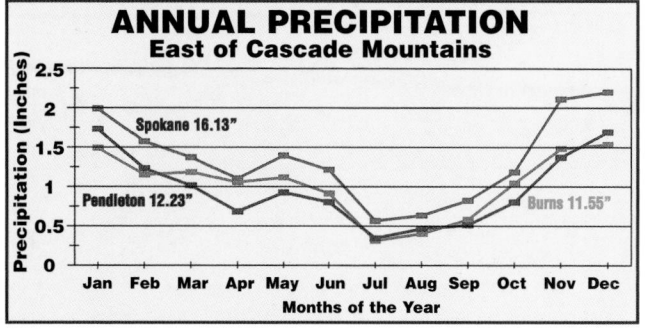

Figure 11.24 With a westerly flow of air clouds that may obscure the west entrance to the Columbia River Gorge (top) decrease rapidly east of the town of Hood River toward The Dalles (bottom).

pine, birch, and fir. Several different forecast zones exist in this area, their boundaries dictated by elevation.

Precipitation east of the Cascade Mountains, although showing a winter maximum, is often spread out more over the entire year. Burns and Pendleton, Oregon, and Spokane, Washington all show a weak maximum of precipitation in the spring. The westerlies and frequent storms account for the cold season precipitation, while showers and occasional thundershowers account for the precipitation in the warmer spring and summer months. Annual precipitation for three locations east of the Cascade Mountains—Burns and Pendleton, Oregon and Spokane, Washington—is shown in Figure 11.25. This area, when given additional

Figure 11.25 Precipitation east of the Cascade Montains often shows a weak maximum in spring in addition to the winter maximum.

moisture through irrigation, is very productive due to the warm days with abundant sunshine, although higher elevations are subject to both late frosts in the spring and early frosts in the fall.

The effect on precipitation of even small changes in elevation can be seen in comparing annual values from the city of Burns to readings taken at the airport. The city location receives roughly half an inch more annually than the airport although only a few miles separates these two locations. The city is slightly higher and closer to the hills to the west.

In addition to precipitation, temperature is a strong factor in determining climate. The average January temperature at Seaside, Oregon is 43.9°F compared to 25.1°F degrees at Burns. In July, Burns is much warmer with an average of 67.5°F compared to Seaside's 59.5°F. This illustrates quite clearly the impact of the Pacific Ocean in moderating the temperature. In addition to the seasonal variations there are also variations in the daily high temperature to the daily low temperature. The average high in July at Burns is 84.6°F compared to 67.2°F at Seaside.

Average minimums in July show a value of 50.3°F for Burns compared to 51.8°F at Seaside. The spread is greater for January average minimum temperatures. Burns has a chilly 15.6°F compared to a mild 36.9°F for Seaside. Air east of the Cascade Mountains is much drier with less cloudiness. Thus, more solar radiation is allowed to strike the earth's surface to warm the air next to it. This absence of cloudiness allows for greater nighttime radiation resulting in cooler minimum temperatures. Figure 11.26 shows monthly average maximum and minimum temperatures for Seaside and Burns, Oregon.

Temperature differences in Washington from west of the Cascade Mountains to east of the mountains are similar to those in Oregon. Stations such as Wenatchee and Yakima located just to the east of the Washington Cascades will have a climate that is similar to the climate around Bend and Redmond in central Oregon, although these two Washington stations are slightly lower in elevation. Spokane, in the eastern portion of Washington, has a climate similar to that of Pendleton, Oregon. Figure 11.27 graphs the average monthly temperatures for Aberdeen and

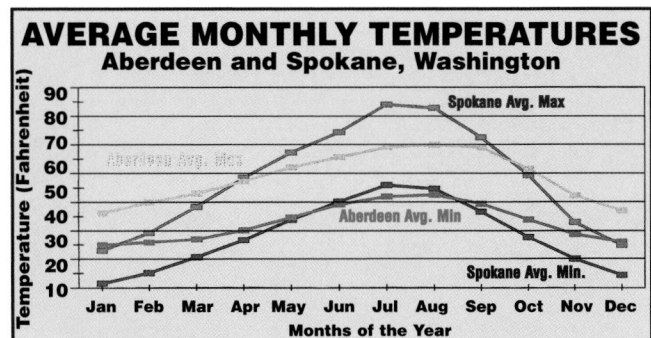

Figure 11.27 Average monthly temperatures show a distinct marine influence between coastal locations in Washington and those in eastern Washington

Spokane in Washington. In the two graphs, 11.26 and 11.27, the average maximum temperature for both Seaside and Aberdeen levels off during the months of July, August, and September while values east of the Cascade Mountains show a slight decrease in August with a sharper drop in temperature during September. Once again the influence of the Pacific Ocean is apparent. Decreasing northwesterly winds along the coast allow for more surface heating in the coastal strip as a result of less upwelling. Meanwhile, a decrease in the hours of sunlight, along with drier air east of the Cascade Mountains, results in much cooler nighttime temperatures which brings the average temperature in these areas downward in August and September. Ocean beaches often experience their most favorable weather during September and early October before Pacific storms begin pummeling the coast.

Elevation also changes the annual temperature values. The average temperature in January at Government Camp, elevation 3,980 feet is 29.5°F, while at Portland it is 39.6°F. In July the difference is still eleven degrees, with Government Camp showing a value of 56.8°F compared to Portland's 68.1°F. This difference is roughly equivalent to the standard atmospheric lapse rate of around 3.6°F decrease per 1,000 feet. Similar differences are observed when Seattle, Washington is compared to Stampede Pass, located to the east near the crest of the Cascade Mountains at 3,960 feet.

Large variations exist in the snowfall over the Pacific Northwest as elevation and latitude play the dominant roles. Crater Lake National Park Headquarters at 6,500 feet receives an average of around 530 inches of snow per year. The value at Government Camp, just under 4,000 feet mean sea level, is 275 inches per year. In Washington, Paradise Ranger Station in Mt. Rainier National Park, at 5,600 feet, averages 675 inches each year. Farther north, Stevens Pass (elevation 4,100 feet) averages 494 inches of snow a year. Mountain snowfall values vary greatly with each season. Government Camp has recorded less than 200 inches total accumulation during a year while recording close to 600 inches in other years. Similar variation exists at Stevens Pass where close to 800 inches has been recorded as

Figure 11.26 Average monthly maximum and minimum temperatures for a station with marine influence and a station east of Cascade Mountains.

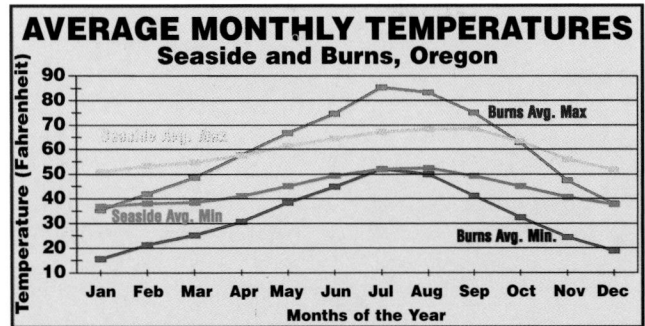

opposed to less than 225 inches for a year. During the 1998-1999 snow season (July 1 through June 30) the Mt. Baker ski area in the northern Washington Cascade Mountains captured the title of "Most Snowfall ever Measured in the United States" with a value of 1,140 inches falling. Remember, however, this is what fell during the entire year, not what was on the ground at one time. Snow settles and melts during the year and maximum snow depth in the mountains of Washington and Oregon does not occur in the middle of winter as some would believe, but during late March or early April.

At valley locations both east and west of the Cascade Mountains, annual snowfall shows great variability. Many lower elevation stations west of the Cascade Mountains record zero or trace amounts on many years. On other occasions, severe winters with several arctic outbreaks will bring over 20 inches of snow to these locations which makes an average figure almost meaningless. At Portland the average yearly snowfall is a little over six inches while Medford's annual snowfall is near seven inches annually. Yet Portland recorded over 40 inches during the winter of 1949/50 and over 60 inches during the snowy December, January and February of 1892/1893. Annual snowfall at the Seattle-Tacoma Airport is nearly 12 inches but farther north, Everett Junior College records less than 6 inches annually. Still, this six- to twelve-inch value is an average figure for locations in the inland valleys west of the Cascade Mountains, including the Puget Sound area. The average annual snowfall at Olympia of 18 inches is likely due to precipitation from advancing winter frontal systems starting out as snow with brief accumulations, then turning to rain.

East of the Cascade Mountains, snowfall is also highly variable and dictated by elevation, but values are higher than west of the mountains. An average annual value of 20 inches could be selected arbitrarily, but it would certainly not account for the large geographical variations. The value at Pendleton is slightly over 17 inches annually, 24 inches at Yakima and slightly over 40 inches at Spokane. Pendleton, however, recorded 80 inches during the winter of 1921-1922. There is very little correlation of seasonal values of snowfall between stations east and west of the Cascade Mountains.

Snowfall at coastal locations is even less than inland stations due to the moderating effect of the Pacific Ocean. Again, an average of five inches could be selected, but that would certainly not reflect any kind of yearly value. Lewis and Clark with the Corps of Discovery recorded that amount while camped at the mouth of the Columbia River during the winter of 1805/1806. Snowfall, however, is a rarity on the southwest Oregon coast. This area is far removed from sources of cold arctic air, and temperatures rarely fall to below the freezing point. The area boasts itself as the "banana belt" of Oregon. The climate here is mild, which accounts for a large number of Easter Lilies that are marketed in the United States being grown there.

Snow Level and Freezing Level

These two terms are not synonymous. By definition, the freezing level is that elevation measured by weather instruments, mainly the radiosonde, where the temperature of the atmosphere changes from a value above 32°F to a value below 32°F. Snow level as mentioned in weather reports and forecasts, means the lowest level that snow is expected to fall before it melts. Depending on the atmospheric conditions, snow can occur at surface temperatures as high as 37°F. An average value used for snow level is 1,000 feet below the freezing level because snowflakes begin melting when they encounter temperatures above freezing.

Yet, often in the Pacific Northwest snow occurs 1,500 to even 2,000 feet below the measured freezing level and sometimes even lower. This is mainly due to the air for several hundred feet below the freezing level being just slightly above the freezing point. In Figure 11.28 the actual environmental sounding as measured with radiosonde equipment may look like the dashed line. In this case, the actual freezing level is near 4,000 feet but the temperature of the atmosphere is only slightly above freezing, 34°F, down to an elevation of 1,500 feet, increasing only to 37°F at the surface. In this case, snow could occur down to 1,000 feet.

Many times Cascade Mountain passes will be recording snow when the freezing level is 1,500 to 2,000 feet above them. Cooler temperatures east of the Cascade Mountains will be bringing colder air westward, resulting

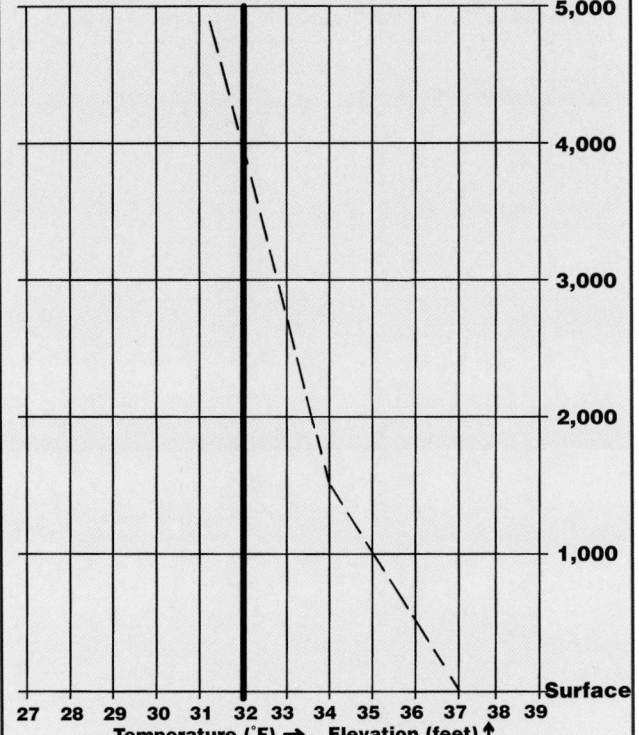

Figure 11.28 An environmental sounding with the temperature only slightly above freezing 2,000 feet below the actual freezing level near 4,000 feet.

in an atmospheric distribution of temperature that is just barely above freezing.

Often when the atmosphere is unstable and showers are occurring, the freezing level can lower markedly. In this case, cold air that is below freezing plunges down out of the base of the cloud, actually bringing the freezing level of the free air down to a lower elevation. This is shown in the schematic diagram in Figure 11.29. In this case the snow will often be in the form of snow pellets or graupel. Hail, which is produced from clouds in a very unstable atmosphere, can fall several thousand feet through the atmosphere and undergo very little melting before it strikes the surface. Hail less than one-eighth of an inch in diameter is often referred to as ice pellets.

Some Pacific Northwest Weather Peculiarities

There are many peculiarities to the weather in the Pacific Northwest, and local residents will cite their own phenomena. Only a few, however, are covered in this section. One that has recently been studied is the Puget Sound Convergence Zone. This weather pattern can account for large variations in rainfall or snowfall in the area from Bellingham, Washington, on the north to Olympia, Washington, on the south. Basically, air enters Puget Sound through three corridors: (1) from the Pacific Ocean through the Strait of Juan de Fuca, (2) from the Pacific Ocean through a gap in the Coast Range Mountains east of Hoquiam, and to a lesser extent, (3) from the Strait of Georgia in southwestern British Columbia, and these air corridors are shown in Figure 11.30.

Converging air streams at the surface produce a lifting of the air mass. That is precisely what happens along the Puget Sound Convergence Zone. Where the air streams come together is where the greatest amount of precipitation will fall. This zone is not stationary, but moves as the large scale pressure patterns that affect the air streams entering Puget Sound also move. Stronger, or higher, pressure to the north will move the zone south. This is often the case after a frontal system moves through the area. Winds will have shifted to a more northerly component at the north end of Puget Sound but remain westerly from the Pacific Ocean into the Olympia area through the gap in the coastal mountains east of Hoquiam, turning southwesterly as they approach the Tacoma area.

Rather than a convergence type of pattern, a divergence pattern is associated with strong easterly winds flowing out of the Columbia River Gorge. After accelerating through this gap in the Cascade Mountains, the air "fans out" as it enters the Portland area and locations to the north and south. This is shown in Figure 11.31. During weather regimes with a strong east wind, the flow south of the Portland area will be from the north or northeast as the wind moves up the Willamette Valley toward

Figure 11.30 The Puget Sound Convergence Zone. Air enters Puget Sound through three corridors. Where the northerly component meets the southerly component is where the heaviest precipitation occurs.

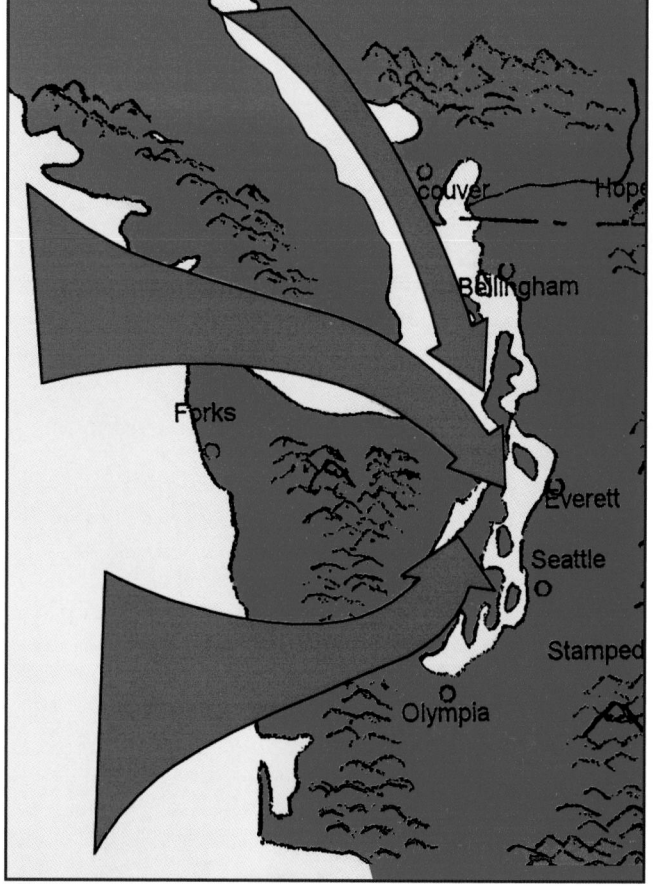

Figure 11.29 Heavy showers in an unstable atmosphere can lower the freezing level as well as the snow level.

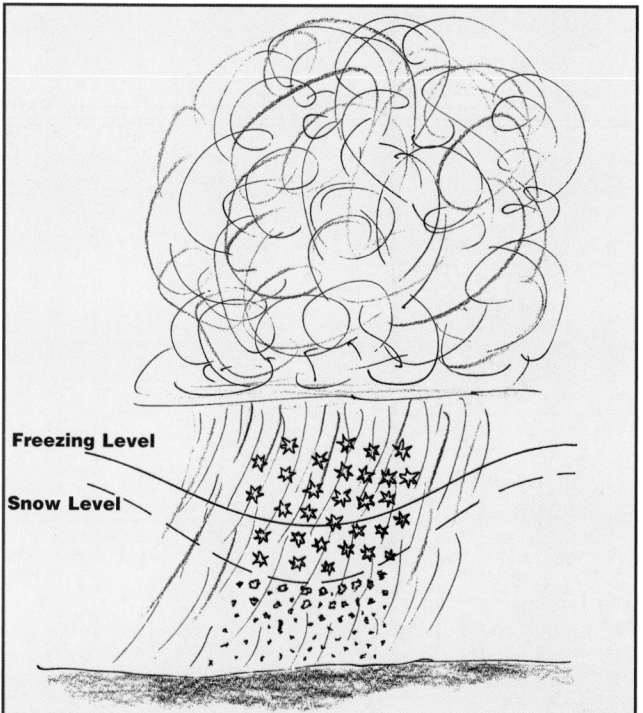

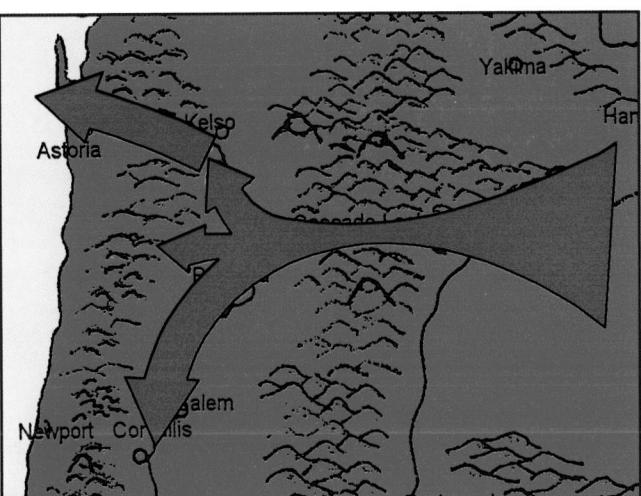

Figure 11.31 Air flowing out of the Columbia River Gorge can be diverted north or south, depending on the location of the lower pressure offshore and geography.

Figure 11.32 During the colder months of the year strong southeasterly winds can occur at several locations in the Pacific Northwest due to higher pressure east of the Cascade Mountains and over the Great Basin to lower pressure offshore.

Salem and Eugene. The reverse is true north of Portland along the Columbia River where the flow is from a more south-southeasterly direction. This is especially true in the area from Woodland, Washington, north to Kalama, Washington, where the hills crowd the river and again funnel the flow. An area at the mouth of the Columbia River Gorge just to the north of the Columbia River in Washington, behind a low range of hills, will not experience the strong east winds that may be occurring in the Portland area. This low range of hills is enough to divert the wind.

This wind pattern has a profound effect on temperatures throughout the northern Willamette Valley and southwest Washington, especially in the area just north of the Columbia River and west of Portland near Forest Grove where winds may be light or calm. With temperatures near freezing, wind prevents overnight lows from dropping below the 32°F mark in late spring and early fall. This serves to lengthen the growing season in the windy locations as opposed to those places that do not experience the wind and may have cooler overnight temperatures. The reverse occurs during the day. The areas where the wind is light or calm such as Forest Grove, Lake Oswego, and the area north of the Columbia River near Battle Ground will be warmer than locations near the Portland Airport. Temperature differences as much as 6 to 10°F degrees can be experienced between windy and non-windy locations.

There are several other locations in the Pacific Northwest that experience localized strong winds. They include the areas around La Grande and Ashland, Oregon, and Enumclaw, Washington, Figure 11.32. Virtually all of these strong winds occur during the colder months of the year as surface high pressure becomes established in southeastern Idaho, northwest Nevada and northern California. Approaching low pressure areas from off the Pacific create strong pressure differences that

produce the winds in the Enumclaw area. In the La Grande area the cold, heavier air to the southeast with higher pressure refuses to budge as a low pressure center moves into the Columbia Basin. Near blizzard conditions can occur in this area due to strong winds and blowing snow, creating hazardous driving. The Ashland case is also due to higher pressure to the south and lower pressure just offshore of the Oregon Coast. Often these winds do not surface in the Rogue River Valley near Medford and only affect the Ashland area.

These are but a few of the weather phenomena that make the weather in the Pacific Northwest unique in many respects. All of the weather elements mentioned in the first chapter either combine, or make themselves scarce, which accounts for the large variability in the climate of this region. In the Pacific Northwest, the cliche, "If you don't like the weather we are having, just wait a short time, or move in a slightly different direction and it will change" is very true.

Chapter 12
Climate Change

Is our climate changing? Were the rains and snows heavier in great-grandma's and great- grandpa's days? Were the winters colder and the summers hotter? Some are fervent in believing that global warming and a changing climate are here. Others are not so sure. Currently, there is a growing

majority of scientists who now believe that the earth's climate is changing and that it is warming. Some computer models are forecasting a warming of 3° to 10°F over the next 100 years. Global warming has become a common household phrase. How does a person separate fact from fiction? Did Sir Francis Drake actually see the land along the southern Oregon coast covered with snow in June? Was it so cold that the ropes of his ship were frozen and the precipitation that fell also frozen as was entered in his log? That would certainly be a drastic change from today. One thing we do know for certain is that the climate of the earth has changed in the past.

Clues to the Past

The earth's climate has only been measured with instruments for 500 years at the most, and then, only in very small areas. References before that are in terms such as when the cherries bloomed in the spring or when the first frost of fall occurred or recollection of a major snowstorm or windstorm. Many of these "observations" were recorded in diaries or journals. Others were handed down from generation to generation. Europeans were the first to actually record weather data, and a few of these observations still exist. The record is not as long on the North American continent. The first systematic weather observations in the New World were taken by John Campanius Holm, a Lutheran minister, in the mid 1600s. There is some recorded data from the 1700s in America. Thomas Jefferson was a "weather buff" who kept daily records even during long, hot congressional sessions.

In the western part of the country there are references to weather events in the logs of mariners who visited the Pacific Northwest Coast in the 1500s, 1600s, and the 1700s, such as those words from the journey of Sir Francis Drake. Lewis and Clark and other members of the Corps of Discovery kept

meticulous daily records of the weather during their journey to the Pacific Ocean and back. This included temperature measurements until they broke their one thermometer in what is now Idaho. There were some military posts that took weather observations in the 1840s in Oregon and Washington, but continuous readings go back only 100 to 150 years at the most in these two states. Official records were started at Portland, Oregon, in 1871 and in Olympia, Washington, in 1877. Earlier observations were recorded at Walla Walla, Washington, and The Dalles (Dalles), Oregon. So with data from such a short period, how can climate change be detected?

Proxy Data

Mother Nature has left us with many clues to the past, and scientists are only beginning to unlock the secrets she has left. These clues are called proxy data, or literally a substitute for the measured data used today. The study of tree rings, or dendro-climatology, reveals some clues regarding the past climate. This has been done in many locations in North America and in Europe, using trees that were preserved and some still growing, such as the bristlecone pines of Arizona that have survived for several thousand years as have some giant sequoias. The giant Sitka spruce found near Seaside, Oregon, Figure 12.1, has been growing for hundreds of years. The growth rings from these ancient forest dwellers can put a few pieces of the puzzle in place regarding past climates as to whether they were wet or dry.

Varves are another indicator. These are thin layers of clay and silt with contrasting colors that correspond to growth rate and pollen distribution of various plants. Some are found on the edge of former lakes that provide a small piece to the puzzle since they reflect past lake levels that are indicative of past climate regimes.

Ice cores from glaciers in Greenland and Antarctica are also very revealing such as the Vostok ice core from the continent of Antarctica. They give clues to the amount of carbon dioxide present in the air during past climates, as well as other trace gases that can be correlated with what the atmosphere was like several thousand years ago. Ocean sediments and deep-sea cores also provide some clues regarding the climates thousands of years ago as organisms died and settled to the ocean floor.

The Little Ice Age

This period in the history of the earth's climate has been quite well documented. Most scientists place the period from around 1350 to the mid 1800s. However, when this period actually began and ended is under speculation and not the important part. What is important is that it had some drastic effects on the earth and its inhabitants. During this period the earth's glaciers showed a marked advance. Many small villages in the Alps were either destroyed by avalanches, or they were abandoned. Most of the vineyards in England died or were severely damaged. Charles Dickens wrote his famous "A Christmas Carol" around this time. Near Geneva Mary Shelly was inspired to write "Frankenstein" and Polidori "The Vampire." Did the weather motivate them? The Thames River froze over many times during The Little Ice Age. The potato famine in Ireland forced many immigrants to this country during the latter part of this period.

Figure 12.1 This giant Sitka spruce has survived hundreds of windstorms over hundreds of years.

Vikings who had settled in Greenland and actually farmed there abandoned their colonies somewhat hastily around 1400. Were they driven out by a climatic change as some scientists believe? The American colonists suffered through many cold winters. The Little Ice Age was a definite cold period in the very recent climate of the earth and the cause is still not known. Yet even that cold period was interspersed with warm years.

The Greenhouse Effect

The increase in carbon dioxide in our atmosphere is receiving considerable attention. The "greenhouse effect," however, has been with us a very long time. Indeed, if we did not have a greenhouse effect, we would not be here. It preserves life on earth. Carbon dioxide and other gases such as methane and water vapor in the earth's atmosphere allow the sun's shortwave radiation to reach the earth's surface, but they intercept the earth's longwave radiation from returning to space. Figure 12.2 shows the re-transmission back toward the earth, although carbon dioxide and water vapor do not necessarily appear in layers as drawn. The term greenhouse effect is actually a misnomer, since a greenhouse (the one used for growing plants) does not trap radiation, but prevents the heated air within the greenhouse from circulating or mixing with air that is outside.

Carbon dioxide is the gas most frequently referred to when the greenhouse effect is mentioned. Water vapor also absorbs the earth's radiation and retransmits it back to earth. There are other gases such as methane that are beginning to attract attention. Carbon dioxide is measured in parts per million (ppm). It has shown a steady increase from around 315 ppm when it was first accurately measured by instrumentation at the Mauna Loa Observatory in Hawaii in the late 1950s until today where it stands at near 370 ppm as is shown in Figure 12.3. This upward trend appears to have shown some acceleration during the last 100 years. Estimates during the 1800s were only slightly less than 300 ppm. There are two major processes that generate carbon dioxide. One is through the burning of fossil fuels and the other is deforestation. Plants take in carbon dioxide and release oxygen, which is why carbon dioxide in the atmosphere decreases during the Northern Hemisphere summer

Figure 12.2 The greenhouse effect. Shortwave radiation reaches the earth, but longwave radiation is prevented from escaping back out into space.

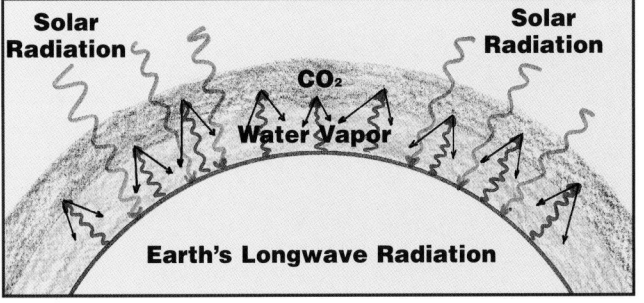

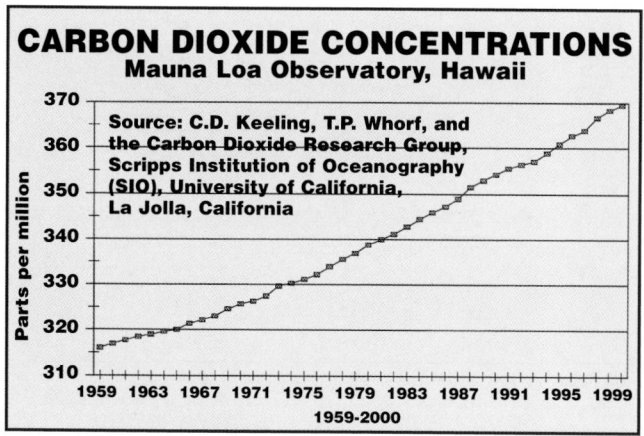

CARBON DIOXIDE CONCENTRATIONS
Mauna Loa Observatory, Hawaii

Source: C.D. Keeling, T.P. Whorf, and the Carbon Dioxide Research Group, Scripps Institution of Oceanography (SIO), University of California, La Jolla, California

Parts per million

1959-2000

Figure 12.3 Carbon Dioxide values have increased from around 315 parts per million in 1959 near 370 parts per million in 2000.

and increases during the Northern Hemisphere winter. Since carbon dioxide intercepts the earth's longwave radiation and prevents it from escaping to space, some speculate that increasing the amount of carbon dioxide will warm the planet. Others believe that more heating would increase the ability of the air to contain moisture, thus causing more clouds which would reflect the sun's radiant energy back into space and cool the planet.

Global climate models indicate a warming trend. The models used to generate forecasts of future climates operate on a much larger grid spacing than the computers used to forecast daily weather patterns for several days. Hence, their results are general and cover wide areas. The models forecast that most of this warming will occur at higher latitudes with very little change in the equatorial regions. Warming at the poles would begin melting the polar ice caps and glaciers which many believe would lead to an increase in mean sea level. The peninsula that protects Tillamook Bay from the ocean was mostly reclaimed by the

Figure 12.4 Many years ago the Pacific Ocean reclaimed this stretch of seashore along the Bayocean Peninsula in Oregon. Will it do so again including many other areas near the ocean because of rising sea levels due to global warming?

Pacific Ocean many years ago (Figure 12.4). The cause was mainly due to the construction of a single jetty. But will increased sea levels and Pacific storms reclaim it again, along with other areas in proximity to the ocean?

During the last ice age, sea level was much lower than it is today. Some speculate that the earliest North American inhabitants crossed over from Asia via a "land bridge" and migrated down the exposed coastal areas along southeast Alaska and British Columbia.

Many scientists believe that the warming, should it come, would be gradual. However, some of the latest data from ice cores and sediments is revealing that there have been only 5 to 10 years between some climatic changes. If the climate is warming this fast, the earth's inhabitants may not have much time to initiate actions.

Milankovitch Theory

Past records reveal that there have been several climatic changes over several hundred thousand years. What may have caused these changes? The Milutin Milankovitch theory on climate change is rather intriguing. Mr. Milankovitch, a Yugoslavian astronomer/mathematician first proposed the theory around 1930. It was given little credence until twenty or thirty years ago. Mr. Milankovitch calculated that the earth is going through several motions as it moves around the sun. First of all its orbit is not circular, but more elliptic, being closer to the sun around the first part of January than it is around the first of July. In January that distance is about 91,400,000 miles and in June 94,500,000 miles. But this varies as the earth's orbit changes on a 100,000 year cycle from elliptic to more circular. This is referred to as the "eccentricity of the earth's orbit," and it places the earth closer to the sun when the orbit is more circular. This motion, although highly exaggerated, is shown in Figure 12.5.

The obliquity, or angle of the earth's axis, also changes. This tilt is currently 23.5 degrees from the vertical and accounts for the seasons as the earth travels around the sun. The tilt varies over a 41,000 year cycle from 22.1 degrees to 24.5 degrees. A greater tilt of 24.5 degrees means that the polar regions would receive sunlight that is slightly more direct or intense than with a smaller tilt of 22.1 degrees. That is not much change, but it becomes significant when the sun's radiation is considered. That tilt, again slightly exaggerated, is also shown in Figure 12.5.

In addition to the above motions, the earth, as it revolves around the sun and spins on its axis, is wobbling like those tops we used to spin as children. That means that the direction its axis is pointing changes. It completes a "wobble" approximately every 21,000 years and this effect is called precession. Currently the axis is pointing toward the North Star, or Polaris. In 14,000 years it will point toward the star Vega. As the precession changes, so will the seasons and they will be reversed.

When these phases are put together, they produce one of the strongest cases for climate change. Put the earth closer to the sun, tilt it more towards the sun in the summer, and you increase the amount of radiation received from the sun.

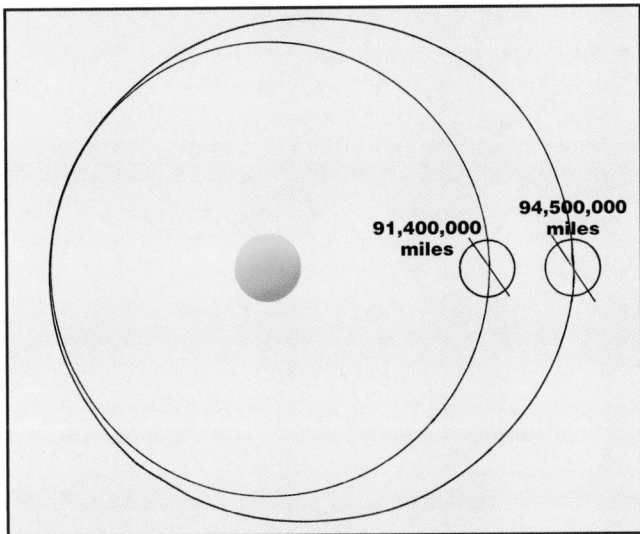

Figure 12.5 The Milankovitch Theory. The earth's orbit changes from elliptical to more circular every 100,000 years. The tilt of its axis and direction the axis is pointing also change over 41,000 and 21,000 years respectively. (Diagram not to scale.)

Thus it should be warmer. Cycles of 100,000, 41,000 and 21,000 years do show up in the proxy data climatologists have studied.

Weather Cycles

Many times I have been asked the question, "Does weather operate in cycles?" Cycles do exist regarding the weather, but the answer is always supplemented by saying that weather cycles are like dropping a stone into a clear, still pond. Ripples will be created that will extend out from where the stone is dropped into the pond as shown in Figure 12.6. The ripples can be traced for several feet or yards, but they eventually dampen out. Additionally, if another stone is dropped into the pond, or something else causes ripples at a different location, when these different

Figure 12.6 Weather cycles are like ripples that result from a stone being dropped into a pond. The ripples expand outward but eventually die like many weather cycles. Different ripples or cycles that meet often enhance or dampen the other.

ripples meet they become confused. Some are enhanced and others will dissipate. Drop more stones into the pond and soon the whole area is confused. This analogy emphasizes that there are many factors that control weather and climate. To say that one effect is the blame for all climate changes is folly.

The cause for a weather cycle, unlike the ripples on a pond, is never entirely known. There are just too many variables. I have plotted thousands of values of weather data. Often I have felt that I had the answer. "Wait, there seems to be a cycle developing!" Then, the entire study would collapse and the cycle would diminish to nothing. Thousands of computer and man hours have gone into this topic, and I know of no cycle that continues to perform flawlessly year after year. Perhaps the best is what is called the quasi-biennial oscillation (QBO) or an oscillation every 2.2 to 2.8 years. But is this a cycle or just a natural variation of the weather?

Another cycle that has received much attention within the last ten to twenty years is the 18- to 20-year cycle that is often called the "lunar cycle" since it is related to positions of the sun and the moon. It is called the Pacific Decadal Oscillation (PDO), and it shows up in weather data that has been "smoothed" or averaged over a period of years. The PDO relates to changes in the North Pacific Ocean sea surface temperatures and pressure. Some meteorologists subscribe to the fact that the last 15 to 20 years have been relatively dry and mild and that we have entered a new 18 to 20 year cycle of wetter and stormier weather. Perhaps, but that does not mean that every year for the next 15 to 18 years will be wetter and colder than normal. Anomalies appear even in smoothed cycles which simply means there are many factors working to influence the weather.

Does a cold winter follow a warm summer and vice versa? Many accounts can be found in historical references to this theory, yet there is no sound basis for it, other than perhaps Mother Nature just wants to "even things out" over a period of time. The Pacific Northwest has suffered through several cold winters in a row interspersed with different summers. There have also been several mild winters in succession. A forecast such as this will be correct 50 percent of the time, but you could do the same by flipping a coin.

Sunspots

Sunspots are cool areas on the sun's surface with a temperature of around 4,000°C as compared to the sun's normal temperature of near 6,000°C. There is an 11.2 year cycle to sunspots that can vary from 7.5 years to 16 years. The intensity also varies. There have been numerous studies trying to correlate sunspots with just about anything from the stock market to the rabbit population in Australia. Sometimes it works, and sometimes it doesn't. A few of the many long-range weather forecasts that are now in existence use sunspot data to derive weather forecasts one or even two years in advance.

Recent satellite observations have been able to measure very accurately the sun's output, which is extremely important to weather. These observations reveal that the sun's radiation received on the earth can vary by 0.04 percent. That does not sound like much, but a small value accumulated over a long period of time could account for some minor change that could be enhanced by something else minor occurring at the same time.

Volcanic Eruptions

Do volcanic eruptions cause variations in the climate? There is some validity to this theory since volcanic particles trapped in the stratosphere have a tendency to reflect solar radiation back to space. Calculations have been done regarding the effects of Mt. Pinatubo in the Philippines in 1991 and El Chichon in Mexico in 1981. Some scientists believe the amount of sulfur dioxide that was placed into the stratosphere was enough to have a cooling effect on the earth by possibly as much as $1/2°C$.

Those two volcanoes are located in the tropical latitudes. The tropopause is higher in this area than in middle latitudes, making the level of the stratosphere higher. Once particles are placed this high, their return rate to the earth is slowed. They remain in the atmosphere for longer periods of time. Mount St. Helens in Washington State erupted on May 18, 1980, but it is located in middle latitude. Most of the particles it placed into the atmosphere from the crater shown in Figure 12.7 did not rise high enough in elevation, and the westerlies dispersed them more quickly. The lighter winds aloft in the tropical areas did not disperse the particles released by Pinatubo and El Chichon. Many of these particles found their way into the stratosphere and remained there for many months.

Two other volcanoes during the last 200 years may have had an effect on the earth's weather. In looking at weather records after the eruption of Krakatoa in the Indonesia area in 1883, one can marvel at the many references to bright orange and red sunsets and sunrises throughout the United States. These remarks continued for almost two years after this eruption. The eruption of Tambora in 1815, also in the Indonesia area, has been blamed by many for the "year without a summer" in the New England area in 1816. Snow and frosts plagued New England during June, July, and August of that year and virtually all crops were lost. There was a famine in Europe, and the potato famine in Ireland, some believe, was a result of this eruption. This event also occurred toward the end of the Little Ice Age.

El Niño

El Niño, or "The Boy Child" in Spanish, was the name given by Peruvian fishermen to an event that would occur with some regularity around Christmas time each year. The ocean off the coast of Ecuador and Peru is generally quite cold due to upwelling caused by the southeasterly winds blowing along the coast around the large area of high pressure in the Southern Hemisphere. These winds are influenced by the Coriolis effect and cause warm ocean water to be pushed offshore and replaced by the colder water from deeper depths in the ocean. It is the same effect that occurs off the Pacific Coast. (Remember, in the Southern Hemisphere, winds blow counter-clockwise around an area of high pressure and the Coriolis effect is to the left.)

The warming referred to by the Peruvian fishermen was due to the invasion of much warmer water from the west due to weaker, or sometimes non-existent southeasterly winds. The Peruvian fishermen took this in stride and instead of fishing for anchovies, as they normally would, the time would be used to mend their nets, repair their boats and be with their families. They knew that soon the southeasterly trade winds would return and with them colder water and the anchovies. Figure 12.8 shows the normal wind flow in the tropical Pacific Ocean throughout the year.

That was the original definition. Since then, scientists have learned that this phenomenon did not only affect the northwest coast of South America, but other areas as well. Now the scientific definition of El Niño is a marked warming of the tropical Pacific Ocean from the International Date Line eastward to the northwestern coast of South America. Thus, simply by definition, the Pacific Northwest

Figure 12.7 Particles from the explosion of Mt. St. Helens in Washington did not rise high enough in the atmosphere to have much effect on the weather. (Photo courtesy Jack Bird, Medford, Oregon)

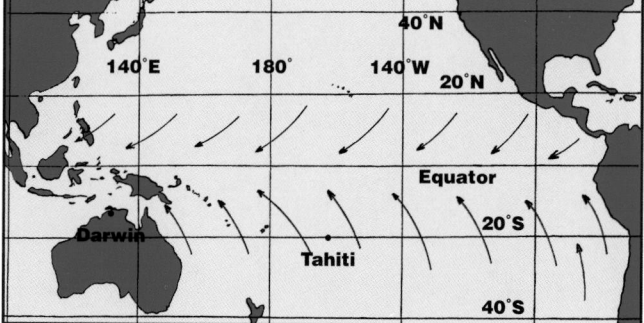

Figure 12.8 Normal wind flow in tropical and subtropical Pacific Ocean.

does not experience El Niños. However, this warming of the ocean from the International Dateline to the northern coast of South America can have effects on the weather that are felt around the globe. Those effects include the Pacific Northwest.

The trade winds are one of the major wind belts around the globe. Southeasterly trade winds are blowing around the large area of high pressure in the Southern Hemisphere, and northeasterly trade winds are blowing around the large area of high pressure in the Northern Hemisphere. These areas, of course, fluctuate with the seasons.

Constant blowing of the trade winds pushes the warm tropical water toward the west. This warm water piles up in the area around Indonesia, Figure 12.9. Under normal conditions, this area contains some of the warmest water in all of the oceans. Here, ocean temperatures are in the low 80s. Warm water takes up more space than cold water. Thus, the advection of warmer water into the area, and the effect of warm water taking up more space, results in a mean sea level in the western tropical Pacific Ocean that is anywhere from one to two feet higher than it is along the northwest coast of South America or the eastern Pacific during normal conditions.

When the trade winds decrease (or in extreme cases, reverse and blow from a westerly direction) all the warm water that has accumulated in the Indonesian area wants to slosh its way back eastward toward the northwest coast of South America, Figure 12.10. The same effect can be created in a bathtub by trying to push all the water to one end and then letting it go. This, in essence, creates a mini-El Niño in your own bathtub! During strong El Niño events, the much warmer water can work its way eastward to the coast of South America and then spread north and south. Those are the conditions that exist during an El Niño event. But what causes these events and how often do they occur?

Wind blows from high pressure to low pressure. In the Southern Hemisphere, Tahiti is located in the northern part of the sub-tropical high pressure area over the South Pacific Ocean. Farther to the west, Darwin, Australia is located on the northern coast of this continent, close to that warm ocean water. On the average, Darwin has a lower air pressure than Tahiti. Thus, the wind will normally blow from

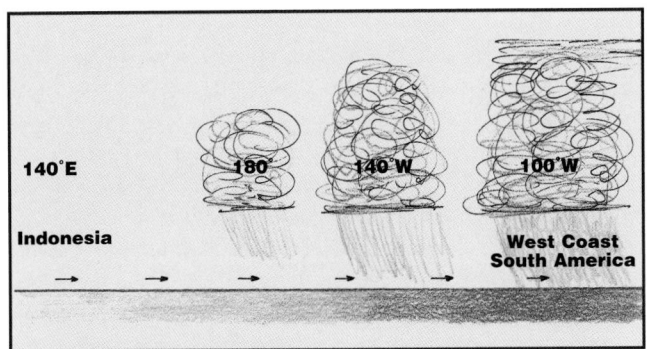

Figure 12.10 Reversal of a normal easterly flow to a westerly flow in the tropical Pacific Ocean pushes warm water east toward the northwest coast of South America, resulting in heavy precipitation in normally dry areas.

Tahiti to Darwin. The result is the trade winds. Figure 12.11 is a graph of the yearly sea level pressures at Darwin and Tahiti.

Scientists have given a name to this difference in pressure, or variance from the average values, between Tahiti and Darwin, and it is called the Southern Oscillation Index (SOI) or simply SO. Simply stated, higher than average pressure at Tahiti and lower than average pressure at Darwin will produce positive values. Lower than average pressure at Tahiti and higher than average pressure at Darwin will produce values near zero, or in extreme cases minus values, meaning that Darwin's pressure is higher than Tahiti's. It is the latter case that produces the strong El Niño conditions. Lately, much to the chagrin of some oceanographers and meteorologists, scientists have begun referring to the strong "normal" events as "La Niñas." That is, a higher than average pressure at Tahiti and a lower than average pressure at Darwin, or a large positive variance in their respective average pressure difference that produces stronger than normal trade winds.

Air rises at the equator, partly due to the effect of surface heating and partly due to the converging northeast and southeast trade winds. This convective activity is enhanced in the Indonesian region because of the warmer ocean temperatures. In 1997 and early 1998, however, that was not the case. The surface pressure at Darwin was slightly higher

Figure 12.9 Trade winds and warm ocean temperatures cause mean sea level to be higher in the western tropical Pacific Ocean than in the eastern tropical Pacific Ocean near the coasts of Peru and Ecuador.

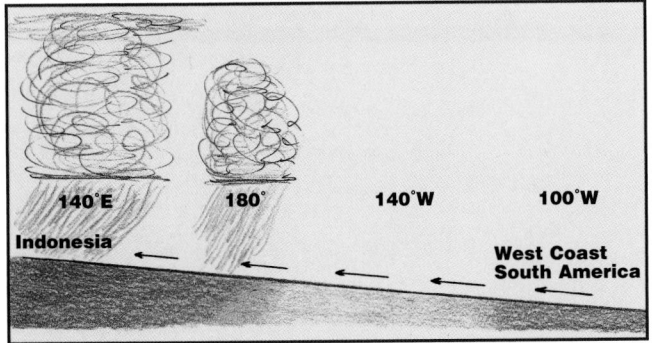

Figure 12.11 Average monthly sea level pressure at Tahiti and Darwin.

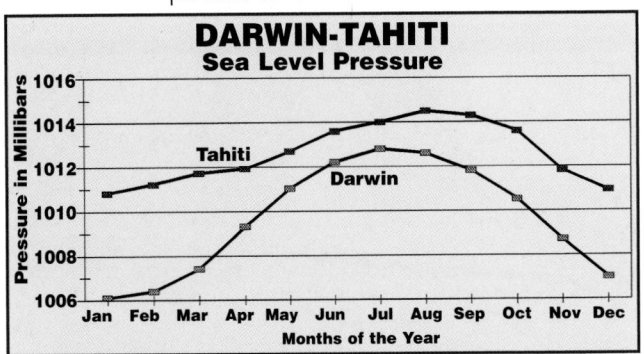

than the surface pressure at Tahiti. Drought occurred in the Indonesian area and forest fires burned millions of acres there and in Australia. Disastrous floods occurred in Peru and Ecuador. It was a very strong El Niño event that some have termed one of the strongest in recorded history.

Because of the normal upwelling along the coasts of Ecuador and Peru, this area is dry. A cold ocean is not conducive to convective activity. The land area records only scant amounts of precipitation but conditions change when the warm ocean water sloshes up against the Peruvian and Ecuadorian coasts. Heavy rainfall results and there have been some devastating floods in this area during El Niño events. Other effects of El Niño are droughts in Central America, Africa, India, the East Indies and Australia. Heavy rain and flooding often occur in southern California, along the Gulf Coast of the United States, in Chile and Argentina. El Niños have also been associated with a fewer number of hurricanes in the Atlantic Ocean. And, due to the warmer ocean temperatures, Pacific hurricanes and typhoons drift out of their normal areas and follow paths that can lead them to the Hawaiian Islands and Tahiti which normally are hurricane- or typhoon-free.

There is an average of four years between El Niño events, but this can vary from two to seven years. There is an average of nine years between strong events, and an even higher period of time between very strong events. For instance, over the last 200 years strong to very strong events were recorded in 1997/98, 1982/83, 1972/73, 1957/58, 1940/41, 1932, 1925/26, 1917, 1911/12, 1899/90, 1891, 1884, 1877/78, 1871, 1864, 1844-46, 1828, 1814, and 1803/04. Thus, some El Niños last more than one year, and the period of time from one event to the next is highly variable.

Above normal rainfall in Southern California and along the Gulf of Mexico is caused by a slightly southward displacement of the jet stream and subsequent storm track during strong El Niño events. This allows the jet stream to tap moisture sources near the equator in the central tropical Pacific Ocean associated with strong convective activity in that area. Often a split in the jet stream occurs over the central Pacific Ocean, Figure 12.12, with one storm track into southeast Alaska and northern British Columbia and another storm track farther south into California. With this type of pattern the Pacific Northwest and southwest Canada are not as susceptible to storms. On the average these areas will normally receive below average precipitation, including snowpack during strong El Niño events. This generally results in a lower spring run-off on the Columbia River. This by no means suggests that the jet stream is always located in these positions during El Niño events. During winters without El Niño events, the jet stream is located on the average near its normal path across the Pacific Ocean, Figure 12.13, tapping sub-tropical moisture sources farther west towards Indonesia. The result is more rain and storms in the Pacific Northwest and fewer storms with less rain in southern California. Little correlation has been established between El Niño and La Niña events and Pacific Northwest summer weather.

A former Oregon State University oceanographer, Dr. William Quinn, now deceased, looked very strongly into the occurrence of El Niños. He traveled in many areas around the globe looking for signs of historic El Niño events. Many documents were translated. He investigated events recorded well over a thousand years looking at logs from early maritime explorers, journals of other explorers, and evidence from early native populations about sea surface temperatures and heavy precipitation in the Peru-Ecuador area. His studies even correlated El Niño events with the flow of the Nile River in Egypt. Perhaps, as he once mentioned to me, Joseph's interpretation of the Pharaoh's dream regarding seven fat cows, then seven lean cows coming up out of the Nile was seven years with good crops followed by seven years of bad crops or a manifestation of an El Niño/La Niña period.

No two El Niño events are the same. Sometimes they will occur very quickly and decrease the same way. At other times they will last for a couple of years, or drop off after one year, only to appear again the next year. Today an array of deep water buoys, drifting buoys, and research vessels that report atmospheric and ocean conditions are situated across the tropical Pacific Ocean. Weather satellites also

Figure 12.12 Location of the jet stream(s) in winter during many El Niño events.

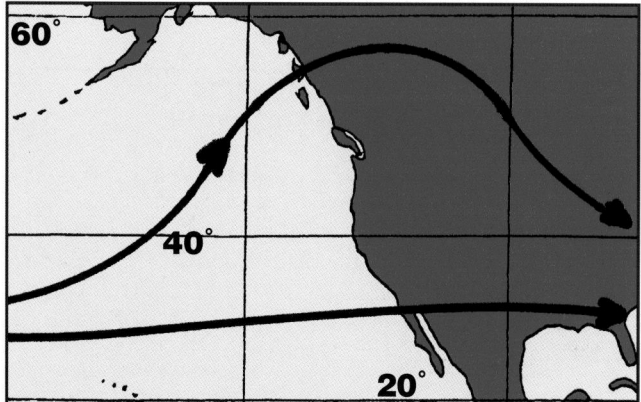

Figure 12.13 Normal position of the jet stream during winters without El Niño.

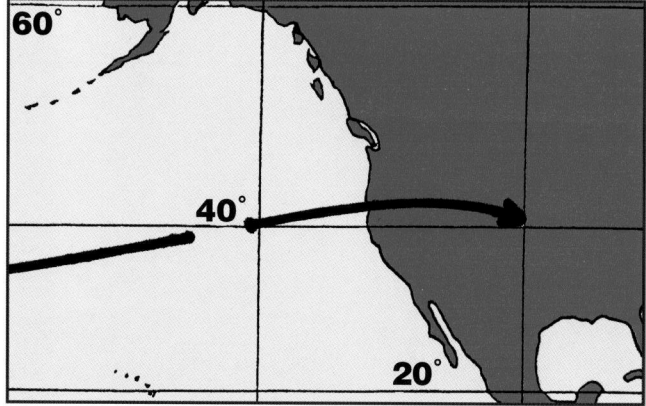

monitor the longwave radiation from the earth. The amount of longwave radiation escaping from the earth is decreased by extensive cloudiness. Thus, under normal conditions, longwave radiation would be greater over the central and eastern tropical Pacific Ocean than the western tropical Pacific Ocean because of the absence of cloudiness. With these data one of the ways scientists are able to detect when an El Niño event is beginning is by a decrease in the longwave radiation over the central and eastern tropical Pacific ocean and warming of ocean temperatures in the same area.

El Niño events are not something new. They have been occurring for thousands of years, at least. They are a marked warming of the central and eastern tropical Pacific Ocean as the trade winds weaken or reverse. El Niños do not occur off the coast of the United States. La Niña events have also probably been around as long as the trade winds have been blowing. As with El Niño events, they come and go. In any case, it seems incorrect to point to some striking weather phenomenon such as a bad snowstorm, tornado, hurricane, or other severe weather events and blame these occurrences on El Niño or La Niña. Factors controlling the weather and climate are far more·complicated. However, since El Niño events do have an effect on global weather, any increase or decrease in these events would likely bring about some changes to the earth's climate.

Something Measured

Official weather observations began at Portland in 1871. Snowfall records since then show an interesting trend. Ten-year cumulative snowfall values since 1871 show a marked decrease in the number of inches of snow. Table 12.1 shows the cumulative snowfall for ten-year periods, beginning with 1871/72-1879/80 and continuing through 1990/91-1999/2000. For about the first 30 years observations were taken in downtown Portland at several locations from Front Street to 6th Avenue between Pine and Alder Streets. In 1902 the observation site was moved to the Customs House between Davis and Everett on Park Avenue. It remained here until the climate office closed in 1963.

Airport observations began in 1940. Thus, for two ten-year periods duplicate observations were taken downtown and at the airport location. The late 1800s show much larger accumulations of snow than in the 20th Century where values continued to drop, except for a very slight increase during the 1990s. Between the location downtown and the location at the airport there is little elevation change. The data is shown in a graph in Figure 12.14. Critics will remark that this is like the old saying, "You're comparing apples and oranges! Data from one location cannot be compared with data from another location." Perhaps, but to the author, the decrease is striking. Climatic change? If your grandpa or great-grandpa was around in the late 1800s and early 1900s, and you heard him remark, "Now back when I was a boy you should have seen the snow drifts!" he may have been right!

SEASONAL SNOWFALL PORTLAND
10-year Cumulations November - April

Winter of...thru winter of...	Downtown Location	Airport Location
1871/72 - 1879/80	182.9 inches	
1880/81 - 1889/90	196.1 inches	
1890/91 - 1899/00	163.7 inches	
1900/01 - 1909/10	75.7 inches	
1910/11 - 1919/20	117.6 inches	
1920/21 - 1929/30	94.8 inches	
1930/31 - 1939/40	92.3 inches	
1940/41 - 1949/50	81.9 inches	91.3 inches
1950/51 - 1959/60	94.7 inches	84.9 inches
1960/61 - 1969/70		67.4 inches
1970/71 - 1979/80		50.1 inches
1980/81 - 1989/90		40.0 inches
1990/91 - 1999/00		48.7 inches

Table 12.1 10-year seasonal snowfall cumulations for Portland, Oregon for downtown and airport location.

Does the same snowfall trend at Portland, Oregon show up at other locations? Similar data was plotted for Seattle, Washington and this is shown in Table 12.2. Observations at this location started about 20 years after data began in Portland, and thus much of the late 1800s is not shown in the Seattle data. The decrease is not as pronounced but the large values at the end of the 19th Century are definitely apparent. There is a greater distance separating the Seattle downtown location from the airport location than for Portland. Whereas elevation changes at Portland are minimal, at Seattle the airport is approximately 300 feet higher. This data was also graphed and it is shown in Figure 12.15. If snowfall values have decreased, what about precipitation? Is there a similar trend? Not really. Since snowfall values are for a November through April period, the same period was used for precipitation. Those values for Portland, Oregon are shown in Figure 12.16. Except for the large amounts recorded in the late 1800s, there seems to be little trend.

Figure 12.14 Snowfall at Portland, Oregon was greater during the latter part of the 19th century.

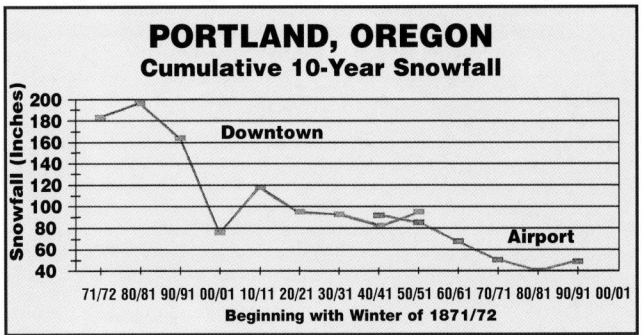

SEASONAL SNOWFALL SEATTLE, WASHINGTON
Federal Building Downtown vs. Seattle Tacoma Airport
10-Year Cumulative Values November-April

Winter of...thru winter of...	Federal Building	Airport
1892/93 - 1901/02	212.3 inches	
1902/03 - 1911/12	100.9 inches	
1912/13 - 1921/22	125.5 inches	
1922/23 - 1931/32	88.1 inches	
1932/33 - 1941/42	57.3 inches	
1942/43 - 1951/52	104.4 inches	150.3 inches
1952/53 - 1961/62	81.7 inches	113.4 inches
1962/63 - 1971/72	105.4 inches	178.5 inches
1972/73 - 1981/82		63.9 inches
1982/83 - 1991/92		60.8 inches
1992/93 - 1996/97		44.8 inches*
* Indicates only 5 years of data		

Table 12.2 10-year cumulative snowfall amounts for Seattle, Washington.

Rainfall and snowfall are only two ways to track climate. Temperature is also a definite factor in climate change. The author has classified winters at Portland, Oregon, since weather records began in 1871, using an "M-scale" from M1 to M8. This scale incorporates maximum and minimum temperatures as well as snowfall for November through April, Table 12.3.

During an M1 winter the minimum temperature does not fall below 20°F, there are no days when the maximum is less than 32°F, and cumulative snowfall for the winter is less than 3 inches. For a winter to be classified as an M2, there must be 1 to 3 days with a minimum temperature of 14°F to 19°F, or 1 to 3 days with a maximum less than 32°F, and less than 3 inches of snowfall. An M3 winter occurs when there are 4 or more days with a minimum temperature 14°F to 19°F, or 4 or more days when the maximum is less than 32°F, or 3.1 to 6 inches of cumulative snowfall. An M4 winter lowers the temperature scale and increases the snowfall. In this

Figure 12.15 10-year cumulative snowfall values for Seattle, downtown and Seattle, Tacoma Airport.

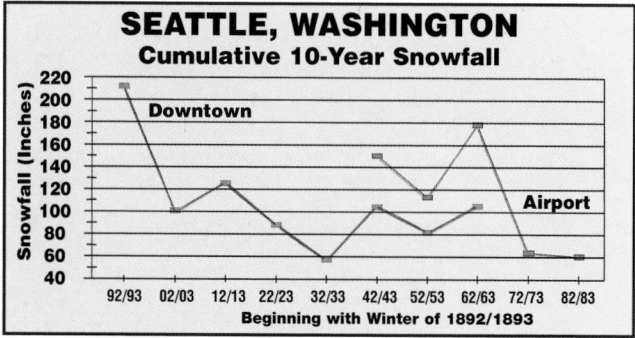

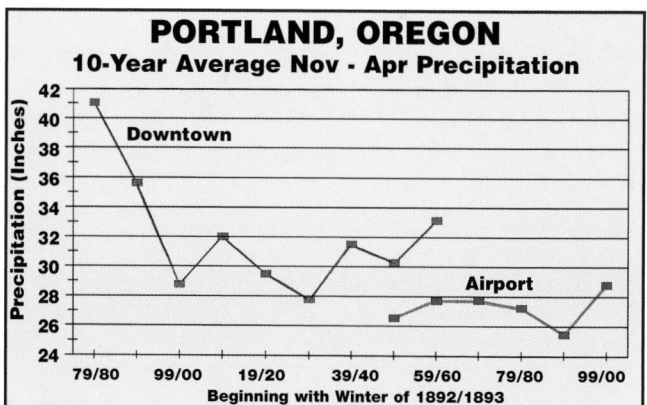

Figure 12.16 10-year average precipitation, November-April for Portland, Oregon for period of record 1871-2000.

category there are 1 to 3 days with a minimum temperature 7°F to 13°F, or 1 to 3 days with a maximum less than 20°F, or 6.1 to 11 inches of snow. M5 winters become slightly more severe with 1 to 3 days having minimum of zero to 6°F, or 4 or more days with a minimum 7°F to 13°F, or 4 or more days with a maximum less than 20°F, or 11.1 to 16 inches of snowfall. M6 winters only include snowfall of 16.1 to 24 inches with no reference to temperature. An M7 winter must have a snowfall of 24.1 to 36 inches. For an M8 winter, the very worst, a minimum temperature of less than zero must be recorded or a snowfall of greater than 36 inches.

Throughout the latter part of the 19th Century, the winters appear to have been much more severe with several falling into the M6, M7 or M8 categories. During the last 50 years, the classification shows only two winters falling into the most severe, one M6 and one M7. Indeed, one could remark that the last severe winter in Portland was the winter of 1968/69 when 34 inches of snow was recorded at the airport, the minimum temperature dipped to less than 10°F and for 10 days the maximum remained below 20°F. Historical references often reflect on the nature of severe winters in the 1800s. Writers in the 19th Century often refer to a severe winter every 7 to 10 years. The above data substantiates this remark but it disappears in the last half of the 20th Century.

An article in the February 2001 issue of the Bulletin of the American Meteorological Society (BAMS) complements the above assertion. The article correlated high stream flow with heavy precipitation events in the contiguous United States. In the western portion of the country, this study indicated a reduction in snow cover leading to a slight decrease in maximum run-off and a slight shift of the latter to earlier in the year. A similar study recorded in the March 2001 issue of the BAMS reveals an earlier bloom date to lilacs over the western portion of the United States.

This trend, should it continue, would have ominous repercussions for the Pacific Northwest. A decrease in mountain snowpack would lead to an earlier and lower maximum run-off in Pacific Northwest streams and rivers. This upsets the normal conditions for juvenile salmon returning to the ocean. A lighter snowpack means less water for recreation, irrigation, and normal use.

This chapter has taken a brief look at the topic of global warming and climatic change. The debate regarding this issue will continue for many years, with some arguing that humans are altering the climate and others stating that change is a natural occurrence. It behooves the reader to keep informed of studies and articles relating to this topic. It must be noted that an overall warming trend will be interspersed with years that are cooler than average. My philosophy is that we need to frequently remind ourselves that we are stewards of the planet and what we do, or do not do, will have long-term effects for those who follow.

Table 12.3 The author's "M-scale" of Portland, Oregon winters incorporating snowfall and temperature.

10-Year Period	M1	M2	M3	M4	M5	M6	M7	M8
Winter of 1871/72 through 1879/80	-	1	1	-	2	1	3	1
Winter of 1880/81 through 1889/90	1	-	-	1	2	1	3	2
Winter of 1890/91 through 1899/1900	1	1	-	3	1	3	-	1
Winter of 1900/01 through 1909/10	2	1	2	2	3	-	-	-
Winter of 1910/11 through 1919/20	2	1	1	2	1	2	-	1
Winter of 1920/21 through 1929/30	1	-	4	-	2	3	-	-
Winter of 1930/31 through 1939/40	3	-	2	2	2	-	1	-
Winter of 1940/41 through 1949/50	6	1	-	-	-	2	-	1
Winter of 1950/51 through 1959/60	1	2	1	2	3	1	-	-
Winter of 1960/61 through 1969/70	5	-	1	2	1	-	1	-
Winter of 1970/71 through 1979/80	3	1	1	4	1	-	-	-
Winter of 1980/81 through 1989/90	3	-	2	5	-	-	-	-
Winter of 1990/91 through 1999/2000	4	-	2	3	1	-	-	-
Totals	32	8	17	26	19	13	8	6

Data incorporates both downtown and airport data. Since 1995 snowfall observations taken at Gresham, Oregon, elevation 410 feet.

Chapter 13
Use of Meteorological Data

Differential heating, global winds, temperature extremes, storm events, along with several other topics. How is all this information used? The use of meteorological data is increasing very rapidly each year. Its uses include environmental

planning, forensics, construction, calculating the amount of energy used, when to plant your peas and beans, global warming, to mention only a few. Meteorological data is now a part of our daily lives. This chapter offers a brief look at how to use it.

Averages

Television weather people refer to the average high temperature or the average low temperature for that day, or the average precipitation for a month. An average is a figure that is compiled from data over a period of time, normally several years. The average high temperature for a certain day would be all the high temperatures recorded on that date, divided by the number of observations. Minimum temperatures are figured the same way. Average yearly or monthly values of precipitation incorporate data from many years or many of the same months, again divided by the total number of years or months. Realistically, however, weather does not often follow averages. It is either too wet, or too dry. The temperatures are too high or too low.

The spring of 1999 in the Pacific Northwest was a good example of weather not following the average. It was cold and wet. The precipitation was above normal. Snowfall set a United States record at the Mount Baker ski area in the northern Washington Cascades during the winter of 1998/1999. The rim road at Crater Lake National Park in

Oregon had one of its latest openings on record. Ski areas ran out of skiers long before they ran out of snow. The winter of 2000/2001 was just the opposite. Far below normal precipitation fell throughout the Pacific Northwest and southwest Canada. Storms that approached the coast headed south and entered the continent in California. Climatologically we average the weather for a day, month, or year, but seldom does Mother Nature follow the script.

This is illustrated in Figure 13.1, which is a plot of actual high and low temperatures for Portland, Oregon for March 1999 along with normals (1961-1990) for each day during the month. Not one day did the actual high temperature equal the normal, or average, maximum for that date. On only two days was the actual minimum temperature equal to the average for that date, or what we refer to as normal. The temperature values were either above or below the average. These daily values can often show great variation during any month of the year. Ten, twenty, or even thirty degrees or more above or below a daily value are not uncommon for stations located in middle latitudes. The longer the length of record the more large variations there will be, since longer records incorporate a better chance of extreme values.

The average temperature for a particular day is simply the highest recorded for the day added to the lowest recorded for the day, and the total divided by two. At my home I take high and low temperature readings each day. In the late evening I observe the maximum temperature and minimum temperature from the thermometers in my instrument shelter described in Chapter 1. The highest temperature and the lowest temperature since the last reading approximately 24 hours ago are recorded. Hundreds of cooperative weather observers around the Pacific Northwest and thousands around the

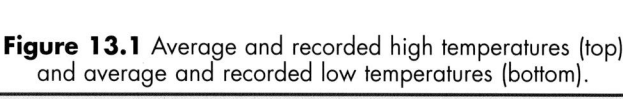

Figure 13.1 Average and recorded high temperatures (top) and average and recorded low temperatures (bottom).

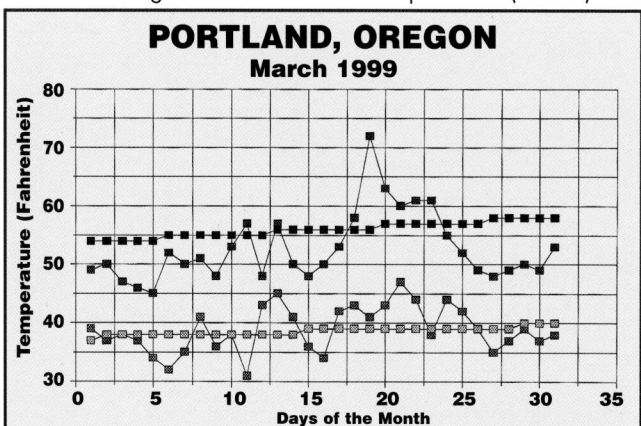

world take similar readings once a day. Some take them in the morning, some in the late afternoon, and some in the evening. The average for a day is computed by adding the highest to the lowest and dividing the sum by two. For the most part, this will be a good approximation of the average temperature for that day. But is it a true average? In most cases, yes. The march of temperature over a 24-hour period usually follows a nice smooth curve from high to low.

> **Earl Stewart, Cooperative Weather Observer**
>
> *Earl Stewart (1902-1996) of Cottage Grove, Oregon was one of the premier Cooperative Weather Observers for the National Weather Service, which enlists the services of over 10,000 such individuals. Earl began taking the weather readings under the direction of his father in October 1917. In October 1992 he was presented with an award that is named after him, "The Earl Stewart Award for Serving 75 or More Years As a Cooperative Weather Observer." It was the first such award ever given to a Cooperative Weather Observer. Earl was highly deserving of this award, the highest given to a cooperative weather observer.*
>
> The Author

The lowest temperatures are normally experienced around sunrise. The temperature rises during the day and reaches its highest value during mid afternoon and then begins falling. It continues to fall after midnight to the lowest value around sunrise, assuming clear skies, little wind and no change of air mass. Figure 13.2 is a thermograph trace of daily temperatures from my home for a six-day period. For the most part, the rise and fall of temperature is a nice sinusoidal-type of a curve with some minor fluctuations in the afternoon and around sunrise, probably due to wind or partial cloud cover. It is easy to derive an average temperature for the day from these data.

But what if the temperature hovered in the low 30s for most of the day with a minimum reading of 30 degrees, and then took a jump to 50 degrees shortly before I took my readings? The average for the day would still be 50 plus 30, divided by 2, or 40 degrees. It might not represent the "true average" for the entire day, but by meteorological definition, it is the average temperature for that day. In determining average daily values then, it does not matter how long the temperature remained at a value, only that it reached that value. The number of observations is not taken into account, only the highest and the lowest to determine an average for the day.

The average high or average low temperatures for a certain period are calculated by adding all the values and dividing by the number of days. For example, the average high temperature for a month would be obtained by adding all the high temperatures and dividing by the total number of days in the month. The same is true for the minimum. This gives an average high temperature for the month and an average low temperature for the month. The average for the month can merely be determined by adding these two values and dividing by two. A similar figure can be determined by adding up the daily averages and dividing by the total number of days in the month. Either method should result in the same value, or perhaps a tenth of a degree difference. Figure 13.3 is a copy of a monthly record from my

Figure 13.2 With no change in air mass, little wind, and clear skies daily temperatures follow a sinusoidal-type curve.

Figure 13.3 The daily temperature and precipitation form used by local observers with the Bonneville Power Administration observation network.

U.S. DEPT. OF ENERGY—BONNEVILLE POWER ADMINISTRATION

DAILY HIGH / LOW TEMPERATURE READINGS

MONTH: March YEAR: 2006 NAME: George Miller

DAY OF MONTH	TEMP HI	TEMP LO	PCPN AMT	SNOW FALL	SNOW DEPTH
1	52	35			
2	52	43	0.29		
3	49	37	0.01		
4	46	38	0.82		
5	45	33			
6	51	34	0.03		
7	51	33	T		
8	50	38	0.13		
9	56	36	0.01		
10	55	39	0.27		
11	52	40	0.06		
12	55	33	0.01		
13	59	39	0.43		
14	51	37	0.09		
15	55	31	0.03		
16	55	43	0.59		
17	48	39	0.05		
18	50	42	0.34		
19	48	38	0.20		
20	55	42			
21	63	43			
22	52	42	0.58		
23	56	39	0.01		
24	62	32			
25	53	40			
26	63	33			
27	50	42	0.15		
28	50	42			
29	54	34			
30	66	35			
31	70	37			
Total					
Average	54.0	37.7			
Extreme	70	31	4.10		

Remarks:

BPA 1458 OCT 1981

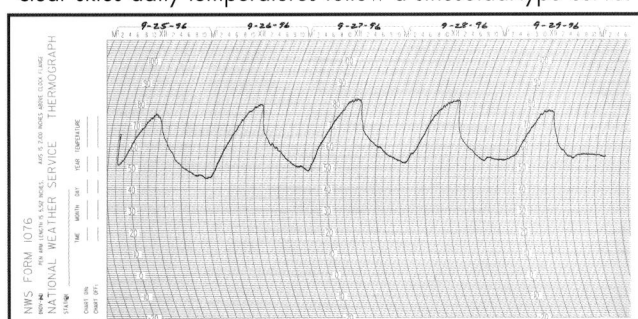

home on a form used by the Bonneville Power Administration network. Cooperative Weather Observers and official National Weather Service stations use a slightly different form that is sent to the National Climatic Data Center (NCDC) in Asheville, North Carolina.

Most records are kept at NCDC. There are six Regional Climatic Centers across the United States such as the one for all western states which is located at the Desert Research Institute, 2215 Raggio Parkway, Reno, Nevada 89512. Most states also have a State Climatologist. For Oregon, the Office of the State Climatologist is located in 326 Strand Agricultural Hall, Oregon State University, Corvallis, Oregon 97331-2209. The State Climatologist's Office in Washington is located at the Atmospheric Sciences Department of the University of Washington, AK-40, Seattle, Washington 98195. Climatological information from cooperative weather sites as well as many other locations in each state is readily available from each of these locations.

Every ten years, "30-Year Normals" are determined for each station reporting their records to NCDC. The 30-Year Normals can change by a few tenths of a degree in temperature or a few hundredths of an inch in precipitation, depending on whether there was a prevailing warm or cool cycle or a wet or dry cycle to the weather during the last ten years. The averages that are most often referred to are the 30-Year Normals. These are sometimes referred to as the 30-Year Means in some publications.

The total average for a station can be determined by averaging all the observations since that particular station began recording data. This does represent a true average for that particular station. Often, from these data, climatic trends can be developed. Reporting locations with long historical records and little if any movement are referred to as Benchmark Stations in the Cooperative Observer Program of the National Weather Service.

Temperatures can also be averaged over an area such as a state. These values, however, are sometimes misleading, especially for Washington and Oregon where the Cascade Mountains dissect these two states resulting in great variations from west to east. The longer the period of time and greater the area covered, the lower will be any departure from the average. You may have heard that the last few years were the warmest the earth has yet experienced since accurate records were kept. That value was less than a degree. That is a small value, but it was over the entire earth that included thousands of observations and for many years of data. Long term averages tend to smooth out the extremes.

Temperature extremes, however, are also useful, especially for those in construction. How cold or how hot has it been at a location? What are the fastest winds that have been recorded? How low do relative humidity values reach? Data such as this is readily available at either NCDC or the Regional Climatic Centers.

Precipitation is generally averaged on a monthly basis, in addition to a calendar year basis. The term "water year" is now being used consistently. It represents the total precipitation beginning with October 1 and continuing through September 30 of the following year. This is especially true for stations that have a winter maximum and a summer minimum of precipitation. An October 1 through September 30 period will encompass the entire rainy season, or the colder months of the year when most precipitation falls. If the precipitation is totaled at the end of the calendar year, it divides the rainy season into two periods that cover different years. Precipitation values include all types such as rain, snow, ice pellets, hail, and other forms.

Degree-days

Degree-days (actually quite a misnomer) are used by heating and cooling companies, electrical companies, and gas companies. Degree-days are based on a value of 65°F. For instance, if the high temperature for a certain day was 50°F and the low temperature was 30°F, the average would be 40°F. To compute the degree-days for that day, 40 is subtracted from 65 to get 25. That value is the amount of heating degree-days for that day. The inference is that your home had to be heated on that particular day, and the 25 is an indication as to how much. Suppose the high for the day was 90°F and the minimum was 60°F. The average would be 75°F. In this case 65 is subtracted from 75 for a value of 10, or 10 cooling degree-days. Once again, the inference is that you used air conditioning, or some other means, to cool your home or business. Heating or cooling degree-days are always rounded to the higher value. That is, if the high temperature for the day was 60°F and the low was 31°F the average temperature for the day would be 45.5°F. This value would be rounded to 46. Degree-days are often summed up for a period such as a week, month, or even a year. Figure 13.4 shows temperatures for a seven-day period with degree-days computed.

Growing Degree-days

Agriculturists will often use a "growing degree-days" figure for various plants. With growing degree-days, however, the

Figure 13.4 An example of computing heating and cooling degree-days from seven days of data.

High and Low Temperatures for a 7-day Period with Degree-days Computed					
	High	**Low**	**Avg.**	**Degree-days (cooling)**	**Degree-days (heating)**
Day 1	50	30	40		25
Day 2	57	38	47.5 (48)		17
Day 3	64	44	54		11
Day 4	72	48	60		5
Day 5	80	58	69	4	
Day 6	82	60	71	6	
Day 7	75	58	66.5 (67)	2	
Average	68.6	48	58.3		
Totals				12	58

base figure can vary according to the plant variety. Peas and wheat have values that are around 40. By totaling the number of growing degree-days based on a value of 40 since planting, the estimated date of maturity or harvest can be calculated. The growing degree-day value, however, is still based on daily temperatures. If, for instance, the daily low temperature was 35°F and the daily high was 55°F, that computes to an average for the day of 45, or a total of 5 growing degree-days for peas. The base value is always subtracted from the daily average. Individual varieties respond or grow better with warmer temperatures. The growing degree-days base value for sweet corn and beans is around 50 and for cotton and rice it is around 60. Growing degree-days are also being used to determine when various insects become active or hatch, which can then be a factor in their control. Again, the base value depends on the insect.

Wind is also highly used in climatological data. Lately, hurricane and tornado damage across the United States has generated stricter building codes that use the maximum wind speeds a location may expect. This data is then incorporated into engineering designs. Most construction along coasts must be done to withstand a sustained wind of 100 mph. "Wind roses" are also used in planning. A wind rose indicates the percentage of time that the wind blows from a certain direction and the frequency of various speeds. They are usually determined on a monthly basis. For instance, a wind rose for the Portland Airport would indicate a prevailing wind from the east-southeast in January and from the northwest in July. At coastal stations in the Pacific Northwest a wind rose would show a prevailing direction of southerly in January and north to northwesterly in July. Local features such as mountains, hills, valleys, canyons and other geographical features can have a great influence on prevailing winds at a theoretical location. Figure 13.5 is an example of a wind rose for a theoretical station for July.

Meteorological data has value in many different areas. These data are readily available from NCDC, the Regional Climatic Data Centers as well as from local State Climatologists. Each location has data on file from many locations in the Pacific Northwest.

Figure 13.5 A wind rose for a theoretical station for July. In the example 22% of the time the wind is less than 4 mph; 30% of the time it blows from the northwest at 4 to 12 mph; 14% of the time from the northwest at 13 to 31 mph; 15% of the time from the north at 4 to 12 mph; 10% of the time from the west at 4 to 12 mph and percentages of less than 5% for the other directions.

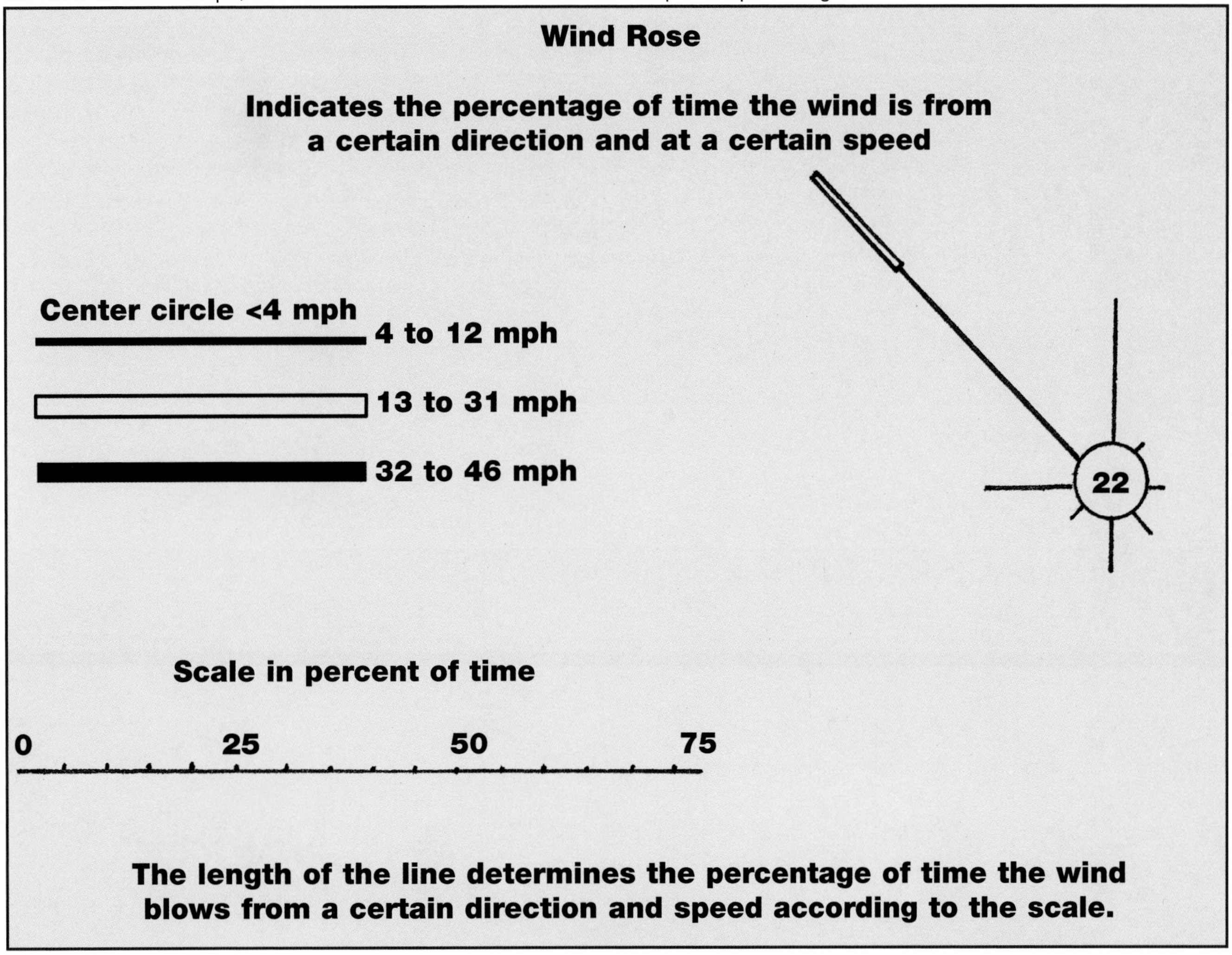

Wind Rose

Indicates the percentage of time the wind is from a certain direction and at a certain speed

Center circle <4 mph
4 to 12 mph
13 to 31 mph
32 to 46 mph

22

Scale in percent of time

0   25   50   75

The length of the line determines the percentage of time the wind blows from a certain direction and speed according to the scale.

Chapter 14
Weather Forecasting

"If you can't see Mt. Hood, it is raining. If you can see Mt. Hood (Figure 14.1) it is going to rain." I am not sure who developed this statement, or "weather forecast," but if the rule were to be applied over a long period of time, it could very well be true— for the most part. However, weather forecasting is much more sophisticated than just looking out the window, although many times I am sure you have listened to a weather forecast, looked out the window,

> ### Weather Cannot Be Foretold
> *"The most accurate and minute meteorological observations continued for half a century in different countries, have proved that, though the moon affects the tides, it has no perceptible influence on the weather, and that predictions what the weather will be on particular days are pretense and delusion."*
>
> *The Oregon City Argus,* March 28, 1857

and wondered why the meteorologist who made the forecast did not look out a window before the forecast was made.

As the Oregon City Argus so stated nearly 150 years ago, sometimes it is with pretense and delusion that weather forecasts are made. But they are made, and their accuracy is far better than it was 150 years ago and more accurate in the 21st Century than in the latter part of the 20th Century. The 48-hour prediction today is better than the 24-hour prediction 15 years ago. I certainly believe that the Argus reporter who penned the statement nearly 150 years ago would be amazed with today's forecasts that often are very accurate 10 days into the future. Yes, I have heard the

comment, "Only a fool and a newcomer predict the weather in the Pacific Northwest." Well, I consider myself neither. I was born and raised in southwest Washington, and I won't let myself be thrown into the former category.

There is no question that weather forecasting is difficult, but what makes it so difficult? First of all, take a body that is very nearly a sphere and begin rotating it on its axis. Tilt that axis 23.5° and begin revolving it around a star. Put a shallow film of air around it that contains many gases, some of great importance but only in minute quantities. Heat it at the equator and cool it at its poles. Make about 70 percent of its surface water and move the water around. Randomly place continents over the remaining 30 percent. Put mountains and valleys over the land surfaces and then intersperse those with smaller bodies of water. No small wonder that you can hear a forecast of "partly cloudy with a few showers" while it is sunny and warm, or raining when the barometer says it should be fair.

Basically, the atmosphere must be measured in its initial state both vertically and horizontally before a weather forecast can be made. This is done through a host of measuring devices from weather satellites, to radiosonde balloons, to weather radar, to an individual taking an observation at a remote site on an island in the ocean. This information is placed into a computer which then computes values at grid points both vertically and horizontally around the globe. If your entryway has square tile or if your kitchen linoleum has a square pattern to it, the grid points would be at the four corners. Figure 14.2 is an illustration of this.

Observations of the weather do not always fall at the grid points, or at the letters A through F in Figure 14.2. They will be at the numbered locations in the figure. Thus, for the computer to generate a value or "observation" at

Figure 14.1 "If you can't see Mt. Hood, it is raining. If you can see Mt. Hood, it is going to rain." Obviously, from the photo, the forecast is rain!

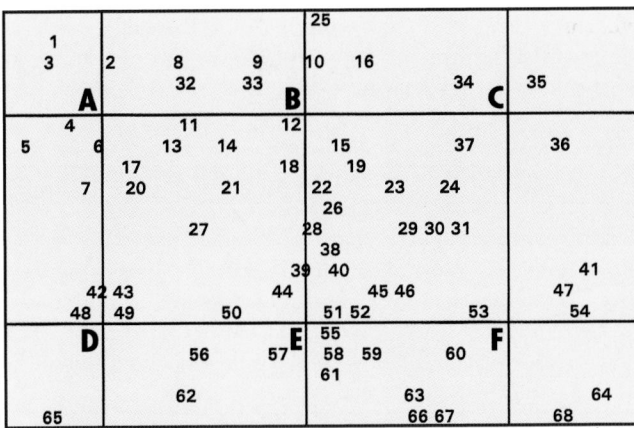

Figure 14.2 For a computer to generate a numerical forecast, it must first compute values at grid points (letters) from the measured data (numbers).

point A it looks at the values surrounding this point such as 1, 3, 2, 8, 4, 11, 5, 6, 13, 17, 7, and 20, giving more weight to those that are closest and less to those farther away. This calculation is done for each grid point A, B, C, D, E and F.

The atmosphere is also measured at various levels above the surface. It is like stacking several layers of tile or linoleum one on top of the other like the grid points shown in Figure 14.3. Observations above the surface of the earth, however, are far more skimpy, coming mostly from

Figure 14.3 Values at each grid point are also computed for many levels in the atmosphere from data available at that level.

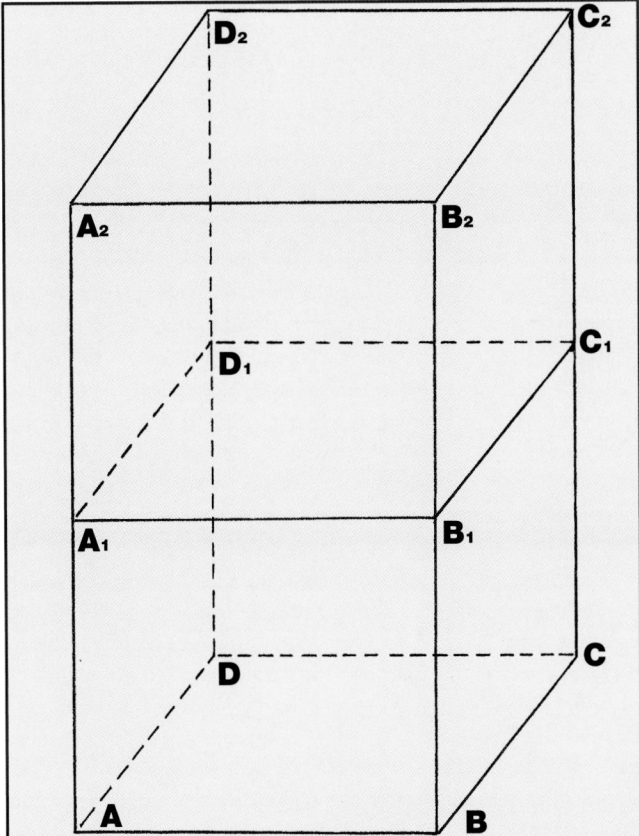

radiosondes, airplanes and satellites, than those at the surface. Thus, there are many levels with many grid points where the initial conditions of the atmosphere must be determined.

The atmosphere operates on a series of equations. Knowing the initial state of the atmosphere at these grid points both horizontally and vertically, the computer, using mathematics, can then integrate those values forward in time. The computer does this in short time increments. Thus, air with certain qualities or characteristics at some point in the atmosphere is moved forward in time. The computer lifts it or causes it to descend, depending on the stability. If winds from a location with more or less moisture intersect the parcel, moisture is either added or subtracted. If the parcel of air moves over a continent, theoretically smoothed mountains are put into the equation, and the parcel is then forced over the mountains. Additional variables of sun angle, surface condition, time of year, snow cover and several others are incorporated. There are several computer models that may analyze and integrate the weather in a slightly different manner, perhaps using smaller distances between grid points. The principle, however, remains the same although the outcome may differ sometimes with only minor variations and sometimes with large variations.

The result is what the pressure pattern (location of highs and lows) and upper air contour lines should look like 6, 12, 18, 24, etc., hours after the initial time. (Figure 14.4 is an example of a Medium Range Forecast (MRF) model output for 24 hours from initial time.) As the speed and capacity of computers have improved over the last 20 years, so have the weather forecasts. From very basic models 30 years ago, meteorologists have refined the equations by adding more variables, reducing the spacing between grid points, adding more observations, and including more accurate descriptions of mountains. The result of all this is a more accurate forecast and forecasts that project the weather, that is, the location of high and low pressure areas, troughs and ridges, further into the future. Figure 14.5 shows the same MRF forecast 48 hours after the initial time. This model now extends the output to 10 days.

Figure 14.4 A Medium Range Forecast model (MRF) for 24 hours from initial time. Solid lines represent isobars; colored areas 500mb contour heights or lines. (Chart taken from Unisys Weather Web Page.)

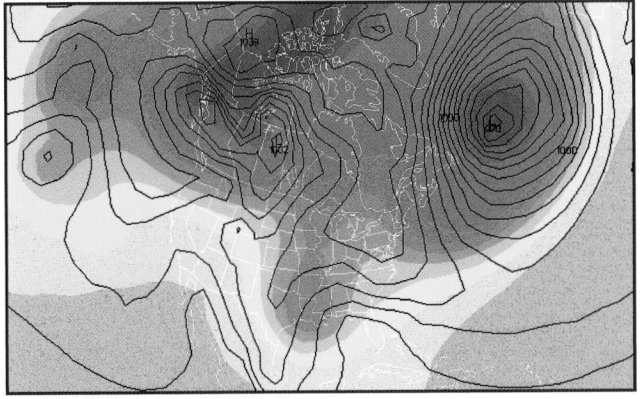

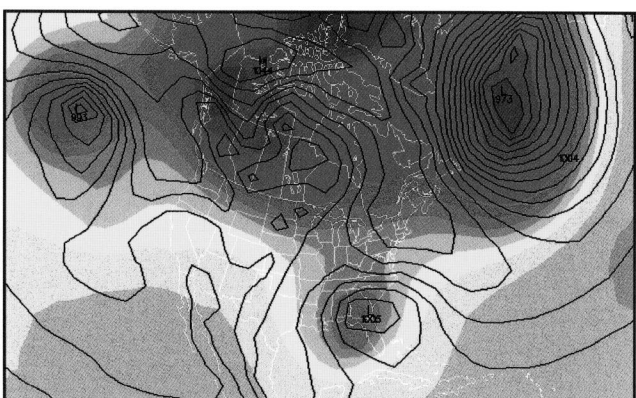

Figure 14.5 The MRF forecast for 48 hours after the initial time in Figure 14.4. Note the intensification of surface lows in the Pacific and over the southeast U.S. (Chart taken from Unisys Weather Web Page.)

Weather forecasters refer to this information as "guidance." Once the computer has reached its final product, it is up to the local meteorologist to interpret that data and add local peculiarities to the forecast since every hill and valley cannot be included. For the Portland area it might be the Columbia River Gorge, or the Willamette Valley, or its proximity to the ocean. In California it might be a refinement of the Sierra Nevada Mountains or the Sacramento Valley, and in the Seattle area the Puget Sound Convergence Zone and/or Olympic Mountains.

The above forecast is called a "numerical" forecast since it incorporates real time data and meteorological equations to

what is happening "now" will continue to happen several hours from the present. Jesus in Luke was using a nowcast in speaking to the multitudes about showers coming from the west. Nowcasts are issued in short time increments since what is happening now will likely not continue beyond several hours. Or, if a storm front has been moving consistently at 20 miles per hour, it will continue to move at that pace. This moves into another type of forecast called a "persistence forecast." During the dull, warm, clear days of summer in many parts of the country this forecast merely states, "What you got today, you will get tomorrow!" A forecast of rain in the western valleys of Washington and Oregon in winter might be a good persistence forecast.

Climatology is also used as a forecast or a forecast tool, especially for months in advance. Jesus was using climatology in the quote from Luke 12:55. In the Holy Land, when the wind blows from off the hot, dry desert, extremely warm temperatures are experienced. We know that the climatology of an area is the average of the weather in that area for a long period of time. It quite often is a good forecast in the tropics or desert areas of the globe where extreme values are rare.

Meteorologists also use analogues in forecasting. No two weather systems are exactly the same, but there are similarities. Similar storms will often result in similar weather conditions. If the weather pattern that exists resembles one that happened several years ago, the meteorologist can draw conclusions from the similarities.

Weather forecasting is still an inexact science. Several years ago the idea of "probability" was incorporated into the forecasts. A probability forecast means that with similar con-

---

Jesus Christ Speaking to the Multitudes

He also said to the multitudes, "When you see a cloud rising in the west, you say at once, 'A shower is coming': and so it happens."

Luke 12:54; Harper Study Bible
Revised Standard Version

Jesus Christ Speaking to the Multitudes

"And when you see the south wind blowing, you say, 'There will be scorching heat'; and it happens."

Luke 12:55; Harper Study Bible
Revised Standard Version

---

arrive at a forecast. Numerical forecasts, or forecasts using mathematical deductions, have been on the minds of meteorologists for almost 100 years. It was early in the 20th century that Europeans first had the idea. Then a brilliant meteorologist by the name of L. F. Richardson actually tried it in the early 1920s. He used two equations, but his task was formidable. A desk top calculator and slide rule are a far cry from today's computer power. But Richardson's idea caught on. He was just a little ahead of his time. Today, the power of computers to make calculations is unbelievable. But a computer model is only as good as the data that is fed into it. And the further out in time a computer model projects the weather, the greater threat there is that the final product will not verify with the final isobars and contour lines. This is especially so if the atmosphere has not been measured accurately in its initial state.

There are other types of forecasts that meteorologists use. One is called "nowcasting." This forecast means that

ditions there is a probability of a certain event occurring. Precipitation is often expressed in probabilities. A 60 percent chance of rain simply means that given the same conditions, it will rain six times out of ten at a particular location. Probability values are especially valuable in the construction and engineering fields. When used with climatological values, they take on additional meaning. A forecast of 60 percent chance of rain when the climatological value is only 15 percent is a significant confidence factor in the forecast.

A forecaster often gets a "feel" for the weather. Some call it intuition. I know that after several days off and away from a weather map, the first forecast that I made after returning to work was not always my best. It would take a couple days of "getting a feel for the weather" before my confidence factor increased again. Weather has a tendency sometimes to repeat itself, and successive storms often follow the same track.

So far, the discussion has been about precipitation. But does it rain all the time in the Pacific Northwest, at least west

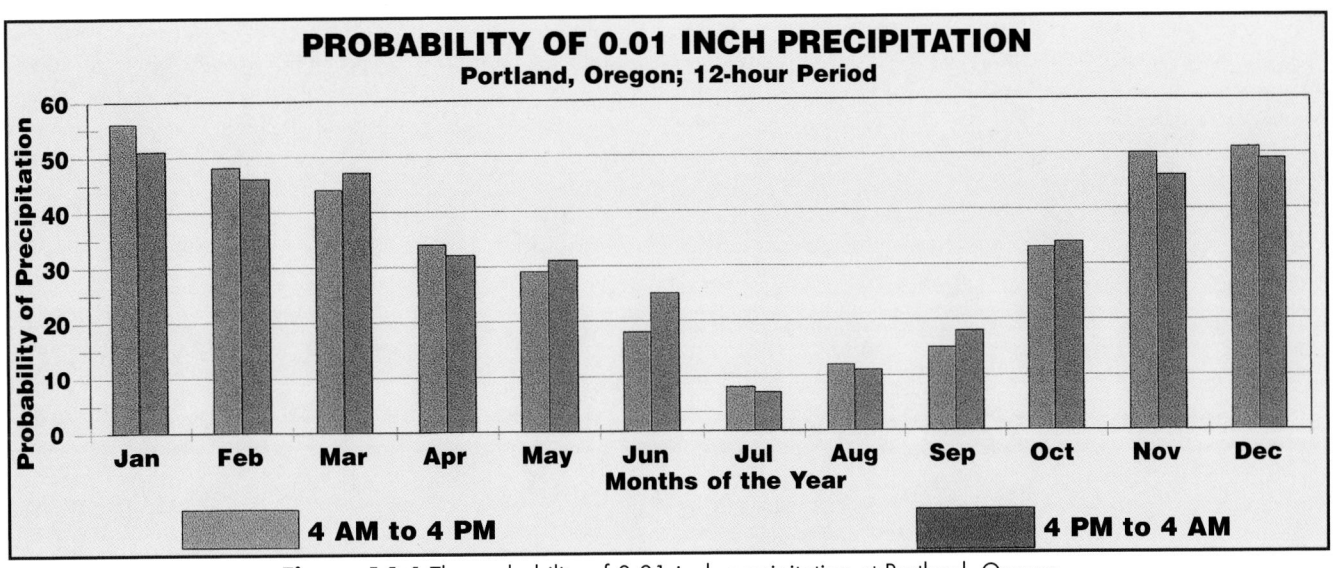

Figure 14.6 The probability of 0.01 inch precipitation at Portland, Oregon never exceeds 60% for a 12-hour period and falls to less than 10% during July.

of the Cascade Mountains, as some people think? The answer is unequivocally, NO! Even in the middle of winter when the Pacific Northwest is seemingly deluged with precipitation, the probability of receiving 0.01 inch of rain at the Portland Airport in a 12-hour period is just over 50 percent. In the middle of summer, that value for a 12-hour period drops off to less than 10 percent. Figure 14.6 shows the variation throughout the year. The values from 4 AM to 4 PM are slightly higher in most of the spring months due to shower activity that generally dissipates during late afternoon.

Pendleton, Oregon is representative for several lower elevation locations east of the Cascade Mountains. At this location, Figure 14.7, the value for December and January is around 30 percent for a 12-hour period. This value drops to less than 5 percent in July. No, it certainly does not rain

all the time. Weather forecasts, however, might lead one to believe that it does. Forecasters can verify a high percentage or probability for precipitation if only 0.01 inch falls during that forecast period. Thus, even throughout the 12-hour period if it was mostly sunny and clear and then 0.01 inch of precipitation fell at the very end of the period, the forecaster would verify. But was that the true representation of the weather for the 12-hour period? No. I believe that if the Pacific Northwest received all the rain that was forecast, the inhabitants would be living in arks! As a former colleague of mine used to say, "This place would be a jungle if we received all the rain that was forecast." Rain is definitely over-forecast in the Pacific Northwest.

On the lighter side of forecasting, in addition to the statement about Mt. Hood to open this chapter, there are

Figure 14.7 Probability of precipitation for a 12-hour period is far less east of the Cascade Mountains, such as at Pendleton, Oregon than it is west of the mountains.

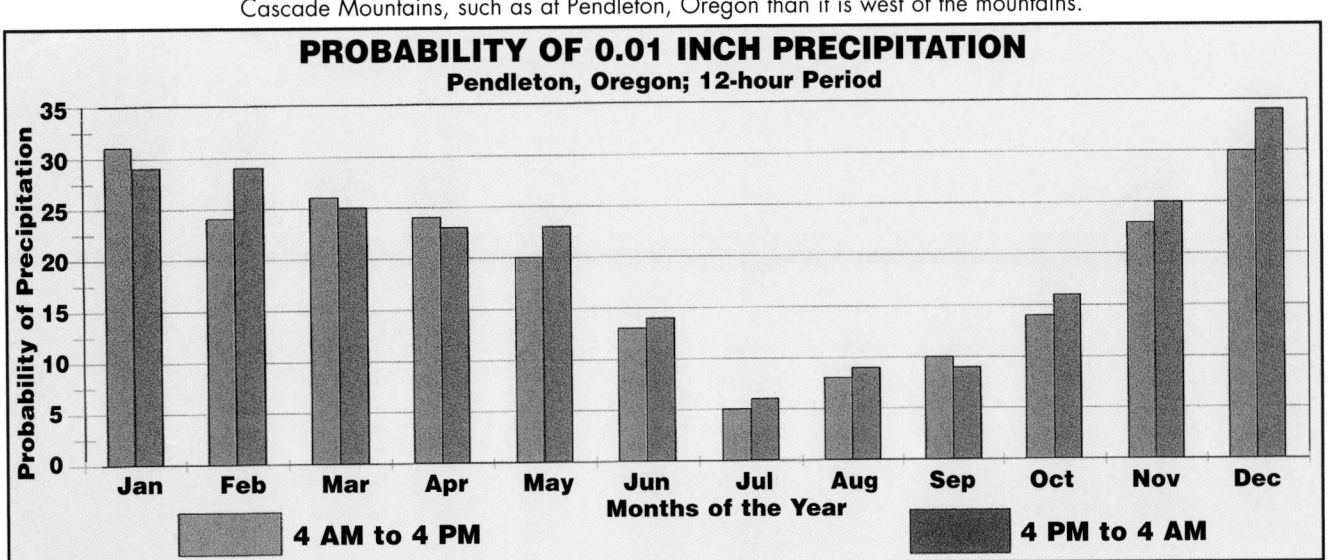

other facetious "rules" among meteorologists. One is that "Highly advertized events rarely happen." This could be more a media hype than a missed forecast. But if a big storm is forecast with much publicity regarding the event, as there seems to be now, and the event does not happen, the critics abound.

His Banjo a Barometer

There is a young man about town who is always prepared for all kinds of weather. No matter if he attends a function when the night is cloudless and rain falls before he goes home, he is always on hand with an umbrella, much to the delight of the girl with him.

For a long time his secret remained undisclosed, and he was looked upon as a weather prophet who could give points to the local bureau. However, it is no longer a secret, for the young man confessed not long ago the reason for his invariably correct prognostication of nasty weather. He is a very fair banjoist, and it was noticed that he always played on his instrument before going out at night. When the plaintive sounds were muffled, he never neglected to take his umbrella, but if, on the contrary, the sound was sharp and clear he went without it.

The head, or sounding board, of a banjo is made of sheepskin, and in damp weather it expands, and the head becomes tight as a drum. This is the reason for his invariable good luck in 'picking' the weather, for he owns a natural barometer.

Corvallis Gazette, December 25, 1900

Heavy rain and strong winds do occur many times together. At other times, the wind may blow hard but very little rain occurs, or there may be copious rainfall and very little wind. Thus, the saying, or verification is, "The wind blew all the rain away!" or "Hey, it rained a whole lot just north of here!"

"Big storms always happen on weekends and holidays." Well, anyone who finally received a long weekend off after having worked a large number of days in a row knows this to be absolutely true! And from the staffing standpoint at a weather office, there are usually fewer people on duty over the weekend and on holidays than there are during the week.

"Clouds tend to form at sunrise." Of all the sayings, this one probably holds the most grains of truth. First of all, if you are a weather observer in the middle of the night with no moon, your first glimpse of clouds may come with the first rays of dawn. And certain particles in the atmosphere seem to become hygroscopic when sunlight strikes them. This could result in cloud formation.

"Fair weather accompanies each full moon." My sister and I have been battling this one for years and years, and I give her credit for being right 100 percent of the time—

somewhere! But locally, it is no more than 50/50. She still swears by it, however, and plans her vacations in accordance.

And then there are several "forecast clues" that persons living near the coast have mentioned to me. One is regarding gulls. Supposedly, if they are up and flying around the

---

An Unusual Well

"On the mesa of Juniper Flat, Oregon, there is a well having unusual characteristics. In addition to furnishing a plentiful supply of very good water, it also serves as the barometer of its proud owner..."

'Twelve to twenty-four hours before a storm arrives a gentle draft begins to come out of the well, the intensity increasing rapidly to almost a roar.

"Throughout the duration of a storm the well continues to 'blow', sometimes so violently as to emit a cloud of water vapor. Within 12 to 24 hours after the storm has passed the well will cease blowing and begin to inhale and air will continue to flow into it until equilibrium is reached or a new period of exhalation begins."

Monthly Weather Review, January 1927

---

weather will be fair, but if they are all huddled together on the beach, then look for a storm. Well, one day while riding with a fire control official along the coast, we rounded a bend in the road and had a good view of the beach where several gulls were huddled together. However, just as many were flying around in the air. "Tom," I said, "now what's

---

Fickle Oregon Weather

"However of the principle characteristics of this fickle, slippery Oregon is the extreme uncertainty of its weather. In no other state, I believe, is this so apparent. Thermometers become perfectly exhausted with the rapidity with which they have to jump from Zero upward, and then down again, and Barometers are disgusted with their failures in attempting to point out a change before it takes place, and like a fussy little old gentleman who stamps from side to side in the vain attempt to discover which will convey the full extent of his irateness, they are sorely puzzled in which way to turn when it rains, snows, hails, blows, clouds and shines in the same hour."

So Far From Home: An Army Bride on the Western Frontier, 1865-1869 Gillis, Charles J. (1993)

---

going to happen? There are as many gulls flying as there are huddled together." His reply was, "Looks as though they are just as confused as you are, George, and don't know what is going to happen!"

The other coastal forecast involves sea lions or seals. Supposedly, they beach themselves when a storm far out at sea has created large swells that they have difficulty swimming through. The storm, moving from west to east, will then arrive at the coast a day or two later. Well, perhaps, but I believe they just get tired and need a rest, storm or no storm. Wouldn't you be tired if you had been swimming in the ocean all day?

And, of course, no reference to weather forecasting is complete without mentioning the Roseburg Goats. During the mid 1960s the official U.S. Weather Bureau station at Roseburg, Oregon was closed. Not to be denied a forecast, the local residents began observing goats that grazed on the side of Mt. Nebo and were easily seen by most residents of the town. Reportedly, when the goats grazed near the top of the hill the weather would be fair. However, when the goats stayed low and out of sight, there was a change in the weather coming or it was already stormy. Now, I give the goats credit. Why graze at the top of the hill where it was windy, cold, and wet when the protection of the trees below offered some shelter? And, when the weather is sunny, don't we seek a location where the sun is warmest and there is a refreshing breeze? As for moving to the top of the hill on a rainy, windy day that is to be followed by a sunny, warm day. Na! Goats are smart, but not that smart. They will, however, probably go where the grass is greener despite the weather!

Forecast Clues

Banjos, wells, gulls, goats, full moons, seals, and so forth offer a bit of humor to weather forecasting. There are, however, some clues that a layperson can apply that will give him an indication of what the weather might be.

Self-predicting the weather is as old as man has been observing it. Jesus Christ in the book of Matthew was speaking to the Pharisees and Sadducees. But obviously the people of that time had observed the weather long enough to know that the sun shining from the west and creating colorful clouds meant that the sky was clearing, since weather generally moves from west to east. In the morning with the sun shining toward the west and off

Jesus Christ Speaking to the Pharisees & Sadducees
"When it is evening, you say, 'It will be fair weather; for the sky is red.' And in morning, 'It will storm today, for the sky is red and threatening.' You know how to interpret the appearance of the sky, but you cannot interpret the sign of the times."

Matthew 16:2-3,
Harper Study Bible, Revised Standard Version

threatening clouds, it could mean that stormy weather was approaching.

There are a few other indicators that a person can use to "self-predict" the weather in the short term, usually less than 24 hours. Many pertain to the characteristics of cold fronts, warm fronts, and occlusions. In the Pacific Northwest a wind veering from the south into the northwest and rising barometric pressure usually means clearing skies and a day or two of clear weather. These are two of the characteristics of a cold front: rising barometric pressure and clearing skies. In the summer months, however, this rule is not always the case, certainly west of the Cascade Mountains. Frequently, after a period of warm or hot weather, a west or northwest wind accompanied by rising barometric pressure signals an invasion of marine air or a marine push which then results in extensive low cloudiness the following day in the valleys west of the Cascade Mountains. Afternoon clearing will usually occur if the marine layer and clouds are not too thick. East of the Cascade Mountains, a northwesterly wind is usually a downslope wind with associated clearing of the clouds. This is especially true after a few days of thunderstorms and above-normal temperatures in the summer. A northwest wind is bringing in drier air.

Generally in any month of the year throughout the Pacific Northwest, a southerly component to the wind accompanied by falling barometric pressure is an indication that a Pacific storm front is approaching. Clouds are usually increasing with these conditions that eventually lead to rain, snow if the air mass is cold enough, and if the storm front is relatively strong.

Clear and cold weather usually accompanies an east or northeast wind with rising barometetric pressures in the winter at many locations west of the Cascade Mountains such as Portland, Oregon and Bellingham, Washington. This is very likely the case east of the Cascade Mountains in winter. A northeast wind and rising barometric pressure are an indication that an arctic front has passed. In this case, look for colder weather. However, very warm weather accompanies an east wind and falling barometric pressure especially in the area around Portland and valleys west of the Cascade Mountains and at coastal locations during the summer months. In winter an east wind with falling barometric pressure usually indicates increasing clouds followed by snow, rain and ice.

In fall, winter and into early spring, clearing skies after the passage of a cold front in the late afternoon will usually lead to the formation of fog the next day. The clear skies that often follow a cold front or cold occlusion will allow the earth to radiate its heat, cooling the air next to the surface to the dewpoint temperature with condensation the result. If the dewpoint temperature is below freezing, frost will be the result. These are generalizations and weather forecasting is certainly not this easy. Local influences such as the Columbia River Gorge and Puget Sound have their own peculiarities.

Clouds As Weather Indicators

Certain clouds can often be used as forecasting tools. The altocumulus standing lenticular clouds (ACSL) in Figure 14.8 seen at sunrise from the author's home in Gresham,

Figure 14.8 Altocumulus standing lenticular clouds at sunrise that indicate increasing moisture and possibly strong winds aloft.

Figure 14.9 Altocumulus standing lenticular clouds over and to the north of Mt. Hood in Oregon and the presence of weak rotor clouds on the north slope.

Oregon are indicative of relatively strong winds aloft and the presence of moisture in the middle and upper levels of the atmosphere. The appearance of these clouds after several days of cloudless skies means that air with a higher moisture content is being advected into the middle levels of the troposphere.

I distinctly remember many years ago on a fishing trip to the Mt. St. Helens area before the eruption. While taking a boat across Spirit Lake, we looked back at a beautiful lenticular cloud covering the top of Mt. St. Helens. The rest of the sky was clear and blue. "How long you fellas gonna be campin'," the boat operator asked? "Oh, 3 or 4 days if we catch some fish," we answered. The old fellow looked back at the mountain, shook his head and said, "You boys gonna get wet." We were both young, upstart meteorologists who thought we knew all there was to know about the weather and simply laughed. The next day we woke to a threatening sky and by evening it was raining. After a wet night we left the next day with our soggy backpacks. Needless to say, we did not take the boat back across the lake.

Altocumulus standing lenticular clouds, however, are not moving along with the wind. They are stationary. As air is forced up and over an obstruction such as a ridge or mountain, it undulates downstream. At each wave crest downstream from the obstruction where the air is rising, a lenticular cloud will form much like those shown in Figure 14.9 to the north of Mount Hood in Oregon from a strong southerly flow of air up and over the mountain. Altocumulus standing lenticular clouds move or change only as the wind direction and speed and moisture values change. As the source of moisture is depleted, they will dissipate, or if additional moisture is added, they can soon be obscured by other clouds. Figure 14.9 also shows a rotor cloud. These clouds are sometimes present below lenticular clouds as the air flows up and through the lenticular clouds and then descends. The wind often reverses direction, in this case blowing from the north at the surface. The air makes a complete circle, rising again to form the rotor cloud as depicted in the Figure 14.10. Rotor clouds are very prevalent to the lee of the Sierra Nevada Mountains in California and the Rocky Mountains in Colorado.

Often the winds associated with altocumulus standing lenticular clouds are apparent at the surface. Figure 14.11 shows well-formed lenticular clouds. Note the trees in the lower portion of the photograph leaning toward the left because of strong surface winds. The atmosphere where altocumulus standing lenticular clouds are forming is normally a stable atmosphere and the flow is quite laminar. Showers and thundershowers would not likely form in this type of vertical temperature distribution. But the presence of these clouds can be a valid indicator of strong winds aloft.

There are other clouds, however, that do indicate an unstable atmosphere and can lead to entirely different weather episodes. Altocumulus castellanus clouds resemble castles or turrets, hence the name. Two photographs of these clouds appear in Figure 14.12. These clouds are indicative of a layer of instability and moisture present in the atmosphere that is of sufficient depth to cause air to rise and condense. Their bases can be quite dense as seen in the right photograph. Their sister clouds, altocumulus floccus, appear in Figure 14.13. These clouds resemble fluffs of cotton, and their presence is also indicative of an unstable layer of air at mid-levels in the troposphere with sufficient moisture present to form clouds. When seen at sunrise or in the early morning hours, these clouds could portend thunderstorms later in the day as surface air heats up and convective currents begin, assuming

Figure 14.10 Rotor clouds, A, often form beneath lenticular clouds.

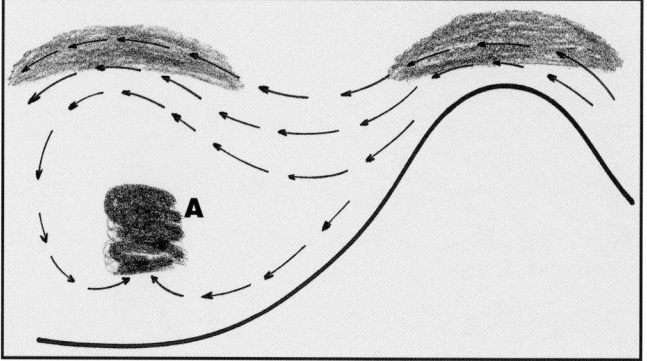

Figure 14.11 Lenticular clouds often indicate strong surface winds as shown by the trees in this photo.

Figure 14.13 Altocumulus floccus clouds resemble fluffs of cotton and indicate an influx of moisture at middle levels of the atmosphere.

the supply of moisture is maintained. The appearance of these clouds can change quickly as atmospheric qualities of moisture and stability change.

Cirrostratus clouds are formed at high elevations in the troposphere, usually above 20,000 feet and offer a milky-whitish appearance. Often these clouds will show a distinct halo around the sun or the moon as shown in Figure 14.14 due to light passing through ice crystals. Their presence indicates moisture at very high levels in the atmosphere perhaps from an advancing warm front or occlusion. If these clouds begin to thicken and lower into altostratus clouds, rain or snow will likely follow. It has often been stated that the presence of a halo is followed 24 to 48 hours later by rain or snow. With halos the red appears on the inside of the ring and the blue or violet on the outside. With rainbows, red appears on the outside and blue or violet on the inside.

Cirrocumulus clouds are also high-level clouds above 20,000 feet composed of a combination of supercooled water droplets and ice crystals. Their presence indicates wave motion and possible turbulence aloft. In Figure 14.15 the contrail from a jet aircraft has caused a disruption to these clouds and a slight enhancement over a portion of the

contrail. Often the presence of cirrocumulus clouds portends a change in the weather.

Altostratus clouds are often forerunners of rain or snow. The dull gray appearance they portray is usually the result of small supercooled water droplets. These droplets produce a hazy, gray appearance with no halo, as opposed to the ice crystals in cirrostratus clouds that do produce halos. Altostratus clouds can usually be found slightly ahead of Pacific frontal systems. Should altostratus clouds continue to thicken and lower, precipitation will follow. Soon after the altostratus clouds in Figure 14.16 were photographed, it began to rain.

No weather watching or short-range forecasting would be complete without mentioning cumulonimbus clouds. Often, the direction in which the anvil top of the cloud is pointing will give some indication of storm movement. But the anvil is caused by the column of rising air reaching the tropopause and flattening out. Winds at this level could be different than lower level winds that are steering the storm. In Figure 14.18 the anvil at the left of the picture could indicate movement from left to right. A better indicator, however, would be the tilting of the cumulus congestus cloud in the center of the photograph which also shows a definite tilt to the right, indicating storm movement in that direction. In

Figure 14.12 Altocumulus castellanus clouds resemble castles or turrets.

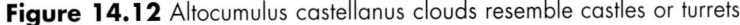

Figure 14.14 Halos around the sun or moon are caused by light shining through a thin film of ice crystals in the higher levels of the atmosphere.

Figure 14.17, however, the anvil of a cumulonimbus cloud in the background of this photograph when taken by the author, had spread out evenly to the left and right. The cumulus congestus cloud also has no apparent tilt to it. This could indicate movement toward or away from the observer or very little movement. In the case of Figure 14.17, the clouds were moving away and slightly to the right from where the picture was taken.

Cumulus and stratocumulus clouds often appear together as in Figure 14.19. The cumulus clouds in this picture will not likely grow into showers. Stratocumulus above cumulus often indicate the presence of an inversion or isothermal layer in the atmosphere that prohibits vertical development. In this photograph the stratocumulus clouds are already beginning to dissipate.

Clouds can be short-range indicators of approaching or future weather conditions or an indication of atmospheric conditions aloft. Continued observation of existing sky conditions and the types of clouds can help with short-range weather forecasting. Longer range forecasts are better left to the computers.

Figure 14.16 If altostratus clouds continue to thicken and lower, rain or snow will soon follow.

The morning rain had quit and the few cumulus clouds that had formed during the afternoon had rapidly dissipated due to lack of surface heating and the absence of moisture. The cold occluded front had passed. A light southerly wind earlier in the day had shifted to a light northwesterly wind which was also beginning to weaken. The air was clearing. Stars sparkled through an atmosphere that contained very little moisture. The dewpoint was dropping. A distinct October chill was in the air.

Figure 14.17 Cumulonimbus, cumulus congestus and cumulus clouds that were moving slowly away from the observer.

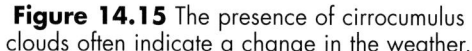

Figure 14.15 The presence of cirrocumulus clouds often indicate a change in the weather.

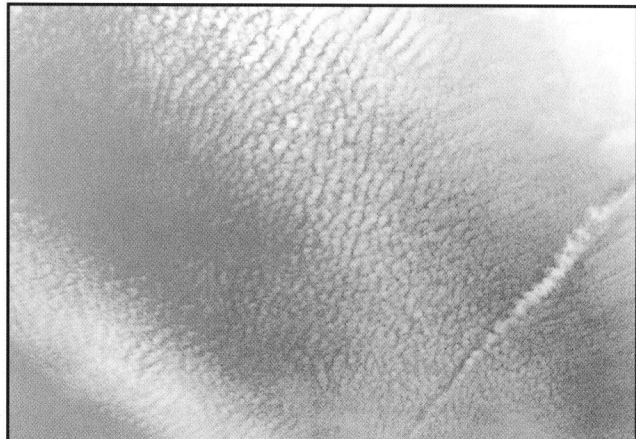

Figure 14.18 The anvil of the thunderstorm in the left portion of the photograph could indicate movement from left to tight. A better indicator might be the slight tilt of the cumulus congestus cloud in the center.

The few house plants that had been placed outside earlier in the summer were brought up on the front porch. Here, radiation from the house would keep the overnight temperature well above the freezing point, the same effect those large buildings downtown would have tonight in keeping the minimum temperature there also above freezing.

My thoughts turned to what I might expect for the forthcoming winter. Would a deficiency in precipitation be replaced by a year with copious amounts of rain and snow? How much protection should I take to prevent freeze damage? Would it be another mild M1 winter or would Mother Nature throw a curve and send an M6 or higher at us? Would that type of severe winter ever happen again or has global warming shifted the main storm track north of the Pacific Northwest.

Questions, questions! The weather, and climate, are always providing us with many. But it remains fascinating, even to the layperson. It does so because it has an effect on almost everything we do. What we wear, where we go, the price of vegetables, and so forth all are weather-dependant. It is simple, yet complex. It is benign, yet at times very violent and destructive.

Hopefully, this book has given the reader a few answers to their questions about the weather in the Pacific Northwest. Ah, what a wonderful, crisp fall day it turned out to be. Gosh, I hope the climate doesn't change! And yes, the barometer was indicating FAIR!

Figure 14.19 Cumulus and stratocumulus clouds appearing together often lead to sunny skies in the afternoon.

Bibliography

Books

Ahrens, C. Donald, *Essentials of Meteorology, An Invitation to the Atmosphere*, (1998) 2nd Edition, Wadsworth Publishing Company, A Division of International Thompson Publishing Inc.

Allen, John Eliot, M. Burns, (1994), 3rd Printing, *Cataclysms on the Columbia*, The Timber Press, Inc., Portland, Oregon.

Aviation Weather, (1975), U. S. Government Printing Office, Washington, D. C.

Barry, Roger G., Richard J. Chorley, (1982), *Atmosphere, Weather and Climate*, Methuen, London and New York.

Beals, Herbert K., (1989), *Juan Perez on the Northwest Coast*, the Oregon Historical Society, Portland, Oregon.

Bradford, Marlene, (2001), *Scanning the Skies: A History of Tornado Forecasting*, University of Oklahoma Press, Norman.

Burroughs, W. J., (1992) *Weather Cycles: Real or Imaginary*, Cambridge University Press, New York, New York.

Chase's Calendar of Events - 2002, Chicago, Contemporary Books; A Division of McGraw-Hill Companies.

Clark, Ella E., (1953), *Indian Legends of the Pacific Northwest*, University of California Press, Berkeley, Los Angeles, London.

Coues, Elliott, *The History of the Lewis and Clark Expedition, in Three Volumes*, Dover Publications, Inc., New York. (An unabridged republication of the four-volume edition published by Francis P. Harper in 1893.)

Drake, Sir Francis, (1854), *The World Encompassed*, Compiled by Francis Drake, nephew of the admiral, printed for the Hakluyt Society, London.

Duxbury, Alyn C., (1977) 2nd Printing, *The Earth and Its Oceans*, Addison-Wesley Publishing Company, Reading, Massachusetts.

Fagan, Brian (2000), *The Little Ice Age: How Climate Made History 1300-1850*; Basic Books, A Member of the Perseus Books Group, New York, New York.

Forrester, Frank H. (1957), *1001 Questions About the Weather*, Dodd, Mead & Company, New York.

Geiger, Rudolf (1975) 5th Printing, *The Climate Near the Ground*, Harvard University Press, Cambridge, Massachusetts.

Gillis, Charles J. (1993) *So Far From Home: An Army Bride on the Western Frontier*, 1865-1869; Edited from a transcription by Charles J. Gillis with Introduction & Annotation by Priscilla Knuth; Oregon Historical Society Press, Portland, Oregon.

Glickman, Todd S. (2000) 2nd Edition *Glossary of Meteorology*, American Meteorological Society, Boston, Massachusetts.

Grove, Jean M. (1988), *The Little Ice Age*, Methuen, London and New York.

Haynes, B. C., (1947), *Techniques of Observing the Weather*, John Wiley & Sons, Inc., New York, Chapman & Hall, Ltd., London.

Kelsey, Harry, (1986), *Juan Rodriguez Cabrillo*, San Marino, California, Huntington Library.

Ladurie, Emmanuel Le Roy (1971), *Times of Feast, Times of Famine: A History of the Climate Since the Year 1000*; Garden City, New York, Doubleday & Company

Lakeside Classics (The), *The Fur Hunters of the Far West*, edited with historical introduction and notes by Milo Milton Quaife, The Lakeside Press, Chicago, R. R. Donnelley & Sons Company, Christmas, MCMXXIV. Narratives of Alexander Ross while with the North West Company in the Okanogan.

Lee, R. Kump, James F. Kasting, Robert G. Crane, (1999), *The Earth System*, Prentice-Hall, Inc., Upper Saddle River, New Jersey.

Life Application Bible, The Living Bible, (1988) Tyndale House Publishers, Inc., and Youth For Christ/USA, Wheaton, Illinois.

Lindsell, Harold, (1978), *Harper Study Bible*, Revised Standard Version, Zondervan Bible Publishers, Grand Rapids, Michigan.

Linsley, Ray K., Jr., Max A. Kohler, Joseph L. H. Paulhus (1958), *Hydrology for Engineers*, McGraw Hill Book Company, New York, London, Toronto.

Lowry, William P., (1988), *Atmospheric Ecology for Designers and Planners*, Peavine Publications, McMinnville, Oregon.

Lutgens, Frederick K., E. Tarbuck, *The Atmosphere, An Introduction to Meteorology*, (1995), 6th Edition, Prentice Hall, Englewood Cliffs, New Jersey.

MacGregor, Carol Lynn, *The Journals of Patrick Gass, Member of the Lewis and Clark Expedition*, (1997), Mountain Press Publishing Company, Missoula, Montana.

Meteorological Office, (1969), *Observer's Handbook*, Third Edition, Her Majesty's Stationery Office, London.

Middleton, W. E. Knowles, (1969), *Invention of the Meteorological Instruments*, The John Hopkins Press, Baltimore, Maryland.

Moulton, Gary E. (1998) 3rd Printing, *The Journals of the Lewis & Clark Expedition*, Volume 6, University of Nebraska Press, Lincoln and London.

O'Donnell, Terence, (1988), *That Balance So Rare, The Story of Oregon*, Oregon Historical Society Press, Portland, Oregon.

Parmenter, T., R. Bailey, (1995), *The Oregon Ocean Book. An Introduction to the Pacific Ocean off Oregon Including Its Physical Setting and Living Marine Resources*, Oregon State Department of Land Conservation and Development, Salem, Oregon.

Price, Larry W., (1981), *Mountains & Man, A study of Process and Environment*, University of California Press, Berkeley, Los Angeles, London.

Quaife, Milo Milton, *The Fur Hunters of the Far West*, The

Lakeside Press, Chicago, R. R. Donnelley & Sons Company, Christmas, MCMXXIV.

Robertson, John W., (1927), *Francis Drake & Other Early Explorers Along the Pacific Coast*, The Grabhorn Press, San Francisco.

Schaefer, Vincent J., J. Day, *A Field Guide to the Atmosphere*, (1981), Houghton Mifflin Company, Boston.

Schultz, Stewart T., (1990) *The Northwest Coast, A Natural History*, Timber Press, Portland, Oregon.

Spiegel, Herbert J., A. Gruber, *From Weather Vanes to Satellites, An Introduction to Meteorology*, (1983), John Wiley & Sons, New York, Chichester, Brisbane, Toronto, Singapore.

Spray, Sharon L., Karen L. McGlothlin (2002), *Global Climate Change*, Rowman & Littlefield Publishers, Inc., Lanham, Boulder, New York, Oxford

Stull, Roland B., (1995) *Meteorology Today For Scientists and Engineers*, West Publishing Company, Minneapolis/St. Paul, New York, Los Angeles, San Francisco.

Taylor, George F., Ph.D., Colonel, USAFR, (1964) *Elementary Meteorology*, Prentice-Hall, Inc., Englewood Cliffs, N. J.

Turco, Richard P., (1997), *Earth Under Siege, From Air Pollution to Global Change*, Oxford University Press, Oxford, New York.

Viessman, Warren Jr., Claire Welty, (1985) *Water Management Technology and Institutions*, Harper & Row, Publishers, Inc., New York.

Wagner, Henry R., (1926), *Sir Francis Drake's Voyage Around the World, Its Aims and Achievements*, John Howell, San Francisco, California

Ward, Roy, (1978) *Floods, A Geographical Perspective*, Halsted Press, a Division of John Wiley & Sons, Inc., New York.

Webber, Bert, Margie, (1989), *Bayocean: The Oregon Town That Fell Into the Sea*, Webb Research Group Publishers.

Williams, Ira A., (1991), *3rd Edition, Revised, Geologic History of the Columbia River Gorge*, Oregon Historical Society Press, Portland, Oregon.

Williams, Jack, *The Weather Book, An Easy-to-Understand Guide to the USA's Weather*, (1997), 2nd Edition, Vintage Books, A Division of Random House, Inc., New York.

Brochures, Manuals and Manuscripts

Chief of Engineers to Secretary of the Army 1949 Report.

Felton, Dana, NEXRAD Weather Service Forecast Office, Seattle, (1998), *Climate of Seattle, Washington*, NOAA Technical Memorandum NWS WR-257.

Heat Wave, A Major Summer Killer, U.S. Department of Commerce, National Oceanic and Atmospheric Administration, NOAA/PA 85001.

Johnson, D.M. and J.O. Dart, Department of Geography, Portland State University (1982) *Variability of Precipitation in the Pacific Northwest: Spatial and Temporal Characteristics*, WRRI-77.

Keeling, C.D. and T.P. Whorf (2000) *Atmospheric CO2 records from sites in the SIO air sampling network. In Trends: A Compendium of Data on Global Change*. Carbon Dioxide Information Analysis Center, Oak Ridge National Laboratory, U.S. Department of Energy, Oak Ridge, Tenn.

Miller, George R. (1987), *The Oregon Coast Storm, July 4, 1986*, paper presented by author at Marine Symposium, October 1987, Halifax, Nova Scotia.

Miller, George R. (1994), *The St. Paul-Newberg Tornado, December 8, 1993*, paper presented at the Oregon Academy of Sciences Annual Meeting, February 1994.

Mazza, Patrick,(1999), *In Hot Water-A Snapshot of the Northwest's Changing Climate*, A Climate Solutions Special Report, Olympia, Washington.

National Weather Service Operations Manual, C-40, 95-2, 3/24/95, 5-8.

National Weather Service Operations Manual, C-42, 92-5, 9/14/92, 4, 5.

Oregon Task Force on Global Warming Report to the Governor and Legislature, 1990 (Draft), Part One: Possible Impacts on Oregon from Global Warming.

Quinn, William H., College of Oceanography, Oregon State University, Corvallis, Oregon, *El Nino*, Paper given to author by Mr. Quinn.

Quinn, William H. College of Oceanography, Oregon State University, Corvallis, Oregon, *Climatic Variations in Southern California Over the Past 2000 Years Based on the El Nino/Southern Oscillation*, Paper given to author by Mr. Quinn.

Quinn, W. H. and V.T. Neal, *The Historical Record of El Nino Events*, Reprinted from "Climate Since A.D. 1500," edited by R.S. Bradley and P.D. Jones, Routledge London (1992).

Quinn, William H. and V.T. Neal (1987) *El Nino Occurrences Over the Past Four and a Half Centuries*, Journal of Geophysical Research, Vol. 92, NO. C13, December 15, 1987.

Report on the Pacific Northwest Wind Storm November 13-15, 1981, Prepared by Western Region Headquarters, National Weather Service, Salt Lake City, Utah, May 1982.

Reports to the Nation: El Nino and Climate Prediction, a publication of the University Corporation for Atmospheric Research pursuant to National Oceanic and Atmospheric Administration Award No. NA27GP0232-01.

Rocky, Clinton C.D., National Weather Service Forecast Office, Portland, (1996) *Climate of Portland, Oregon*, NOAA Technical Memorandum NWS WR-239.

Schlesinger, Michael, 1989, *The Greenhouse Effect: Theory or Fact*, Proceedings Global Warming: A Northwest Perspective,

Symposium held February 9, 1989, Olympia, Washington, PNL-SA-17905, CONF-8902158, UC-402.

Tornadoes...Nature's Most Violent Storms, U.S. Department of Commerce, National Oceanic and Atmospheric Administration, National Weather Service, September 1992.

Winter Storms, the Deceptive Killers, A Guide to Survival, U.S. Department of Commerce, National Oceanic and Atmospheric Administration, National Weather Service, Warning and Forecast Branch, November 1991.

"True Story of a Flood as Told by Mary Higley Hopkins," Mss 1509, Oregon Historical Society Archives.

The Journals of Cyrus Locey, Mss 2968, Oregon Historical Society Archives.

Periodicals

Bulletin of the American Meteorological Society, Vol 82, Number 1, January 2001.

Bulletin of the American Meteorological Society, Vol 82, Number 2, February 2001.

Bulletin of the American Meteorological Society, Vol 82, Number 3, March 2001.

Corvallis Gazette, December 25, 1900.

Daily Astorian, January 10, 1880.

Daily Oregonian, November 11, 1861.

Fourth Biennial Report of the Oregon Weather Bureau, (1897), Legislative Assembly, Nineteenth Regular Session, Central Office, Portland, Oregon, B.S. Pague, Director, Salem, Oregon: W.H. Leeds, State Printer.

Henson, Robert, 2002, Scientists Search for an Index That Fits the Chill, *Weatherwise, January/February, 2002*.

Kuo, Ying-Hwa, R. J. Reed, 1988, Numerical Simulation of an Explosively Deepening Cyclone in the Eastern Pacific, *Bulletin of the American Meteorological Society, October 1988*.

Long Creek Eagle, June 8, 1894, Long Creek, Oregon.

Lynott, Robert E., Owen P. Cramer, Detailed Analysis of the 1962 Columbus Day Windstorm in Oregon and Washington, *Monthly Weather Review, Vol 94, Number 2, February 1966*.

Mass, Clifford, 1981, Topographically Forced Convergence in Western Washington State, *Monthly Weather Review, Vol 109, June 1981*.

Miller, George R., 1990, The Brookings Effect, *Oregon Coast, January/February 1990*.

Miller, George R., 1999, The Great Willamette River Flood of 1861, *Oregon Historical Quarterly Summer 1999*, Oregon Historical Society.

Monthly Weather Review, May, 1889.

Monthly Weather Review, December 1895

Monthly Weather Review, October 1898.

Monthly Weather Review, December 1898.

Monthly Weather Review, January, February 1902.

Monthly Weather Review, March 1909.

Monthly Weather Review, February 1915.

Monthly Weather Review, June 1917.

Monthly Weather Review, April 1918.

Monthly Weather Review, March 1921

Monthly Weather Review, January 1927.

Monthly Weather Review, February 1930.

Monthly Weather Review, August 1930.

Monthly Weather Review, November 1935.

Monthly Weather Review, October 1938.

Monthly Weather Review, March 1943.

Morning Oregonian, January 10, 1880.

Roden, Gunnar I., 1965, A Modern Statistical Analysis and Documentation of Historical Temperature records in California, Oregon and Washington, 1821-1964, *Journal of Applied Meteorology, Vol. 5, No. 1, February 1966*.

Oregon City Argus, March 28, 1857

Oregon City Argus, April 18, 1857.

Oregon Statesman, December 11, 1865.

Statesman, Salem, Oregon, February 27, 1862.

The Oregonian, Portland, Oregon, May 24, 26, 1971.

The Oregonian, Portland, Oregon, October 10, 2000.

(The) Sunday Oregonian, February 12, 1888.

USDA, Climate and Crops: Oregon Section, July 1900.

USDA, Climate and Crops: Oregon Section, February 1903.

USDA, Climate and Crops: Oregon Section, June 1903.

USGS Water Supply Paper No. 96, *Destructive Floods in the US in 1903*.

Personal Conversations

Many conversations were held with agriculturists, fishermen, fire control officials and local individuals throughout my years as a meteorologist. Several of those conversations are the basis for statements that are included in this book. The names of the individuals, however, are forgotten. I came to realize, however, after accompanying fishermen on their boats and agriculturists on their daily excursions through an orchard, that they know much more about local weather conditions than they are given credit for. That statement is true as well for local individuals who are neither farmers nor fishermen. These individuals, if they have lived at a certain location long enough, know about the weather. They may not know the reason behind a particular weather phenomenon, but they can tell you all about "their" weather.

Glossary

Adiabatic. A thermodynamic process where there is no transfer of heat across the boundaries of the system. For simplicity, it simply means no gain or loss of heat. In an adiabatic process, compression results in warming and expansion results in cooling.

Advection. Movement in the horizontal of some atmospheric property such as heat, moisture, fog, air mass, etc.

Albedo. A ratio of the amount of radiation reflected by an object or surface compared to the amount it receives. It is normally expressed as a percentage.

Altocumulus castellanus. Mid-level clouds that often occur in rows. The appearance of these clouds suggests towers, turrets or castles, indicating atmospheric instability.

Altocumulus floccus. Mid-level clouds that give the appearance of flocks of cotton. The appearance of these clouds suggests atmospheric instability.

Ambient air temperature. The actual temperature of the air as expressed in degrees Celsius or Fahrenheit. It is often noted as the "free air" temperature.

Anemometer. A meteorological instrument used to measure the velocity of the wind.

Aneroid. Without liquid. An aneroid barometer has no liquid in it.

Anticyclone. A large circulation where the winds are blowing clockwise in the Northern Hemisphere.

Aphelion. The point in space on the orbit of the earth where it is farthest from the sun.

Apparent temperature. The temperature that a person "feels like" due to the effects of wind or humidity. Wind will make the body "feel" cooler than the actual or ambient temperature. High humidity will make the body "feel" warmer or hotter than the actual or ambient temperature.

Arctic air mass. An air mass that originates over land surfaces at northern latitudes having the characteristics of low temperature and low moisture values.

Arctic outbreak. An invasion of cold arctic air into the Pacific Northwest.

Automated surface observing system (ASOS). A weather station that automatically reports and records the weather elements except amount of snowfall.

Avalanche. A large area of snow that is dislodged and moves down a mountain or steep slope.

Azimuth. Horizontal direction from true north as measured in degrees.

Bankfull. A level at which a river or stream can contain no additional water without overflowing its banks.

Barograph. A device that records the barometric or air pressure on a chart.

Barometer. An instrument that measures the air pressure.

Beaufort wind scale. A wind scale from zero (calm) to twelve (hurricane) used in the 1800s to denote the speed of the wind at sea using a ship's sails.

Bimetallic strip. A thin strip of two metals whose expansion rates are different that are bound together. The expansion rate of the strip is converted to temperature on a chart.

Blackbody. A hypothetical surface that absorbs all the radiation that strikes it and then emits all that radiation.

Boundary layer. A thin layer of the atmosphere directly above the earth's surface above which the effects of friction on the wind are minimal or zero. It is sometimes given at the 50 millibar level above the surface.

Bretz floods. A series of disastrous floods that occurred along the Columbia River and many of its tributaries at the end of the ice age 10,000 to 14,000 years ago due to the periodic breaking up of an ice jam holding back Lake Missoula.

California Current. A southward flowing ocean current along the Washington and Oregon coasts that causes upwelling. The current often reverses in the winter becoming light southerly.

Calorie. A unit of heat or energy. For simplicity, it is the amount of heat required to raise the temperature of one gram of water one degree Celsius.

Cap cloud. A lenticular cloud lying over the top of a mountain or over the top of a rising column of air within a cumulus congestus cloud.

Carbon dioxide. A colorless gas resulting from the combustion of organic material including fossil fuels.

Celsius. A temperature scale in which the boiling point of water is 100° and the freezing point of water is 0°.

Centrifugal force. In a rotating system, the force that deflects objects outward from the center of rotation.

Chinook wind. Currently, the name given to any downslope wind to the lee of mountains where the air is warmed dry adiabatically. Original definition in the mid 1800s was a warm wind blowing up the Columbia River from its mouth at the Pacific Ocean towards Portland, Oregon.

Cirrocumulus. A high level cloud composed of ice crystals and supercooled water droplets giving the appearance of patches or small bunches.

Cirrostratus. A high level cloud giving the appearance of a thin, whitish veil. These clouds often produce a halo around the sun or moon.

Cirrus. Any high level cloud giving a white appearance that is composed of ice crystals.

Clear-air turbulence. Turbulence occurring at high levels in the troposphere or lower stratosphere due to wind shear.

Climate. The average of weather conditions over a long period of time at a particular location.

Cloudburst. A heavy fall of rain over a small area from a large cumulus cloud. In earlier western terminology these were referred to as waterspouts.

Coho wind. A wind blowing from the east through the Columbia River Gorge that results in cooling in the winter and warming in the summer in areas near the mouth of the Gorge.

Cold front. A boundary between two air masses where cold air is replacing warm air.

Cold wave. A rapid fall in temperature associated with the invasion of an arctic air mass.

Conditionally unstable. A state of the atmosphere where the air is stable if it is unsaturated and unstable if it is saturated.

Condensation. The process in the atmosphere where water vapor changes from a gas to a liquid such as dew, fog, or cloud.

Condensation nuclei. Very tiny particles in the atmosphere such as salt, sand, and dust that serve as the building blocks of cloud droplets as water vapor condenses onto them.

Conduction. The transport of energy (heat) through the motion of molecules.

Confluence. The coming together of individual air streams.

Constant-pressure surface. A surface in the atmosphere where the pressure is the same but at different elevations above mean sea level.

Contour line. Lines on a weather map that constitute equal height above mean sea level of a constant pressure surface such as 500 millibars, 700 millibars, etc.

Convection. Atmospheric motions that are vertical in nature.

Convergence. The coming together of air motions (wind) in the horizontal.

Cooling degree-day. A value based on an average daily temperature of 65°F. Average daily temperatures above this value are subtracted by 65 to determine the number of cooling degree-days.

Cooperative weather observer. An observer for the National Weather Service who records daily high and low temperatures and precipitation.

Coriolis effect. An apparent force acting on particles in motion caused by the rotation of the earth. The effect is to cause particles in motion to curve to the right in the Northern Hemisphere and to the left in the Southern Hemisphere.

Cubic feet per second (CFS). A unit of volume that is one-foot by one-foot by one-foot.

Cumulonimbus. A cloud of sufficient vertical extent as to cause lightning and thunder. A thunderstorm cloud.

Cumulus. A cloud showing some upward motion that results in condensation.

Cumulus congestus. A cumulus cloud with strong vertical development that resembles towers.

Cut-off high. An area of warm temperatures, usually resulting from a ridge of high pressure, that has been displaced from the normal westerly flow.

Cut-off low. An area of cold temperatures, usually resulting from a trough of low pressure, that has been displaced from the normal westerly flow.

Cyclone. A large circulation where the winds are blowing counterclockwise in the Northern Hemisphere.

Datum plane. A reference level used to indicate the height of a river or stream.

Deepening. A term used in meteorology in reference to the lowering of the central pressure of a surface low or to the lowering of heights on a constant-pressure surface.

Degree-day. The departure from a given standard of the daily mean temperature. The standard is normally 65°F for heating or cooling degree-days, but different for growing degree-days.

Dendroclimatology. The concept of using tree rings to determine past climates.

Density. The ratio of the mass of a substance to the volume it occupies.

Deposition. The process where water vapor molecules are converted to a solid at the earth's surface.

Dew. Water condensed on objects at the earth's surface as a result of the temperature falling to the dewpoint temperature.

Dewpoint. The temperature to which a parcel of air must be cooled in order for saturation or condensation to begin.

Diffluence. The diverging of individual air streams.

Divergence. The spreading out of air motions (wind) in the horizontal.

Doldrums. An area on the earth's surface near the equator of very light winds where the northeast trade winds and the southeast trade winds come together.

Doppler radar. A radar that detects the change of frequency of a return signal from an object that is either moving away from the radar or towards it.

Downburst. An area of strong winds flowing out of the base of an active thunderstorm.

Downvalley wind. A nighttime wind that flows down a valley due to radiational cooling of the air next to the surface.

Drifting buoy. A buoy that has been placed on the ocean surface or below that transmits data to a satellite passing overhead. These buoys drift with the ocean currents.

Drizzle. Very fine water droplets that can be seen floating on wind currents. Along the coasts of Washington and Oregon it is often called mist.

Dry-adiabatic lapse rate. A lapse rate where temperature either increases or decreases at 5.4° per 1,000 feet depending on whether air is descending or rising.

Dry-bulb temperature. The temperature of the air as recorded by the dry-bulb thermometer in a sling psychrometer.

Dryline. The boundary between dry continental air and moist Gulf of Mexico air.

Dry thunderstorms. See high-level thunderstorms.

Dust devil. A small rotating column of air having no association with tornadoes. They are often called whirlwinds.

El Niño. A warming of sea surface temperatures in the central and eastern tropical Pacific Ocean.

Electromagnetic spectrum. The array of electromagnetic waves or radiation from wavelengths of several hundred meters to as short as fractions of micrometers.

Environmental lapse rate. The actual distribution of temperature with elevation in the atmosphere.

Environmental sounding. The actual vertical distribution of temperature and moisture in the atmosphere as measured by a radiosonde or other device capable of detecting temperature and moisture content.

Equinox. That point in the earth's journey around the sun when the sun appears directly over the equator at which time each hemisphere receives the same amount of solar radiation. The spring equinox occurs around March 22 and the fall equinox around September 22.

Evaporation. A physical process where liquid water is transferred to the gaseous state.

Fahrenheit. A temperature scale developed in the early 1700s by Daniel Fahrenheit. He assigned 32° as the freezing point of water and 212° as its boiling point.

Flash flood. A flood, usually on a narrow stream, where the level of the water rises and falls rapidly as a result of heavy precipitation over the stream's watershed. Flash floods are also caused by dam breaks.

Flood. The rise of a river or stream beyond its normal channel that results in damage to the area being flooded.

Flood stage. A level above a reference point (datum plane) at which a river or stream overflows its banks and begins to cause damage.

Foehn. A warm dry wind that descends the lee slopes of the Alps in Europe.

Fog. Water droplets that constitute a cloud with its base at the earth's surface where visibility is reduced.

Freezing level. The level in the atmosphere where the free air temperature lowers to 32°F.

Freezing rain (drizzle). Liquid water droplets (rain or drizzle) that freeze upon contact with a surface that is below freezing.

Front. The dividing line between two air masses with different characteristics, one of which is displacing the other.

Frost. Ice crystals that are deposited at the surface when water molecules change directly from the gaseous state to the solid state.

Fujita scale. A scale that relates tornado intensity to the damage to structures or vegetation. It is also called the F-scale.

Funnel cloud. A protuberance extending from the base of a convective cloud due to condensation of a violently rotating column of air. If the violently rotating column has an effect on the ground it is called a tornado.

Gale. In meteorology a wind with speeds of 32-54 miles per hour.

Gale Warning. For marine interests a warning of sustained winds of 28 to 47 knots.

General Circulation Model (GCM). A numerical model of atmospheric circulation that is time-dependent. GCMs can be used for climate predictions.

Geostrophic wind. The horizontal wind produced as a result of the pressure gradient force being balanced out by the Coriolis force. Geostrophic winds usually blow parallel to contour lines on constant pressure surfaces.

Gradient wind. The horizontal wind produced when the pressure gradient force balances out the Coriolis force and the centrifugal force. Gradient winds can be applied to curved contour lines on constant pressure surfaces.

Graupel. Snow particles clumped together that are often called snow pellets. They bounce very little when striking the surface as opposed to hail which bounces higher.

Greenhouse effect. The warming of lower layers of the atmosphere due to trace gases that absorb and retransmit the earth's radiation.

Growing degree-day. A type of degree-day index used in agriculture that relates to the planting and growth of various crops and also insect and disease development.

Gust. A sudden increase in the speed of the wind more prevalent over irregular terrain.

Hadley cell. A simple circulation of the earth's atmosphere where air is rising near the equator and descending near 30°N and 30°S. The simple one-cell circulation has sometimes been expanded to the entire earth showing air rising at the equator and sinking at the poles.

Hail. Precipitation in the form of ice produced by turbulent action within a convective cloud.

Halo. A whitish ring around the sun or moon caused by the refraction of light through ice crystals.

Haze. Suspended small particles in the air that reduce the visibility.

Heat index. An index that incorporates temperature and relative humidity to give an apparent temperature, or how hot one "feels."

Heat lightning. Distant lightning that reflects off clouds but is too far away for the thunder to be heard.

Heat low. See thermal low.

Heat wave. An extensive period of hot, humid weather.

Heating degree-day. A value based on an average daily temperature of 65°F. Average daily temperatures below this value are subtracted from the base of 65 to determine the number of heating degree-days.

Heavy Snow Warning. (See winter storm warning)

High index pattern. A weather regime that features very strong westerly flow. A strong westerly jet stream.

High-level thunderstorm. A thunderstorm occurring at such high levels in the atmosphere that its precipitation mostly evaporates before striking the surface. Strong gusty surface winds often accompany these storms.

Horse latitudes. An area on the earth's surface where the winds are very light or calm, usually near the center of sub-tropical high pressure areas around 30° north and south latitude.

Humidity. A general reference to the amount of moisture in the air.

Hurricane-force wind. A wind with a sustained speed of 64 knots (73 miles per hour) or greater.

Hydrograph. A plot of river height, or flow in CFS, vs. time at a gauging station.

Hydrologic cycle. Basically, the pattern of water evaporating from the oceans, transported thousands of miles as water vapor, falling as precipitation over land, and then returning to the oceans via rivers and streams.

Hygrister. A humidity sensing device that measures changes in the electrical resistance.

Hygroscopic. An acceleration of condensation on certain particles in the atmosphere.

Hygrothermograph. A device that measures temperature through a bi-metallic strip or liquid filled tube and relative humidity through the expansion or contraction of human hair. Both values are recorded on a chart through a series of linkages.

Ice crystals. Ice occurring or falling in the form of needles, platelets, columns or their combinations

Ice jam. Broken sections of ice that accumulate in a channel causing an obstruction to the flow of a river that could result in local flooding.

Ice pellets. Liquid precipitation or raindrops that have frozen. Often referred to as sleet.

Ice storm. A heavy accumulation of ice on objects due to freezing rain.

Indian summer. A period of warm, dry weather in the fall following several days of stormy, cold and often frosty weather.

Infrared radiation. Electromagnetic radiation that has a longer wavelength than visible light, but shorter wavelength than microwave radiation.

Inversion. An increase in temperature with elevation as opposed to the normal decrease with elevation.

Isobar. A line along which the pressure is the same. Isobars are often expressed in millibars.

Isohyet. Lines drawn to indicate equal amounts of rainfall.

Isotach. Lines drawn to indicate equal wind speed. Isotacks are often drawn to reveal the core of the jet stream.

Isotherm. A line indicating equal temperature.

Isothermal. Having the same temperature distribution either in the vertical or horizontal.

January thaw. A short period of mild weather that often occurs in late January. Some speculation surrounds the term.

Jet stream. A band of strong winds in the upper troposphere, sometimes referred to as the westerlies. The jet stream is often broken up into segments.

Kilometer. A unit of measure equal to 3,281 feet or 0.62 miles.

Kinetic energy. The energy that an object or body possesses because of its motion.

Knot. A unit of wind speed equal to 1.15 statute miles. One knot is one nautical mile per hour.

Köppen classification. A classification of the world's climates developed by Wladimer Köppen.

Kuroshio current. A warm ocean current flowing northeastward off the coast of Japan.

La Niña. A condition where the northeast and southeast trade wind component is stronger than normal over the tropical Pacific Ocean.

Lake breeze. A condition similar to a sea breeze where the wind is blowing from the lake which is normally cooler to a land surface which is warmer.

Land breeze. A breeze occurring at night that blows from the land to a body of water where the land is cooler than the water.

Lapse rate. The decrease of an atmospheric variable, usually temperature, with height.

Latent heat. The heat that is either released or absorbed by a substance as it changes from one phase to another such as from liquid to solid or solid to liquid.

Lifting condensation level (LCL). A level at which the temperature and the dewpoint temperature become the same resulting in condensation or cloud formation.

Little Ice Age. A period from around 1350 to around 1850 that was marked by glacier advance and relatively cold episodes around the globe.

Long wave. A large scale feature in the atmospheric circulation marked by either clear , warm weather (long wave ridge) or cold, stormy weather (long wave trough). See Rossby wave.

Longwave radiation. Radiation in the longer wavelengths from infrared to radio waves and commonly referred to as radiation from the earth.

M-scale. The author's scale of the severity of Portland, Oregon winters based on seasonal snowfall and minimum temperature, with M1 being the mildest and M8 the most severe.

Mammatus clouds. Protuberances from the base of a cloud in the form of pouches or bags.

Marine push. An invasion of cool marine air into the valleys west of the Cascade Mountains.

Maritime air. An air mass originating over water with high moisture content especially in the lower layers.

Maximum temperature. The highest temperature experienced at a location for a certain period, usually 24 hours or a day.

Maximum thermometer. A thermometer that records the highest temperature for a certain period.

Mediterranean climate. A climate usually on the west side of a continent between 30° and 45° latitude where the winters are wet and mild and the summers hot and dry.

Meteorological bomb. A storm system in middle latitudes where the central pressure is falling at a rate of at least one millibar per hour and often faster.

Methane. One of the trace gases in the atmosphere primarily released through the decay of vegetation and from cattle and termites.

Microburst. See downburst.

Midwest. For the purposes of this book, that section of the United States from Kentucky and Ohio on the east to the Dakotas, Nebraska and Kansas on the west, and including the area around the Great Lakes.

Milankovitch theory. A theory used to explain some climatic changes that incorporates the earth's distance from the sun, the tilt of its axis and the direction to which the axis is pointed.

Millibar. A unit of pressure used extensively in meteorology. The abbreviation is mb.

Minimum temperature. The lowest temperature experienced at a location for a certain period, usually 24 hours or a day.

Minimum thermometer. A thermometer that records the lowest temperature for a certain period.

Missoula floods. See Bretz floods.

Mist. Precipitation consisting of very small droplets that often appear to float on the wind and that usually fall from low stratus clouds.

Moist-adiabatic lapse rate. The rate of temperature decrease with elevation of a saturated parcel of air. In the lower layers of the atmosphere this decrease is 3.3°F per 1,000 feet.

Moisture. As used in meteorology, the water vapor content of the atmosphere.

NEXRAD. An acronym for Next Generation Weather Radar.

Nimbostratus. A uniform gray-appearing cloud from which either rain or snow is falling or will soon begin falling.

North Pacific Drift. A relatively warm ocean current flowing eastward across the north Pacific Ocean.

Norther. A cold northerly wind. The term is applied to areas east of the Rocky Mountains during the late fall through early spring months as the winds bring cold arctic air into the region.

Nowcast. A short-term weather forecast of only a few hours.

Numerical forecast. A weather forecast of atmospheric conditions that incorporates the use of mathematical equations.

Occluded front. A frontal surface occurring during the latter stages of cyclone development. Generally it is where a cold front overtakes, or catches up with, a warm front.

Offshore wind. A wind that blows from the land to the sea.

Onshore wind. A wind that blows from the sea to the land.

Orographic. The effect that mountains and ridges have on the wind flow.

Overrunning. A situation where warm moist air overruns colder air with precipitation the usual result.

Ozone. One of the trace gases in the atmosphere that intercepts the sun's ultraviolet radiation.

Pacific decadal oscillation. A fluctuation of sea surface temperatures in the North Pacific Ocean that is believed related to minor climate changes over adjacent areas.

Pacific high. An area of relatively high pressure located between 30°N and 45°N over the North Pacific Ocean that migrates slightly north in summer and retreats slightly south during winter.

Partly cloudy. In weather forecasting where 0.3 to 0.6 tenths of the sky is expected to be covered by cloudiness.

Peak gust. The highest instantaneous wind speed recorded at a station during a specified period.

Perihelion. That point in the earth's orbit where it is closest to the sun.

Pineapple express. A jet stream originating near tropical latitudes that brings copious moisture into the Pacific Northwest.

Polar air mass. See Arctic air mass.

Polar easterlies. Generally spoken of as one of the earth's major wind belts where air subsiding near the poles is deflected to the right (left) as it moves toward lower latitude in the Northern (Southern) Hemisphere.

Polar front. Generally speaking the semipermanent boundary between air of arctic origin and air of tropical origin that occurs at middle latitudes.

Potential energy. The energy that a system has relative to its position.

Powder snow. Snow with relatively small quantities of water that is fluffy and light.

Precipitation. All liquid water and ice particles that fall to the earth and collected for measurement.

Pressure center. On a weather map the point of highest pressure or lowest pressure given to an anticyclone (high) or cyclone (low) respectively.

Pressure gradient. The difference in pressure between two designated points separated horizontally. The greater the pressure difference the steeper the gradient.

Pressure pattern. In meteorology the distribution of pressure or height fields as depicted by isobars at the surface and contour lines at levels above that.

Pressure reduction (correction). The correction of pressure readings at elevated stations to a value that would correspond to mean sea level using temperature and standard atmospheric calculations.

Pressure tendency. The change of pressure at a location over a specified period of time.

Prevailing wind direction. The primary direction of the wind over a period of time.

Probability forecast. A forecast used to express the probability of an event, usually precipitation.

Prognostic chart. A forecast chart derived mainly from numerical calculations that shows relative positions of high and low pressure areas and attendant cloudiness and precipitation.

Proxy data. Data used to determine past climates using biological and geological features.

Psychrometer. An instrument used to measure relative humidity. See sling psychrometer.

Pulse. As used with radar, a short pulse or burst of energy by the transmitter.

Quasi-biennial oscillation (QBO). A period of 2.2 to 2.8 years over which there are cyclical fluctuations of some weather parameters.

Quasi-stationary front. A front that shows little movement over time and may oscillate back and forth.

Radar. A device used to detect distant objects through the use of a reflected signal. In meteorology rain, snow, hail and other forms of precipitation.

Radar frequency. The electromagnetic frequency at which the radar operates.

Radiation. The propagation of electromagnetic energy through space.

Radiation fog. Fog that forms overnight as the earth radiates heat and the surface cools, thus cooling the air to the dewpoint temperature for condensation to begin.

Radiational cooling. Cooling of the earth's surface due to radiation off its surface.

Radiosonde. An instrument carried aloft by a balloon that measures temperature and moisture content of the atmosphere and is tracked to determine azimuth and elevation angles the difference of which relate to wind speed and direction.

Rain. Liquid precipitation with drops that are larger than mist or drizzle.

Rain gauge. Any device used to measure precipitation.

Rain shadow. An area to the lee of a range of mountains or hills where the precipitation is markedly reduced.

Rain shower. A brief and often moderate or heavy fall of liquid precipitation usually from a convective-type cloud.

Rainfall. The amount of precipitation falling. Often used synonymously with precipitation which is the preferred term.

Rating table. A table that converts river gauge height to flow in CFS and vice versa.

Recording rain gauge. A device that records the amount of precipitation falling over a certain period of time.

Reflection. The change of direction of electromagnetic or acoustical waves that may result in a change of frequency. Reflection is usually thought of as off an object.

Refraction. The change of direction, often referred to as "bending," of electromagnetic radiation as it passes through a medium.

Relative humidty. The ratio of the amount of water vapor in the air compared to the amount it is capable of "holding" at that temperature.

Retrogression. In meteorology the backing up of long wave features (Rossby waves) in a normal westerly flow in the atmosphere.

Return period. A calculated return period of a defined event.

Ridge. An elongated region of relatively higher atmospheric pressure in the atmosphere that is often associated with clear, dry weather.

Ridge line. A line that connects points of maximum curvature of lines with equal height values that are defining a ridge.

Rime. Deposits of ice giving a milky or white appearance that are due to the deposition of supercooled water droplets striking the surface and freezing.

River basin. An area drained by a river and associated tributaries.

Rossby wave. A long wave feature in the atmospheric circulation.

Rotor cloud. A cumulus-type cloud often seen to the lee of a mountain or mountain range due to air being forced up over the barrier, descending then ascending. Rotor clouds often appear beneath altocumulus standing lenticular clouds.

Runoff. Water resulting from precipitation that finds its way into a river or stream.

Saturation. A condition where the air contains all of the moisture it can "hold" at a certain temperature. The relative humidity is 100 percent.

Saturation vapor pressure. The pressure exerted by water vapor molecules when the air is saturated.

Scattering. A term applied to radiation from the sun that is dispersed in various directions when striking a medium.

Sea breeze. A local wind that blows from the ocean to land that is caused by differences in temperature between the two locations.

Sea level pressure. The pressure as measured at sea level or corrected to sea level from elevations above sea level.

Sea surface temperature. The temperature of the ocean as measured a few feet below the surface.

Severe thunderstorm. A thunderstorm that produces a tornado, winds of at least 58 mph, and/or hail at least three-quarters inch in diameter.

Short wave. A meteorological term used to denote a relatively small scale perturbation in the atmospheric flow that is often associated with cloudy, stormy weather.

Shortwave radiation. Radiation usually thought of as wavelengths near that of infrared and smaller in the electromagnetic spectrum. It is often referred to as the sun's radiation.

Silver thaw. See ice storm.

Sling psychrometer. An instrument with two thermometers mounted side-by-side connected by a chain to a handle. One of the thermometers is covered with cloth which, after being moistened, the instrument is twirled to obtain the wet-bulb temperature.

Small craft warning (advisory). For marine interests, sustained winds of up to 28 knots that could affect performance of small vessels.

Snotel. A remote site that measures the weight of snow and transmits it via satellite to a receiving station. It is an acronym for snow telemetry.

Snow. Precipitation consisting of ice crystals and usually thought of as hexagonal in nature. Several of these coming together is thought of as a snowflake.

Snow Advisory. Generally an advisory of snowfall that could affect operations within an area. (Local criteria vary and reader should consult nearest National Weather Service Office.)

Snow flurry. A short burst of snow lasting for only a short period of time.

Snow level. The lowest layer in the atmosphere where snow is falling before it melts.

Snow melt flood. A flood caused by the melting of a snowpack over an area.

Solar radiation. The radiation in the electromagnetic spectrum emitted by the sun.

Solstice. The two points in the earth's orbit around the sun where one hemisphere and then the other receives more solar radiation. In the Northern Hemisphere the summer solstice occurs around June 21 and the winter solstice around December 22.

Southern oscillation. Normally thought of as the variance in pressure between two locations, usually Tahiti and Darwin, Australia.

Southern oscillation index. A measure of the variance of the southern oscillation.

Split jet stream. An area where a relatively continuous westerly jet stream will split into two branches, one traveling in a northerly direction and the other in a more southerly direction.

Squall. A sudden onset of very windy, rainy weather often associated with thunderstorms.

Squall line. A line of active thunderstorms.

Staff gauge. A staff on which a scale in feet is placed that indicates the height of a river above a datum plane.

Stage. A shortened term that indicates the height of a river at a location.

Standard atmosphere. A computed vertical distribution of temperature using gas laws. The term is often stated as standard atmospheric lapse rate or standard lapse rate.

Station pressure. The atmospheric pressure measured at a location. Stations above sea level must apply a correction to the station pressure to obtain a value that is relative to sea level.

Stationary front. Same as quasi-stationary front.

Steam fog. Fog that results when the temperature of the air is much colder than the water surface over which it is lying.

Steppe climate. An area with low annual precipitation but enough for sparse vegetation to occur.

Storage gauge. A remote gauge that is filled with an antifreeze solution that collects precipitation and visited once a year by a technician. These gauges are slowly being discontinued.

Storm track. In meteorology a path along which successive storms may travel.

Storm warning. For marine interests sustained winds of 48 knots or greater.

Stratocumulus. Low clouds that often appear rounded or dark at the base and generally with limited vertical extent.

Stratosphere. A layer of the atmosphere that is directly above the troposphere. The temperature of the stratosphere generally remains constant or increases slightly.

Stratus. Low clouds that give a dark appearance with uniform flat bases.

Streamflow. The flow of a river or stream usually measured in CFS.

Streamline. A line along which the wind is blowing. Streamlines can come together as opposed to isobars or constant height lines that do not come together.

Sublimation. The process whereby water molecules change from a solid to a gaseous state. The term is often used to indicate the reverse process as from a gas to a solid.

Subsidence. A sinking of air in the atmosphere occurring over a large area and normally associated with high pressure areas.

Subtropical high pressure areas. Areas near 30°N and 30°S where the air is descending and winds are relatively calm. They are often referred to as the "horse latitudes."

Subtropics. A somewhat indefinite area that lies between the tropics and middle latitudes.

Suction vortices. Small vortices within a tornado complex that rotate around the main tornado column. They are often observed occurring with large dust devils.

Sunspots. Relatively cooler areas on the sun's surface that occur on a relative 11-year cycle.

Superadiabatic lapse rate. An environmental lapse rate that is greater than 5.4°F per 1,000 feet.

Supercell. A very strong thunderstorm that may persist for several hours that is capable of producing severe weather such as large hail, strong winds or tornadoes.

Supercooled water. Water droplets occurring in the atmosphere when the temperature is below freezing.

Teleconnection. The correlation of weather or atmospheric conditions at one part of the globe with that at another.

Temperature. The weather element measured by a thermometer. Temperature represents the average speed of molecular activity.

Temperature inversion. See inversion.

Terrestrial radiation. That radiation emitted by the surface of the earth.

Thermal low. An area where intense surface heating has created an area of low pressure due to rising air.

Thermal. A rising column of air due to heating of a surface area.

Thermistor. A type of thermometer that measures electrical resistance of a material and relates that to temperature.

Thermograph. A type of temperature measuring device that records its values on a chart.

Thermometer. A device used to measure the temperature.

Thunder. The sound heard from the rapid expansion of air due to heating by a lightning bolt.

Thundercloud. The term often applied to a cumulonimbus cloud.

Thunderstorm. A storm that is accompanied by lightning and thunder.

Tipping bucket rain gauge. A recording device used to measure precipitation consisting of two small balanced buckets where one tip of the bucket on one side correlates with 0.01 inch precipitation which allows for the other bucket to begin filling.

Tornado. A violently rotating column of air that is in contact with the ground.

Towering cumulus. A term that is synonymous with a cumulus congestus cloud.

Trade winds. One of the earth's major wind belts that blows toward the equator from the areas of subtropical high pressure in both latitudes.

Tropic of Cancer. A point on the earth's surface where the sun is directly overhead at noon in the Northern Hemisphere.

Tropic of Capricorn. A point on the earth's surface where the sun is directly overhead at noon in the Southern Hemisphere.

Tropical air mass. An air mass having the characteristics of warm temperature and high moisture content.

Tropopause. The boundary between the troposphere and the stratosphere.

Troposphere. The lower portion of the atmosphere between the tropopause and the earth's surface.

Trough. In meteorology an elongated area of low pressure.

Trough line. A line along which the pressure at sea level is lower than the surrounding air. At levels above the surface it represents a line along which the height values of a constant pressure chart are lower than the surrounding areas.

Ultraviolet radiation. Electromagnetic radiation in the wave length shorter than visible light but longer than x-rays.

Unstable air. Air that has the ability to rise freely in the atmosphere because it is warmer than the surrounding air.

Updraft. A rising column of air. The term is frequently applied to the upward motion within a convective cloud.

Upper air. In meteorology generally the middle to upper regions of the troposphere.

Upper low. An area of relatively lower height, if in reference to a constant pressure surface, in the upper air.

Upper high. An area of relatively higher height, if in reference to a constant pressure surface, in the upper air.

Upslope fog. A fog caused by relative moist air flowing gradually up a slope cooling adiabatically to the dewpoint so that condensation occurs.

Upslope wind. A wind that flows up a slope. Upslope winds are often caused by surface heating.

Upvalley wind. A wind that flows up a valley due to heating of surface air in the lower and middle portions of the valley.

Upwelling. The process whereby ocean surface water is transported away from the shore due to the Coriolis effect and replaced by cooler water arriving from greater depths.

Urban heat island. An area within a city that experiences higher average daily temperatures due primarily to higher minimum temperatures. The warmer temperatures are due to heat radiated from buildings, stone, cement and other surfaces within the city.

Vapor pressure. In meteorology the pressure exerted by water vapor molecules.

Varves. Sediment layers deposited in lakes or large bodies of water that differ in color and texture and that give some inclination of past climates through analysis of the sediment.

Veering wind. In meteorology the change in wind direction in a clockwise direction in the Northern Hemisphere.

Venturi effect. The increase of wind and decrease in pressure as the wind passes through a constriction.

Visual flight rules. In aviation flying using visual observations. The height of clouds and horizontal visibility are factored into visual flight rules.

Virga. Gray streaks of precipitation falling from a cloud and evaporating before the precipitation reaches the surface. When the precipitation is solid, as in ice crystals, the process is called fall streaks.

Warm front. A boundary between two air masses where warm air is displacing cold air.

Water content. The amount of liquid water present within a snow sample.

Water equivalent. In meteorology the amount of liquid precipitation produced by melting of solid forms of precipitation.

Water vapor. One of the trace atmospheric gases that varies from near zero to near 4 percent by volume. It is considered to be the most important atmospheric gas regarding meteorology.

Water year. The total amount of precipitation occurring during the period October 1 of one year through September 30 of the following year.

Watershed. See river basin.

Waterspout. A tornado occurring over a body of water. In pioneer days in Oregon the term was synonymous with cloudburst. See cloudburst.

Wave cloud. See altocumulus standing lenticular.

Wavelength. The distance from one wave crest to the next or one wave trough to the next.

Weighing rain gauge. A gauge that records the amount of precipitation falling in a bucket that is placed on a scales.

Westerlies. One of the earth's major wind belts occurring in the middle latitudes of both the Northern and Southern Hemispheres.

Wet-bulb temperature. The temperature air assumes by the evaporation of water into it.

Wet-bulb thermometer. The thermometer in a sling psychrometer that is covered with cloth.

Whirlwind. The term often applied to a dust devil.

Wind rose. A diagram that indicates frequency of wind direction and speed at a location.

Wind shear. A sharp variation in wind speed or direction in either the horizontal or vertical.

Winter storm warning. Generally at low elevations, a fall of snow 4 inches or more expected over a 12-hour period, or 6 inches over a 24-hour period. (These criteria vary especially in mountainous terrain and local National Weather Service Offices should be consulted for extra values.)

X-ray. In the electromagnetic spectrum radiation that has a shorter wavelength than ultraviolet.

Zenith. A point in the celestial sphere that is directly above the observer.

Zonal flow. A strong westerly wind flow. See high index pattern.

Appendices

Table 1. Fahrenheit to Celsius

°F	°C	°F	°C	°F	°C	°F	°C	°F	°C	°F	°C
-40	-40	-13	-25	14	-10	41	5	68	20	95	35
-39	-39.4	-12	-24.4	15	-9.4	42	5.6	69	20.6	96	35.6
-38	-38.9	-11	-23.9	16	-8.9	43	6.1	70	21.1	97	36.1
-37	-38.3	-10	-23.3	17	-8.3	44	6.7	71	21.7	98	36.7
-36	-37.8	-9	-22.8	18	-7.8	45	7.2	72	22.2	99	37.2
-35	-37.2	-8	-22.2	19	-7.2	46	7.8	73	22.8	100	37.8
-34	-36.7	-7	-21.7	20	-6.7	47	8.3	74	23.3	101	38.3
-33	-36.1	-6	-21.1	21	-6.1	48	8.9	75	23.9	102	38.9
-32	-35.6	-5	-20.6	22	-5.6	49	9.4	76	24.4	103	39.4
-31	-35	-4	-20	23	-5	50	10	77	25	104	40
-30	-34.4	-3	-19.4	24	-4.4	51	10.6	78	25.6	105	40.6
-29	-33.9	-2	-18.9	25	-3.9	52	11.1	79	26.1	106	41.1
-28	-33.3	-1	-18.3	26	-3.3	53	11.7	80	26.7	107	41.7
-27	-32.8	0	-17.8	27	-2.8	54	12.2	81	27.2	108	42.2
-26	-32.2	1	-17.2	28	-2.2	55	12.8	82	27.8	109	42.8
-25	-31.7	2	-16.7	29	-1.7	56	13.3	83	28.3	110	43.3
-24	-31.1	3	-16.1	30	-1.1	57	13.9	84	28.9	111	43.9
-23	-30.6	4	-15.4	31	-0.6	58	14.4	85	29.4	112	44.4
-22	-30	5	-15	32	0	59	15	86	30	113	45
-21	-29.4	6	-14.4	33	0.6	60	15.6	87	30.6	114	45.6
-20	-28.9	7	-13.9	34	1.1	61	16.1	88	31.1	115	46.1
-19	-28.3	8	-13.3	35	1.7	62	16.7	89	31.7	116	46.7
-18	-27.8	9	-12.8	36	2.2	63	17.2	90	32.2	117	47.2
-17	-27.2	10	-12.2	37	2.8	64	17.8	91	32.8	118	47.8
-16	-26.7	11	-11.7	38	3.3	65	18.3	92	33.3	119	48.3
-15	-26.1	12	-11.1	39	3.9	66	18.9	93	33.9	120	48.9
-14	-25.6	13	-10.6	40	4.4	67	19.4	94	34.4	121	49.4

Table 2. Wind Speed Conversion

(mph=miles per hour; knots=nautical miles per hour; kph=kilometers per hour.
1 statute mile = 1.15 nautical miles = 1.61 kilometers)

mph	knots	kph	mph	knots	kph	mph	knots	kph	mph	knots	kph
2	1.7	3.2	52	45.2	83.7	102	88.5	164.2	152	131.9	244.7
4	3.5	6.4	54	46.9	86.9	104	91.1	167.4	154	133.7	247.9
6	5.2	9.7	56	48.6	90.1	106	92	170.7	156	135.4	251.2
8	6.9	12.9	58	50.4	93.3	108	93.7	173.9	158	137.1	254.4
10	8.7	16.1	60	52.1	96.6	110	95.5	177.1	160	138.9	257.6
12	10.4	19.3	62	53.8	99.8	112	97.2	180.3	162	140.6	260.8
14	12.2	22.5	64	55.6	103	114	99	183.5	164	142.4	264
16	13.9	25.7	66	57.3	106.2	116	100.7	186.8	166	144.1	267.3
18	15.6	29	68	59.1	109.4	118	102.4	190	168	145.8	270.5
20	17.4	32.2	70	60.8	112.7	120	104.2	193.2	170	147.6	273.7
22	19.1	35.4	72	62.5	115.9	122	105.9	196.4	172	149.3	276.9
24	20.8	38.6	74	64.3	119.1	124	107.6	199.6	174	151	280
26	22.6	41.8	76	66	122.3	126	109.4	202.9	176	152.8	283.4
28	24.3	45.1	78	67.7	125.5	128	111.1	206.1	178	154.5	286.6
30	26.1	48.3	80	69.5	128.7	130	112.8	209.3	180	156.2	289.8
32	27.8	51.5	82	71.2	132	132	114.6	212.5	182	158	293
34	29.5	54.7	84	72.9	135.2	134	116.3	215.7	184	159.7	296.2
36	31.3	57.9	86	74.7	138.4	136	118	219	186	161.4	299.5
38	33	61.2	88	76.4	141.6	138	119.8	222.2	188	163.2	302.7
40	34.7	64.4	90	78.2	144.8	140	121.5	225.4	190	164.9	305.9
42	36.5	67.6	92	79.9	148.1	142	123.3	228.6	192	166.7	309.1
44	38.2	70.8	94	81.6	151.3	144	125	231.8	194	168.4	312.3
46	39.9	74	96	83.4	154.5	146	126.7	235.1	196	170.1	315.6
48	41.7	77	98	85.1	157.7	148	128.5	238.3	198	171.9	318.8
50	43.4	80.5	100	86.8	160.9	150	130.2	241.5	200	173.6	322

Table 3. Millibars to inches of mercury

Millibars	Inches of Mercury	Millibars	Inches of Mercury	Millibars	Inches of Mercury	Millibars	Inches of Mercury
1043	30.8	1021.4	30.16	999.7	29.52	978	28.88
1042.4	30.78	1020.7	30.14	999.0	29.50	977.3	28.86
1041.7	30.76	1020.0	30.12	998.3	29.48	976.7	28.84
1041.0	30.74	1019.3	30.10	997.7	29.46	976.0	28.82
1040.3	30.72	1018.7	30.08	997.0	29.44	975.3	28.80
1039.7	30.70	1018.0	30.06	996.4	29.42	974.6	28.78
1039.0	30.68	1017.3	30.04	995.6	29.40	974.0	28.76
1038.3	30.66	1016.6	30.02	995.0	29.38	973.3	28.74
1037.6	30.64	1016.0	30.00	994.3	29.36	972.6	28.72
1036.9	30.62	1015.3	29.98	993.6	29.34	971.9	28.70
1036.3	30.60	1014.6	29.96	992.9	29.32	971.2	28.68
1035.6	30.58	1013.9	29.94	992.2	29.30	970.6	28.66
1034.9	30.56	1013.3	29.92	991.6	29.28	969.9	28.64
1034.2	30.54	1012.6	29.90	990.9	29.26	969.2	28.62
1033.6	30.52	1011.9	29.88	990.2	29.24	968.5	28.60
1032.9	30.50	1011.2	29.86	989.5	29.22	967.9	28.58
1032.2	30.48	1010.5	29.84	988.9	29.20	967.2	28.56
1031.5	30.46	1009.9	29.82	988.2	29.18	966.5	28.54
1030.9	30.44	1009.2	29.80	987.5	29.16	965.8	28.52
1030.2	30.42	1008.5	29.78	986.8	29.14	965.2	28.50
1029.5	30.40	1007.8	29.76	986.1	29.12	964.5	28.48
1028.8	30.38	1007.2	29.74	985.5	29.10	963.8	28.46
1028.1	30.36	1006.5	29.72	984.8	29.08	963.1	28.44
1027.5	30.34	1005.8	29.70	984.1	29.06	962.4	28.42
1026.8	30.32	1005.1	29.68	983.4	29.04	961.8	28.40
1026.1	30.30	1004.4	29.66	982.8	29.02	961.1	28.38
1025.4	30.28	1003.8	29.64	982.1	29.00	960.4	28.36
1024.8	30.26	1003.1	29.62	981.4	28.98	959.7	28.34
1024.1	30.24	1002.4	29.60	980.7	28.96	959.1	28.32
1023.4	30.22	1001.7	29.58	980.1	28.94	958.4	28.30
1022.7	30.20	1001.0	29.56	979.4	28.92	957.7	28.28
1022.0	30.18	1000.4	29.54	978.7	28.90	957.0	28.26

Index

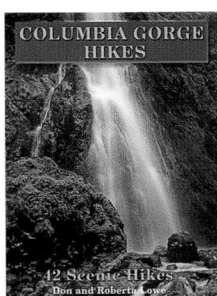